Life and Death in C

C000003162

LIFE AND DEATH
IN CHANGI

+

The War and Internment Diary of Thomas Kitching
(1942 - 1944)

edited by
Goh Eck Kheng

◇LANDMΔRK◇BOOKS◇

Editorial note

In transcribing the diary, most of the numerous abbrevia-
tions which Thomas Kitching used have been spelled out in
full. However, titles of books and names of newspapers and
ships have not been italicised to keep to the style of the
original diary. Similarly, inconsistencies in capitalisation
have been retained. Editorial comments and explanations
are given in italics within brackets. Much of these and the
background information at the beginning of some chapters
were researched and written by George K. McMillan.

Copyright © Brian Kitching 2002

All rights reserved. No part of this publication may be reproduced
or transmitted in any form or by any means, electronic or
mechanical, including photocopy, recording or any information
storage and retrieval system, without prior permission in writing
from the publisher.

First edition privately published, 1998

LANDMARK BOOKS PTE LTD
5001, Beach Road, #02-73/74, Singapore 199588

**National Library Board (Singapore)
Cataloguing in Publication Data**

Kitching, Tom, 1890-1944.
Life and death in Changi : the war and internment diary of Thomas
Kitching (1942-1944) / edited by Goh Eck Kheng. – Rev. ed. –
Singapore : Landmark Books, c2002.
p. cm.

ISBN : 981-3065-63-X

1. Kitching, Tom, 1890-1944 – Diaries. 2. Prisoners of war –
Singapore – Changi – Diaries. 3. World War, 1939-1945 –
Prisoners and prisons, Japanese. I. Goh, Eck Kheng. II. Title.

D805.S55
940.547252092 — dc21   SLS2002024360

Printed in Singapore by Loi Printing

DEDICATION

~

To Tom and Nora's grandchildren:
Alan, Ian, Nora, Richard, Trevor, Dawn and Neil

who were deprived of the wonderful
grandparents they would have been.

CONTENTS

PREFACE

This is the diary of Thomas Kitching, the Chief Surveyor of Singapore when the Japanese attacked the island on 7 December 1941. It tells the story of Tom's experiences in the last desperate days before the fall of Singapore and in the two years and two months he spent in Japanese hands right up to his death from cancer in Changi Gaol on 14 April 1944.

It is not known where the diary was between Tom's death and the end of the war in August 1945. It was probably hidden in Changi Goal when the civilian internees were moved out in May 1944 and retrieved by Tom's friend and fellow internee, Jack Snoxhill, after the war. The diary was then handed to Hugh Bryson, another family friend also interned in Changi, who gave it to Joan Kitching in London in late 1945.

Tom was born on 1 March 1890 and his wife Nora on 24 November 1897. They had three children – Colin, born 28 October 1920; Joan, born 8 November 1922; and Brian, born 5 November 1932. All three survived the war. Colin was in the United Kingdom when the Japanese attacked Singapore; Brian and Joan were evacuated from Singapore. Nora refused to leave her husband's side and stayed on in Singapore nursing the casualties of the battle. She finally left on one of the last ships which sailed from Keppel Harbour before Singapore was surrendered. Unfortunately, the ship was bombed and she did not survive the evacuation.

Tom's diary, which he faithfully and meticulously kept throughout his internment, was contained in one small pocket memo diary (measuring just 7.5 x 12 cm) and three jotter books. He has succeeded in recording not only all the vicissitudes of life in a Japanese internment camp – the horrors, the deprivations, the cruelty and capriciousness of their jailers and the extremes of suffering endured by so many, but also the remarkable resilience of the human spirit faced with this dreadful reality – the rapid return to a civilised routine with a flourishing library and educational organisation, active dramatic, musical and literary groups and a very enthusiastic participation in sports.

His success is summed up in a letter to my brother Colin from Stanley Jones, who was Colonial Secretary until just before the fall of Singapore. After reading part of the diary, Jones wrote on 27 January 1947:

'I have retained your father's diary a very long time, I know, but the reason is that, when it first came and I began to glance through it, I was so deeply affected that I put it aside and it was a very long time before I could bring myself to pick it up again. I did so the other night and read it through at a sitting, as I have always done when reading Tommy's other diaries. He was a born diarist with an outstanding faculty for riveting your interest to simple doings and thoughts and making people you had never met and very likely never would meet your friends.'

Stanley Jones admitted that he did not initially think the diaries 'would be such poignant reading as this'. However, upon reading it, every sentence brought up familiar scenes and many passages dealt with people he knew well.

'One of the traits which attracted me to your parents was their habit of taking up hobbies which, being suited to the surrounding circumstances of their lives at the time, enabled them to be happy and busy and pursue interesting lives wherever they were stationed.... Another endearing characteristic was Tommy's fondness for system and method and there are many illustrations of this in his diary. For me, they brought the diary to life and, in the delight the encounter gave me, I forgot that the author would never again interest and enchant me by those traits of character as he had done in life.'

I was 9 years old when my father started writing this diary. I am now 68 so we have been slow in doing anything with it. Over the years, at least three members of the family started transcribing it, but gave up because it was so time consuming and depressing. Colin sounded out a few publishers soon after the war but none were interested.

Probably nothing would have been done to publish this book but for the interest of George K. McMillan. He approached me in about 1992 and said he was interested in working on the diary as a retirement project. Colin and I agreed that he should do so. George spent nearly 6 years firstly transcribing the diary and then editing it with background material added on World War II. This material preface some chapters, and, where it appears within the text of the diary, is set in italics within parenthesis.

The original document contains about 253,000 words written in a density of about 70 words per 2.5 square cm. It is massively abbreviated and the task of transcribing it was therefore enormously difficult.

In turning the diary into a book, some material had to be omitted mainly on the grounds of repetition. It is broadly as follows:

My mother. Father analysed every scrap of evenly faintly relevant information about her fate. Much of the repetition and misinformation have been left out.

Repatriation. The internees were continuously speculating about this and seem to have been encouraged to do so by the Japanese. About 70 references to it are omitted, but plenty are still included!

Exercise. When my father was fit enough he ran at about dawn on most days. A few references to it have been retained.

Only representative samples have been retained of entries about games of cricket, playing bridge, behaviour of the Japanese, rumours, my father's weight, descriptions of his throat problems, visits to doctors and other recurring themes.

When George completed his task in 1998, he handed me the script saying, 'I have enjoyed doing this. You do what you like with it.' I then tried about 9 publishers without success. I finally decided to publish the book myself. The printers, William Culross & Sons, of Perthshire, Scotland, provided very satisfactory service and when the initial edition of 500 copies were sold out, a small reprint was ordered.

After the book was published, my brother Colin found the 'fair copy' version of father's diary of 1 January – 18 February 1942 mentioned in the entry of 29 August 1942. This contained an expanded version of the diary, hand-written in a hardcover notebook. This 'fair copy' version has been used in this edition of *Life and Death in Changi*.

This publication in Singapore is the result of a recommendation by John Bastin, Reader Emeritus in the Modern History of South-East Asia in the University of London. In his view, Thomas Kitching's diary is the most detailed and important that has survived describing the life of civilian internees in Changi.

The revised index of internees of this edition, based on the register of those interned at Changi at the beginning of the Japanese Occupation, has been prepared with the cooperation of the Imperial War Museum. I wish to record my thanks to Roderick Suddaby of the museum for facilitating the loan of a microfilm copy of the Changi Register.

I am greatly indebted to George McMillan and the late David McKay who gave me an enormous amount of help in presenting this book.

Brian Kitching
2002

– Prologue –

THE FATEFUL DECISION

Colin Kitching stood forlornly on the northbound platform of Lancaster Station, waving goodbye to his parents, brother and sister. His family was travelling to the Clyde to join the S.S. *Sarpedon*. Colin was returning to his studies at Oxford. As he watched the train disappear into the distance, Colin wondered whether he would ever see his loved ones again. For, at 19, Colin was soon to enlist in the Royal Navy and he doubted whether he would survive. It was wartime and Colin was right to be sceptical of his own chances of survival. At least his family would be safe enough, apart from the initial threat from submarines on the voyage out. His father, Tom, was a surveyor in the Colonial Service. He was sailing back with his wife, Nora, his daughter, Joan, aged 17, and his younger son, Brian, aged 7, to his post of Chief Surveyor of Singapore. The month was September, the year 1940.

The S.S. *Sarpedon* did manage to elude the U-boats and the Kitching family arrived safely in Singapore. Malaya remained peaceful, there was a job to be done and the family's future seemed more secure there. The U.K., on the other hand, was still in imminent danger of invasion from across the Channel where the all-conquering German Wehrmacht awaited the order to board the invasion barges. In Malaya, it looked to Tom Kitching as if Nora, Joan and Brian would be safe. The Japanese had taken Shanghai, but the war between China and the Japanese had been dragging on for so long that few Westerners paid it much attention. They had enough troubles of their own in Europe.

In Singapore, Tom and his family took up residence again in their spacious bungalow at 24, Mount Rosie Road with its beautifully-kept lawns and flowerbeds, the large, airy rooms, all run so efficiently by Nora with the assistance of the half-dozen Malay and Javanese servants. The family still had their two cars, the Morris 8 and the Morris 14, and their chauffeur, Ali. Tom, Nora and Joan were members of the Royal Singapore Golf Club; they also played tennis and had their own court in front of the house and Tom had his many hobbies including photography and philately. There were also frequent visits to the Singapore Swimming Club and Joan attended the dances organised by the various clubs. Schoolboy Brian pursued the usual hobbies of young boys; he remembers particularly fishing at a lake on the golf course and keeping moth cocoons until they hatched.

Compared with the situation in the U.K., life had changed little in the Malaya Tom had known since his arrival there at the age of 23. He was the third child and only son of Thomas and Brenda Kitching. His grandfather, Samuel Kitching, had moved from North Yorkshire to Morecambe in connection with his job as a stone-mason with the London and North Western Railway. Brenda was a Baxter, a family identified with fishing in Morecambe Bay for generations. Tom's father, Thomas Kitching senior, was the only bookseller in Morecambe. To take advantage of the booming holiday trade, Thomas Senior's shop also stocked what were known as fancy goods, meaning a variety of souvenirs ranging from leather purses to pottery. Tom happily admitted that his three sisters, Brenda, Phyllis and Nellie, indulged him greatly during his youth, a period he much enjoyed.

Tom Kitching was educated at Lancaster Royal Grammar School, where he made a name for himself academically and on the sports field – notably at rugby and hockey. From there he went up to Peterhouse, Cambridge in 1909 and made the most of his three years as an undergraduate. Although not a big man, Tom was sturdy, stocky and a keep-fit enthusiast. A keen sportsman, he played rugby, hockey, cricket and soccer for the college. Yet he managed to devote enough time to studies to be awarded a second-class honours degree in the Natural Sciences Tripos. Throughout his life, his knowledge of geology, geography and botany remained considerable.

At that time, the Colonial Service was a huge employer of young graduates, the British Empire being at its peak. Having come down from Cambridge in the sum-mer of 1912, Tom applied for a post as a surveyor with the Colonial Service. In due course, he was accepted and, in January 1913, he reported to the Ordnance Survey Department, Southampton for training. On qualifying, he chose to go to the Feder-ated Malay States in preference to British East Africa, Uganda or Ceylon. How much easier Tom's closing years would have been had he chosen Ceylon, for in-stance, or, for that matter, any of the other alternatives! Tom arrived at Penang in June 1913 and was posted to Seremban in the state of Negri Sembilan. There fol-lowed five arduous, but satisfying years involving survey work in primitive jungle conditions.

The outbreak of war in August 1914 created an embarrassing situation. Like most young men, Tom felt it was his duty to return home and join the Forces. He was not allowed to do so. The Colonial Office which had been obliged to suspend recruiting because of the war laid down that Colonial Service officers must remain in their posts. Ironically, it was not until August 1918 that the Colonial Office approved Tom's application to return home and join up. He was interviewed by the General Officer Commanding, Malaya, who agreed to recommend him for the RAF. Tom sailed from Singapore on 2 November and, nine days later, while he was still at sea, the Armistice was declared.

Tom disembarked at Gravesend on 15 December 1918. There was now no ques-tion of joining the Services and Tom began a well-earned period of leave in Morecambe. It was while playing mixed hockey that he found himself at centre forward with a Miss Nora Altham at inside left. Dark-haired and slim, with big, brown eyes, Nora was the daughter of William and Georgina Altham. William, a member of a well-known Morecambe family, was a master butcher with a shop on the corner of Green Street and the central Promenade. The romance between Tom and Nora blossomed and they became engaged, but, to everyone's consternation, at the end of May, Tom was ordered by the Colonial Office to sail from Tilbury on 6 June. A special marriage licence was applied for and granted and the wedding took place in Morecambe Parish Church on 3 June.

Tom found himself posted back to Negri Sembilan and resumed a particular survey assignment at precisely the point he had left it the previous year. The domestic priority was somehow to find a berth in a ship for his wife. After much activity, the object was achieved: Nora arrived in Penang on 31 December 1919 and she and Tom settled comfortably enough in Seremban. It was a new and strange environment for Nora, but she adapted quickly. Settling-in was interrupted, however, by the birth of son Colin in 1920 and the arrival of a daughter, Joan, two years later.

There was home leave in 1924. On return to Malaya, Tom was posted to Kuala Lumpur in Selangor. This was the time elder son Colin remembers – the bungalow on top of a hill, approached by a circling road, his mother's Irish terriers and the Selangor Club, generally known as the Spotted Dog, where Joan and Colin played with other children. Home leave came again in 1928. Colin was approaching the age of eight, Joan six. A heart-rending decision had to be made by Tom and Nora. At that time, it was universally accepted that European children ought not to remain in the tropics after about eight years of age. Although Joan might well have returned to Malaya for another tour, her parents decided it would be best for the two children to stay together, so Joan and Colin went to boarding schools in Arnside, at the head of Morecambe Bay.

Tom and Nora went back to Malaya, bereft and upset. But it has to be realised that, in those days, thousands of families found themselves in this distressing situation. In the Kitching's case, Joan and Colin had the inexpressibly good fortune to be provided in the school holidays with a wonderful and loving home by their maternal grandmother, Georgina Altham.

Tom's posting in 1928 was to the then little-known state of Trengganu, on the east coast of Malaya. So isolated was Trengganu that there was no access by land, only by sea. It was, however, different and delightful as a place in which to live and work. Tom and Nora, according to their son, Colin, probably enjoyed this posting more than any others. They liked Malaya and the people around them – European, Malay, and Chinese. In their leisure time, they had an active social and sporting life – the social club, golf, tennis and, for Tom, his cricket. More than most, however,

Tom and Nora relished exploring the country, sometimes venturing where no white man or woman had trod.

Home leave in 1931 was the best of all home leaves. Joan and Colin were at school in Arnside; their parents rented a house in the village and the children became day pupils for that summer. The four Kitchings were able to live together as a family for the whole of the leave, much to the delight of Colin and Joan, not to mention their parents' joy to be close to their children again. The key part of these periods was the schools' summer holiday. For these two months, the Kitching family made the most of their time together. Colin remembers a cruise to Norway and another round the Western Isles of Scotland. There was also a touring holiday of Scotland and a trip to London and the south coast of England. Excursions like these apart, much of the time was spent by Tom, Nora and the children walking and climbing in North Lancashire and the Lake District.

Tom's next posting was to the state of Johore. During this stay, the main event in the family's calendar was the birth of Brian in 1932. Home leave followed in 1934, and then Tom received an appointment as Superintendent of Surveys in Kulim, Kedah.

In 1937, Tom was posted to Malacca, then the final move to Chief Surveyor of Singapore came in late 1938. This important appointment was due recognition of Tom's 25 years of dedicated service in the Malayan Survey Department. When he went out in 1913, the country was largely un-mapped, land ownership boundaries were chaotic and the road system rudimentary. By the outbreak of World War II, these basic needs had been substantially met, to the great benefit of Malaya and its peoples. Tom Kitching's contribution to this immense achievement is his memorial.

The last home leave began in the early spring of 1940, before the so-called phoney war was brought to an abrupt end by the German onslaught in the West. With the subsequent collapse of France, Britain was left in a dire position. It was the general expectation that Germany would invade before the autumn. As far as the Kitching family's position was concerned, Tom had reached the Colonial Service retirement age of 50 and Nora was looking forward to her husband's retiral and settlement in the U.K., especially as Brian was approaching the critical age of eight. However, Tom had been asked by the Colonial Office to consider going back to Singapore for one more tour and this was a serious option. Joan was on the point of leaving Harrogate College and Colin was already an undergraduate at Oxford. The fateful decision was made. Brian and Joan accompanied their parents to the Far East and Colin was left waving goodbye and wondering what the future would hold.

Throughout the remainder of 1940 and most of 1941, life in Singapore continued much as before, with measures for defence and security causing some disrup-

Nora, 1937

Colin, c.1941

Joan, c.1940

Brian, c.1940

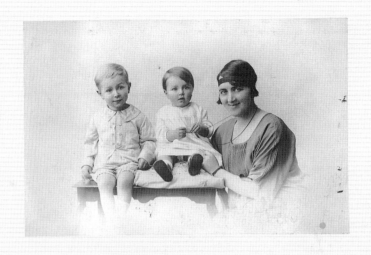

Colin, Joan and Nora, c.1922

*From left: Tom, Colin, Nora and Joan with friends
Christmas 1925*

Tom and Nora, 1940

Brian and Tom, 1940

Nora on honeymoon, on top of Gunong Angsi
January 1920

Diary reproduced in actual size.

DECEMBER 1942 — Thursday 17

KP.T./ Veg. Soup. F.B.F.T. 8 P.M.

Menus last 3 days indicate meat without biscuit, is
vegs vs. More details voyage Wigglum open boat, made with
Bunphy + Trevessa. Boarded 7.3.42. Guvan British. White-
ouse from Bygonia, Rwts. Total crew 48. 26 lifeboat, with
survival + the compass seabaut fleet. 100 2lb ships biscuit.
12 tins evap milk, 50 small tins beef, 10 FISEBALDER, 10
sweet biscuits, 5 veg soup, 10 2s, choc. Slabs coconut-oil
50 galls water. Small Primus. 3 rain. 2 bats milk with
Spirit. 10 sets oilskins in two paddles. Sgt said for X-mas I.
Lost after 10 days no landfall, wind changes. Australia. For
6 days av. 5 knots initial then sighted, changed to S.E.
14 days in heavy seas drifted S-W. N-W, wind veered fur-
thest S, 23°. Child + infant, wind forced them to make
for Ceylon so sailed N.W. in 30° S. have several days
absolute calm broken by SW monsoon wind carried them NE
until they sighted (early) Muny Mungle Ceylon. Sailing Mupe
a straight they saw a barloon + made a pier, believing this
was a ship; seeing a path it was at her stern. Red E sugar
Thought they with joy. A coconut lathe + pint of wind unfurled
the N. flag....... they tried to row to pier too weak and to
towed too weak.... Rain. at 15 a gill of water, one inscr.
or 1/6 pt. badly alterose days. After 10 days this halved.
Water inc. 50 grammes + in 20 rainless days. the last SW
monsoon got extra in a sail. Occasional seagulls caught,
drunk blood, boiled + ate. Also small flying fish much. 3 Eng.
+ an Estlonians picked up after bombing with fractd flight
died after 70 days in bottom of boat. All the the died. Thirst
difficult to control (I expect they wanted go. Jam all the
seems to them) wet wet within wetting the land of land by
in water ration. Many started to drink sea-water + went
raving mad, often loss all interest in life + appeared to make
as the stricken Woolgan plunged bow first + her stern shook
upwards. Mrs Woolgan flag which had been floating limp
at the stream, was caught + in a whiff at air and a stiff flutter-
4 ag. invisible cord, straightened out on a proud gesture of
distance, as she disappeared with colours flying, that is
the ship which lived long treasure.
Mrs Inst. memory of these ship, carried to hosp. Felt, ¾ allot-
Party a squad al noon, carried to hosp.
10 9

DECEMBER 1942 — Friday 18

KP.T./ R.M. Stew. C.V.L S.P.T. F.B.F.C.M.   305 days

Helen Bell's letter from S.A. to James is like a (snort of fresh
Spring air in the (arny Gad. They have moved to a cottage
5 miles from Stellenbosch, in farming country. It stands on a hill
with a view of mountains all round. God! What would I not
give if Nora was here too – not in my respect at all. Attached to the house are acres of vineyards, apple, plum, apricot
trees, a veg, garden. Lots of wire fences neighbours + hedgings
of wild-fire. KNEBPOCH. Evacuee from Madm school, etc.
has 2 children. Primus. Ting. Shook got to school today
Car returning to farmers neighbours. 5 miles. Lunch time, milk.
5.20. On Sundays, B, T like is the farmer i got his milk.
Letter dated 15/8, shall the news of us, we learned that you
are (being well posted, i might it's true.) Last week it was
anxious weeks of clothing c/o to smth. (James got ins)
                                                     Nora well, it is Rab.
I am getting 1/2 doz. Sunday.... New exile.
Frome, that at last received that in the children. Now existing on M/g a shirtane at g/d Grower, 1/- each. complained
Hes N. got within a serious difficult few. / of us, on
Counl refund. Deratisli now communicated Jany again, to move
from nausea up as soon as help ready, expected to be 15-1
tried, again. Re give list maximum (judgn) efforts mum
which earth.? Re overcrowding, we are made off with 20
commissariat todays c water saves (other) Mum has offer 20
internment camph is last mitted (where) Second although
have been made to move as yet. is due to dialing. Many have
not mean carried out. / SS. 16) mentions Edens address
aggression that man work (central by 28 US R. the 19-
called counter-offensive of US. E. forces fast actively legiti-
Scismans.... A.B.C. an Foreign lighting a proved
campaign for the recovery of Burma. Going a voice a
split N forces / Leaders. In the flight of repaired G. gas-
remited in Turkey Plat line horrifoated night will not be viol-
ated as long as the remain absolutely neutral. the (Allied)
suggestion that T. might be invaded by G seems somewhat
childish. Shudder of Holland December Norway. Belgium
say 1. He gave my neck a good break this morning.
I found the swollen in a elastic sep... We oped a tin saret
ones at night + I we Nora milk biscuits with little... moments
nce. Bet 4 vs Brions Flake from shop $10.
10 8

tion to normal routine – Tom, for instance, became more and more involved in turning out maps for the military and he also became responsible for the fire-fighting arrangements at his place of work in the Fullerton Building and for the wartime censorship office, where Nora also worked – but the attention of most was focussed on the war in Europe and North Africa, with only an occasional thought for what the Japanese might be up to. The Japanese had been struggling to subdue the Chinese for years already and appeared to be making only slow headway against such an apparently weak, divided nation. If Japanese sabre-rattling was growing louder, there was the comforting presence of the massive might of the American Navy and Air Force at Pearl Harbour in Hawaii and the American bases in the Philippines. Besides, the Royal Navy, the RAF and the British Army were present in force in Singapore and Malaya and hadn't the battleships *Prince of Wales* and *Repulse* just arrived in Singapore, ready to see off any possible threat from whatever quarter, German, Italian or Japanese?

But all their dreams of peace and security were to be rudely shattered on 7 December 1941, when Japanese aircraft carriers launched 360 fighters, bombers and torpedo planes in a surprise attack on the American pacific Fleet in Pearl Harbour. This brought America into the war, but was to destroy for ever the colonial way of life and the Pax Britannica and was to bring four years of suffering and death to countless thousands of people throughout Asia. Included in this number were Tom and Nora Kitching.

– I –

INVASION

At Pearl Harbour, the Japanese succeeded in sinking or damaging five battle-ships and 14 other ships as well as destroying more than 200 aircraft. Luckily for the Americans – and the rest of the free world – most of the American aircraft carriers were safely at sea and survived unscathed. These were to form the nucleus of their later war-winning battlefleets. For this as the Japanese and Americans had realised, but not the British and Germans – was the age of the aircraft carrier and the torpedo bomber. For the moment, however, the balance of power in the Pacific had swung from the Americans to the Japanese and the colonial empires of Holland and Great Britain lay wide open to attack, invasion and conquest.

Japanese forces struck at Malaya and Hong Kong and, a few days later, opened a full-scale assault on all British, American and Dutch colonial territories in the Far East, forcing western nations out of a vast area of the Pacific and Indian Ocean and even threatening the coasts of Ceylon, India, Africa and Australia.

The Japanese leadership had placed General Tomoyuki Yamashita in command of the 25th Japanese Army, whose objective was to invade Malaya without warning and capture the British naval base of Singapore. The officer in charge of espionage in Malaya was Major Nakasoni. He sent reports of suitable landing-places directly to the War Ministry in Tokyo. The landing-places were to be in the neighbourhood of the Isthmus of Kra, the narrow neck of land which joins Thailand to Malaya. After several months' exploration, he signalled details of three small fishing ports on the East Coast. Two, Singora and Patani, were in Thailand, about 50 miles from the Malayan border; the third was Kota Bahru, the most northerly port on the east coast of Malaya, ten miles south of the Thai border and situated at the mouth of the Kelantan River. Imperial Headquarters decided to make the main landing at Singora. There would be simultaneous landings at the other two sites, but in slightly lesser strength, to confuse the British Army as to where the main thrust would develop.

Tom Kitching would have been interested to know that, at this stage, Yamashita was concerned that the Japanese Headquarters had not supplied him with any large-scale maps of Malaya. They had none. The invader of Singapore planned his attack with maps of the type found in a school atlas. Since they did not show airfields, he had to make crosses where Major Nakasoni and other Japanese intelligence officers had pinpointed them. It was not until six weeks after the first landings in Malaya that the Japanese managed to capture some military maps of Singapore; they found packages of them scattered in an abandoned British railway car.

The British Army were aware of the likely landing sites and had drawn up a plan to meet Yamashita and his troops. It was as follows: as soon as there was definite news of Japanese invasion forces approaching the 11th Indian Infantry Division, stationed in North Malaya, the Division would cross the Thai frontier 24 hours ahead of their enemies and wait for them on the beaches of Singora and Patani. Unfortunately, the definite news came too late and the Japanese landed with only token resistance from the Thai forces and none from the British.

From Singora and Patani, the Japanese 5th and 18th Divisions drove south towards the western coast of Malaya, reaching Penang by 16 December and the Perak river-line and defences by 17 December, then broke through these and reached Ipoh by 26 December. Whenever an assault against defensive positions was mounted, only one-third of the Japanese force would make a frontal attack, while two-thirds swept round the flank to the rear positions. Time and time again, the tactic worked and the British were pushed even further down towards their last defences and Singapore.

Tom's diary of events in Singapore after the Japanese invasion starts on 1 January, 1942. But, in a letter written on 2 January to his sister, Brenda, and other members of his family in England, he includes his diary of 8 - 31 December 1941:

This letter will have to be passed round. It is the first I have composed since our Japanese allies of the last war made the carefully prepared attack on the (very) early morning of December 8th. I am typing it in the Fullerton Building *(headquarters of the Survey Department and other government services)* at 9 p.m., being on all-night duty. Well, before I forget, I must tell you that Brian has left for South Africa in charge of Mrs R.K. Bell of the S.S. Police, I mean her husband is. We will cable further details as soon as possible. He was in excellent fettle, there were no pathetic partings, which was a great help. But you will, I know, keep in touch with him as soon as you are able.

Nora and Joan are staying – I think, quite rightly. They are both doing V.A.D. and, before we repulse the Japs, Singapore is bound to have a packet of bombs, with inevitable casualties which must be dealt with. So the experts – or, shall I say, the trainees – ought to stay and I remove my topee *(hat)* to them for staying, because they might have gone. Some have.

I find it very difficult to write a letter like this. There is so much so extremely interesting which just can't be wrote. And one has been so busy too. Never mind; I will a tale unfold when we arrive home early 1943 with the Forces of Aggression torn limb from limb.

8 December 1941: We all awake, sirens are wailing, planes are roaring, ack-ack guns are firing, searchlights are all over the place – what on earth or in heaven is the matter – it sounds like the real thing, but it can't be. The Mount Rosie Road lamps are blazing away and, if it were an enemy attack, they would surely be out... We hear close crumps and bangs. At 6 a.m., get the news: Japan declared war on Britain and America at dawn today. Of course, she beat the sun in this attack and the attack at Kota Bahru began just after midnight. Even the Japanese sun can't rise then. Honolulu has also been attacked, very heavily. I go to the office. A bomb has dropped. There are others, but not much damage. How it deals with glass, though! Manila is also attacked and Patani in Thailand. It is only two days since the Japs assured the Thais they had no intention whatever of attacking Thailand! I had a very busy day organising my fire-fighters and what-not. I was on duty from 6 p.m. to 8.30 a.m. I stayed in the building all night, walked all over it, listened to all the grouses, what a helpless, hopeless lot they are when they are jerked out of their normal routine! I ate a pork pie and a beer in my dark room, where, of course, I could have a light on, and got very hot... A strenuous night, very. We had an 'alert'; I rushed to the roof, but saw nothing.

9 December: Amusing if it wasn't serious – Thailand has surrendered to the Japs after prolonged fighting for 90 minutes five hours after the invasion! And, only three days ago, she was going to fight to the last Thai and scorch the earth etc. etc. Contrary to instructions, most of my *(fire-fighting)* squads left and then we had alerts before normal office staff arrived! I shall have to make a few impassioned speeches... Still, Menon, who is one of my best men, and I had our own bit of fun, for, during an alert, we espied clouds of smoke ascending from an obscure corner of the fourth floor. *(This is probably the Mr Menon who took Brian Kitching to see his father's grave in 1955.)* Marvelling that we had not seen the incendiary drop, we dashed down at breakneck speed and discovered an aged Tamil coolie calmly burning office debris in a home-made incinerator. Joan renounces Pitman's; she is on V.A.D. duty at hospital seven hours daily. I call a meeting of heads of sections and talk myself hoarse, having already got a sore throat. The telephone rings all day and, by night, I can scarcely speak. And, knowing my propensity for hot air, you will realise what an affliction this is, but the family gets a respite.

10 December: Just one damned thing after another – my throat is horrible and, to crown a foul day, at 8.30 we get the incredible news of the sinking of the Prince of Wales and the Repulse, of which I could – and I would – say a lot. Joan rang to say she'd be late; actually, she was at hospital all night; they were very busy fixing up the survivors.

11 December: What a day! So much happened and I was so busy, the diary fails. We are holding our own in Kelantan, there is no advance by the Japs at Kuantan and there is patrol activity on the Kedah border and heavy bombing raids on Penang. Germany and Italy declare war on the U.S.A., the Japs have heavily attacked the Philippines, also Guam and Wake Islands. There is no more Clipper mail, alas.

13 December: Dutch submarines sank four Japanese transports south of Singora. I have been there; we once motored from Kedah – a peaceful spot with a lovely lagoon. It seems our policy must be to attack their enormously long lines of communication. Car immobilisation orders are issued; I did in England last year; now we are at it again!

Sunday, 14 December: Of course, all golf arrangements are off, but I decide to get some exercise and go round – all very weird. I go to my building for all-night duty again. I would like to do some typing of my diary in quiet periods. I have my room blacked out – but people will come in and talk. 600 women and children are arriving from Penang tomorrow at dawn. Is this a sign that we may have to evacuate Penang? Midnight – I go onto the roof – visibility is appalling. I should say there is no chance of a raid tonight.

15 December: Mrs Lawes from Penang rang – can we put her up? Yes – also Mrs Graham from our old house in Kedah; she apparently thinks it is our duty to put up the whole department. 6.15 p.m. – we go to see 'Goodbye, Mr Chips' in aid of King's School Services Fund. We have to go as Nora is on the committee and Joan is selling programmes. It is a good film and I observe a sight I never thought I should see – viz. and to wit, Nora serving hard drinks behind the bar all night to sailors in a dim, religious light!

16 December: The Japs are at Muda River in Kedah. I know it well. I don't see how we can stop them crossing. It seems to me the Taiping bottleneck is a good spot – impenetrable mangrove swamp on the seaward side, jungle-clad hills rising to 4,500 feet on the land side, in between a gap of only 10 miles to defend. The Japs are dropping leaflets saying that everybody in khaki will be shot; everyone else will be perfectly safe! What nonsense!

17 December: The day is just one damned thing after another. I am officially asked if I will interview War Correspondents, answer questions and talk to them about the topography etc. of the Malaya-Thai frontier – yes, I will – means of communication, nature of terrain of present fighting and so forth. They arrive; I hold forth; they write copiously in shorthand. I can't imagine what the result will be like. Reuters and the 'Times' are there, amongst others, so when, my beloved sisters, you read the blurbs in the Home press, you will little imagine they are inspired by your ancient and enfeebled brother. The Japs have landed in Sarawak and we have destroyed the oil wells, of course. We discuss heavily the question of Brian going or staying; we decide to decide tomorrow – putting off the evil hour.

18 December: Brian decides for himself; he is so pathetic about it that we agree, rather against our better judgement, to let him stay. I must admit to a feeling of relief, quite illogical. W.H. Stubington arrives; he says that all Europeans have been compulsorily evacuated from Penang; he has lost everything. He borrows $10 and can I find him a job? Curiously enough, he was able to get a very suitable one the next day – valuations for the Army. It appears that Penang was not defended. I completely fail to understand this and the less said about Penang, the better – in a letter, at any rate – and, even spoken, my language would not sound nice. We have jumped into Portuguese Timor ahead of the Japs – what a dreadful affair. Doubtless Tokyo, Berlin and Rome will hold up their hands in horror at the unscrupulous Dutch and British! The news from Russia and Libya is marvellous. If only this front was more satisfactory, we should be feeling comparatively bon. Well, one must take the broad view.

19 December: Aylward rang. He has arrived from Penang. Can we put him up? Yes. He is Chief Surveyor there; he has lost everything, of course, including his tiger trophies, which cuts him more than anything else does. And two cars left behind. I hear that Clipper mail by an alternative route may be possible. The ginger cat rescued by Brian from the Cathedral precincts and starvation has disappeared – ungrateful beast. Am rather relieved; although quite a nice cat, there is enough to do these days without tewing after cats, as Mother might have said. We buy camp beds, mattresses and pillows for our evacuees. The Hong Kong news is grave; the Japs have landed on the island; it would appear that surrender is only a matter of time. 3 p.m. – the Shipping Office ring: Brian is booked to go very shortly – what about it? We haver again; eventually again Brian decides the issue by being pathetic! And we had a very nice mother to look after him and all.

20 December: A Gazette notification, cancelling all Christmas and New Year holidays and December 29th, which is the big Malay holiday. I have an incessant morning in the office – nothing to do with survey work, of course – all fire fighting (there are 500 in my building). And maps, and people, and binoculars for the Air Observer Corps. Again, we change our minds about six times about Brian, eventually and finally 'No!' Lawes arrives from Penang; we already have his wife.

Sunday, 21 December: What a lovely morning! How we would have striven on that golf course in happier times. Joan goes to the kirk choir; Brian goes to Sunday school. It is worth not having sent him – he is so happy now! We throw a curry tiffin for our now large household; rice is cheap and plentiful. Nora goes to the Red Shield Club (helping the Salvation Army); I go to my building again for the night – 6 p.m. to 8.30 a.m.

22 December: Last night, I got sandwiches from the Singapore Club for dinner – they were bad. I awoke at 3 a.m., did my rounds, felt rotten and got back just in time to be sick in a gentlemanly manner in my office; and again at 6 and 8, after which I felt a bit better. The de Moubray's arrived from Trengganu; they came to tiffin. They walked through to Kelantan – nine days, mostly in jungle – a stout effort. But what a shame to leave Trengganu all to itself. I love the place, as you know, and I had tea with the Sultan here only a few weeks ago. What a tragedy. The Japs are now in Kuala Kangsar where I lived in 1921-23.

23 December: Very busy all day – the telephone never stopped. Can we put up Valerie Stephens and two children, Mrs Johnston and two children, Mrs Himely and three children? No, but we fix them up – and others. I started a new shelter in the garden on the approved RAF pattern as recommended by Aylward's brother. Churchill is in Washington with Roosevelt. The Japs are attacking the Philippines in great force. The situation here is said to be fairly stationary. The Japs infiltrate in pairs, clad in singlets, shorts and tennis shoes. One carries a Tommy gun, the other the ammunition. Someone says the Japs are now due for a wave of malaria. They have certainly been operating in highly malarious country. But someone else says they are doped up to the eyes in atebrin (an anti-febrifuge). Perhaps it's merely wishful thinking!

24 December: The Lawes moved to Raffles Hotel. Nora has left her other work and is going to do V.A.D. as Joan is. I went round most of the island in the morning with Joan, getting urgent data for certain black-out areas. Then I took Joan and Brian to the Singapore Swimming Club. While I co-ordinated my information, Brian had a rapid swim. A quiet Christmas Eve – we let Brian stay up and play records and dine with us and he thoroughly enjoyed himself, which is something from a wrecked Christmas! 9.30 p.m. – Tony Lucas, a nice lad, arrived with a small sack 'for the Kitching Family', to be put on Brian's bed with his stocking. Now there is a big chance of Brian going with Mrs Bell. He likes the idea. I think that getting Christmas over has helped to change the rascal's views about going away too.

25 December: I went to the office as usual, although most businesses and shops are shut. We are said to have inflicted terrific slaughter on the Japs in Perak – 'wave after wave mown down' – still, on they come. There are air raids on Kuala Lumpur. Nora has her first day in hospital. Read is dealing with the unloading of stuff from our Kuala Lumpur office and Aylward with the reception of transferred draughtsmen, quarters etc. I stayed in my building from 2 p.m. to 10 a.m.

26 December: All quiet – a lovely night – the moon shone serenely on the water. I shan't tell the censor. What a crime to be wreaking havoc in this peaceful peninsula! Hong Kong has gone; the Japs bombed the water supply and that finished it. We are busy fixing up Brian's passage; he is definitely going – that is good. 7.30: Moir and Endean ring – they have arrived from Kuala Lumpur: do I know where they can sleep? We put them up. Endean looks like death warmed up and they have brought two bitches – I mean canine.

27 December: The War Correspondents are round again – can I give more advice about strategy in North Malaya 'in view of the most valuable information I gave before and my specialised knowledge' etc. etc.? I do so. Mrs Conolly rang – can we take Pat and herself? And we have promised to take the three Perrins from Kedah – old friends – and Joan Hands (that was Matthews), with a two-month old baby, and her husband are arriving and expecting us to take them. All very difficult.

They duly arrived at 6 and we managed to park them – a pity in a way; we would have liked to put her up.

Sunday, 28 December: I actually played golf, being Sunday, but it was very unreal. Still, one can't cut out exercise altogether. Boxes of matches are rationed – two boxes per week. It won't worry me, but, with our now large family, the cigarette smokers will have to be harshly dealt with!

29 December: Busy, busy – and the Sparkes arrived from Province Wellesley. We put them up. He has been there over 30 years; they have lost almost everything. I was on all-night duty – 16 hours – in my building. Singapore had enemy planes over. I had a magnificent view – ack-ack and searchlights. The family went into the garden shelter. A piece of ack-ack fell in it and Brian proudly waved it as a souvenir when I arrived home, which was at 9.30 a.m. on December 30th.

30 December: The Sparkes got a room in a boarding-house and we took in the Hardings who had a letter from the Perrins who fondly thought we were keeping a suite of rooms for them! However, Mrs Williamson came to see me by appointment. Her husband is somewhere in Selangor; she can't get into communication with him. Can I arrange a passage to Perth, Western Australia and – most important – will the Government pay for it? As he is only on a month-to-month agreement, the latter is unlikely. I undertake to do what I can. She is nervy. In the afternoon, I got Brian's luggage ready; he is full of beans about it. War! Kodak's expect no more film packs, so I can take no more photos; pity – there are many of historic interest which I could take without being hanged, drawn or dodecanesed.

31 December: One long turmoil all day! Ere I go to the office, Mrs Cobon from Johore – 'Will I get her passage letter from the Government? She hears there is a vacancy on a ship and she has an imbecile daughter aged 10 suffering from infantile paralysis. And will I get $100 and change it into Australian currency? And she will arrive shortly and will I go with her and get her ticket?' Then Mrs Robb, a Czech, can't contact hubby; he told her to rely on me and my advice: 'Should she sell the car?' Values are decreasing like icebergs in Hades, owing to drastic petrol rationing and other possibilities. I find it impossible to advise. While dealing with Mrs Cobon, I find that Mrs H. with three children all under six, who is coming to stay with us today, can be got away if she can be ready in one-and-a-half hours. She has no Government passage ticket letter, no money, and no ticket. I get the lot and dump her just in time – she is very grateful. I pant like the hart for a beer and get one. I forgot to say we said goodbye to Brian – no scenes. He was very happy about it and as we are all working it simplifies arrangements for him to be away, apart from any other considerations. Mrs Farrington and one child have also gone, Mrs Stephens and two children, Mrs Gray and three children and Mrs Ward and Shirley. Being the year-end, my account as Chief Surveyor has not a bean in it, with the red-tape winding-up of accounts. Then, if you please, in the afternoon, I receive from fond husbands $2,000 from Farrington, $1,000 from Robb and $400 from Himely. Too late, except in the case of Mrs Robb whom I track to her boarding house and am received with natural enthusiasm. Singapore is declared to be under martial law and an alert about 8 p.m. as we are thinking about dinner provides a fitting close to a bloody year. But the Scots are not daunted. Those on my fire-fighting staff intimate it will be a graceful gesture if I leave them off the roster tonight – and, of course, tomorrow morning also! – Which I do and, next day, the 'Scotch Consul' is very grateful. He had a good Hogmanay, but times aren't what they were.

THE LAST DAYS

By 2 January, the British were back on the Slim River and here on 7 January they suffered a disastrous defeat, which destroyed one brigade and reduced another to one-third of its strength. On 11 January, the Japanese 5th Division reached Kuala Lumpur with its vast warehouses of military stores and equipment. Japanese seaborne forces looped out from Kuala Selangor and took Port Swettenham. Gemas and Malacca fell on 25 January, then Yamashita's men were driving down to Johore Bahru. Churchill had sent a message to the Singapore commander, Lieutenant-General A.E. Percival. It read: 'Want to make it absolutely clear that I expect every inch of ground to be defended and no question of surrender to be entertained until after protracted fighting among the ruins of Singapore City.'

By the end of January, survivors of the fighting on the mainland had streamed back across the causeway onto Singapore Island. General Percival had at his disposal for the defence of Singapore nearly 85,000 men, including many thousands of fresh troops recently landed on the island.

On the night of 8/9 February, Japanese Imperial Guard regiments made a feint at the eastern end of the Johore Strait, while 5th and 8th Divisions crossed at the western end under heavy artillery cover. By mid-morning of 9 February, they had reached Tengah airfield to find it abandoned, but still with neatly parked British aircraft on the runways, meals cooking, tables laid. By 13 February, the Japanese forces had pinned inside a 28-mile perimeter the remaining 80,000 British defenders who now found themselves with no plans for a counter-attack, no morale and no confidence in their leadership. On 15 February, despite Churchill's direct instructions, General Percival ordered a white flag to be hoisted and, in due course, he met General Yamashita in the Ford Factory and surrendered unconditionally.

It was with mounting alarm at the deteriorating situation all around them, but with stubborn faith in the ability of the British to recover and fight back that Tom and Nora Kitching continued to struggle on to keep a semblance of order and civilised life going in their corner of Singapore, helping refugees and wounded servicemen by whatever means at their disposal and lending a hand wherever possible to keep essential services running. It was in this context that both stayed on until it was too late for Tom to do anything else but go into captivity and for Nora to attempt to escape at the last moment. Taking up Tom's diary we find him still dealing with the mounting flood of refugees:

1 January 1942: I can't remember who wrote it, and I can't remember the quotation, but the success of the Japanese attack on Malaya to date has caused me to recall it more than once: 'Thrice armed is he who hath his quarrel just. But watch the man who gets his blow in fust.' It runs something like that. The Japs ushered in New Year with bombs at 4 a.m. We took cover in our new earth shelter, completed yesterday, with a roof: nothing fell anywhere near. No holiday, of course: I went to the office as usual. Somehow one keeps busy all day, every day, practically none of it is normal survey work. The removal of machinery and records from the K.L. (Kuala Lumpur) map-producing branch to here, indirectly gives me fair amount of extra work, although Read goes to the Railway Station and supervises the unloading etc., and Aylward meets the Asiatic staff and tries to house them or find lodgings: they arrive almost daily from K.L., some with families and some without. Joan to General Hospital, M.A.S. duty, 7 a.m. – 2 p.m., Nora ditto, 2 – 9 p.m. An alert 9.30 p.m., we adjourned to shelters with servants, but nothing happened: so to bed. Russia is making headway in the Crimea, recaptured Kerch. Something unexpected has certainly happened to the Nazi Army: and in Libya we still progress. But on this front the Japs are very near capturing Manila, while we are said to be holding them in Perak – Winston, who is in Ottawa, when asked by a reporter if he thought Singapore would be held, replied 'I sure do'; and the new Commander-in-Chief, Far East. Gen. Pownall says we will fight every inch of the peninsular, and 'considerable' reinforcements are en route. Brian's report is candid, if not so flattering as of yore. Composition, Grammar and Literature are 'Good', Spelling 'Poor' (and so say all of us), Writing 'Untidy and messy, could be good', Maths., 'F.G.', French 'V. Fair', History 'F.G. indeed', Physical Training 'V.G.', Athletics 'Good, not sufficient control over his actions – but tried hard'. Boxing, 'I'm afraid Kitching misses the finer points'. Form report: 'Brian is not making the progress of which I feel he is capable. He seems to lack energy'. Well! Well! We've never noticed that at home. I wish he were here now – we all miss him a lot – but children are better away from this shemozzle.

2 January: Full moon, so we anticipate some aerial activity, and got it, an alert from 1.50 a.m. to 2.40 a.m., but I stayed in bed and damned the consequences. The others all went to shelter. There were a number of bangs, either anti-aircraft fire or bombs or both, but they were a long way off. Mrs Conolly, who is still staying at the Sea View Hotel with young Pat, rang up, can I arrange a passage for them, either to South Africa or U.K. This isn't so easy. In the meantime we invite them to live with us, she is windy about Sea View attack by sea or air. To office, an alert about 11 a.m., I am in my usual spotting place on the roof of the Fullerton Building, but only saw a small dog-fight not far from Bukit Timah: our planes were soon up and roaring round the skies. The subordinates from K.L. (Photo-Litho Branch) 'refuse' to turn out for all-night Fire Watching duty: I interview them, they have no valid reason – living in lodgings: can't leave their wives all night, etc. They are all Malays, and one or two very Bolshie. I tell them they will have had plenty of time to settle in by next Wednesday: and it's only approx. one night per week: so they will be on the fire watching roster from 7th onwards, and, if they don't turn up, will take the consequences. Manila has fallen. Urgent wire from K.L. to take over the Methodist Girls' School on Mount Sophia for our Photo-Litho Branch from K.L. tomorrow morning! And the girls are still at school! Despatch Read to get on with this, ring up Sennett, and get a requisition to take over the building. In accordance with prearranged plan for preservation of records, start moving thousands of Field Books out of 'Strong Room' (which isn't at all strong): they were to go to my quarters, but now I may change plans and send them to Mount Sophia. Latish, Doris Bridges rings to say a 'mob of women' arriving in the morn, evacuated from K.L.; I don't see what I can do about it, our home is full, so are all the other Survey Dept. houses. Can only refer to the Billeting Officer Leslie Forbes. On duty all night in Fullerton Building. 3 alerts, the last about 4 a.m., but saw nothing except signs of conflagration in the direction of Tengah Aerodrome, and a few A.A. shells bursting over Kallang.

3 January: Left office 9.30 after dealing with mail, back 11. Mrs Conolly and Pat arrive from Sea View. To Singapore Cricket Club midday, met Forbes, Middlebrook, Dohoo and so home after a few drinks. Everyone fairly optimistic about local situation. Paid 15th instalment on refrigerator, only 5 more to go. Joan Hands round in the afternoon, and Andrew and the baby. A quiet night, one alert around 10 p.m. Joan duty 7 – 2, Nora 2 – 9 hospital.

Sunday, 4 January: Helen D. rang from St. Andrew's School, just arrived from K.L. Have to tell her we can't possibly put her up. Nora on duty 7-2, Joan 2-9, at General Hospital. Spent all morning typing my diary, with frequent intervals at the telephone, etc., mostly concerned with the transfer of machinery and staff from K.L. Read and Aylward dealing with most of it under my instructions. As Aylward has no car – having lost it in Penang – it can be rather awkward. Taxis are almost impossible to get, I think the drivers object to being bombed – and we are rationed as to petrol and Ali, the syce, has a very long day anyway. Colonial Secretary, S.W. Jones, dropped in for a chat 11 – 12. The Perak and Selangor Malay Volunteers were given the option – do you wish to defend your country or not? Almost with one accord they said, 'NOT'! So were disbanded. So much for all the time and money spent in training them. I did more typing in the afternoon, 1941 Dairy, it is very interesting and will run two volumes. At 6.15, Nora and I to S.W.J's for a drink. G.M. Kidd and Heywood-Waddington are staying there. We had a discussion, have we made the Malays soft? I think definitely we have not: they never had much stomach for real fighting. A British Officer and a handful of Sikhs captured the stockade at Bukit Pilah, the top of the pass to Kuala Pilah, well over

50 years ago, without bloodshed practically: the Malays just bolted from one of the strongest defensive positions in Malaya. An alert about 4.30 a.m., ack-ack fire, and planes very visible in the beams of the searchlights. A very bright moonlight night. I hear there were two raiders, and both were shot down by A.A. fire (Nipponese forces landed at Kuala Selangor 2.30 p.m. on 4th, and caused our army to retire further south).

5 January: Another very busy day. Nora on duty 7 a.m. to 2 p.m. and Joan 2 p.m. to 9, but Joan was late back, casualties from the front were arriving, Indian troops, about 60, some very nasty wounds she says. I must say for an untrained girl of 19 she is standing up to it extremely well. And Ali, the syce, does very well at driving in the blackout with the regulation lights, I don't like it a bit myself. Nor does he appear to be afraid of the bombings. In fact, Ali, not previously considered to be one of our shining lights, is coming out of this period of stress with full marks. Circularised all Depts. in Fullerton Building, again stressing the importance of getting rid of useless scrap paper and other inflammable material: and also called a meeting to fix the hours 'off' for office workers who are on all-night fire-watching duty. They want the afternoon before off, and the morning after! Which is absurd. They get, or should get, plenty of sleep during the night, as they are all provided with camp beds, and there are 3 to each squad, only one of whom has to be on watch, so they get 4 hours sleep in every 6 – if they want it. Unless awakened by bombs! We make it uniform for all workers in the building, they can go off at 7.30 a.m. and return at 10.30 a.m. Lunched at Singapore Club with Andrew Hands, he has got his 8 month's leave on the grounds that there are no local supplies of insulin for his diabetes. I am glad Joan and her baby are getting away. We partake of several gins pre-lunch, very pleasant. A quiet night, one short alert about 4.30 a.m. but I did not move out of bed.

6 January: Hugh Cobon arrived from K.L. to look after map-producing etc. I completed the removal of Field Books to the Girls' School! Well, well: who would have thought it. The idea is to split essential records in case of destruction, and the Fullerton Building is considered to be particularly liable to bombing form the air – or bombardment from the sea for that matter, being right on the water front. Maj. Nicholson takes over from McKerron as Chief Censor, Malaya: I don't know why, or what McKerron is to do instead. As usual, a very busy day, everything but my own job. Gibson arrives. Joan to tiffin at Singapore Swimming Club with Moule and to hospital. Duty 2-0, same as Nora. Got extra petrol coupons, 12 gallons, for the Morris 8, making a total of 19 for that and 10 gallons for Morris 14, which I use very little now as she does only 20 miles to the gallon. On duty all night in Fullerton Building. One alert 6 p.m. which spoilt my stengah in the Singapore Cricket Club and nothing happened: went round whole building 11 p.m. and 2 a.m. to see if all in order and fire-watchers on duty. All correct.

7 January: Barbara Moor arrived to stay with us. Her parents are living in Singapore, but she and Joan were at school together so will be excellent company for each other. She is ycelpt BIM, I obtusely wondered why until I saw her suitcase – B.I.M. Still full of busy-ness, innumerable problems arise with the spectre of actual warfare growing ever nearer to Singapore. One is, all shops now demand cash instead of allowing monthly accounts: so the staff, who are paid by the month, want to know if they can draw their salaries in advance, or get a cash advance. 5 p.m. M. to see me re J. – will I say how long hence we consider she might be able to be engaged, or have an understanding or what you will: I am very sorry, he is intensely keen, but I absolutely refuse to put any sort of limit or anything else, as that might be considered tantamount to an 'understanding': when J. gets home 9.30 I am glad to say she confirms this and although she likes M. does not want to go the length of letting him think she is prepared to marry him, limit or no limit. After all, if I said 'One year' or 'Two years', and then at the end of that period said 'Nothing doing', he could reasonably say 'Well, what was the use of giving me a time limit then?' Got $^1/_2$ case of whisky, 31 dollars.

8 January: Met Mrs Bryant in Battery Road. She is going to Australia: says George will be here shortly! I express surprise, but she says Malacca has no defences, and no troops, in fact nothing to stop the Japanese walking in at their own sweet will. This is very disturbing, I had hoped the southward flight would be arrested before it reached Malacca but she seems to be quite certain it won't. The official communique says our line of defence is now along the Slim River, this is further north than I thought. Another very hectic day, cables and telegrams and 'phone calls, and people. Rob is in hospital in Johore Bahru, with A.I.F. wounded. Mrs Robb is an Esthonian, and very excitable. She comes to office to see me, yes, she certainly is extremely agitated – her husband, who is a New Zealander, is to be sent to South Africa in a hospital ship, and what for would he be wanting to go to S.A., and what would she, a grass widow deserted and left in Malaya, do, and what do I propose to do about it? Well, strictly speaking it has nothing to do with me, but rules don't count in these days, but I can ring up the Chief Medical Officer, Johore and he assures me there is not the slightest intention of sending Robb to S.A. So Mrs Robb departs, mollified but not satisfied. I have an inkling that I shall see her again. 4.30 a.m. an alert, I stay in: Nora and the others go out to the shelters, except Bim and Joan, who join each other in bed, they chatter and giggle so loudly that I can't hear 'planes arriving or shell fragments dropping, which is my signal for departure to shelter: 'Is that a plane?' 'Don't know' they reply, and start giggling again. I hear snatches of conversation – 'He has blue eyes and a wispy moustache...' etc. etc. Planes, bombs and ack-ack leave them entirely cold.

9 January: We have bombed Bangkok heavily and the Thais are quite annoyed about it. Wonder if our pilots used the Target Map we prepared last year. Our line of defence is still said to be along Slim River, and the Japs make some progress at Kuantan, where they have captured the aerodrome. They now hold no less than 15 which we have obligingly constructed for them at terrific expense. Why, God only knows, if we were not able to produce troops to hold them and aeroplanes to put on them... I am very busy all day but with such a multitude of various things it is impossible to recall or chronicle. Consult M.E.O. re a remittance of £15 per month for Brian's maintenance in Cape Town, they tell me I must arrange it thorough my bank. The whole Survey Dept. will be here in a day or two, and housing problems and wives are hellish. Everyone's first action of course, is to ring me up, or come and see me. One female arrived, I know I ought to know her – she says archly 'Now don't say you don't know who I am!' 'Of course not' said I foolishly on the spur of the moment, trying frantically to remember. 'Well, who am I then?' 'Mrs X' – picking evidently her pet aversion in the whole Department! 'Indeed I'm not, I'm Mrs Y.' Most indignant. Anyhow, I proceed to intimate that we could not possibly put her up; but this was quite useless, it was my duty to do so and she practically announced her intention of arriving at the house and staying put underneath it if I could – or would – not give her a bed. Her husband is still up-country and what am I going to do about it? However, I managed to find someone who had a spare mattress and the danger was averted. Victor Perrin arrived 4 p.m. and we were able to put him up, a camp bed in Aylward's room, this would not have been at all suitable for Mrs Y. He has been working in the A.F.S, Kuala Lumpur, but they are all evacuated now and even the fire engines are here. It looks very bad, as if K.L. is given up as lost. Sirens 2 a.m. but nothing happened. We have dropped millions of leaflets over Paris, etc., exhorting the French to be of good cheer.

10 January: I must see F.B. Sewell, he has still not returned the AINSWORTH book out of my Malayan collection, which I foolishly lent him 3 months ago and he swore a solemn oath to return it. Why do people have that complex about books? I have asked him for it at least a dozen times. Mrs Robb is in the office again: her husband must be got out of the Military Hospital, where he is being slowly starved, to the Civil Hospital. She details what he gets for every meal, concluding 'What do you think of that?' Actually, I thought it sounded very reasonable, but I give her an official note to the Principal M.O., Johore, and she departs joyously... Robb was acting as guide to a bunch of A.I.F. who laid an ambush on the road, a car with 7 officers drove into it and they threw hand grenades into the car which crashed and the whole septette were killed, either by the grenades or the crash. Japanese sharp-shooters in the rubber trees wounded R. in the arm as they were dashing away from the scene. An alert 10 a.m. but saw nothing at all: later it transpires it was a recon-naissance plane over the Naval Base, our fighters brought it down. A letter from Brian postmarked Tandjong Priok 2.1.42 and opened by the Dutch censors. He is en route to South Africa with Mrs Bell and 2 children, both younger than Brian, I suppose they will go via Sunda Straits. He is very fit and enjoying life, Mrs Bell says he is being very useful and a model! Synchronises his watch daily with ship's time, takes Tony down to meals punctually, complete with lifebelts and as they have 3 sittings, this is a great help. His spelling is appalling! He says 'right a letter' … 'Dad was rong abought the cabbins' … 'went on bord' … 'peple are sliping' (sleeping) … However, many great men are born bad spellers! Got my 1920 Diary bound in book form, very nice, that makes 8 vols. completed, 1913 – 1920 … Ordered 5 lbs tea, 5 coffee, 20 sugar, flour, case condensed milk and a bag of rice. This is part of the policy of food dispersal and the laying in of stocks by household-ers – and as the shops all demand cash, Government is paying all its officers draw-ing less than 200 dollars a month, twice a month, and will advance up to 30 dollars for the purchase of the above foods. The whole staff of course immediately want this advance. Vernon Conelly arrived, with one Scott, from K.L. We are not going to defend K.L. and in pursuance of the 'scorched earth' policy he helped to destroy 51,000,000 cigarettes (1,700 cases of 30,000), 50,000 dollars worth of whisky, 800 tons of meat in Cold Storage. As I am on all-night duty in Fullerton Building he is still able to stay the night with us. The line we intend to defend is said to be roughly Muar-Gemas – well, it should be possible: the Muar River is a big obstacle any-where near its mouth, and the only other roads through come round the back of Mount Ophir, and the main trunk at Gemas. But there's always this 'infiltration' bogey, and if you once admit that, they can 'infiltrate' anywhere, through jungle, through rubber, through anything. What I fail to understand is why infiltration should all be on one side. Why can't we infiltrate in the reverse direction? And I should have thought there was no better line to hold them than Taiping – Port Weld, on the west side of this Peninsular, only 10 miles of it, with mangrove swamps and the sea on the west, and steep jungle-clad hills running up to 4,500 feet on the East. Yet this was apparently given up without a thought. That was the line I indicated to the War Correspondents when they were sent round to me by the Director of Informa-tion, and no doubt was cabled to all the Home papers! We were at that time sup-posed to be holding a line along the Muar River in Kedah. I did my rounds in Fullerton Building. And discovered what 'donkey-rigged' means. A long alert 4.25 a.m. to 5.40, I am up on the roof but see nothing, except one of our fighters go up from the Airport.

Sunday, 11 January: Hear Tungku Mat Jewa is Sultan of Kedah, and that Tengku Abdul Rahman, D.O. Kulim, made an anti-British Broadcast from Penang. He was married to a Sheffield lass when I was in Kedah. I remember her inviting me behind the scenes at an official dinner in Alor Star 'where we can get a really good stengah'. He has divorced her since. She was real Yorkshire. On the whole, one is forced to the conclusion that the Malays are showing up very badly: I don't know that anything else could be expected, they always take the easy line. Joan to

early service and so home with me, 9.30. Nora on hospital duty 7 a.m. – 2 p.m. …
C. Noble arrived from K.L., says civil population there completely out of hand, the
Police force is disbanded. Robinson's and John Little's premises looted. Husband's
car was stolen, he had locked it and removed the ignition key, but they removed the
floor boards, opened the doors – a bit of wire and away with it! We had a large
curry tiffin – Joan and self, 3 Conollys, Jo and Vic Perrin, Moule, Chambers,
Aylward. Mrs Perrin has arrived with Ethne, just married in K.L. to C.S.K. Bovell
of the Police, he is here too … I did not go out again, felt very tired and went to bed
9 p.m.

12 January: This week Nora on duty 7 a.m. – 2 p.m. and Joan 9 p.m. – 6 a.m.
… An alert 8.20, lasted until 10.30, 125 Jap planes over in 3 groups, saw them very
clearly from our garden, but didn't hear any bombs: lots of ours were up too, and
ack-ack all over the place. So did not get to office until 10.45, very busy. Lots more
of the Dept. arrive, G.D. Barron, Bedlington, etc.… Another alert 1-3 p.m., but I
got tired of waiting for the all-clear, drove to hospital and collected Nora 2.30,
then to office – Squadron Leader Lewis in, I saw very interesting R.A.F. photos for
Target Map, over SINGORA… He flew to Kuantan the other day in 50 mins., the
Japs spotted him and he came back hell-for-leather in 35 minutes, with several
planes after him – he was on reconnaissance only. Got home about 5, should have
played tennis with Joan, but down came the rain so we hiked cross country to Jim
Noble's and back, with letters for W.F.N. Bridges – The Perrins and Ethne and
Bovell are now living in Malcolm Road.… Japanese have K.L. and the fighting is
now reported to be on the Negri Sembilan border – there's damned little fighting
about it, judging by the rate they're moving. We must be retreating to this wonderful line, wherever it is, we are certainly not trying to hold anything just now. A.M.
Pilter came in to see me this afternoon, why should he be ordered to leave Cameron
Highlands? He's about 60, and his settled home is there. Now he hasn't got a bean.
I can't see why people like that should not stay where they are.… Farrington says
he heard a locally printed Trengganu stamp was issued only a few days before the
evacuation – wonder if this is true – if so will it be valuable.

13 January: McEwan in to office, re a survey very urgent, of a new electric
transmission line to the Naval Base, for the Admiralty. These things always are
frightfully important and urgent, it seems a bit late only to be starting to survey the
location of the line now. However, this is no time for red tape, everything must give
way to Service needs. I manage to get hold of Wong Seck Pung and another surveyor, and arrange they meet McEwan on the ground tomorrow. Clark-Walker,
my district Surveyor, is much too busy to attend to it. He is Chief Air Observer,
Singapore and has just got orders to employ about 150 Europeans who are here
from up-country, mostly planters. An alert 11.20, I was in the middle of a T.A.B.
injection with Noel Bridges. The raid lasted about 1 hour, 50 bombers and 20 naval

fighters. I think they went for a convoy, saw about 30 bombs dropped, which made our building quake, but I believe all fell in the sea. The ack-ack keeps them pretty high. The convoy is said to be bringing reinforcements. One bomb fell in Malcolm Road, about $\frac{1}{4}$ mile from our house, there were no casualties but the road is closed to traffic. 12.30 another alert, a short one: we carried on to the house and then sent the car to hospital to fetch Nora. Office again, still with people arriving – Neil by plane from leave in Australia! Himely – too many to remember, and things happening so rapidly, just one damn thing after another all day and all night – at any rate I should have a quiet time in the Fullerton Building tonight, no plane could see 10 yards. But not so quiet, first BAKRI arrived, his brother was killed by a bomb at midday in Meyer Rd. about a mile from the airport, can he be excused from fire-watching tonight? Of course I let him go. Then several times during the night sundry Chinese F-W's came to say they has heard the sirens, an alert, I should be on the roof: I heard nothing at all, peered out of the windows into the wind and the rain and the pitch blackness – impossible! But they insist, so eventually I telephoned A.R.P. H.Q. and they confirm that there has been no alert all night. So the windy Chinese depart but with heads unbowed and no apologies for giving me a night of unrest. About 55 casualties in today's raid, mostly wounded.

14 January: No postal communications with Negri Sembilan or Malacca … Tampin and Gemas bombed. We capture Sollum. Left Office 9.30, 10.45 just about to return when the sirens went. All clear 11.20. I saw a few puffs of A-A fire and several of our planes, but never yet have I seen a formation to bear comparison with the Japs as they fly over. Are we short of planes or what? In office saw Dick Howitt (driven out of Alor Star very early on), J.B. Ferguson, Chris. Mustard. All these people arriving from up-country have lost everything, and it is wonderful how little grousing they do. 2.30 a meeting with S.W. Jones and most Heads of Depts. in Fullerton Building to decide what measures we should take to ensure that essential work goes on during an alert, staff only to stop work when danger is imminent…. We agree to vacate Floors 5 and 6 as far as possible – certainly all essential workers can be accommodated below – 4, 3, 2, 1 and ground floor are considered reasonably safe. But Gilliam, Macnab and I are a sub-committee to mark safe areas on these floors … We already have a system of Klaxon horns, operated from the roof by my 'spotters'. In future 'essential' workers – already ensconced in comparative safety on Floors 4, 3, 2, 1 – will take no notice of the sirens. They will carry on until they hear our own warnings, three short sharp blasts on the Klaxons, when they will take cover in the 'safe' areas marked on the floor by us, which they can reach in 10 seconds or less. So it's up to me and my spotters not to let them down, or they will lose confidence… And the P.W.D. (Public Works Department) are ordered to get on with what we want doing, quam celerrime. This includes the ruthless knocking out of all glass in the building, which I have been trying to achieve for weeks. There is great argument, should all Europeans have fled to Singapore before the advancing wave of Japanese: I say No. Most people say Yes. Understand reinforcements have arrived, and planes – Home 5 p.m. J.A. Dean came in …. Quiet Night.

15 January: Notice in the Press, the Australian Govt. has relaxed restrictions and will allow Chinese, Eurasians and European neutrals to immigrate during the present crisis. Also a notice that valuables can be sent away. How and where is not stated – by air presumably: I must investigate, and if possible send my diaries 1921 – 41, and photographs and stamps. Should have attended a meeting of the Rural Board this morning, but had an urgent meeting with Macnab and Gilliam – we went all over Fullerton Building with Thatcher of P.W.D., and fixed 'safe' areas on each floor, arranged for blast-proof bunds where necessary, and all glass to be removed and that right quickly without paying respect to the glass! And there is some glass! All this would have been done months ago if I could have forced it, but there was too much red tape, it needed the explicit and forceful instructions of the Colonial Secretary himself to get action. Of course the alert went at 9.30, but as we started on the basement that didn't matter – it was crammed with people, all the censor's staff, etc…. The alert ended at noon, we had 2 'imminent danger' signals from my roof spotters, but nothing dropped near. The official report says there were about 50 Jap planes, and 'slight damage' to military objectives. It seems to me that one of our big troubles is going to be stopping them putting all our aerodromes out of action on this small island – but why should we not use our wide straight roads for taking off, if this temporarily happens? It would be a marvellous way of dispersal too, and concealment in the rubber at the roadside. The enemy wouldn't have the foggiest idea where the planes were parked. Saw Neil again, why on earth it was considered necessary for him to fly back at this juncture I can't imagine. Singapore is lousy with surveyors, so he is going into the Volunteers, with the R.E. at Changi, I understand. What a shemozzle when I get home. Bim's mother has been round, and packed all her things, the two are to sail tomorrow and she has already taken the luggage on board: and Bim who knows nothing whatever about it, is doing highly confidential work at Fort Canning for the Navy – which she has been promised she will be allowed to carry on (by her parents) as long as she likes. Telephones and Tears – what shall I do – I won't go! Eventually Father arrives – Mother won't go if Bim doesn't , and Bim won't and the luggage is on board and can't be got off – eventually it is decided they won't go! I must say I think they could hardy expect Bim to go in such circumstances, without even time to return to Fort Canning…. Of course we hear the usual gup, it's the very last chance of escaping from Singapore, etc, etc…. Joan duty 9 p.m. – 2 a.m., Nora 7 a.m. – 2 p.m.

16 January: Mrs Conelly and Pat left 6.30 a.m. for the boat to Australia, the one Bim should have been on. I got a room on the 2nd floor for my 'essential' workers, so now they can carry on except during the brief 'imminent danger' periods. They are chiefly engaged in computing co-ordinates in checking gun positions in connection with ack-ack fire. We offered to do this months ago, but were more or less told to mind our own business. Now it appears there is a screw loose somewhere and we are to find it. A circular from H.E. says 'The day of minute papers are gone... etc.' In effect, quick communications and quick decisions. You must make them and if you can't take the responsibility, out you go! It ends 'Seniority is of no account'. Revolutionary for Government! The Australian Imperial Forces at last move into action with a flourish. I don't know where, from the communique it would appear to be the Mantin Pass. Gorden-Bennett tells the Press they are itching to get at the enemy, and he has the utmost confidence in them etc. etc. But in the Singapore Cricket Club I met Mo Pennefeather, she has been ordered out of Rengam, which is 150 miles South of the Mantin Pass, and she says the ultimate line of defence is Batu Pahat – Kluang – Mersing. Well, I don't know what it is, but I know it's high time someone did.... I also saw poor old Abang Braddon – if any European would have stayed put I would have nominated Abang. Well over 80, been out here 50 years or so, could surely have gone to Jelebu where there will be no fighting and there are all his interests.... Also saw Bedlington, P.W.D., and gave him a lift to Malayan Motors. How remarkably fat he has got. A slim youth when he arrived in Seremban in 1913. Gilliam, Macnab, self meet again at 10, and again there is an alert on the stroke. We carry on, this time we have a representative of Brig. Simmons with us. This is to accelerate everybody in getting a move on, our chief problem is to get some sort of obstacle in the way of bombs dropping down the 3 big light wells and playing hell on the ground floor. We find no answer to this.... Draft final notices for the Building for essential work to be carried out – the execution thereof now rests with Heads of Depts. I am on all-night duty in Fullerton Building, no chance of raids I think, new moon and foul weather.

17 January: But we have a raid, there was an alert at 4 a.m. but nothing fell near us, heard a few bangs in the distance. As usual I shaved in the office early, then Hugh Cobon arrived, and Aylward, and about 9 we had another alert, but my essential workers carried on uninterruptedly and we completed a most curious-looking chart for the R.A.F. I went home during another alert, about 11, just in time to see a beautiful sight, about 50 Jap planes flying in perfect formation right over our house. Strange that such horrid engines of destruction should look so beautiful, flashing in the sun, silver silhouettes moving slowly across a cerulean sky.... Joan and I sat in the open shelter with cushions on our heads: the roofed one was very muddy so we chance it, but the next house got a large lump of A.A. through the roof so it's not really safe. This raid caused 150 casualties in the town, but most of the eggs were dropped on the Naval Base judging by the direction of the noise, and this was confirmed by reports later.... I got back to office at noon, had a Saturday morning snort at S.C.C., and so home. 5.30 walked to Bryson's with Conolly; Joan H. and family still there…. Bim had night out with 'George' from Fort Canning so I stayed awake to lock up – midnight. Got a distinct shock when a large tree crashed in the garden. Russia still progressing. We captured Halfaya, the last pocket of resistance in Cyrenaica…. Home papers furious about Malaya, but the height of absurdity is reached by the 'Daily Express' which says 'Whisky-swilling planters and military birds of passage forgot that the Malay has the makings of the finest soldier in the Far East'…. Ye Gods! Even for the 'Daily Express' this is the utterest of utter tripe. The Malay Police have ratted all over the place, the Volunteers have refused to fight, what the Malay Regiment are doing I do not know. *(On 13 and 14 February 1942, in one of the fiercest battles for Singapore, the 1st and 2nd Battalion of the Malay Regiment fought fearlessly to defend Pasir Panjang Ridge in hand-to-hand combat.)* H.E. has issued a circular, a bit late methinks – nobody seems to have taken the responsibility of issuing orders to Residents and Advisers about staying at their posts or not.

Sunday, 18 January: In all morning, 2 alerts. Joan to Kirk, in the choir. She brought back Mark Metcalfe, so we had him and Conolly and Aylward to tiffin. Also Dorothy Hirst. Nora to hospital duty. The A.I.F. are fighting at Gemas: the Japs have crossed the Muar River <u>at Muar</u>! It seems incredible, opposition can only have been very feeble. However, now we have some Hurricanes and they are much better than the slow, squat whistling Buffaloes…. The Naval Base was bombed again this morn and petrol tanks fired…. Meanwhile my surveyors carry nobly on with the survey of the new line to it… very urgent. 2 p.m. S.W. Jones rang me up, tells me he is 'sacked' – reason, not enough co-ordination between the Services and the Civil Administration. I am deeply moved…. If there is not the co-ordination, whose fault is it but that of the Services? Look how the Survey Dept. for example, have tried to co-operate with them, and failed except when we were able to force them into it…. It is a year almost since the Surveyor-General and I, at the behest of the C-in-C, attended a meeting at the Naval Base, the general purpose of which was the discussion of Maps of Malaya. Navy, Army and R.A.F. were all represented. After a fairly abysmal display of ignorance they agreed to a programme and policy outlined by us, which we have been trying ever since to get carried out properly. One of the most important items, the formation of a Field Survey Unit for the rapid production of maps under war conditions, is still in embryo. Then we have supplied literally hundreds of thousands of maps which Malaya Command have asked for, but their organisation for using and distributing them appears to me to be very elementary, to put it mildly. For the Navy, I have done topographic surveys which were represented to be of the extremest urgency – only to have them cancelled within a week of, or even before, completion. For the R.A.F. we have devoted a great deal of time and thought to the production of Target Maps, yet it seems impossible to get any efficient co-operation from them. No: my experience has been that in spite of giving them every possible priority and consideration, attempts at 'co-ordination' with the Services are highly disappointing: and if I had to give a reason in a sentence, I would say that no single individual with whom one dealt, really seemed to know what he was driving at. Mark and Joan to Kirk: on my way back picked up Nora at hospital. S.W.J. came round 5.30 and we had a long talk. He is, naturally, very cut up that this should be the end of over 30 years in Malaya, when he had attained the highest possible position in the M.C.S. He has offered to stay on in any capacity but been refused, and is flying home shortly. Hugh Fraser takes over. Our cook says the police are seizing all the bicycles they can lay their hands on: wants a 'surat' *(letter)* to protect his. So I ring up the Police, it is true, the military have requisitioned 5,000 and they just seize any bike in good condition unless the rider can produce evidence on the spot that he is in an essential service such as M.A.S., A.R.P., A.F.S. etc. So our cunning old cook deflated his tyres when he heard what was going on, and saved his bicycle. But what high-handed action. Tony Lucas arrives, he has been as far North as Seremban, the bulge in the line which he was going to create hasn't materialised! They destroyed everything they could when leaving, he did some looting out of a railway truck, a silver coffee set and two toast racks which he has left with us. It was all being destroyed, so he chucked it into his car. He arrived 9.30 p.m. as volatile as ever, fed and stayed the night.

19 January: 'THE OBSERVER' of August 31st 1941 delivered! 141 days.... Office, a perfect panic about bikes – survey coolies, peons, clerks, all want protection chits – and W.S. Pung doing the urgent Admiralty line survey has been bombed and machine-gunned daily, he says he can take it, but naturally wants tin hats for himself and coolies. Discover the true story about the bicycles. The Army ordered 1,200. The Police, to be on the safe side, stole (what other word fits?) 1,500. Then the Army found they had made a mistake and they only want 100. So 14 out of every 15 bikes which have been pirated can now be got back, theoretically, by the owners asking for them. But what a panic has thus been caused without reason, as if there wasn't enough to put up with. Joan has a day off duty and spent it at the Swimming Club with Moule. Nora at hospital 2 – 9 p.m., but got home 8.30. Conolly started Mine-Watching duties, 5.30 p.m. to 7 a.m. (mines dropped by parachute at sea). What a world. Aylward's brother Jack to dinner with another R.A.F. from Tengah – Thomas. They say all our bombers are to be stationed in Sumatra – sounds a good idea, more dispersal – certainly can't keep large numbers on this island. Most interesting item of news today is that U SAW, the Burmese Premier who has just been on a visit to Britain, is proved to have been in communication with the Japanese and is not allowed to return to Burma.

20 January: Mat gives notice to leave at end of this month. A queer lad.... An alert before we left the house, to office, immediately another alert. I dashed up to the roof, soon spotted 18 Japs in formation, but not in our direction, lots of A-A fire, some close but they were over 20,000 feet. Then 6 Hurricanes came right over the Fullerton Building; we watched them, and a little Buffalo struggling up – when suddenly 27 Japs came straight out of a cloud immediately overhead, had just time to sound the imminent danger hoots, and beat it off the roof, and almost simultaneously a salvo of bombs dropped, but nothing very close. Still it was a close shave for warning the 'essential' workers of danger. 10.35 Arumugan rang up from Rumah Miskin Police Station saying they have bombed Middle Rd., Orchard Rd., and elsewehere, can we have a loan immediately to build an air-raid shelter? L.D. Gammans in a speech – In House of Commons? – says it is a wicked thing to speak of whisky-swilling planters and blimpy Govt. Officers – we have turned Malaya in 50 years from a lawless, jungle-enveloped peninsula, into the Empire's richest colony. Hear Hear! There is fighting round Muar, we have put a lot of tanks out of action and destroyed many barges, says the official news. I can't help thinking, tanks should never have been able to get there. There is much damage in Town. Quite indiscriminate bombing of Orchard Rd., Cairn Hill Road, Newton Circus. 'Draycot', which used to be the residence of one of the R.A.F. Chiefs, Bukit Timah Rd., etc. At midday I could not get along Clemenceau Avenue, but got home via Cavenagh Road, although 16 bombs fell in Government House Domain. Should think there will be a lot of casualties.... They got near enough to the Cold Storage premises in Orchard Rd. to damage some plant and cause a release of ammonia, which produced tears from the customers and led almost to a panic – GAS! Mrs. Perrin was there at the time, the acrid fumes were certainly most alarming. On duty all night in Fullerton Building. Another survey coolie in, with the same story as was sprung on me the last time, and it worked that time – a bomb killed his 'abang' *(brother)* this morning and there's nobody to look after his widow and children ... etc. 5.30 p.m. too late for me to get a substitute. Nothing doing this time, I don't believe it, too much like the office boy and his grandmother's funeral. So having explained matters to him, he goes on duty quite happily. About 50 killed and 150 injured in today's raids. A night without incident. Willmot tells me there is a new 25 dollar Straits Settlements stamp out, I must get one.... Later I found out from G.P.O. this is not so.

21 January: What a day. Nora arrived at Fullerton Building about 9 a.m. from hospital duty: we were just about to leave for home when the alert went, and we decided it was safer to wait, which was just as well. The alert continued, with a very brief intermission, until 11.30, planes and bombs were all over the place. A direct hit on Clyde Terrace Market caused an indescribable shambles: the Singapore Cricket Club padang was pitted with bomb craters, and one blew a car into the billiard room of the Singapore Cricket Club. The P.W.D. building, an old one, got it hot, and all along Connaught Drive, where many cars were blasted and blazing. There were more fires in the direction of Raffles Hotel – yet relatively, no vast damage appears to be done.... Their bombs seem to be pretty small.... I saw no sign of air opposition on our side, though the A.A. was deafening. We brought down I am told, 9 by A.A. fire. Bombs fell very near the Fullerton Building, the nearest was about 50 yards away, in the mud beside Anderson Bridge – and the remarkable thing is that the mud splashes came high over the roof, say 150 feet high, bespattered the walls of the inside light wells, and bomb-splinters made three small holes in the walls of the Meteorological Office and one on the 3rd floor.... No further alerts except a short one soon after we got home.... During one of the lucid intervals, I got my 2nd anti-typhoid (T.A.B.) injection over. No ill effects whatsoever, with either of them.... The crowd in the Fullerton Building behaved very well, no panic and our marked 'safe' areas were very useful. Nora and Joan to hospital 2 – 9, a lot of work, many ghastly casualties coming in.... Jack Aylward turned up again from Tengah aerodrome, 128 bombs there today he says, no great damage, but he stays the night in our house, so I wonder. Offical, 304 killed, 625 injured plus 100 treated outside. Mostly in Clyde Terrace Market where a large number were crowded, mistakenly taking shelter contrary to all advice.... Tokyo Radio killed us with its mouth today 'Fullerton Building is destroyed'.

22 January: Roof-spotting today for me, there were 2 alerts, during the 2nd spotted 27 Japs coming straight at us, and then sounded the Klaxons: they got the airport all right, and dropped some eggs near us, but no danger as far as I saw. But it's disturbing, one never sees a formation of our planes at all comparable to the Japs. Odd ones seem to go up and fly around and come to earth again without doing anything. It seems a pity, the staff and in fact, the population generally, are standing up to it remarkably well, and it would do an immensity of good if they could only see a few of ours in the sky, smashing up the hated Japs. Joan has a bad cold, Nora takes her duty 2 – 9 p.m. They are wonderful, I don't know how they stand up to it. Problems of the day – sandbag shelter for roof-spotters very necessary but how to get it up to the roof? We have the sand and the bags on the ground floor, but no labour. The P.W.D. coolies won't come up to scratch, they don't like the roof – the moment the alert goes, they bolt like shot rabbits and are never seen again – I don't blame them much.... Will I keep bicycles off the steps in the Fullerton Building? They cause congestion and in a panic might be a serious obstruction: I put up notices all over the place.... Will I stop the crowding of people in the marked 'safe' areas on each floor, as this stops the 'essential' workers dashing to their havens of refuge when the Klaxon goes.... Forest Office can't hear the Klaxons.... Cook can't get transport to bring firewood to house, will I get it? Chief Clerk eventually gets 2 lorries for 20 dollars, colossal price, but we must have firewood, especially as electricity might be put out of action anytime.... What is Macnab to do about his

Fire-Watching squads, his men continually being taken for other duties. Will I find a job for Mo Pennefather, her husband is on duty in Johore with Volunteers and she must have something to do…. A Wahid has not turned up for duty as ordered, he is to be prosecuted – actually I think he has bolted and probably trying to get back to K.L.… Wong Seck Pung again bombed at work at Seletar on the new Naval Base line: he is really very plucky about it, but I wish I could reproduce his description and above all his manner with it. 'One bomb fell very near me today, Sir – I threw myself flat on the ground, there are no ditches, it comes ZZZZZZZZZZ – think my last day has come, it is within 30 yards and it doesn't explode!' Mailvaganam, my senior Asiatic surveyor, has his coolies' house in Palembang Rd. hit yesterday, and some women were killed…. To Brysons, saw Joan and Andrew Hands, and the Boswells who said how they enjoyed my broadcast, now over a year ago! Jack Aylward slept in our house again. Another raid-free night. Casualties today, killed 58, injured 170.

23 January: My Chief Clerk says Geylang caught it hot yesterday, many old shophouses damaged, but not many casualties. Two alerts, but nothing very near us, although we had to sound the Klaxon once: if the sky is cloudy and you can hear the planes droning away somewhere near, it's safer to give the 'imminent' signal, otherwise they may dart out of a cloud and be on you before you can give the alarm; and if we once let the 'essential' workers down by letting bombs fall any-where near the Building before we have sounded the Klaxons, then it's goodbye to any work during the whole period of alerts. I took a number of photographs with Conolly's Rollieflex. Singapore Cricket Club has half a car in the billiard room, 8 bomb craters on the Padang within 200 yards, but the Club itself practically un-scathed. I took them to Kodak's for development, they will have to pass the censor. Busy afternoon again, bikes off the steps! And will I tell the Fire-Watchers not to clutter up the Co-op. Office with cigarette ends at night? I will not…. What about First Aid, now that workers shelter on each floor instead of congregating in the basement, where the main First Aid Post is? Fix this matter with M.A.S. Another quiet night. Jack Aylward slept with us, but was phoned to leave 5 a.m. tomorrow. Ethne and Victor came round for an hour…. The Jap sappers, they say, are marvel-lous, bridges, etc., repaired in double-quick time.

24 January: Fixed Brian's remittance to S. Africa, monthly with Hongkong Bank. The Banks are rushed off their feet, people going away, people wanting cash, drafts, sterling (almost unobtainable), and the ever-present 'alerts' combine to make an incredible picture…. And Nora's passport has expired and is not renew-able for a further period: the Passport Office, of course, is besieged all day too. What am I doing about cutting off the gas in the Fullerton Building in an emer-gency, asks the secretary of the Singapore Club? Nothing: when I made previous enquiries I was told no gas was used in the Building, now I find they use it for cooking, so I cannot cut it off permanently: the Singapore Club is chock-a-block with people from up-country, you can walk in and see the finest collection of Ancient Monuments ever gathered in Malaya. It's an awful shame, really.... This gas question is going to be very difficult, the meter, etc., are in a most curious little locked cubby-hole under the bottom of one of the lifts – I had considerable trouble locating it. Saw Macnab re sandbags on roof and elsewhere, he is in a very incensed condition, and with good reason – he came to office on Wednesday last, sent his car away on some business, when the syce returned, he found a military car, securely locked and with nobody in charge, parked in the space allotted by Government to the Surveyor-General of Ships, i.e. Macnab, and so marked. So he took Mac's car and parked it near the Singapore Cricket Club and it got the blitz and was severely damaged, while the military car was untouched. So Mac has no car and swears someone will have to pay compensation, but who, he doesn't know. Curious how one swears so much more than usual at a time of great stress like this, not in anger, but merely – well just swearing. At the Singapore Cricket Club midday, drinks, Forbes and 'Margie' Kellagher, G.L. Howe.... Nora to hospital 2 – 9, on her return she tells me another ship has been blown up by a mine in harbour (or near it), coming in with munitions, one of a convoy, I understand. Many of the crew killed, but they got some of the casualties in hospital. The Japanese announce over the radio that Singapore is in for a real hammering on Sunday, Monday and Tuesday. Opinions are divided as to whether they mean it or are just bluffing to terrorise the people. My own opinion is that if they contemplate a special effort, they won't advertise it. Took Joe and Victor Perrin to the Royal Singapore Golf Club. It is a hive of Services now and special passes required to get in, but I wanted to show them the place, they had never seen it before. About a dozen golfers were actually playing, but greens and fairways are very unkempt. It seemed incredible sitting there in peace and quietness, sipping stengahs and admiring the beautiful prospect of lake and jungle, that stark warfare is so close – but a large A.A, gun near the ninth green and ferns camouflaging all the bunkers, and armed troops all over the place, supply reminders if required. Joan has a cold, still off hospital duty. Official, we are holding the Japs at points north of Kluang and Mersing and at Batu Pahat.

Sunday, 25 January: Total killed in Wednesday raid now officially given as 383.... Nora to hospital 7 a.m. – 2 p.m.... We had 2 alerts, nothing happened near the house, but they dropped a lot of bombs in the sea, again near Keppel Harbour: we are told there is no damage.... A dull, cool day. I spent most of it typing 1941 Diary. 5.30 to Colonial Secretary's house. Nora, Joan and I said our farewells to S.W.J.... Present were Mrs M.C. Hay, Hugh Fraser, Haji Cussen, Arthur Worley, Mrs. Forbes, F.W, (Dato) Douglas, R. Boyd, A.B. Jordan, Col. Rae, Heywood-Waddington.... Chatting to Douglas, he spoke of a map of Cameron Highlands, made by Cameron and preserved in Raffles Museum; so I mentioned an 1875 map of the Malay Peninsular which I discovered in my Singapore office and handed over to Raffles to preserve…. '1875' says he, 'H'm. Yes, I was living in this house then' I nearly jumped out of my skin! 'What! In 1875?' But it is so: he was born 31.12.1874, and his mother was living in the house! We returned home 7 p.m. ere it got dark: an alert about 9 and another after midnight, but no bombs near us.

26 January: Bought, at Kelly and Walsh, a most seductive book of pictures of the Lake District, 11 dollars and worth it, but it causes acute nostalgia… Roof spotting today, we had an alert at 10; at 10.30 heard planes in the clouds round about, so sounded 'imminent danger', but whatever they were passed over without us seeing them. Bought 100 gunny bags, 37 dollars! and started making a shelter on the left of the front door, under the house: filling the bags with earth from the garden, using Chan Chan Swee and coolies. He is doing a useful job in one of the A.R.P. centres. We are undone! Thailand, probably annoyed by our bombing of Bangkok has declared war on Great Britain and the U.S.A.! Another short alert 2.45 – 3 p.m., saw nothing …. 5 – 6 p.m. Nora and I visited the Sparks who are now installed in a room in a wealthy Chinese towkay's house which has been converted into a sort of boarding house. He is now on the Defence Security Staff, or some such title, but I have the impression that they will be getting away soon. An alert again after dinner, nothing to worry about though – my experience on the Fullerton Building is useful, one has a pretty fair idea now, by sound and sight, whether bombs can fall near or not. Heavy firing 3.45 a.m. We are out of Batu Pahat…. Jap vessels observed off Endau – why don't we bomb them; …. We are retiring a little in Libya, may evacuate Benghazi …. Russians progress …, Japs are in New Guinea, have had heavy losses in the Macassar Straits, warships and transports – surely that is their vulnerable point, these far-flung lines of communication? Saw J.A. Black today, he is in charge of the export of valuables to a safe place: as I thought, it is by air, and intended for small and highly valuable articles, so I have abandoned the idea of getting away my diaries and other personal records of 30 years in Malaya by this means.

27 January: A short alert 8.30, then another 9.15, and again 10, unloaded a lot of bombs on what appears to be Seletar: I saw 27 Japs very clearly from Fullerton Building roof, flying in perfect formation, apparently too high for our A-A to shake them…. 11.30 sounded the 'imminent' signal, lots of bombs dropped and the Building shook, but on emerging to the roof again, the nearest visible damage is on the airport, one plane is blazing on the ground, and there are vast clouds of smoke round the Hotel and hangers…. The next excitement is the tanker blazing away a few miles out to sea – a terrific column of smoke and flames – whether it was bombed or not, no one knows, may have hit a mine. Then I had just sallied forth into Battery Rd. when I spotted 27 coming straight at us from the S.W. Ran for it to the Fullerton Building and got there just as they dropped a lot more, probably in the sea, and a number in the Kallang Airport area again; the all clear went at 12.30, but where the hell are our planes? Our spotting system worked excellently, and we were only off work for an aggregate of perhaps an hour, instead of the whole morning. I get my exercise now running up and down the steps of the Fullerton Building seeing that things are in order. The de Moubrays arrived for tiffin. George is attached to the A.I.F., Katherine stays with us…. Pawan Teh, our old Malay boy, came to see us. He has been working at the Naval Base, but is afraid to stay there any longer and I don't blame him! And Hitam is back again, she only got as far as Kuala Lipis, on her way to Trengganu. I told him before she started there was no hope of her getting there. On duty all night at Fullerton Building. 6 p.m. they send up the meteorological balloon – it is observed by theodolite for upper air currents. I have an idea it would make an interesting photograph, so I got ready, up come the 2 Chinese observers, clad in shirts, shorts and shoes, no socks. After a whispered consultation, one comes along – 'Are you going to take a photograph, Sir?' 'Yes, that is the idea, just as you let the balloon go up.' 'Will you please not include anything from the knees downwards, Sir – we are so improperly dressed without socks.' An alert 9.15 p.m. I dash up to the roof, search-lights are stabbing the sky – near to us. There is a strong wind blowing – the tanker is still blazing away out to sea, it has drifted East – I hear planes, see nothing, but find it prudent to sound the danger signal for the benefit of the G.P.O. workers and the Singapore Club. Give 'Raiders passed' 10 minutes later. One must be on the safe side…. Today in the Singapore Club have seen Abang Braddon, Freddie Cunninngham, Vallentine, H.T. Piper. 9 p.m. Nora rang me up: Joan and Andrew Hands are leaving for Australia (?) early tomorrow, so I rang the Brysons and said farewells. Joan is very insistent that I should get our Joan away and also Nora if possible – I don't know what to say, they are both doing very useful work in the Hospital, casualties from battle and air raids are pouring in – No, I think and think, I cannot see the fairness of bolting yet again when you have been training for the very emergency which has arisen.

28 January: Managed to wrangle a haircut in the lucid intervals, and fixed up the Fullerton Building gas problem. I have a duplicate key and it will have to be cut off if necessary: can't do any more. It is announced that H.M.S. Barham was sunk by enemy action on Nov. 25: We are now fighting at Rengit, S. of Senggarang, and Ayer Hitam, and the threat to the Singapore water supply from Gunong Pulai is very grave. But we have enough in the Pierce and McRitchie reservoirs on the island, to keep us going if we have to. A large convalescent camp for A.I.F. has suddenly appeared behind our house. Most of them look fit enough, but the panic when the siren goes is ridiculous: a clear blue sky, not a plane in range of sound or sight: no matter, there is a sauve qui peut, a terrified undignified scramble to get into our shelters, and they stay there one hour, two hours, until the all clear sounds.

We haven't a look-in. Nor our servants nor their womenfolk and children. It is disgusting. I have remonstrated, I have said 'Take 2 out of the 3 shelters I have built for myself and staff, if you can't or won't make your own, just leave me one.' They agree to do it 'Next time', but the next time the siren goes, there's the same frantic panic-stricken rush. There is no discipline and there appear to be no officers. And of course the servants are terrified, if this goes on we shall lose the lot. 5 p.m. I picked up the Wrigleys at 11, Nassim Rd. and they came to tea. She and the boy, aged 5, only arrived in S'pore Dec. 8, and he was in Bangkok. He had a most adventurous time getting away: Dec. 9 a jump ahead of the Japs, with a party. They travelled by foot and bullock cart, lorries, canoes, were guided through the jungle and over the mountains by aborigines (Karens) and eventually reached Tavoy. Thence by ship to Rangoon, and plane to the Andamans, Sabang, Singapore Jan 11, where he met his family. Katherine and George de M. stayed the night, making a total of 8, and Tony Lucas dropped in to dinner.

29 January: J.R. Neave announced killed, G.M. Kidd missing. Sad. I met G.M.K. seeing his wife off, on the boat Brain left by, Dec. 30.... Roof-spotting again: 9.15 a reconnaisance plane flying very high passes overhead, and at 10, 27, in formations of 18 and 9, dropped bombs on the Naval Base, but the smoke soon subsided. One plane, probably hit by A-A, was emitting smoke. Two of our Hurricanes dived into them and they turned and fled North. Saw all this v. clearly from the roof of the Fullerton Building. A big convoy in, about 6 large ships, we estimate there might be 10,000 men in it.... 11.30, 27 Jap planes bombed Seletar aerodrome, then sheered off, glittering in the sunshine, surrounded by A-A fire but very high. Johore Bahru is evacuated – and has been heavily bombed, there is no electricity, power station is either hit or put out of action: the police are disbanded and the military have taken over.... The official communique mentions fighting at Layang-Layang. What a night! The Brysons rang up at 11 p.m., there is a ship or ships leaving tomorrow and Ida is going. She has been working in the hospital.... So after prolonged discussion we decide Joan must go. I got the car out, pick up the Moors and take Bim and Joan and them to the P and O Office, which is now at Cluny Park. Luckily there is a bright moon and driving in the blackout is simple. Cluny Park at midnight is a seething mass of cars and people, there is a big queue: I discover a big trooper is going to the U.K. so book both Nora and Joan to go, tomorrow. We get away 1.30 a.m. and home 2 a.m..... Break the news to Nora, she will not go. 4 a.m. the telephone again, the P and O this time, does Bim know about this ship? I tell them she is booked. And to put the lid on a disturbed and disturbing night, Nora gets up at 5.15 and says it's 6.15. So I get up too. There were some early alerts as well, and bombs dropped near the hospital. Churchill says Hess came to Britain, to contact certain elements which it was believed would help him throw out the Churchill 'clique', and enable Hitler to dictate a magnanimous peace.

30 January: We discuss the question of Nora's going. Duty says 'Stay': common-sense says 'Go'. Is Singapore going to fall? If we can believe our experts it is not: but there will be frightful casualties. Are the people who have been training to help, to go away now? Reason says 'Of course not!' So where are we? And the civilian morale in Singapore is magnificent. Asiatics of every race are doing their duty most nobly. Medical Auxiliary Services, Air Raid Precautions, Auxiliary Fire Services, all the rest – are working efficiently and without panicking. Then what are we to say if the European personel deserts, to put it plainly? I do not know what to say. Nora makes her own decision, she will not go, I inform the P and O; I think they think I am bats! Commons pass a vote of confidence in the Churchill Government by 464 to 1, I do not know who the hardy 1 was. An alert at 9, and again at 10. At 11.15 planes in the direction of the docks, an immense number of bombs fall – no doubt they are after the ships which came in yesterday – As it clears a little I can see the masts and funnels, intact and at the same angle as before! This long alert is a nuisance, I want to get home and fix up Joan's luggage. At last I chance it and go during the alert. Ali is nothing loth, a lot of syces are. He has a tin hat now and bombs daunt him not at all. We arrive at the docks 1.30: a direct hit on something has caused a large fire, our normal route to Joan's ship (The Empress of Japan by all the Gods!) is closed. 200 yards of sea has to be crossed in a tender to get to it. This is an appalling business, there is an indescribable scrum of men, women, children, luggage and no porters. The tender fusses back and forth across the strip of water, but makes no apparent impression on the dense mob. Then after $1^{1}/_{2}$ hours hard jostling and shoving – Ali helping nobly with Joan's large trunk – the 'alert' sounds! I feared it all along. Those big ships are much too tempting a target. Joan, at any rate, is across. Nora and I take refuge in an Air Raid Shelter close by – then I hear there are women and children outside who can't get in, so out I go and nestle coyly alongside a godown, where there is a very narrow concrete drain…. Then the A-A gun crew shout 'Get down' – and I horn myself into that drain somehow, so does another gent a few seconds later, and puts his feet on my head. All most unpleasant and dirty. However, no bombs fall near, the all clear goes, and eventually we get the luggage on to the tender. In the big trunk are my bound diaries 1913 – 1920 inclusive, 8 vols. And part of my stamp collection. At any rate our car was not stolen – Moorhead's was, and several others. Joan was very brave about it all, she didn't really want to go. It is a blessing there is not a large proportion of children on board. Our new office for printing maps in Ho Chiang Rd. got a direct hit, I think there were no severe casualties, but all the chemicals are burnt and there is some damage to machinery…. And Weisberg, the Financial Secretary, rang me up this morning to ask if we can do some security printing of notes, money is running short owing to Army requirements, and no doubt paying cash for purchases helps too. Needless to say, we cannot print them. We got home 4.30, very tired and thirsty

– Ray Wilson and Bedlington, from Johore, there. And discover Aylward has gone, in Joan's convoy doubtless. He is retired on medical grounds, certainly he is a nervous wreck. Victor Perrin joined us, so we have lost 3 (J., Bim and Aylward) and gained one.... I must say our old Chinese cook is turning up trumps in this emergency, although we have been within an ace of parting company more than once. Shopping is difficult, what with alerts and what not, and he has a full house to cook for, but he produces satisfactory food with great regularity. An alert about 10 p.m., nothing happened, I slept, having had only 2 hours sleep last night. The weather was grand for the ships getting away, rain and poor visibility.

31 January: Joan's ship is away. Curfew 9 p.m. – 5 a.m. starts in Singapore. The morning was stiff with alerts – 4, no less – but there was no interruption of work in the Fullerton Building We have struck water in the well I am making in the garden, and it looks good. This is in case our water supply fails .... A. Wahid, the bolshie, has definitely bolted to Johore, doubtless to help the Japs – and he owes me 11 dollars 50 which I advanced for his board and lodgings when he arrived from K.L., damn him! Amusing this morn, Bedlington, who certainly has a liking for a bottle of beer, or even two bottles, dropped into the G.H. intent on beer at 10.59, the bar opens at 11, so the boy said 'One minute more' (and in that minute the alert sounded, the whole staff vanished, and he never got his beer.) Stark War, we felt, so I took him into the Singapore Club, with R. Wilson, and we had a beer there, thanks to our system of Klaxons the service only stops during imminent danger periods. Nora to hospital 7 a.m. – 2 p.m.: she is now working in the hostel, and Katherine also goes at 7 to the blood transfusion section: Victor at 6.45 to Food Production and Vernon Conolly on all-night Mine-Watching every alternate night. I had a lie-off, and went to Fullerton Building. 5 p.m. for all-night duty. The Naval Base is evacuated and handed over to the Army. So much for all the millions spent on it: just when it ought to be proving of the utmost use – we have to destroy it. This war in Malaya is proving yet again the absolute necessity of Air Supremacy. Two alerts before 9.30 p.m., nothing happened. It's rather amusing really, the 2 Europeans, Willmot and I, dash up to the roof, and meet the Fire-Watching squads all rushing down to the 4th Floor, which they are quite entitled to do, by my in-structions, until any necessity for their services arises. But there are some damned good ones too, not on duty tonight – Menon, Ah Bee: after 11 another alert, a lone Jap, searchlights stabbing the sky all over the place. I could hear it: there were a few A-A shots, then a fire started in the direction of the airport, but away past it. All clear 1.55. You can never tell by appearances. T. Kandiah was up on the roof with us, all the time, and he's a miserable-looking specimen, while all the rest had bolted to the 4th Floor. A lovely sunset through light rain, I took several photos, on spec, looking towards the Singapore River, an eerie sight in the declining light, with its black water, houses in utter darkness, a blood-red sun behind, and fires and smoke rising to the Heavens all round.... No more alerts this night, but a constant artillery fire in the Johore direction. We expect the causeway to be blown up at any moment now, and with it, of course, the water supply from Gunong Pulai. (The Japanese Army reached Johore Bahru).

Sunday, 1 February: Mileage: Morris 8, 14,550 = 914 miles. Morris 14, 48,033 = 111 miles. The Johore Causeway was blown up yesterday, and the BATTLE OF SINGAPORE BEGINS. The Argylls piped the last batch of troops across, and all are successfully on the island.... We have destroyed the Naval Base... Incredible.... Nora to hospital 7 a.m. – 2 p.m. 10.15 an alert. Victor arrived at 11, very excited – a bomb fell within 30 yards of him on the road, he had heard it coming and was lying flat, behind a rubber tree; but one of his coolies was killed outright, another had both legs blown off below the knee, and a third badly injured. A pretty shattering experience for Victor, he got the injured ones fixed up, and as work was naturally all finished, came home, rang up 'The Boss' and reported what happened, whereupon said Boss told him it was his duty to go back, (about 10 miles), put the body in his car and take it to the mortuary! A little hard, 'pon my soul, as Stanley Fetherstonhaugh Ukridge would have said. Anyway, he didn't go. Having rung up H.J. Fein, the Dutch Consul, I went to the Consulate to get Nora's passport visa for the Dutch East Indies 'just in case' – Terrific mob there, waited over an hour, then they told me the passport was out of date and wouldn't do anything. However, I sent Ali to our Passport Office and got it made valid for one journey to anywhere outside British Malaya. Then ruthlessly sorted out my most cherished possessions, books, scrap books, reports etc., and finally got everything I value most of all, into 1 suitcase. There is a most varied collection of photos, taken by me all over the Peninsular in 30 years – many unique and unobtainable now – and negatives, all duly catalogued and in negative albums – my original Diaries 1921 – 1941 which I also think are unique in Malaya – and a few personal documents, stamps, securities. And I hope to be able to get this suitcase away, if it comes to that. If it comes to that. I wonder, we must have 60,000 troops on the island. I doubt if they can prevent Japanese landings here and there, but they should be able to drive them off again. On the other hand we seem to be frightfully short of planes. They never appear in droves like the Japs. And if they are allowed to come and bomb the Island, and Singapore Town, when they like and where they like, A-A fire alone cannot stop the frightful devastation and probably destruction of water supplies. But surely more planes are on the way, and until they arrive our forces should be able to hold on, 60,000, men fully equipped. R.B. Horner came in, he has buried his stamp collection in a sealed box in his garden in Kuala Lipis! To Noble's 6 p.m., saw Noel and Doris Bridges, and to Gilliam's to see how he is arranging the bags for a shelter under his porch, which is just like ours.... Early bed, and marvellously a quiet night, full moon.

2 February: Alerts 8, 10, 11 a.m. I am roof-spotting, saw nothing. The sky is grotesque, thick with haze from an enormous pillar of black smoke from oil burning at the Naval Base, whether fired by us or the Japs I know not. I also hear Seletar aerodrome and all it contains, is being destroyed as untenable. Of course you can't 'destroy' these places in the sense that they are completely useless, there must be an incalculable amount of stuff left at the Naval Base. After 11 another alert, we spot them coming in our direction and sound 'danger imminent'. They dropped at least 8 bombs in the sea front aiming at shipping; actually they were not far off a destroyer, but no damage was done. I could see the patches in the sea where the bombs fell. Continuing, they hit a small ship lying alongside in Telok Ayer Basin, there is a terrific blaze, I think it must be a tanker: and several cars and lorries near by are burning furiously. And 2 more large fires started in the same direction, but these were under control after tiffin.... The most astonishing thing is that there seems to be absolutely no opposition from our aircraft, although some A-A fire. Where are they? Have they all gone away? Rumour has it they are busy up-country, attacking communications. About 3 p.m. another alert, we saw 3 planes, presumably Jap, diving in but they came nowhere near us. Today my coolies dammed the drain in my compound which luckily is at the head of a small watershed: my idea is the water can be used for bathing, flushing W.C.'s, etc, if it becomes necessary.... Frozen meats and butter are to be rationed as from Feb. 8th. A quiet night.

3 February: Our well is finished. It has about 3 feet of water in it and it looks quite good water. A long alert 9.30 – 11.15, lots of Jap planes all over the place: none of ours: and curiously, spotting is rendered extremely difficult by the monstrous canopy of smoke and haze from the inferno in the Naval Base: from our eyrie on the Fullerton Building we can see it spreading in all directions. They dropped a lot of bombs at Kranji, and in the docks area, where they started 4 fires, of which 2 were under control fairly quickly. I got what should be unique photos, but can I get them developed? Most places are closed, and Kodak get little work done as staff can't work during the alerts. No news of fighting on the Island. It seems to me to be a matter of communications: if we can't interrupt them, it is only a question of time before they are in a position to overwhelm us by sheer weight of men and materials. We have done a lot of damage to a convoy in the Macassar Straits.... The enemy forced down a Qantas plane at the W. end of Timor and 13 passengers and crew drowned.... Air mails to Australia are suspended.... Dutch Naval Base at Sourabaya bombed for the first time, by 26 bombers escorted by many fighters. 'Rather considerable damage to material' says the official report; and many aircraft lying on the water were damaged. The West Coast Area of Singapore is gazetted as a Battle Area, and has to be evacuated by all civilians by noon on Thursday next. A typical repercussion of my efforts to make things comfortable for the Asiatic Fire-Watching staff in the Fullerton Building at night, is that they have started a gambling school on Floor 3, they congregate there from all floors, in the room I have had blacked out for them so that they can see to read etc. And stay up all night, lose more than they can afford, and in the morning complain that they are much too worn-out by their excessive exertions at Fire-Watching to be able to get back to office by 10.30! It's an uphill business! I have warned them it will not be tolerated.

4 February: An alert just before 10, usually we get this long before there are any planes actually near the Town. On this occasion by great good luck I happened to spring immediately up on to the roof, and again luckily, at once spotted 27 planes coming straight at us at about 25,000 feet, so was able to sound the 'imminent danger' signal about a minute before a whole bevy of bombs fell into the sea near the dock area but close enough to have created considerable alarm if no warning had been given. I presume they approached from the sea, hence the short notice given by the alert. At noon I had just got home, the alert had sounded enroute – we heard planes overhead as we got out of the car, and they dropped a packet fairly close to our house, where I don't know yet. 'All clear' 12.15. I instructed 'Fuzzy' Furze, Jas. Laird and 2 others in the gentle art of roof-spotting – the New Supreme Court is beginning to think about building up an organisation like mine in the Fullerton B! About time, one thinks…. In the noon raid Moorhead's house had a direct hit, also Birtwhistle's, but he had previously moved. No casualties. The boy walked out on us today. He is 'takut' *(afraid)*. Asked permission to go for a haircut and never came back. Artillery fire all night, bang, bang, bang, bang. Nora to bed very early, had her third T.A.B. injection and a slight temperature…. Russian news is good, Libya not so good.

5 February: Alert 5.30 a.m. but nothing near us…. War is responsible for some curious changes in habits of thought – in the morning now I take a look at the sky – if it is brazen I think 'Ha! We'll be able to spot the ******* today': if cloudy, 'H'm, going to be difficult today'. A long alert 10.20 – noon, but we only had the staff off work for 10 minutes, which shows how essential the roof spotters are. A big flight went over us and bombed the airport, but there were only 4 small fires, and I think little damage…. After this, single planes were in the vicinity, over Alexandra Barracks or in that direction, dive-bombing: we watched – the ack-ack seemed useless against it, rather naturally the burst seemed always too late. McConnechy P.W.D., in, very urgently, from Man-Power Bureau, all available European able-bodied men are to help immediately in demolition work at Naval Base, denial of materials to the enemy. I haven't any available at all, Clark-Walker is very busy on Air Observer Corps work…. Does this mean they expect the enemy to gain a foothold in the Naval Base? It looks remarkably like it. Cable from Colin, despatched from England 8th Jan…. Recd. 29th Jan…. delivered to me 5th Feb!!! It runs: 'Cable received awaiting more news all well here thumbs up.' Sent 'Casual Leave' and 'The Northern Circuit' home to England, by registered post (parcel) addressed to Tannie: I saw them through the censorship personally, so there will be no delay in that quarter, and I asked the Controller of Posts and he was quite reassuring about mails getting away. Victor out at work this morning as usual, heard shells swishing over and discovered they were not ours but Japs shelling Bukit Panjang! After that he did not enjoy the swishes so much.... On the way home from office at 5, bought 12 tins of sardines 2.40 dollars, 12 ginger ale (Special Dry) 2.10 dollars, 2 bots. Salt 1.10 dollars. Salt is hard to get, and I couldn't get any large sodas. Tony Lucas rang, he still has not got the letter Joan wrote before she left almost a week ago.... Mat, the skulker, sent his wife round to get his gaji *(salary)*, he is supposed to be still ill, I don't believe it, I think the rumour is gaining ground that servants who have been working for Europeans will get it in the neck!

6 February: Alerts at 4 a.m. and again 5 a.m., we saw and heard nothing, but Nora and I went downstairs to the inside shelter under the staircase, where we have mattresses, cushions etc., always ready. She is still on 7 a.m. – 2 p.m. duty. Another air attack on Sourabaya, and our communique also says our artillery is shelling enemy transport in S. Johore, and the enemy is massing troops: how do they manage to shell transports when, as far as one can see, they have practically no planes to observe with? Of course we have given them co-ordinates, so they have the range of all important objectives such as road junctions. Still – one doubts. The communique adds there was some dive-bombing yesterday and damage to shipping, I very much fear it is the Empress of Asia, coming up the Straits off Pasir Panjang – that is exactly the direction of the dive-bombing we watched yesterday. I hear there were 2,000 troops on board, and all were saved except 30, but I suppose all the equipment is gone, and the modern soldier isn't much use minus his accessories.... And Hurricanes intercepted and turned back a bombing squadron yesterday too. Moulmein is evacuated and the Japs are trying to cross the Salween River: it's a huge obstacle, surely if we have any forces worth the name they can hold them there? It's only 100 miles from Rangoon, some official ass of a spokesman says over the wireless 'They will never take Rangoon', and then goes on to say that if they do, it doesn't much matter, as China has so much war material now, she can carry on for years. Japs are very annoyed about our 'scorched earth' policy, especially in the oilfields, they threaten to 'exterminate' the Dutch forces at Balik Papan if the oilfields there are destroyed. Two alerts this morning, saw a dive-bomber in the direction of Changi, but no bombs fell that we could see. The oil at the Naval Base is blazing away more fiercely than ever, it is now announced that the Japs have hit it with a bomb. The sky is positively weird, as blue as blue but a pall of smoke hangs over everything: a most peculiar dawn, I took a snap, and also another of 'The End of the Naval Base'. The convalescent camp at the back of our quarters is quite a large one and certainly increases our chances of being bombed: and Indian troops are digging a well almost on top of the ridge! How they ever hope to get down to water I can't imagine. Alert 2.30 – 3 p.m., saw nothing. Sent 'Leave 1940' and 2 others by Reg. Post to Tannie.

7 February: Our well water has turned black! It is absorption from the atmosphere created all over the island by the burning naval Base. Who would have thought it possible when we dined on board H.M.S. Glasgow there, only a few short months ago? The place was colossal, a city in itself, and the amount of machinery and engineering paraphernalia generally, positively bewildering. These soldiers continue to fill all my carefully built shelters and we will lose all our staff if it goes on, they are all Aussies – I had a talk with them during an alert. <u>Of course</u> they can't make their own shelters – but they will get out of mine! I get a very unfavourable impression of the ability of the Aussie soldiers to 'take it', and although they can move like rabbits or racehorses when the siren goes, and <u>look</u> as fit as coalheavers, the officer I spoke to said 'Oh! We are much too ill to be able to dig' etc. etc. The Royal Singapore Golf Club course is now the home of hundreds of Bali cattle: the R.A.F. have nearly all gone, and the Navy (ex naval base) occupy the Club House. Alert 9.30 – 10 a.m., we could hear planes in a cloud so gave the 'imminent' signal, and then 27 popped out in the usual formation and loosed bombs on the airport, but the only damage I could see (through x10 binoculars) appeared to be one Hurricane burnt out, but the pilot is safe – I saw him get out and run. Lt. Gen. A.E. Percival made a statement to representatives of the World's Press last night. He told them Singapore will be defended at all costs. There should be no uneasiness about the removal of planes from the Island. Obviously they can't operate from aerodromes under enemy shell fire. We are hitting back every night. The public should also realise that the Naval Base could not operate when subject to shell fire. Permanent black-out starts tonight…. Noel Bridges starts as Survey Directorate at Fort Canning on Tuesday, and is wondering whether to relinquish the Surveyor-General Post or not. I say not – not yet any rate. He is to have the rank of Colonel. So what we have been trying to achieve for a year is accomplished at last. Too late? He tells me Doris – and about 2,000 others – were due to leave by the 'Empress of Asia', sunk on Thursday. When I get home, I find a new menace has arisen – artillery shells from the mainland. Conolly says shells went whistling over the house – he had four officers in, all shattered to bits – nerves – by it, so they finished my beer…. Shells dropped near Manor House, and in Balestier Rd., Lt. Gerrard stayed on, to tiffin and tea. These officers were not Aussies. The congestion in house is not so great now, so many have left, and our party is reduced to Nora and myself: Katherine de Moubray: Connolly and Victor Perrin…. A lie off, and to Fullerton Building 5 p.m. for all-night…. I am weeding out old negatives to get them into smaller compass. About 8 an explosion at the airport, saw it plainly from the roof – would it be a shell? Willmot tells me his wife and child should have sailed last night for India, the passes for the boat were in four batches alphabetically, starting at 6 p.m. They were 9 – 10 p.m. and it took $2^1/_2$ hours to do half-a-mile in the black-out and amidst the queues of cars so when they reached the ship she was moving, to get away before the moon was up. Very bad luck. North-Hunt came to see me, one of his staff has been deliberately disobeying orders and evading Fire-Watching duty, so we are going to fine him two day's pay. The first case. Letters from Colin and Tannie, and a photograph of C. posted Nov. 22. Colin was about to go to Brighton for a final vetting to see if he is a fit and proper person to be an officer in the Navy! He has done over six months as Ordinary Seaman on the Edinburgh – I've always thought what a terrific change it was, from living in your own rooms at Oxford, to being an O.S. on a cruiser.

Sunday, 8 February: A very peaceful night last night in the Fullerton Building and now a lovely dawn over the town and river: it seems incredible that 15 miles away 100,000 men are waiting to kill each other, armed with every conceivable engine of destruction. 'Lord, what fools we mortals be.' In the morning, did some more blackout in the house, in view of this permanent blackout, managed to buy the stuff at Whiteway's yesterday. Bombers passed overhead but dropped nothing near us. Nora to hospital 2 – 9 p.m. We all went to bed early, and there was a most infernal racket the whole night long: suppose it was nearly all our own artillery, and the noise unimaginable if one had not heard it. The house literally shook all night. Nora and I went downstairs. Wonder what they are shooting at – I suppose they know. A dreadful night. The Japs have landed on Pulau Ubin, and also I hear on the West Coast of the Island, but this is not announced. The permanent blackout is now held in abeyance, I don't know why: and official rationing of frozen meat and butter is postponed for a week. The Cold Storage actually have been rationing butter on their own for some time. An American claims to have loosed the Atomic energy in uranium – wish it were true, we would finish this war off in a week or two. And an Aussie claims an invention to stop torpedoes hitting a ship.

9 February: My Royal Singapore Golf Club bill is 10.04 dollars, of which 8 dollars is subscription, and Swimming Club is 4.50 dollars, all subscription! I'm all in favour of supporting them in this time of crisis, but they should cut down the subscription when you get absolutely nothing for it. The Singapore Cricket Club is full of troops and what-not. Half-a-dozen shells whistled over the house at 8 a.m., very disturbing: later I met Hamilton, who is living at Dunearn Road end of Chancery Lane, the shells dropped about 100 yards past his house, so that's about 750 yards past ours, as the shell flies. Their objective may be Newton Circus or Government House – if so they are 500 yards off one and 1000 yards off the other. Shells on Newton Circus would certainly disorganise traffic a lot. Alert 10 – 10.40. I am spotting, we see 24 Japs but they wheel away to W. and N. and are obviously not interested in us. 7 Hurricanes and 2 Buffaloes were up from the Airport before they arrived. Today's Government Gazette includes amongst the notifications

'… orders that all pigs in Province Wellesley be kept confined in sties, and prohibits movements of pigs about Province Wellesley except with the written permission of a Government Veterinary Office'!! The height of absurdity. We are sending our Federated Malay States Standard Sheets to Java for safe keeping: but this morning's paper says the Japs are working up to a large scale invasion of Java! So what? Another alert 12.30, 27 Japs, I saw them clearly, they wheeled over Bukit Timah and dropped bombs in the direction of Kranji, starting a fire which looked like an oil tank. Meeting in my office, S.G. Photo-Litho Section, etc., arrangements re destruction of maps, printing machinery and so on, if it becomes necessary…. Japanese landings between Sungei Kranji and Pasir Laba on the West coast of the Island, in the dark hours of last night, are officially confirmed…. I cannot understand it, they seem to do what they like when they like and where they like. At tea Katherine brought Lt. Paterson, he is on the staff at Fort Canning and says it's a 9-1 chance that we hold the Island…. Well, I hope he's right: I can't see it. We haven't the air support, apart from anything else. About 6 p.m. nine shells whistled over the house, very close, exploded almost simultaneously with the whistle, it's not at all pleasant, I much prefer bombs! One soldier in the camp was killed, about 100 yards away from our house…. Mailvaganam who is surveying small plots for food cultivation not far away, had 3 near him this morning, and Bovell arrived shortly to say one fell near his house, 13 Malcom Rd., that's 250 yards from us, and blew out all his blackout! After this we had a comparatively peaceful night. The Aussie troops still bolt for our shelters like homing rabbits when the siren sounds or shells are about. The servants won't stand it. The dhobie has now thrown his hand in. (Gleaned from Jap. Newspaper 14.2.43: Zero hour was midnight: and at 12.16 a.m. 9th, Jap troops landed on Singapore island. By 7 p.m. they had captured Tengah aerodrome.)

10 February: Ayah sends a 'phone message she is not well and will not be coming to work today. Yet another defection I fear. Still, it was decent of her to let us know and I would not blame her – what with the troops and the shells, the life in this house is no picnic for them, especially as we are out most of the day. The 7.30 commuique says the Japs 'INFILTRATE' further on the Island, and we have executed a further withdrawal…. It seems hopeless…. 'Infiltrate' – maddening word! Why don't we exfiltrate a bit? Apparently every time a few Japanese soldiers manage to bypass our Army, which is the easiest thing imagineable in this country – they are 'infiltrating', and the Army withdraws. It's disgusting. Alert 11 – 11.30, 27 flew over but not near us…. Still the most extraordinary cloud and haze affects over the Naval Base. This morning we saw a quaint sight, a stout gent in khaki, with a long, gray unkempt beard and moustache, and hair six inches long – it was M. Baker of 'offal' fame – see my 1920 diary. I return home 12.30 to find my compound completely occupied by an Australian R.A. Battery: they have made themselves quite at home, dug or are digging a pit laterine above the tennis court (nice for my well); our servants are shattered to bits, they have been all over the house, drunk all the beer they could find, in spite of the cook's frantic protests: been through all the bedrooms and annexed various articles, including Victor's razor and scissors, and my Winchester electric torch. They all look very hale and hearty, nobody has even a scratch, and I gather they have left their guns at Bukit Panjang, and beat it in lorries as fast as they could get away: the lorries are all in our garden now. Tony Lucas, who is a gunner himself, came round in the afternoon to park his luggage in our house, although there is no guarantee that we can keep it safe. He found our place full of the Australian Battery, all our shelters even including those in the house – when I protested, one gent asked me if I was going to object to the Japs occupying them! Tony tried to find out what happened – but it all seemed very vague and appeared to boil down to the simple fact that they had seen a few Japanese soldiers in the distance, who appeared to be coming in their direction, 'so we thought it about time we left'. 'But hadn't you got any rifles?' says the bewildered Tony. 'Rifles? Of course we had some rifles – can't you see them over there?' So Tony asked in horror-stricken accents 'and you just left your guns?' 'Oh yes, we left them'!! Eventually I struck a bargain about shelters – they can have the whole bloody lot, including that under the porch (this is tactful of me, for I haven't the slightest chance of keeping them out) but the cubby hole in the house, under the stairs, they will keep out of. And I tell the servants they can use it as well as us. The news is bad – there are more Jap landings on the Island and we 'withdraw' again – one is really forced to the conclusion that our troops are not fighting hard, making every allowance for dive-bombing and inadequate or total lack of air support. After all, if troops are at really close quarters, dive bombing seems to me to lose its value. And to put the lid on everything, an urgent 'phone message 11 p.m. from Noel Bridges, to vacate house and go to live in Fullerton Building at once – tomorrow may be too late, the news is very bad he says. So I arouse Katherine and the rest, we hold a mass meeting and do a lot of essential packing, but decide No! we will not flit from the house like a lot of thieves in the night: we will sleep fully clothed, and if conditions are so bad 9 hours hence that we can't get to Town – well, we'd better just stay where we are. After all, the servants are standing by very well, that is the old cook and Ali, and Osman the old Javanese gardener, and Amat his son, and I would hate to be 'flown' in the morning. But we certainly pass a most uncomfortable night, trying to sleep under the stairs, with large guns – ours or theirs – pooping off all night and rattling everything to blazes. And the Government – bless 'em – today issued ration books covering the next 26 weeks!!! Let's hope their optimism is justified. (Japs attacked the line Bukit Panjang – Bukit Timah 'the last line of defence' and captured Bukit Timah at night after bayonet and fiercest fighting of the whole campaign.)

11 February: Rapid packing and Nora and Katherine left in the Morris 8 for hospital, K. driving: I was to wait for her returning, but the alert sounded soon after 7 a.m., I thought she might be delayed and so might I, I'd better get away. Gave cook 20 dollars, and Osman 10 dollars, and Amat 10, they are all behaving splendidly, of course sent their womenfolk away because the soldiers overran the house and pinched the shelters. Put a lot of stores in the car, and also left a lot, my aim in packing has been to have enough either in the house or the Fullerton Building to enable me to stay in either for some time. So I got to Fullerton Building about 8, with Ali. The Japanese forces appear to be approaching from N.W. I don't know where they are, but Fullerton Building is full of people who have left their homes as we have.... This is a hell of a day: innumerable alerts and imminent danger signals from us. No oppostion at all bar A-A fire. They appeared to hit the oil tanks at Pulau Samboe and Pulau Bukum (though later I heard we started these fires ourselves – and started fires at the docks, and in other places.) Caldbeck Macgregor's is burnt out, the stocks of drinks had been mostly destroyed, anyway, but the populace had a glorious time getting what booze they could. It was set on fire purposely. Lunched at John Little's with Victor, and Birtwhistle, their 'Raiders overhead' signal went off about six times during lunch, but we got ours largely by helping ourselves: it is true John Little's would be a most uncomfortable place to be if a bomb fell on it, and one can't blame the boys for beating it when the signal goes. I returned to our house at 2 p.m., all is normal – the staff had locked everything up and departed. The refrigerator is ticking over and the house clean. I switched off all electricity, collected a few things and returned to Fullerton Building. There are troops everywhere in Town, it seems peculiar there should be so many doing absolutely nothing, when you'd expect every sound man to be in the front line, resisting this advance. There's nothing visibly wrong with them. What is the explanation? If it's the obvious one – desertion – we are finished. I cannot understand it at all. To General Hospital 6 p.m., saw Nora, she decided to stay there: I would have liked to show her my menage in the Fullerton Building, but it is wise to stay on the spot. Took Katherine back to our house, she collected a few things and drove her car away.... There is a boat out today, Nora could have got away on it, but would not. However, I told Willmot about it and he got his wife and child away. Destination unknown.... Noel is now a full-blown Colonel, attached to Fort Canning, Malaya Command G.H.Q. All transmitters and accessories of the Malaya Broadcasting Corporation were destroyed this morning – now our only means of communication with the outside world is a secret Military transmitter which connects with G.H.Q. London. Yet Government is still buying suitable private cars! How can one reconcile these seemingly irreconcilable facts. Victor and I dined off a tin of Camp Pie, and had bread and peaches and milk which I brought from the house.... Sleep in my office, on a mattress on the floor. A very disturbing night with artillery fire but no alerts.

12 February: Should have been a Rural Board meeting 10 a.m.! Postponed....
My Chinese clerk asks, can I not get away? He thinks I ought to, for the first time
he fears the worst. I tell him no, I don't propose to run away and leave the staff
without a Head and to face whatever may be going to happen. My staff have backed
me up jolly well and I'm very pleased with them. The 'Singapore Free Press' is
reduced to a single sheet 11 x 8 inches. It says 'Enemy held on all fronts', and
contains an announcement by the Governor, all spirits in anybody's possession are
to be destroyed by noon tomorrow! Six months or 2,000 dollars is the penalty for
infringement.... I shall probably risk it! My office has the most wonderful hiding
places. It may be a precaution in case we have to capitulate, we don't want drink-
inflamed Japanese soldiers about the place – but a contributory cause is certainly
some heavy drinking by our own men – the Navy rifled the drink stocks when they
took over the Royal Singapore Golf Club, and the Aussies put the lid on it yesterday – they have broken and behaved very badly. The town was full of them last
night, many were tight and many were demanding to know when they are going to
be evacuated! And these are the men, who when we entertained them in our house
before the War reached Malaya, used to have one stock remark: 'all we want is a
chance to get at them bloody little Jappos before we are sent back to Australia!
D'you think I can get 2 on one bayonet?' Yesterday the Japanese invited us by a
polite letter to a parley, no use carrying this resistance on any longer, they said. We
were to send a car with a special flag along Bukit Timah Rd. We refused. Today
destroyed all important maps, including hundreds of Aviation maps of Malaya,
Rhio Archipelago, topo. maps etc. An alert at 8 a.m., bombs at Changi, and another
at 9, 10 and 11 – a fire in the direction of Bukit Timah – the town is literally ringed
with fires. Oil tanks at Alexandra appear to have gone up, and I watched them dive-
bomb a small vessel, but they never hit it. Nora is the only Survey Dept. wife left,
Doris Bridges has gone and Mrs. Fendall left yesterday.... We tiffin off herrings
and baked beans then to hospital, saw Nora and Katherine – and drove to our house
once more. There are all sorts and sizes of guns round it, Chancery Lane and Mt.
Rosie Rd. are bristling with them, hiding under the trees by the roadside, but there
are no troops in our compound now. The house and its contents are intact, but
Victor's car is stolen, and Shotter's left in our compound for safety, reposes in the
drain about 100 yards down the road, doors open, uselessly sabotaged.... The Aussie
troops seem in many cases to be completely out of hand. They have looted Clark-
Walker's house, drunk 4 cases of booze and eaten a case of tinned food.... Nelson
went down from the Fullerton Building this evening to look at his car, which is
parked just across the river in Empress Place. It was immobilised, and he arrived
just in time to see them tear out all the wires and ruin it generally – when they saw
him approaching they took pot shots at him as well, so he beat it, very incensed. So
I thought I'd go do down and have a look at my car, the little Morris 8, but they all

said NO! The Aussies are down there in force, full of booze, and they take pot shots at anybody. (It is after 9 p.m. and there's a curfew at 9) so I don't go.... We have tried to rig up a wireless in the Fullerton Building, but it is D.C. so no good: Wilson's and Hamilton's have been burnt out already.... This is the most extraordinary day for rumours – the Japs are pushed off the Island – Chinese have landed at Port Swettenham – Americans have landed at Mersing and captured Penang! They have bombed every aerodrome in Malaya into little pieces with Flying Fortresses! The one certain fact seems to be that the Aussies have been incredibly lacking in morale, discipline, and guts. The Singapore Club has a historic evening, the last stengahs are being quaffed prior to the destruction of stocks, they have over 200 cases of whisky alone, which must be got rid of ere noon tomorrow. Obviously the members can't drink it, but they have a good try. I went down from the 5th Floor to assist in the obsequies. Just imagine a Singapore Club in which you can't have a stengah! All the Fathers of Singapore will turn in their graves, and a new name will have to be found for the time-hallowed 'stengah shifter'.... It's an astounding scene, wish I had the pen of Frankau to describe it. The Club of course is absolutely filled to capacity with refugee members from up-country and Singapore members washed out of hearth and home by the ever-advancing wave of the hordes, of Nippon: all the fossils of Malaya are there, paleozoic (Abang), mesozoic (E.N.T.C.) and cainozoic (me): all the boys have disappeared, except one faithful retainer, dumping out stengahs behind the Bar, with Braodbent, the Club Steward, perspiringly assisting. And what stengahs! You still go through the formality of signing for them (though I doubt if anyone now expects to get his bill at the end of this month) but you can have 'em any strength you like, it matters not, one, two, three, four fingers, take what you want, the rest will be down the drains and into the Singapore River before noon tomorrow.... I met Pop Wiseman, Stringfellow, Scott, from Malacca, and lots and lots of others. Inspected the Building for Fire-Watchers, found none on 6th, 5th, 4th floors, five on the 3rd, and two on the 2nd! So much for my organisation. Press Censors, Dept. of Information and Publicity, Cable and Wireless, left for Java today. And 'Singapore Free Press' ceased publication – they have got no gas at night.

13 February: Amin my peon arrives bright and early, stout fellow! and, as ever, his first act is to turn the calendar – watch him and find it is Friday the Thirteenth. Umph. He is very faithful, and if by a miracle we pull through, I shall not forget it. Nine a.m., the pounding begins again with the bombing of Stamford Rd. and vicinity: can't see how much damage, but it looks bad.... Bombing and shelling incessantly. The shells are worse than the bombing. You never know when you are going to get a whistle, BANG! And be blown to bits. Nora rang me up at midday, she has orders to go. On what ship, or whither, it is not known. So I went to the General Hospital in the Morris 8, see Dr Bowyer the C.M.O. – he knows no more than I do about the vessel: says this is the saddest day of his life, and I can well believe it. Casualties are arriving by the hundreds, and God knows how many of his nursing staff are leaving this afternoon. We discuss again and again, Nora has got to go, and rightly decides to do so. Katherine will stay, George has been wounded and is in hospital. So I drive Nora to the docks, 3.15, what a mob! Women and children first – so we say 'Good-bye and Good luck'! She takes my precious suit-case, lucky there's a Tamil porter available: I stand on the top of a car near the barrier, and as she disappears round the corner, wave a farewell to the last survey wife to leave Malaya.... I wonder when we shall see each other again. I hang about the dock gates in case anything goes wrong and she has to come back. Suddenly bombers come straight overhead, a hell of a raid, and a rain of bombs on the docks and I fear very near her ship. I rushed to the dock gates, they would not let me in, but luckily saw Middlebrook inside, the mob at the gates had dispersed when the bombers came. I explained I was anxious in case my wife had been hit, and he induced the military police to let me in, on my assurance that I had no intention of jumping the ship and getting away. Once inside, I found it was about a mile walk to the place of embarkation. Poor Nora, I had no idea it was so far, I'd never have saddled her with that case of mine if I'd known.... I passed blazing cars and lorries, several wounded, and one corpse, but saw no women amongst them.... When I reached the embarkation place, which is alongside the Laburnam, I found they are being sent out on a tender to the ship, and all the women have already gone, so Nora must be safely on board, thank Heaven: the ship, I am told, is one of the China river steamers *(the Kuala)*. There are crowds of men waiting to board the tender, some in uniform, some not – I spoke to Johnny Walker of the S.U. Club, and thought I might just have a look round to see if Nora's luggage is away – and I find my precious suitcase with all my photographs and diaries in it! So I picked it up and brought it back, luckily managed to get a lift. Returning to the Fullerton Building I find the ground floor has been converted into a military hospital, since morning.... And Noel Bridges has gone to Java. He doffed his Colonel's uniform yesterday, so he was a Colonel for 2 days! Order from Malaya Command, Fort Canning, to destroy all maps of Singapore Island, which seems rather foolish as the Japs have already got thousands and my stock is very small, about 6 – however, they are destroyed, except my own copy, which I must have. Fort Canning has the main stocks. A news sheet compiled from wireless and other sources was produced – the 'Fullerton News', – on a Gestetner, a very creditable effort. We hold a line Ang Mo Kio – McRitchie – Pasir Panjang; and there is hand-to-hand fighting on the Race-course, is the official bulletin. Slept in my office, the others slept elsewhere, said it was safer, no doubt they were right – I had a very disturbed night, it is distinctly disturbing to hear the whine and BANG! of shells all night long and wonder when one is going to zoom through your window. Wonder if Nora's boat is getting through safely.

– III –
THE TRAP CLOSES

As the Japanese began their take-over of Singapore, and Tom Kitching and the thousands of British servicemen and civilians waited anxiously to know their fate, there were others who even then were desperately trying to escape the clutches of the Japanese, some into the jungles of Malaya, but most on board a motley collection of boats and ships, described in the title of a book by Geoffrey Brooke as 'Singapore's Dunkirk'. Some 70 small vessels left the harbour between 10 – 16 February only to be attacked by Japanese bombers and to face the Japanese invasion fleet in the Banka Straits. Most of them were either captured or sunk by naval gunfire or bombing.

Among the flotilla was the *Kuala*. On 14 February, St Valentine's day, Mrs de Malmanche had just finished breakfast: 'I took the empty plates to the galley and, as I was coming back, some planes flew over. We heard the planes go over again and then I opened the door. As I did so, I saw huge columns of water rising around the *Kung Wo* and when they cleared, it had disappeared. Hastily closing the door again, I said, We're going to be bombed and, even as I said it, there was an ear-splitting crash and the roof vanished, leaving us in bright sunlight. Nobody said a word, but we all scrambled to our feet and scattered. The bomb had scored a direct hit on the bridge and saloon and went straight through into the engine-room. Dozens of people were trapped in the wrecked saloon. The casualties in the crowded holds must have been terrible. Within minutes, the ship was on fire, the flames ably assisted by our leafy camouflage. Added to the cries of the wounded was a terrifying shrill scream from the engine-room – probably a cracked boiler. We had to abandon ship by either jumping straight into the sea or sliding down a long rope which the sailors had fastened to the ship's rail. A little boy went down the rope in front of me, so crazy with fear that he wouldn't let go of the rail, but had to be forced; he was drowned. I slid down the rope, but seemed to go an awful long way under water; when I surfaced, I swam about until I was able to grab a piece of wreckage. Someone had brought a boat out from the shore; it was already full and many people were clinging to the sides. I made for it and hung on with the others. There was only one oar, which was being used, not very effectively, by an elderly woman. The planes were still flying backwards and forwards, dropping bombs on the people swimming around…. There was an unpleasant whistling sound and, looking up, I saw a bomb falling straight towards us. We all cringed towards the side of the boat and, the next minute, we were caught up in a huge wave, which flung us on to the rocky beach of the island. Everybody scrambled over the rocks and ran up the steep thickly wooded hillside. Halfway up, the planes came again and we crouched behind trees for protection. Bombs fell and our boat went up in smoke.'

Among the refugees on the *Kuala* was Nora Kitching. She has been carried wounded on a stretcher on board the vessel a day earlier.

Tom, in captivity in Singapore, and her sons and daughter, Colin, Brian and Joan, knew nothing of the fate of the *Kuala* at the time and it was only after the final surrender of the Japanese in 1945 that the family at home knew for sure that their mother had not survived.

14 February 1942: St. Valentine's Day! What a mockery. We still hold the same lines as yesterday, at noon. Some bombing, and the shelling is more or less incessant, I hear 12,000 were killed in the Town yesterday, 1,500 corpses were thrown in one communal pit at the General Hospital. There is still water in the taps, and I have a reserve supply of about 20 gallons in kerosene tins and bottles. Feeding here in my room now are Husband, Sworder, Irving, and Perrin: we have food enough to stand 2 months' siege, and I have acquired a grand oil stove, and some kerosene, so I made tea and had Grape Nuts for breakfast: haven't tasted them since my jungle-camping days. There is a 'Straits Times', a leaflet, the last issue for sometime I imagine – unless we can drive the Japs off the Island, this shelling cannot go on indefinitely without civilian morale cracking. Fisher came in, says the orders are to defend Fort Canning to the last man and the last cartridge – and Malaya Command want all the maps of Singapore Island which I can possibly produce! 'But damn it all, man, they gave me orders yesterday to destroy every single copy.' 'Yes, but now they think they might want them.' 'Well, I haven't got any – haven't you any at Fort Canning?' 'No, they are all destroyed.' 1.40 p.m., two shells on Fort Canning and one on the Old Supreme Court – for the first time. I am proud of my building, it's the only one left functioning with warnings, and my roof-spotters are doing their stuff splendidly. There are no A.R.P. sirens, we do our own spotting and hoot with the Klaxons. Went to see Cellan-Jones the dentist, got a pang or two in the left upper recently, and if I <u>have</u> to be interned, I don't want to add toothache to my troubles. However, he says all O.K., probably recent nervous strain has caused a little neuralgia.... Parked my stamps in what I hope will be a safe place. We must watch the water now, there are bound to be corpses in McRitchie Reservoir.... My Head Computer Elayathamby, turned up this morning, a stout fellow. He broke down and wept – it is very bad luck, he has been here for years and was probably on the verge of promotion to a special post. I console him as best as I can, anything that may happen in the near future is an interlude only. I've given him my two volumes of 'Quaint Trengganu', and 'War Voyage 1940' to keep and post to my home address in better times if necessary.... *(Elayathamby did faithfully return these to the family after the war.)* It's a painful business losing thirty years of records, pictorial and otherwise. It is going to be a difficult proposition to keep Asiatics out of this Building, families (probably rendered homeless by bombing or shelling) are already camping on the staircase, complete with babies and impedimenta, and sanitation will be negligible...; Yet I find it hard to throw them out, and haven't done so yet. 1.50 p.m. shells, shells, shells. 2.15, took photos, on the roof, of shelling: 4 shells into houses between River Valley Rd. and the River, near Hill St. Police Station, and saw one plop into the River, it didn't explode. 2.45, walked round the Fullerton Building, the big bar room of the Singapore Club is now a hospital – the Singapore Cricket Club was converted some time ago. Walked to Raffles Square, bought a few essentials at John Little's and the Dispensary – their stocks are low and buying is restricted – I got small portable things like elastoplast and aspirin. Met an Asiatic calling for troops to go and stop looting of shops in Malacca St. by Chinese. 3 p.m. hear Japs have broken through.... 6, we are counter-attacking, 7, no water, have they got the reservoirs, or is it just damaged mains? By request drove car to Hill St. Police Station to collect a police officer and his baggage, his nerves have gone owing to the shelling.... The Asiatic Police are disbanded; there is an big bomb hole in the middle of the Road, poles and wires all over the place, drains full of booze, broken bottles and cases, getting rid of liquor under the prohibition. What a mess.... And there is no Police Force, Chinese are looting a liquor shop down River Valley Road. I hear the A.I.F. are being sent to deal with them: if so there'll be bloodshed all right, and having driven the Chinese away, the A.I.F. will undoubtedly complete the looting. Return to Fullerton Building with Gilliam and the policeman and his bags. Gilliam and other Post Office men have some idea of getting hold of a boat and beating it for Sumatra, say there would be room for me if I want to go: I don't know what to say, there seems little point of staying if we are to be interned – on the other hand even if Singapore falls – and damn it, it's not down yet – surely we will be of considerable use in restoring normal working conditions or improving the lot of our Asiatic staffs? That at any rate seems to me to be what we are here for, partly: and also it would be very bad if all the Europeans deserted the sinking ship like a lot of rats. No, I shan't go.... On the other hand there's a lot to be said for the school who take the attitude, 'What use are we to anybody in internment? We're Off!' Best, Goss, Clark-Walker are in this category, and they have a boat and say they might have room for me. The danger of large-scale invasion of the Fullerton Building by the populace and/or troops increases hourly: I manage to get one gate locked, the key of the other has been stolen: and the main entrance by the river is stiff with troops bringing in stores, whether legitimately or not I don't know, could not find anyone in authority. This night I moved my mattress to the inside of the Survey Office on the 5th Floor, which has 2 roofs over it and is immune from the shelling if it continues in its present direction. All the Survey Dept., Field Survey Coy. Officers are there too. 9 p.m. made coffee for six on my beautiful stove, and they pronounced it very good, which will tickle Nora if she ever sees this. *(At this point, Nora may well already have been dead, since the Kuala was sunk on that day, Saturday, February 14th.)* And at 9.30 the water is on again, so I wash up: there is no shelling at the moment, is our rumoured counter-attack succeeding? Bed 10 p.m. There are a lot of bangs, it is our guns I think, and an air attack is unlikely, no moon and a pall of smoke. In view of the water shortage I put out a notice all over the building, that all the pull-plugs are to be flushed by water out of the Singapore River, and all garbage is to be dumped there as there no sanitary coolies: the Sikh watchman is still functioning.

15 February: A comparatively quiet night: no news. Heavy artillery fire early morn, shells at Fort Canning and in the direction of Raffles Hotel, but further away, and the Union Building: which also has been hit by a bomb – a curious effect of the bomb was that the tops blew off 10 Thermos flasks in one room, but the glass containers remained intact. Why? Wilton and Irving made an attempt to get away last night, in a Chinese sampan, but the current beat them and they had to come back. They were trying to reach a twakow lying outside the breakwater, on which they had observed a crew. Husband, Clark-Walker, Goss, Best, Nelson, and Edwards of the P.W.D. are going away in Best's small launch – if they can get away. Husband typed out an official memo., authorising them to go – and got me to sign it as Surveyor-General! I gave Best one of the maps before I destroyed the rest, of the islands south and west of Singapore: they intend to make for the Indragiri River and thence overland to Padang on the West Coast of Sumatra. It's possible, both Best and Clark-Walker are excellent yaughtsmen. Japs reach Mt. Keppel, W. of Empire Dock, 'Resistance continued stubbornly' but 3.30 p.m. conference Percival, Yamashita, in Ford works: unconditional surrender 7.50 p.m. (Jap. Paper, 14.2.43) Interpolated. Dive-bombing and machine-gunning in the street most of the morning.... I saw H.E. *(His Excellency, the Governor, Sir Shenton Thomas)* about the water position in this Building, flushing, etc. Midday a heavy air-raid near Clifford Pier along Collyer Quay, lots of cars ablaze – I took what should be very interesting photos. The Fire Brigade were out pretty promptly. 3.30, bombs in Stamford Rd., and round the Cathedral, which looks as though it may be slightly scarred.... I hear we are surrendering at 4 p.m.... If they have the reservoirs – and I think they have – the Town must be finished.... And our troops are all over the place, just loafing, a dreadful sight. Why didn't I go on Nora's boat? I could have walked onto the tender. But I'd promised not to when they let me in. 3.45, a most colossal row of artillery fire, 'they say' we are using up our ammunition, by order. I don't know....

The Japs pump scores of shells into the Town – a lot of it is ablaze – this can't go on. Little's and Robinson's are thrown open to the public, take what you like. They are cleaned out. Dave Nelson is back. He went to the launch with the others, then at the last moment decided he could not go: he is embodied as a Volunteer and it would amount to desertion. Well, I admire him for it.... They found a lot of Aussies occupying the launch and trying to get away in it, and the only thing that induced them to get out was the official memo. signed by me! Which is ironical when you look at it the right way! Dave and I adjourned to the main survey office, where there is a good view of the sea, and through a telescope we described the launch dancing on the waves in the sunshine, well out on her way to sea. Regretfully we turned away – wonder if they will make it? 6.30 p.m. from my window I see a boatload of Aussie soldiers leaving, in a small launch, they don't look as though they'll get far. Sumatra is the only possible objective unless you want to get marooned on some small island.... All is quiet, there must be a cease fire order.... All the Field Survey Company invades my room, some hard words are spoken about certain personages beating it and leaving the others to carry the baby. 11 p.m. Dead quiet. I lock my room and sleep in the main survey office on 4 asprins and a stiff stengah.

16 February: Still all is quiet. I shave and wash, before 8 an officer – don't know his name – comes in and telephones Fort Canning from my office: he tells me all was over at 8.30 last night. So the 'Fortress' of Singapore has fallen in one week! It all seems like a dream. Surely shelling the Town, and the damage to the water supply, was foreseen once they were on the Island – or even from Johore. And if we surrendered on that account, then why did Percival make that confident statement on Feb. 7, and Paterson on Feb.9? We had no 'back door' defence at all: the military pundits must have thought we could stop an attack down the Peninsula. They may have counted on Siamese help – Sir Josiah Crosby up in Bangkok was entirely deceived – but why blame the Siamese when we could achieve so little, they hadn't a hope and probably knew it.... Military plans were certainly based on fighting in the North, I know that from the mapping programme. Our front door had marvelous defences, big guns to blow anything out of the water: mines: the most intricate system of barbed wire and other barriers, for 20 miles along the South Coast, the beach, the docks, the Town. Elaborate arrangements for the evacuation of the civil population from these so-called Battle Areas – where never a shot was fired in anger! On the Johore side absolutely nothing – so the Japanese attacked from that side. Simple. Then, of course, a lot of the Indian troops were raw recruits and should never have been sent here. And many of our own were rushed straight into action off the ships, never having seen tropical conditions in their lives. As for the Aussies, with all the goodwill in the world – the less said the better. An abysmal failure.... And above all, no air support. No one can say what the outcome might have been if we'd had that. And the effect on the morale of the troops – and the civilian population all over the Peninsular – would have been immense. You could see that on the very rare occasion our planes were in the sky, though I never saw a single scrap in the air in spite of constant work on the roof of the Fullerton Building, the finest vantage point in Singapore. And as it proved, there was far too much mechanical transport – they had only to hop into lorries to 'execute a strategic withdrawal owing to infiltration'. Infiltration! How I grew to hate that word on the wireless. And I don't know yet, and never will understand, why it should be only one side which can infiltrate in a country like Malaya, where in almost any place your range of vision is restricted to a few yards. Well, surely at any rate the surrender is not unconditional, with our Army practically intact as it appears to be. Present orders for us are to stay where we are…. Ali reported 8 a.m. He and his wife have been slightly wounded by bomb splinters. He has taken the car with my permission and gone to see our house…. One of the Meteorological Branch Chinese came in too, expressed his sorrow and sympathy, and can I give him anything as a souvenir of myself? Some small personal article, anything will do. I gave him a serviette ring, and he departed immensely pleased with it. Ali came back, couldn't reach the house, stopped by a Japanese patrol on the road. He suggested he should take the car to his quarters, safer there, cars are being looted and stolen and commandeered all over the place. I agree. Still no news, is the surrender unconditional? Hugh Fraser (Acting Colonial Secretary) and Dawson (Secretary for Defence) have gone to the Japanese H.Q. on Bukit Timah Rd. I suppose this will be in connection with the civil population of Singapore – I still have a hope that we may be evacuated. 11 a.m. Hamilton and I left in his car to try to get to our house on Mt. Rosie Rd. It's really a most extraordinary situation. British troops all over the place. Fully armed. And apparently quite contentedly waiting to see what is going to happen next. Lashings of motor transport of every description. And yet we have surrendered. And the number of Jap. troops to be seen is absolutely negligible, what you do see is toughish-looking little chaps. But from whatever angle you look at this debacle, the conclusion is inevitable that these troops don't approach 1914 – 1918 standard, and that the manner of the fall of Singapore provides the blackest page in the History of the British Empire. We found Clemenceau Avenue impassable, a huge hole stops all traffic, it must have been made by us to stop tanks, on the far side are anti-tank defences. So we tried Bukit Timah Rd., and found the same thing. Returned via Orchard Rd., a Jap patrol stopped us. At length we tried Cavenagh Rd. (past Govt. House, there has been terrific shelling all round here), New Cemetery Rd., Thomson Rd., Chancery Lane, but are stopped at the Mount Rosie junction. We indicated by signs that we want to go on, one soldier removed my wrist watch, but by intelligible noises and signs I induce him to give it back. He looks in the car. There is literally nothing in it but Hamilton and me, so at last we are allowed to proceed up Mt. Rosie Rd., and reach the house. It is entirely undamaged by shells or bombs, and nothing appears to have been near it: I open the front door with my keys, we go upstairs – what a sight! It has been looted by our own troops – Aussies – as the various bits of uniform here and there testify. Every desk, drawer, box, wardrobe, cupboard store, has been forced open and the contents thrown all over the house, quite uselessly and wantonly. All the liquor and most of the stores are gone. The typewriter has taken a punch on all the keys simultaneously, which has ruined it for life. Nora's and Joan's dresses, and my clothes, and the bedclothes, and everything else are thrown about as if a herd of elephants had been in. However most things are retrievable, the refrigerator, glass, china et hoc genus omne are intact, so if we are allowed to return to our homes I can soon get things shipshape. Morris 14 is still in the garage and intact, so is the firewood, and even my spare 25 gallons of petrol in a large drum in a corner of the tennis court. There is no point in staying, I can't do anything, so we return to Fullerton Building at noon. There are still very few Japs about. Hear H.E. is to issue a proclamation from the Japanese High Command, that we should return to our homes. That will suit me, but many houses have been stripped absolutely bare and there may be a lot more looting yet. Later the proclamation is cancelled: the Japanese order 'All enemy civilians' (! This really includes the whole population but means Europeans) to parade on the Singapore Cricket Club Padang tomorrow – essential services are excepted. I don't know if I am essential as Head of the Department. I think I should be, if my Asiatic staff are to start functioning again as outlined in yesterday's communique. Those who parade are to take with them clothing sufficient for 10 days, and only what they can carry: no transport will be provided. Take no food, rations will be supplied. This is the gist of a notice circulated officially. So I get things ready, a careful selection of what I can carry (how far no one knows). I pack myself, into a very small case 17" x 12" x 6" and a rucksack addressed to the Director of Geological Surveys and providentially delivered here as the next best place after Perak Postal Services were suspended. There are two, I give Victor one.... Also pack and labelled my personal possessions as far as possible, in the hope that the Custodian of Enemy property, or his Japanese equivalent, may save something from the wreck. Apart from books, I have a canteen of cutlery, reflex camera $1/_4$ plate, a Rolliflex, a new 16 mm Cine-Kodak and about 1,000 ft of beautiful films, and my precious suitcase, with all its diaries and photographs, lots of new clothes, a brand new typewriter, lots of other miscellaneous stuff salvaged from the house and dumped in the car – and enough food and drink for months. And stamps and covers worth about $1000. Nobody has any idea where we are going to, or what will be done with us at the end of ten days, but 'clothing for 10 days' presumably means something.... Victor went down to the river to bring up a bucket of water, wherewith to flush the

W.C.s .... River rather low, he had to balance in a precarious position to fill the bucket – and at that very moment a large seagull glided down and passed over his head – its shadow on the water looked exactly like a plane, and he has never been nearer falling into a river through fright than he was at that moment. After early dinner the Dept. or most of what is left of it, gravitates to my office; it is very hard on the Field Survey Coy. They will all be Prisoners of War I suppose. They are naturally fed up with things; there is lots of whisky, we have a somewhat rorty night on what is presumably our last night of freedom, and there's a good deal of plain speaking about the Survey Dept. and things in general!

17 February: Shrove Tuesday it is – what a day! I must try to describe it as best I can. Firstly in view of a possible long march, which I'd rather do on an empty tummy in this climate, I had no breakfast. Went to see H.E. early; the surrender is unconditional: I must say this surprises me, I had hoped for terms, with such large forces and resources still available in Singapore. H.E. is very sorry, he doesn't think I'm 'essential', I should parade with the rest at 10.30: – 'If the Japanese say "Why is the Chief Surveyor essential" I should find it very hard to say why.' I could say that I am also Surveyor-General and Deputy now, however let's get on with it. H.E. thanks me very much for all I've done, referring especially to Fullerton Building organisation (tho' that was child's play to the initiation of the Singapore Censorship Sept. 1939 – March 1940) – a hand-shake and we parted. So I have one almighty rush until 10.30. My last Official act is to write out a full list of my staff for the Colonial Secretary, the Japs want them with the view of issuing 'passes': this takes up much valuable time which I might have occupied in storing my personal property in safe or inaccessible places, my strong room e.g. But I had one stroke of luck, E.J.H. Corner is in charge of the storage of valuable records etc. to be put in the Raffles Library where they should be safe: he had heard of my 30 years diaries, photographs etc., and came to ask about them. So on his instructions I labelled the suitcase SCIENTIFIC RECORDS OF T. KITCHING. CHIEF SURVEYOR. SINGAPORE. And deposited it in his room, so that's one load off my chest. Next duty is to deliver the staff list to the Col. Sec.'s Office: this isn't so easy as it sounds, there is a barking sentry on the Cavenagh Bridge, he has already dealt ferociously with several pedestrians for no apparent reason – we can observe him from my office. However there's no time to waste, I sally forth and cross the Bridge waving the list as a sort of Open Sesame, and although he waggles his rifle with fixed bayonet in an aggressive manner, nothing untoward occurs and I reach C.S.O. with no hitches. The place is seething with our troops but eventually I discovered a very harassed U.S. and delivered my list. I have been punctilious about this as it may benefit my Asiatic staff and I take it that's what I am here for. Dash back to Fullerton Building, seize my rucksack and case, and Sworder, Victor and I marched to the Padang looking like Christmas trees and arrived punctually at 10.30. I had locked my own office and given the key to O. Watson. The Field Survey Company are still waiting in my main office for instructions as Prisoners of War. On the Padang are hundreds of people, but not so many as I expected. It is extremely hot; I feel incensed at women and children being kept hanging around like this.... We are at length divided into groups by nationalities – British, N.Z., South Africans, Australians, Dutch and so on – why I don't know – and formed into columns of four. We picked up Snoxhill from Asahan, Malacca and decided to stick together as a four.... Another tedious wait, the heat is intense.... A speech by a Japanese officer, translated into English, the gist of it is that the Japanese will observe international law as regards internees, we will be protected, we are to go to a point near Sea View Hotel, and wait there. Transport will be provided for women and children and luggage, the rest can walk (about 5 miles) and we must take our own food. This is very bad, in the notice yesterday we were told food will be provided and most of us have none.... Another prolonged wait, we hang about, eventually make a break for the Singapore Cricket Club and get water, and find a very dry biscuit or two. The S.C.C. is a sorry mess.... Everyone is taking this extremely trying time very well indeed, all chins are up and I never detected a sign of a whimper even amongst all the women and children. Nobody seems to know what the next step is, but we know our immediate destination; Bedlington tells me he has a car and petrol in it, so has Snoxhill – why walk? It's already 12.45, and the only certain thing seems to be, that we are to get to the rendezvous.... So Bedlington, Miller Mackay, Miller and I packed into the car and drove off. The streets are deserted, it is like the city of the dead, all doors are shut. We pass many shelled areas, were stopped by a Japanese soldier at the Lavender St. crossroads, but I think he was more bewildered than us – anyhow after sundry signs we proceeded and pulled up at Meyer Flats about 1 p.m. Passed a body of our troops marching out to Changi – poor devils, they look fresh from home, and I dare say they are. We decide this must be where we are to be put for the next 10 days, the Flats are almost deserted. We picked a suitable one for ourselves and actually got a cold drink out of the refrigerator which is ticking over, however we'd better await orders before moving in! More people arrive in cars, then some Jap officers while we wait.... A car arrives with an irate individual driving, he pulls up, not seeing the Jap officers and starts a tirade about these **** Japanese; one overhears, comes round the car, 'Why do you call us these names? We want to be your friends. You must not talk like that,' – and the gent, in spite of apologies and protests, is forcibly removed from the car, and away he goes. However he returned about an hour later, so presumably only got a bad fright. This hanging about is frightfully tedious.... At length we are told to go to a point on the road about $1/_4$ mile away... more hanging around and here I met Mrs. Grist and Miss Nicolson, who had walked from the Padang, the promised transport not being available. Nearly all the women had had to walk; very trying in the hottest part of the day on the Equator. And quite unnecessary, there was no need to rush us into internment like this: we are all peaceful citizens domiciled in Malaya, even Germans don't intern the civilians in the countries they overrun. An interpreter arrives, no such luck as Sea View and Meyer Flats – men are to go to Joo Chiat Police Station and women to the Sultan of Trengganu's house near the Roxy theatre. So off we got to Joo Chiat Police Station, find a sentry on guard who knows nothing about the arrangement – someone says the alternative is some houses in ? Road – decide this sounds better that Joo Chiat which looks positively horrible – proceed and find the place, 5 big houses in a large compound by the sea, obviously owned by a wealthy Mohamedan, there is a mosque tower. The whole place is absolutely bare, dirty, everything smashed to atoms, very little water, no sanitation, no light: we are the first to arrive, closely followed by other cars and pedestrians until there are about 600 here, and I hear others are in Joo Chiat. We choose a room about 18 feet square and lay out our pitches on the bare wooden floor, nothing to sleep on of course, and no food, only a trickle of lukewarm water to drink. Snoxhill, Sworder, Perrin, myself, Jas. Laird, Geo. McCulloch, W.A. Gutsell and Cyril Ryves in our room: it grows dark, we are all tired, we sleep – or try to – the floor is very hard, it is very hot, the mosquitos never stop biting, we are hungry and very thirsty. I cannot sleep, I ruminate on escape – on the mainland I would make for Ulu Trengganu, but it is hopeless to try to get off this island… had I arranged for supplies via Ali, I believe I could lie doggo in the 20 square miles of jungle covered Catchment area, but I haven't. I've lots of money, and anything would be better than this… At last I snatch an hour's fitful sleep by wrapping myself completely in a sheet, except for my head, and putting a handkerchief over all my face except nostrils and mouth. Final reflections, Brian would like pancakes today…. And so would I.

18 February: NPOTUSPVTLXNOHBIPSEFT. *(This decodes as 'monsterous myopic hordes.' 'Monsterous' and 'hordes' are decoded as one letter in the alphabet before the code letters and 'myopic' by one letter after.)* I rise early, get the first bath 6 a.m., a mere trickle under a tap in the yard, but refreshing; and a shave. There is a meeting to promulgate a communication from the Japanese, in brief it is: The British did not treat the Japanese internees well, they only got rice and salt, but we will be given more than that. We are to be interned for the duration. We can use 5 of our cars with 5 communication officers who will be given passes to go out, and they will get all our food, and that's all we will get, unless we work for it by helping to clean up Singapore…. In camp we must do everything for ourselves, the British soldiers have made it the mess it is. In addition there are two representatives of the various nationalities, whom we will appoint. That is the gist. We meet each house, five in all. We are No. 3. We elect Dr. Bain as our communications officer, and the Rev. A.J. Bennitt, Vaux (a lawyer), Johnny Foster and myself, as House Committee. I start a census of House 3, it's not easy, nobody knows anything about anybody or anything yet! Another general camp meeting to report the results of today's contact with the Japs. We now have five communications officers who have personal passes to go out, and they have to do everything. No one else can go out. There will be no communications with our wives and families, except those interned here, as the Jap internees have had none with Japan. (I expect this will be altered later – there has been no time for communication to be arranged.) We must not go outside the compound, i.e. on the beach, except to bathe. S.S. currency will be accepted for purchases (I presume through communication officers). We appoint a camp Disciplinary Committee, composed of the Chairman of each House and a lawyer as Secretary, Gen. Macrae as Camp Commandant. (He is retired Indian Army I believe). Camp time official, is to be Tokio time, as that has now become Malayan time – so what is 7 a.m. by the laggard sun, is now 9 a.m. Fix camp mealtimes as: tea 9 a.m. brunch 2 p.m. (I think too late) supper 7 p.m. (Tokio time). There was a big scrounge today from adjoining houses – chairs, tables and what not: all I found was two packets of Army biscuits on the verandah of a deserted house – but they were very useful. Rations today were, bully beef, apricots, and a biscuit at midday; rice and jam in the evening. We certainly have a remarkable diversity of talent, in House 3 alone are stewards and cooks from the 'Empress of Asia', electricians, doctors (Bain, Heron, Smith), a dentist (Hanna), Health Officers and even a barber. And I have noticed W.J. Mayson, E.A. Brown, Sir Percy Mc Elwaine, Falconer, Sheehan, Belloch, Shorty Coleman, Dick Howitt, Murray Jack, Justice Aitken and hosts of others I know. Decide to sleep in Bedlington's car, it is a saloon and comfy, but suddenly mosquitoes appear from all the nooks and crannies, so I have to get out, carry the car seat up to our room and try to sleep on it, but the mosquitoes are impossible and I get very little sleep.

19 February: I shave; water is still sparse. A cup of tea is served at 9 a.m. We have a busy morning drawing up the organisation of the house. We have indoor and outdoor sanitation committees and room representatives. We draw up a plan of the house and number all the rooms – 16, leaving out 13! We arrange the cleaning and scavenging. I take a census, the only way is to catch 'em as they come along for meal rations! There are 157 and two doubtful in this house. Sworder and Snoxhill are very useful – Victor too. How tired one gets of this everlasting lukewarm water! What would I give for a cold beer? There is a house meeting at 12 – it is all Jap time now. We elect sub-committees, a librarian etc. For lunch, we have curry, rice and tea. There is more work, then I have a bathe – good. I converse with a Jap soldier in mufti who knows a little English. There are lots of people I know here including, C.C Brown, W.E. Pepys, Belgrave, Birkinshaw, Ivery, Watson, Edwards, Boswell (Forests), Dugan Hampshire and J.W.E. Adams. Fifty-seven more arrived today including: Mayson, E.A. Brown, Sir P. McElwaine, Falconer and Sheehan. I seem to be busy all day, washing up or getting meals for myself or committee work. I wash my shorts by having a bathe in the sea. I'm glad I bought iodine and Dettol – I scraped myself on rusty barbed wire in the sea today. *(Tom goes on to list what he brought with him into captivity.)* Andrews Liver Salts, which are much as Eno's – very good, too, in early morning, elastoplast, toilet soap, two pairs of shorts, three sweat shirts, two pairs of stockings, one pair of shoes, a sheet, my dark blue blazer, one pair of flannels, two handkerchiefs, two sweat rags, shaving tackle, paper, hair brush and comb, aspirin, vitamin pills, plate, mug, knife, fork, spoon, towel, two face towels, serviette (as dish cloth), Asepsa soap and scissors. We have our evening meal at 7 p.m. – rice, fruit and coffee (?). The Jap Commandant arrives. We all listen to a speech on discipline. Some folk have been found living in a room near the camp including Phillips of S. Ramal and Evans. Phillips and others have been most ferociously beaten up! There are masses of bruises on their arms and back. It will be remarkable if there is no permanent damage. Evans was struck in front of us all, because he is moving about at the back of the crowd and not presumably paying attention to the miserable little squirt. It is all very, very hard to swallow. The Commandant says that we are internees. There are internees in Calcutta etc. The Commandant is gratified at the progress made in organising the camp. If we behave like gentlemen, we will be treated as such. Later, we meet and decide the steps to take. The camp buildings are somewhat curtailed and we are not to loiter on the beach; we may still bathe and our latrines made today are there – a long pit in the sand. I sleep in Bedlington's car; there is only one mosquito this time; I kill him. Anyway, he disappears and I have the best night yet – with a dream.

20 February: I awake with a jump – I hear the padre calling the house A to K to turn out and put up a barbed wire fence along a new building. I shave and wash and dash along. Better hands than mine are at work, it is soon up. We have tea and a biscuit at 9 a.m. (all Japanese time) and then a meeting with the General Committee. General MacRae addresses us; it is up to us to conform to Japanese orders and to co-operate with them. We are conquered and must realise it. We should show respect to their officers e.g. by standing up when they inspect and not smoking then and so on. Attempts to escape must be severely discouraged. The faults of one may easily lead to a punishment affecting the whole camp. We are told the results of yesterdays meeting: The chief thing is that the property in the camp will not be interfered with, which is useful. There are 12 at a house meeting and there is a roll call. My census with Sworder was very good, so is the attendance at the meeting. We report, then we appoint officers to deal with fatigues for the various housework, inside and out. Tiffin is herrings, rice, peas and coffee. There are more arrivals. I scrounge an old cash box in the garden to hold some of my things! At 2 p.m., I meet the Governor, Sir Shenton Thomas, and Dawson, the Secretary for Defence.

The latter gives me a small pillow. He tells me they have found the paper dealing with internees and it proves they (the Japanese internees in British hands) have been well treated. This is very good and should alter the attitude of the Japanese authorities. The Governor says that there has been marvellous progress in cleaning up the town. It's marvellous here too – you see people making something out of nothing all over the place. We still have no lights, but our experts are trying to repair them. At 7 p.m., I get a mattress, which I share with Victor. We have added Rowse to our room, so we are chock-a-block. I bathe. For supper, we get rice, spaghetti, bully beef and tea. I give the rice to Hope. I sleep in the car and am devoured by mosquitoes. I must get that net up.

21 February: There are now 192 in this House. I have a mug of coffee for breakfast and two biscuits with the thinnest possible veneer of jam. There is another brazen sky. We have had no rain for ages. Now I go to wash my clothes in a bucket. At 10.30 a.m. – all binoculars, cameras and firearms are to be given up. I have none! Yesterday, I scrounged a large, ornamental flowerpot. If it had had no hole in the bottom, I had intended using it as a water container – but it has, so we turn it up and use it as a seat! I have discovered that washing clothes is not so simple, especially when jealously conserving one tablet of Lifebuoy toilet soap. In the first place, it defies the laws of nature; you half-fill a small bucket with water, then place in it a bath-towel and a small towel and it remains half-full. However, I work from small to large, by which time I have soapsuds in the bucket, then I transfer half into another small tub – memories of youth! The results are not bad. Mother would not have approved. A lorry arrives with Grist and others. I stop the bedding in it being completely scrounged, but I can't hold the whole mob back – some goes. We get mattresses for deserving cases, if not the most deserving. Tiffin is rice and baked beans, then coffee. Then there is a House meeting; we have a central gong – one beat for meals, two for a Japanese visit, three for a camp meeting, repeated beating for a fire. The cigarette ration is sold afterwards 20 for 40 cents. I give eight Empress of Asia people $2 each; they are very grateful. They had nix; I have a lot. I wonder where Nora, Joan and Colin are. Dick H. says the Colonial Office will see to Brian's remittance; this is a relief. I wonder where R. K. Bell is. *(This is the husband of Mrs. Bell who took Brian to South Africa.)* I flick all the mosquitoes (I hope) out of the car once more. Now we have an approximately 1,000-book library. Bathe at 6 p.m.; it's a quaint sight, all in the nood and we're not a pretty lot to look at, I must say: I miss salt badly; I suppose a sea bathe puts some through your pores? And I'd give $10 for a glass of beer. This everlasting tap water is very boring. I'm glad I had the T.A.B. injection. H.B. Clifton is here... He has a bandage over his nose from a bomb. Supper consists of rice and a mixture of tinned vegetables and fruit, then coffee. I go to bed in the car; there is not a hope – the mosquitoes bite me all over. I try opening the window and flapping them out. I try everything; it is no bloody good – the mosquitoes are incredible. 11 p.m. is our curfew hour; I go to Room 16; Victor is under my net; I try sleeping, but they are legion: So I crawl under and we share the net.

Sunday, 22 February: There is communion at 8.30 a.m., lots go. There is tea with two biscuits and jam at 9 a.m. Our five communications officers have worked like slaves and there is a lot of food in store and we need it. There is a Nipponese visit at 11 a.m. Today's last thought – what am I going to do about a diary for 1943? I get a hair cut at 11.30 a.m. He want's to shave my head completely, but I kick at the front hair going. This I am assured on all sides, produces a quaint effect. The complete lack of news at a time like this is distressing. And, most of all, the uncertainty about Nora and Joan, Brian and Colin. How I love them. Perhaps I was not given to showing it enough.... Lunch is rice, bully beef, potatoes and carrots; the latter are sparse. I get half a potato. I had previously asked why on earth the cooks peeled the potatoes and threw the peel away. The answer given is: there was not one each all round. I don't see this answers the question. After tiffin, we get a small ration of chocolate. I am reading 'Peculiarities of Behaviour' by Wilhelm and Stekel. It is curious how these psychoanalysts boil everything down to food urge or sex urge. Eureka! We now have a light! Stout work! I have a bathe, then we eat at 7 p.m. We have rice, cornflour, prunes, (three each) and a chocolate biscuit. There is a church service at 7.45 p.m., We sit around on the grass. The address is by the Rev. Gibson, a Presbyterian. There are three hymns; he reads each verse out. I put my net up; Vic and I are sharing it. Then I sit out in the moonlight and talk to Findall. I hear this is now Syonan, not Singapore. Findall was in the Supreme Court, then he went to Raffles and walked here on Thursday. Lots of police have arrived, latecomers from the Central Police Station. They sleep on the bandstand. The newcomers have cabin trunks and loads of washing. Findall says the water should now be boiled. I have a good night's sleep under the net, my first, but the mosquitoes are bad outside.

23 February: We have oats and milk with early tea at 9 a.m. The camp is very active; there are various fatigues – water, latrines etc. Vic says the police who bolted are to lose pensions etc. doubt if this is true, but there should be a penalty. At noon we receive an issue of a communal piece of washing soap and a piece of Nestle's milk chocolate each. Lunch at 1 p.m. consists of rice, herrings and a biscuit and tea. I discover the fish smell and it is difficult to get rid of the smell after washing up. If you are not careful your fingers and drying cloth stink to high heaven. There is a committee meeting at 1.30 p.m. There are various points: there is a shower, but small.

My mug is used for everything e.g. this morning for a drink, then for shaving, then cleaning teeth, then for early tea. The first button comes off a shirt; I have no needle and cotton. The police are still waiting orders to go somewhere and new arrivals go into the Convent next to 2A. The police have also gone into the Convent. One hundred and fifty of us have fresh meat for tomorrow. There is rice, spaghetti with cheese and a biscuit with jam and a mug of tea today. Our communications officers have done marvellous work. The total in camp i.e. 1, 2, 2A, 3 and 4 is approximately 700. Swadon with his kettle beard and head shaved is quaint; so am I. I shall not stop shaving until I've got to. I talk to Powell and Evans: R.K. Bell is not in yet; he's in Kuala Kerbau. I hear the General Hospital Staff are arriving soon. I wonder what has happened to the two cars SN 614 and S 9355, and Nora's bike. Ali *(the driver)* has Joan's car and my refrigerator and typewriter. *(In 1945 Ali presented the car to the authorities but was told to keep it after Colin had been consulted.)* Fairy has cut down a pair of his white drill slacks. James asks for one leg to make a pillowcase: But he has cut it open and transformed it into mosquito flappers.

24 February: Victor this morning broke the record for hurling false teeth out of the window. He had cleaned the top plate and forgot the bottom was in the mug. Luckily, the teeth were intact. The Salvation Army bring rations. I read the 'Syonan Times'. It says: The era of equality for all in Greater East Asia is at hand. The kitchens are using a lot of firewood. What happens when the compound supply is finished? – I don t know. I suppose there is no petrol for the firewood lorries yet. Vic and I air our mattress; I remark that our wives would approve! We discuss our insurance policies; the general opinion is that premiums are in abeyance while interned, so Brian's education is OK. I paid the premium on January 1st; the next is due on April 1st The Salvation Army arrives; lunch is rice, fish kedgeree, tea and broken biscuits. There is a House Committee meeting at 2 p.m.: all dogs must be put down. We have a vet; they will receive an intravenous injection of Epsom Salts. Mosquito nets are badly needed. We receive 20 copies of the 'Syonan Times' for the camp. I hear the remainder of the Europeans are to parade today at 4 p.m. (Tokyo Time is queer here – two hours different from the sun.) I prove that a black sweat-rag can be returned to its pristine white at least once by good washing with soap and ordinary water – doubts have been cast on this by the room. Cyril scrounged two chairs out of the Convent School last night before the police knew the arch-scroungers were around. Now we have six in our room and one small wicker table. I go to the beach; there are two Malays there, one inside our fence! 'How did you get in?' 'This way, Tuan *(Sir)*,' indicating the fence. 'Well, you can't come in here!' He seemed surprised at this and made his exit under the wire, the same way as he came in – all a matter of course. 'The Syonan Times' says that prices are decreed to be as prior to the outbreak of the Great Oriental War. The sole currency of Malaya is the Japanese military dollar, but for the time being, previous currency will be accepted at parity. We have our first death, Milroy. New arrivals today have trunks, mattresses etc.! I see G. D. Barron and Jarrett. I have a bathe. Supper is a sausage and a tiny portion of mash. I eschew rice; I am slightly constipated; most people are very constipated. It's a combination of diet and lack of exercise. It is also partly aesthetic, for the latrine – a trench on the shore – is horrible; it is also partly due to the stoppage of alcohol. A lovely, moonlight night – the stars look down. I wonder where Nora is. I crawl under my net; Vic is there. The light, though only 15 watt, is a godsend. I get some sleep, though, with nine in the room, it resounds most of the night with snores and snorts or sudden reports. George talks in his sleep, Cyril has a most remarkable sudden snort.

25 February: Up at 8 a.m. – the routine tends to get established. I unfasten the net, fold and roll it up; I fold the mattress in half (it's a seat as well). I go downstairs with a bucket, mug, toothbrush and shaving tackle. I fill the bucket at the tap, shave, clean my teeth and wash. For breakfast, we have porridge, pineapple chunks (four) and tea. I walk with Sworder and Irving by the Convent School to have a look; I see Hugh Bryson, Bagot, Haines, T.E. Upton and others. I am told there are 550 there and the breakfast queue lasts one-and-a-half hours. I pick up an ancient coconut – it has milk, so I split it with an axe and we have a room feast. Cor, meat for lunch: We have a stew and carrot and turnip (tiny). It is very good. Then we have a biscuit and tea. There is a committee meeting. My only pad is disappearing rapidly. Dear me – and I had a stock for my diaries. I watch some bridge – they play half a cigarette a hundred! At 2 p.m., we get an issue of Bata sandshoes. I manage to get a size $6^1/_2$ – not so bad – for $1. I am reading 'Puppets into Scotland' by W. Wilkinson – it makes one very homesick. I wonder how long we will be here? Estimate there are 1,250 here now and 250 in Joo Chiat. Are chances of a swop *(of internees)* receding? We have quite decided that, as there is no news of the European War in the 'Syonan Times', it is favourable. At the committee meeting, we are told that all dogs are to be dead by Sunday. The vet, D.P. White, will help. Dr Macintyre has decided that three good meals are better than seven indifferent ones. The camp shop will be open soon. We need cards, toilet paper and shaving mirrors. Lime juice will be issued daily at tiffin after Saturday, probably. We need it; the water is boring. Macintyre is getting proper cookers for rice. We hope to get firewood from an estate on the Serangoon Road. There are to be no more private fires. We are volunteering to provide labour to clear up all mosquito-breeding places within a half-mile of the camp, if the Nipponese will let us. The main drain outside is blocked with filth. There are 607 in the Convent: The Sultan of Kedah who built this place was the 'Mutton King'. He lost his money after the last war. It must have been a marvellous place. At 6 p.m., the Dutch District Officer of the Rhio Archipelago arrives at our House. He was badly treated and beaten up. You can see the evidence.

26 February: After breakfast of cereal, honey, jam on a biscuit and coffee, I get a dose of salts at the dispensary; I can not remember when that was last necessary. I was ruminating in bed last night – what does one regret losing most? I assume my diaries and photos were saved, my Malayan books and scrapbooks and records of that kind. My clothes will take a lot of replacing. I've presumably lost the dinner service, Joan's desk, canteen of cutlery, books, two typewriters, a Morris 8, a Morris 14, silver cups, cloths, linen, bedding, furniture, movie camera, reflex camera, and telephoto lens, coloured movies, Lewis camera, projector, sewing machine, crockery (Royal Worcester Service), glassware, refrigerator (only four more instalments of $19), all the garden stuff including two mowing machines, two bags of golf clubs and $1000 worth of stamps. We have to be careful of land-mines on the beach; they removed three yesterday. From the Survey Department, the staff interned are T.K Findall, Sworder, Barron, Bedlington, Hamilton, Irving and the Field Survey Company. We have a good tiffin: sardines (some oil) with rice (I take very little), fruit with cream and a biscuit and sweetened tea. At the commit-tee meeting, we deal with the issue of rations. There is a mass issue for the day, so we appoint two officers to apportion it to the various meals. There are to be no ranks in the camp: No colonels, majors etc. Reveille will be at 8.15 a.m. daily. There is to be a notice asking room representatives to put up room lists and it is decided to issue meals by rooms in rotation, to obviate waiting in queues. I am to put up the notices and a roster. We are to have a camp shop and a house shop. In fact, we start our house shop in a bathroom with a squatpan, which does not work. Jack runs it: our stock today comprises soap, razor blades, hand and bath towels, some hooks, buttons, needles, cotton, toothpaste, one sarong and a lot of decrepit toothbrushes which have been in water – all from Gian Singhs. Oh and a roll of mosquito netting. $44^{1}/_{2}$ yards, 90 inches wide- $77 – a great advance, this. I hear that the Civil Government is arriving in a week. At 6 p.m., I bathe. Then dinner consists of fresh meat in a stew and rice, with tea – good. I chat to Belgrave Grist and we yarn far into the night – old stories of Negri Sembilan. *(Where Tom Kitching was posted from 1913 into the Twenties.)* Cyril comes in with the news that A. knows a man who knows a man who met a Nipponese from the Municipality who says negotiations for our exchange are already opened.

27 February: I rise with the Angelus at 7.30 a.m.; it is twilight. I fetch water in the bucket, shave, wash and attend a P. T. class from 8.20 to 8.40 a.m. I watch the first meal being served in rotation by rooms. It goes well and is voted a great im-provement. Jack and I wash up. Our breakfast consisted of oats (good) and a bis-cuit with jam. The room expresses a unanimous desire for Rinso. The idea gleaned from adverts is that you get gleaming white clothes with no expenditure of energy. I have a washing day. I have a first try at shorts in fresh water and at socks – a pair too small for Colin. I hope they don't shrink. Vaux – a lawyer-cum-banker, is sent for by the Japanese today. When he is returning is not said. We buy six yards of netting and are mosquito-proofing our room. With the three windows, we knock out the louvres and cover them with netting, then a double-width for the door. My only fears are rain and the rotting of the netting. We decide that a good solution of the Far East difficulties would be to give Siam and Indo-China to Nippon – they desire nothing better – and free the China coast. We also decide that probably not more than half of our troops fired a shot in anger. For lunch, we have rice and fish curry, then coffee and two biscuits. I hear the Japanese have declared Singapore an open town; this may be true, but not of the Island, though, with its aerodromes and naval base? At the committee meeting at 2 p.m., there is not much business. Fresh fruit is being bought, if possible. Our cooks are not to be paid any more. House shop hours will be 11 a.m. to 12.30 p.m. There is no camp shop at present. I finish the 'Puppets' book; it induced too great a longing for home and freedom and the end of this nightmare the world is plunged into – to appreciate it as I should have done. How easy it is for armed, ruthless force nowadays to hold down any number of unarmed human beings? Stories percolate about the treatment of the Chinese and there must be half a million in Singapore. *(Soon after the fall of Singapore, the Japanese conducted the Sook Ching or 'purification' excercise where males between the ages of 18 and 50 were ordered to present themselves at screening centres. There was no standard procedure, nor was there any clear sign as to what the Japanese were looking for. However, it is estimated that some 50,000 Chinese males were taken away and executed, many taken to beaches where they were shot.)* We finish the mosquito proofing at 6.45 p.m. Probably they will be with us for a night or two; they congregate in a dark corner. I bathe; it is very dirty water and the blocked East Coast Road drain is beginning to flow into the sea with its accompanying filth. Binoculars and cameras are now being returned; the Japanese have enough. This is very surprising; perhaps now they have seen how punctiliously we dealt with enemy property. This island was fortified the wrong way round! The south coast had terrific fortifications, the Straits of Johore nil. Why did they not fell a quarter of a mile of mangrove? It would have been absolutely impassable. We hold committee meetings in a car. Johnny says he's glad his is not here; there are too many happy memories. I feel rather the same. We now have eight houses – with about 1,300 people! And 500 at Joo Chiat. All the Sumatra crowd have probably been caught. We discuss pay; someone says ours goes on. If so, we will have a wad to draw! And those who bolted minus permission lose all – I wonder! *(Tom continued to be paid up to the time of his death. Joan Kitching had an allowance from it, which the authorities tried to stop at Tom's death. Strong representations from Joan and her brother, Colin, allowed it to continue, at a reduced rate.)* The Empire's richest colony has gone in 70 days – what a disgrace! My views on infiltration, as they call it – why was it always one-sided? There was far too much muddle. I wish I had more shorts – two pairs leave no margin.

28 February: The mosquito proofing has been a success; there were just a few nibbles during the night. The sale of footwear has been prohibited in town. Is this because of the needs of the Japanese Army? Eurasians are to be released from internment. We have a large breakfast of cereal and honey, two biscuits, half a sausage, bacon and tea. Washing up bacon plates in cold water is difficult. At the committee meeting, we are told that the Convent Camp have asked that it be treated separately from us. The Japanese agree and both are to be out of bounds to the other. This is foolish. There is rice as part of lunch again today, but I eat little rice now. I bathe – the water is very dirty, the bottom is muddy. Vaux has smoked only Lambert and Butlers Birds Eye since varsity in 1906; now he's stumped – he has only one fill left. We are in bed by 10.15 p.m. by sun it is 8.15 p.m. The nights are very long. Of course Tokyo time is based on 135 degrees and we are 105 degrees. The chat veers to estate strikes – are we too soft? One imagines that, if there are any during the present occupation, the White Queen policy will be adopted – 'Off with his head!' It is very effective for a time, at any rate. I drink a bottle of water; Nora used to say we ought to take two quarts of liquid a day. It was easy with stengahs. Fancy the water is tasting better too. In the long, wakeful hours, I compute our mosquito net – 100 square feet and we bought 150. So what?.

Sunday, 1 March 1942: It is my 52nd birthday and what a one. My roommates all express the pious hope they will not see me on my next birthday. Hope, Fairy, George, James and Gutsell now have camp beds. The tinned butter at breakfast is rancid. I wash up, then wash a hand-towel and a white bath-towel. We scream for Persil and Rinso. I can't get it white this time; I spend half an hour dollying in the soapsuds in the bucket. One gent says it is easier to do it with your feet, but I prefer the bending exercise. James scrounges two planks for shelves. There has been no news of any kind since Tuesday – not even the 'Syonan Times'. I buy a pair of shorts for $3.50; they have a 34-inch waist. They fit where they touch, but I must have a reserve pair. The heads of departments and firms are asked to put their names down to help in the reconstruction. It seems to me I should. There is great argument about it. Vaux says my name as head of the Survey Department goes on the Nipponese list anyhow, so that settles any quisling questions. There will be an election tomorrow, as the Nipponese require names for the organisation of the camp. At the committee meeting, we are told the camp has food for three weeks for 1,400. We have agreed to give rations for three more days to the new camp, then half our rice and any stores brought in. They want the position reviewed after three days. We must remember there will be no imports now except from Japan and occupied territories. How we stand concerning remuneration for internees is not yet known. The cooks are to be allowed to buy at 5 p.m. from the shop. We have five bottles of tomato sauce and eight of lime juice, so we draw by rooms for a bottle each – there are four blanks. We get tomato sauce. George, our camp scrounger, produces a saw, screwdriver and a mattress for a camp bed. We rig up two planks as shelves to hold plates, bottles of water and odds and ends, which were previously kept on the floor. I get the impression that perhaps being in the Camp Police helps George. Today's church service is good; Padre Bennitt, Church of England, preaches on the 'Paradox of Evil'. We take stern measures to suppress flies; they come up through the sand from buried tins. There have been two cases of dysentery already. The Nipponese claim they sank the ships which left on February 11th, 12th and 13th. I hope it is untrue; Nora left on the 13th. They also say about 40 small craft left at the end; they captured 30 and sank some. Best and company were making for Palembang in Sumatra, if they ever got there, they would have been captured. I walk round to J. Jackson, then Hamilton asks me to his room and gives me a tot of brandy for my birthday! Very noble of him; he only has a spot.

2 March: My duty today is to go round the houses. I first go to PT class – good. I scrounge a ground sheet. We receive our first issue of bread at noon – one roll for five people. We being nine get two and gamble for the extra bit; Victor gets it. We also get a bunch of grapes at lunchtime! They must be from the Cold Storage. I play a lot of bridge today. We see some vessels. Whither are they heading? We spend a dull day – I don't mean the weather. Even George fails. We had instructed him to scrounge a pump. We resign as a committee. In the election for a chairman, Padre Bennitt gets 88 votes and Victor 67. The committee formed consists therefore of Victor, Jarrett, Burnham and Coles 59 votes each and me next, 44 votes. There were 11 candidates, so all the old committee who have done the spade-work have gone. Well, we are satisfied with what we've done in 14 days. We now have 700 in camp 1 (Karical), 500 in camp 2 (Joo Chiat), 350 woman in camp 3 and 650 in camp 4 (Convent). General Macrae is the commander for them all. The meetings will be held at the Nipponese Garrison Office in the Cold Storage Building on the East Coast Road. Fresh fish can now be sold at the gate at prices fixed by Nipponese. Nippon declares the enemy countries to be the British Isles (Japan refuses to distinguish between Southern and Northern Ireland), the U.S.A., Australia, New Zealand, Canada, South Africa, Holland, Cuba, Haiti, Guatemala, San Salvador, Honduras, Nicaragua, Costa Rica, Dominica, Venezuela, Iraq, Belgium, Greece, Mexico, Egypt, Brazil, Peru, Bolivia, Ecuador, Uruguay, Paraguay and Iran. We have a contract for 250 loaves a day – 50 to the Women's Camp. Vaux says that the doctors say 2,500 calories a day are necessary; we get 1,500. In a few weeks, we shall be lying about all languid and unable to work! But hope springs eternal. We sit around and, to hear us talk, Hitler is practically finished. The water is alleged to be inferior – should we boil it? There are many practical difficulties. Byron says it is OK to drink the water as it is, if we've had a T.A.B. injection. To bed; I have a good night – only one mosquito. We are remarkably lucky – there are no ants here. It is useless thinking about the family; I have no idea where they are.

3 March: The Bishop is still at large, also the Roman Catholic Bishop, the

Padre tells me. I am room orderly today; I sweep out etc. It is an apology for a broom and I use a bit of tin as a dust receptacle. Still, the floor is the better for it. I have a quiet morning. I play some bridge. There is a grand tide – I bathe. Lunch is served efficiently; the room system for meals is working excellently. I acquire a pillow (no cover), a pipe and some Eno's for $5.60. I observe at our usual post-tiffin chat that my only acquired vice in internment so far is I smoke more than usual. In fact, every day is a Sunday as regards this. I wonder what's happening to our troops at Changi? And to the Volunteers and Field Survey Company? There were about 15 – 20 Europeans in the latter. Stubbs, Bruce, Greig and Booth, the officer commanding, in view of their training, should surely have been amongst the first to be got away. We use a spoonful each of our tomato sauce on the rice; it helps a lot. I give half of my rice away each meal. Victor and Hope, I swear, have bulimia, yet both are as thin as rakes. I spend a quiet afternoon. I play some bridge. The new committee appoint various new officials – a quartermaster and assistant quartermaster. I hear House 4 had to pay $25 for a small mosquito net – price control is not very effective! It is a lovely afternoon; 100 Malay fishermen are busy just outside our fence – I envy them. We have a large dinner; even Victor and Hope don't go for second helpings – cold beef, tongue, peas, rice, a roll and butter and tea. I have a T.A.B. injection. Jack had his second yesterday. I see Hugh Bryson; he says he is bearing up. It is silly I can't go to his camp. They have half our food now. We don't agree, but we want no dissension between camps. The food situation may get serious. Still, there are thousands of Bali cattle roaming the golf course, if they're still there. We had two boxes labelled 'CREAM' in the store. We open them today with a flourish for distribution to the houses. They are found to be full of Anzam cream. And two boxes of 'ham' are found to be full of school slates!

4 March: After PT, I have a trot round the quadrangle. I am now in charge of a fatigue squad of eight. Victor is not so good today – he has pains in his tummy and his bowels are loose. The doctor gives him udapa. Hope and I scrub out our 'side-board.' He strings it up with nails and copper wire. Now we can park our plates etc. off the floor. I have a grand bathe; it is high tide. I buy tobacco and the despised Anzora! No 'Syonan Times' has been seen since Saturday, though we asked for 20 per day over a week ago. Is there any significance in this? At last, our Communications Officer gets bottles of drinks; we shall have one for our room tomorrow. What a change from this infernal water! I play bridge. After dinner – which includes tinned pears as well as the omnipresent rice – we have our usual mosquito strafe; we hound them out with flappers and this and that, then close the windows and door. I walk with Victor; he's a bit down. Bed as usual; we talk till elevenish. I have a pillow now, which adds to the comfort of my mattress on the floor, but no pillow-slip. Shall I cut up my sheet to make one? No, I will put my sheet over the pillow. Can wash the sheet. I hear that at Joo Chiat they are now allowed to bathe in the sea once a day for quarter of an hour; it is a 10-minute walk. George met a man who told him he saw looting in the Singapore Club vaults where lots of barang *(luggage)* was stored, including James's. And I know the third floor was looted. I wonder if they reached the fifth?

5 March: The morning is occupied strengthening Fairy's camp bed; he is 15 stone. Victor's tummy is better this morning. I have a little prickly heat; I use Asapsa. I wash my shorts, towel, handkerchief, using Lux for the first time. Then I bathe – it is a lovely tide. Reports have it that our captors are not so happy just now. I buy from Jack a sweat-shirt, notebook and tobacco (Frontier) for $7.40. We play poker hands for who pays for the fruit juice and toilet paper. At 5 p.m., there is a bombshell: the Padre calls a house meeting – we are to move to Changi jail. The Japanese Notice says; 'the Japanese army is going to accommodate all civilians of enemy nature in Changi Prison according to the treatment meted out by the British Army to Japanese civilians. Internees must prepare for removal today. They will start tomorrow (March 6th) at 10 a.m. from their present camps under the leadership of Ex-Governor Sir Shenton Thomas. There will be four lorries, one from each camp, for the sick, the aged and the infirm. Pregnant, sick and elderly women will also be taken in a lorry. The others will walk. Food and sufficient water for the day will be carried by internees. Bedding, luggage, foodstocks etc. will be carried by lorries.' We return to Room 16 sadly and start arranging packing for the morning. We issue a ration of lime juice for tomorrow and finish our fruit juice; it tastes good. I fill a bottle for tomorrow. All lights are out at 10 p.m. – why, I don't know. We sit around and muse on things. All sorts of people are growing beards. And we've just got a bucket latrine system working beautifully!

IV

WELCOME TO CHANGI

6 March 1942: I rise at 7 a.m. (5.30 a.m. local time) and shave, wash and pack. Breakfast at 8.30 a.m. comprises bacon, porridge and coffee. I eschew the bacon. I finish packing; it is difficult. I put my mosquito net round the old cash-box and wrap the lot up in my ground sheet. I'm lucky – there's lots of old stout string. My mattress rolls up with the pillow inside. My pack is too heavy – about 30 pounds. I take out some food, a sheet, a large plate, then find my small plate broken. Tidapa *(never mind)*. I stack the bedding under the porch, with the luggage outside. We move off at 10.50 a.m.; the sun blazes down. We march via Bedok village and Simpang Bedok. We arrive outside the gaol at 2 p.m. after a walk of seven miles. Only about six people pass out – very creditable. What a picture we make! There are two rickshaws, several trolleys, one with a roller-skate as a fourth wheel! I am not done and sweat very little. We have a long wait – one-and-a-half hours. At last, we get in, then we hang about. Finally, we park ourselves in a big room, about 90 of us; there is a concrete floor. But we can get water from a tap. I scrounge two sacks for Jack and me to lie on. Victor gets some bits of cardboard. Hope, the seasoned campaigner, has his camp-bed mattress; it rolls up. There are 2,000 of us here, excluding women, whom we have not seen yet. I see Clem and Hugh Fraser carrying a tiny tin with water. Jack and I share a tin of bully beef and a hunk of dry bread. By 7 p.m., no luggage has arrived. No pull-plugs are working. What are 2,000 men to do? Findall is in a cell, twelve foot by seven, with two others; there is a squat pan. Our room is 72 feet by 42 feet. Well, I never thought I'd be in gaol, but here I am! Water is short; it will be turned on from 8 to 9 a.m., from 12 noon to 1 p.m. and from 6 to 7 p.m. We retire for the night at 9 p.m.; I am lying on a sack while a sandbag with a sarong, towel and shorts in it makes a pillow. I sleep. The Nipponese are moving all numbers of the houses on the East Coast Road; one would think they had other things to do just now.

7 March: Jack and I are up at 7.30 a.m. I get a mug of water out of the pull-plug reservoir and shave. I hopefully wait for a wash in the laundry at 8 a.m. I am first tap, but no water comes, so I come dirty to breakfast – half a tin of sardines and a drink of water. A large drain at the edge of the padang near the laundry serves as a latrine, but this can't go on. Apart from other considerations, there are flies and there will be dysentery. I meet Wilmot – he has a beard too! He says my office was looted by our own people. It was later occupied by a Nipponese professor; he was very pleasant. He was working with him on the scientific records etc. I join a water queue; there is a cart at the main gate; I fill a bottle and a mug. Then I rush to the laundry – the water is on. We get under the tap and have a bath three at a time; I feel much refreshed. Then I fill a tin Jack finds and wash my towel etc. I see B.W. Upton and R.K. Bell – the remittance should be OK; he has written to his wife. *(This is the husband of the Mrs Bell who took Brian Kitching with her to South Africa. The remittance would be money for his keep.)* The Governor of Malaya, Sir Shenton Thomas, is on the top floor. At noon, there is still no sign of the barang *(luggage)*. The rain begins to pour down. The Joo Chiat luggage is still in the open; they can't bring it in, so presumably is ours at Karikal. I hear that all the cooking here is by diesel oil; it needs a blowlamp to start it. The blowlamp is missing! I start making a crossword puzzle. I eat a small piece of chocolate and biscuit fragments and drink some water at 2 p.m. There is no hope of anything else to eat or drink. I meet Gilham B., Pop Duggan, Mustard, Forbes and dozens of others. I find some coir *(the fibre from coconuts).* Jack and I stuff it between our sacks, sew up the edges using a knife and string – and lo! – We have a mattress! It is a darned sight better than concrete, if dirty. We get a lot of food into store from Karikal. I make a plan of the room and measure it up, allowing eight feet by three feet per man. We can do about 100, allowing for gangways, so I will lay it out tomorrow, using a piece of string as a standard measurement. At 7.15 p.m., we have hot tea. Jack has now scrounged a mineral water box; it is very useful for small impedimenta instead of perpetually shoving it back into a haversack. The water is better now; it has been on all day since it started. The Joo Chiat barang has now been cleared after examination. Rumours – Batavia *(Djakarta)* has fallen.

Sunday, 8 March: I sleep fairly well. I am up at 7.15 a.m. and shave and wash. I split a tin of sardines with Jack. Breakfast is at 9 a.m. – porridge, tea and two biscuits. The fatigue parties for cleaning up etc. are now working. At 11.45 a.m., fatigue parties are called for to clean the quarters for the women who have now arrived, some by lorry. I think they are going to the European block, which is good. The gates are shut; there is no communication with the women. My hair has grown a bit and is respectable again. The Padre announces a service at 8 a.m. and his coir has lice in it, which ours has not. They are possibly from some other place! There is a small boy here about Brian's age. How glad I am he is away, over nine is the criterion for being interned with the men. *(Below nine years of age, boys were allowed to stay with their mothers in the women's section of Changi.)* I see Sir Shenton Thomas, the Governor of Malaya, doing his washing this morning and Georgie Bryant carrying water in a chamber pot! At 4 p.m., we hear that the Governor is moving to cells over the kitchen. H.W. Evans is here too. I thought he got away on Nora's boat; he was in the crowd. For lunch, we have rice and stew; the rice is steamed this time. People say it's better that way. Anyhow, there is more than I can eat. Dinner consists of rice with a few raisins, two biscuits, jam and a little very wishy-washy tea! There is another dysentery case. I see Fawcett and Adolf. They are incensed – they are by no means whatever allowed to glimpse their wives nor their wives them. How glad I am Nora got away; it makes it much easier to bear. I hear that the women who walked to Changi – 120 of them – arrived singing, 'There'll always be an England.' I play bridge and I am composing a cross-word puzzle. More lorries of our own food arrive; we need it for over 2,000. No luggage has arrived yet. I am glad I carried what I did. I can at least shave, bathe, dry myself with a towel and change my clothes. I could do with a pillow and a mattress, though. Jack has to go on a fatigue unloading lorries, so I do the chores and miss church. We can't leave dirty plates about with all these flies and dysentery.

9 March: Five Danes are sleeping on a carpet a yard away, although they are neutrals. I am up at 7.20 a.m.; I have a bath and shave. Early morning in the vegetable garden is the spot, with our bucket, by the light of the now half-moon. There are very few about; it is later crowded. The squat pans which are only three yards away were a nuisance last night – noisy! For breakfast, we are given two biscuits with butter and tea, so we open our last but one tin of sardines. I win a tin plate – very dirty and covered with grease. But, expending much energy and using soap and water and laterite to scrub, I get it clean. I meet an irate Scot; he spent five hours making a ratan mattress. He went away to wash his hands and someone stole it. 'What kin' o' camp is this? If I find yon b— b— , I'll push his feet through his throat, if my hands weren't so sore. Anyhow, I'll get a b— axe and bash his head in!' But there is very little taking, really. At 12.30 p.m., some luggage arrives, but not ours, I think. I see Alexander with a ginger beard; I hardly recognise him. C. Ramsay is here too, so we can do 'The Green Eye'. There are now 21 suspect cases of dysentery, Jack thinks; it is due to overcrowding. I measure the available sleeping areas in the rooms with Jack and King. It works out at less than 25 square feet per person. The barang arrives at 4 p.m. Ah well, we are slightly more comfortable with a mattress. I wish I knew how things are with Nora. Lunch comprises one third of a tin of sheep's tongue, rice and a little tinned vegetable soup. I knew the cork would come out of the iodine bottle in my bag. Luckily, it only stained a towel. We spend a strenuous hour cleaning up and arranging beds. Vic and I share a mattress again. Dinner is a buttered scone and tea. I find a copy of the 'Prison Regulations' for December 1938: European rations total over three pounds daily and Japanese 2lbs 10 oz. I give this in to the Committee as evidence. The women are in the European section of the gaol. We can't see them at all, but I believe it is considerably more comfortable than ours. That's easy! I work on my crossword; it is hard, especially minus a dictionary. An old watch-repairer is in; he was in Chulia Street for years. He sits all day in a corner; he wears black trousers and coat, a white, starched shirt with no collar. He never speaks. Lights Out at 10 p.m. – I go to sleep cogitating on the crossword.

10 March: I dry the mosquito net, which got wet at Karikal. It is lucky there are no mosquitoes here. I ponder on the contrasts – four weeks ago, I was in a comfortable bungalow, then I was in the Fullerton Building for a week. It was also reasonably comfortable. Then I was sent to Karikal; we thought that was the nadir. Now we think Karikal was Paradise! However, we can't get worse than this, except for the food. The ration position is not good and the Japanese guarantee nothing more than rice, soya bean sauce and tea and coffee while they last. For breakfast, we have one pint of porridge and three-quarters of a pint of tea. I note that the porridge is served out of a municipal dustbin. I trust it has been well cleaned! Tiffin is rice and soup mixed with a spot of bully beef. It is polished rice. We shall have to beware of beriberi. And the tinned stuff won't last; and there's nowhere to import it from. Leading a life like this, one must beware of getting too lethargic, I find. I talk to Phillips – his arms are useless. Hope has cracked his dental plate; this is very unfortunate, as there is no chance of a repair. He dare not bite, so he has to eat without it. We play some bridge. Fairy's bed-trestle is apparently not being brought and all his toilet things are in it. He has no toothbrush, razor etc. and no apparent chance of getting any. For dinner, we have a scone, butter, a decent piece of Kraft cheese and tea. We are gradually ousting the prison cooks from the kitchen and 'infiltrating' with cooks from the Empress of Asia. I have been ruminating on Singapore as a port. It is entirely dependent on shipping and its import and export trade. There is none and not likely to be. What will the population do? Exist on each other like Kilkenny cats? It is a very difficult problem for the authorities. I hear the place is far from being cleaned up yet. Lights Out at 10 p.m. I fall asleep ruminating over my crossword. In one wakeful period, I think I feel a cockroach running up my leg; I hope it isn't. If we get them, it won't be funny sleeping on a mattress on the floor. The distribution of belongings is very unfair. Many brought a complete outfit; we, the first batch, brought clothes for 10 days, as instructed.

11 March: I wish they would put the prisoners' showers on. There are about 50 in a row outside our room. I hear that a man just arrived says a Japanese Foreign Office official says parleys about an exchange of prisoners have already started. I wonder. A popular occupation is making fly-swatters out of ratan left by previous prisoners. For breakfast, we get porridge with a little molasses and tea. I put molasses in the tea and it rather improves it! We have a real washing-up. Things are getting a bit greasy. I use soap and water. Then it is washing day – a sarong, shorts and a towel. A gent lends me Lux. I next air all my things in my small case – they were damp. After some bridge, I ascend to the top-floor cells with Jack. We weigh ourselves on the gaol scales: I don't believe it. I haven't been 125lbs. since I was at school.

A squad goes to collect fuel; Jack is in it. I am agog to hear where they go and what happens. The women allocated to Changi are not overcrowded as we are. But how thankful I am Nora is not here. I should feel it intolerable. About 50 men still sleep on the exercise ground in the open under the eaves; it will be impossible when it rains. Six cases of dysentery are allowed out to hospital today. Better news: a prison hospital is to be opened. I finish my fair copy and clues of Changi Gaol Crossword Number 1; I give it to Hope to see how long he takes. There is a very feeble dinner – the tea is dreadful, then we have rice and juice which is a mixture of molasses and prune juice. Later, they discover the prunes and we get two each. Jack comes back with three coconuts, a screwdriver and a fish knife. The fatigue party got six loads of rubber wood in lorries from an estate two miles away. I talk to Abang; he says he will never return to Jelabu; he will live in Singapore. He recalls our walk along the route Kanabu-Ubu-Langit many years ago. 'The Syonan Times' says Java surrendered unconditionally on Monday. Our cells are euphemistically labelled 'cabins'. In fact, the top floor of B-Block has gone the whole hog and made it a ship, with captain, purser etc. Vic has dribbled onto his pillow, which is a cushion, so he gets the last bit of white cloth to make a pillow slip, but he has no needle and no cotton. We offer to lend him some, but he says he can't sew, so he makes a parcel of it!

12 March: For breakfast, we get porridge, molasses and tea, minus milk. I get extra molasses, as I think it is nourishing. It tastes just like the stuff Mother made treacle toffee with, but later lies very heavy on the tummy and apparently has a laxative effect. Vic and I air our beds and the sacking in the sun. The Committee is against my plan for equal distribution of the space in eight foot by three foot lots, so we take ours and they are somewhat peeved! Hope has most ingeniously bound his cracked dental plate with thread. This is to prevent the crack spreading; he can't eat with it, of course. I talk to Jordan, Dr Macgregor, Rae, Dawson, J.G. Watson and others. Jordan says there is no hope of an exchange of prisoners. Writing is difficult; there is no table or chair. So is eating, though we have a wooden box or two scrounged. I hear that 150 engineers and architects are going out on Saturday – what to do is not clear; no surveyors are wanted! Twenty-eight neutrals parade today, by order, including some Southern Irish, but they are sent back – there are too many to deal with. Hope and Victor help to clean out a filthy cesspool outside the gaol; it is connected with septic tanks and they are all clogged up. Luckily, I am playing bridge at the time. Cobly isn't here, or Pennefather. They must be with the troops, I fear. And I have heard nothing of Moule or Tony Lucas.

13 March: It is a cold, very wet morning. Our forlorn people outside sit disconsolately under the eaves. D. Heddle has died in hospital. Abang and Duggan are in hospital too. I hear the Danes were asked if they came in a Danish ship. 'Yes'. Then you must be interned. At last, people outside are moving into the punishment cells.

They are bigger than ordinary cells – why, I don't know. The food policy is announced to be three good as possible meals a day, so that we will be as fit as possible if the time comes when we have to feed on rice only. I see Forbes-Leyne. He prescribes vitamin B, but I can't get it. Clery (from Southern Ireland) is up before the Japanese today as a neutral. He is asked many questions: 'Are the Southern Irish really anti-British?' ('No.') 'Does he particularly want to be out?' ('Not particularly.') Night thoughts – it is remarkable that so many hard drinkers have settled down, with no ill effects, to total deprivation of alcohol for nearly a month now. We have asked the Nipponese about perishable foods in Singapore e.g. flour. There is so much of it that its import was prohibited. It should be made into biscuits. The Japanese representative is non-committal; we are prisoners and don't forget it! Not likely, or not bloody likely. ('Pygmalion.') It is a very cool night; I use a sheet; I have no blanket.

14 March: It is reported that the Empress of Asia ran out of coal, because of stokers' strike. There is no water for bathing; it comes on later. There is a Japanese landing in New Guinea; it is easy. Will the Nipponese attack Australia? I doubt it. Cripps is going to India. *(Tom's news is on target. The Japanese have indeed already landed on the north coast of New Guinea; and Sir Stafford Cripps does go to India and, on 29 March, promises the Indians independence and Dominion status.)* The Nipponese premier in a speech says that now is the time for Australia to reconsider her position; if not, she knows her fate. 'The Syonan Times' also gives a list of Nipponese taking positions as Advisers in various States of Malaya except Pahang. The figures for yesterday's menu are: breakfast – oats – $1^1/_4$ oz each; milk – four 14-oz tins per 100 persons; salt – 2 lbs per 533 persons; tea – $^1/_5$ oz per person; milk (sweetened condensed) – six 14-oz tins per 533; sugar – 10 lbs per 533 persons. The library is now going strong again. I see Hugh Bryson is on the first floor of D-Block. We may be able to use the showers. I wonder how the fall of Rangoon affects the chances of a swop. I wonder if Nora got away from Batavia. We must not be dispirited; we are doing very well. I walk a mile or so with Dawson in the vegetable garden. Now Lights Out is 9 p.m., which equals 7 p.m. by the sun! Is this because of the blackout? It is very tedious, anyway. The Padre makes the following announcements at 9 p.m.: There is to be a roll call every morning at 9, with breakfast at 9.30. Shopping lists may be prepared – necessities only. The vegetable garden will be at our disposal in two days. We will be allowed to bathe once a month (in the sea, presumably) Dawson (the Secretary for Defence) says, 'Don't build any hope on the chances of a swop. The general opinion is that our internees are more useful to the Nipponese than we are to the British Empire. We are useless except in Malaya.' I dispute this. If this is so, then why are officers in the Colonial Service all transferable? I can recall no parallel case of such large numbers of Europeans being held prisoner by an Asiatic race in the tropics. This SHOULD count with the Home Government.

Sunday, 15 March: The following are the orders issued at a meeting between the Garrison Commander and the Head Commandant and Committee of the Changi Internment Camp held on 14.3.42 in the Garrison Commander's office:

1. All enemy civil subjects will be interned in Changi Prison.
2. They will do all necessary work inside the prison for the benefit of the community.
3. The behaviour and attitude of internees towards the Nipponese authorities must be respectful and obedient.
4. The camp will be divided into three male camps, one female, a hospital etc.
5. Gives details of organisation *(Tom does not elaborate)*.
6. The Garrison Commander shall appoint the Head Commandant.
7. Reveille will be at 8.30 a.m., breakfast at 9 a.m., roll call at 9.30 a.m. Absentees are to be reported immediately to the Garrison Commander. Work in camp to start at 10.30 a.m. Lunch will be at 1.30 p.m. Work re-starts at 2.30 p.m. Duties cease at 6 p.m. Supper is at 7 p.m. Lights out at 9 p.m. (by order of the Nipponese High Command). The Head Commandant and the Block Commandants will meet the Garrison Commander daily at 5 p.m. in his office.
8. Communication between the male and female camps is strictly prohibited.
9. When any Nipponese officers come into camp or into rooms, internees must bow and stand to attention. Only those who are sick and aged may remain seated or in bed.
10. Gives the fire and theft precautions.
11. No internees will be allowed out of camp except to collect firewood or, if sick, to go to the Mental/Miyako Hospital and for sea-bathing once a month. Sentries will accompany all such parties.
12. Bread for the female camp will be cooked in the main kitchen. Particular care must be taken to see that infants and children are well fed.
13. The hospital and dispensary will be opened.

Lists of necessary articles will be submitted through the Head Commandant to the Garrison Commander. Medical and dental items must be kept separate. No further food may be bought and the camp is advised to conserve its stocks. The Nipponese authorities are endeavouring to procure vegetable seeds and they propose to open the main vegetable garden as soon as possible. The question of the supply of the necessary tools and provisions is to be considered by them. About 50 Roman Catholics have their Mass at 7.30 a.m., near where we bathe. The crescent moon has dwindled almost to nothing, but we can still see to shave by it in Jack's mirror; I haven't one. We have our first suicide today. There will be more if conditions are not improved. It's Mrs Wallace; she fell out of a hospital window. W.H MacGregor has died in the Mental Hospital, now the European Hospital. He was 67 and came from Mallaig. The Maison Changi Hairdressing Salon is now in full swing! 'The Syonan Times' is still full of Australia at the crossroads and the noxious habits of the degenerate British living in luxury. I do a fatigue at 10 a.m., cleaning the latrines and a drain – a noisome task. I wash some small things, handkerchiefs etc. After tiffin, I do a fatigue in the kitchen, but nobody seems to know what for, so, after humping a few cases of tinned fruit and hanging around for half an hour, I retire. At 6 p.m., we are told the engineers are to go at last; they are to take essential baggage only and no beds. I go to church at 7.45 p.m. The Rev. Tipson takes the service. We hold a spelling bee after Lights Out at 9 p.m. We play for money, but we finish all square. The authentic number of men is 2,199. I get it from the Daily Roll in the kitchen.

16 March: Notice over the bakery – 'Wedding Cakes A Speciality'. I find a tin of powder for films; it may do. A statement about the position as regards the exchange of internees is given by 'The Changi Guardian' (the prisoners' bulletin): no steps have been taken yet and can only be initiated by the governments concerned. The women say they are going to stay with their husbands! Conversation with the women had been possible in the courtyard by going there on various pretexts, then some female complains that so-and-so talked for a quarter-of-an-hour with her husband; why hadn't she? The Nipponese stopped the whole thing. There is a quiz after Lights Out – six-a-side as before. I pick a different six – it is quite amusing. I have a sore throat; it's a cold.

17 March: Miles goes to hospital with stomach trouble. Some rice has arrived from the Nipponese; it is fermenting. It is St Patrick's Day. The irrepressible Irish announce they will entertain us with Irish ditties. There will be a special poteen composed of water, tea, sugar and milk. Vic and I argue about the pronunciation of 'poteen.' I am on the list for heavy fatigues; I trust I can stand them. Refuse disposal: we use an enormous number of tins e.g. with the fish yesterday, for tiffin, we used one tin for three folk (equals 800 tins). They go into a very posh incinerator and come out purged and flattened. They are then buried in the vegetable garden. I don't know what sort of vegetable tins grow! In the afternoon, I am challenged to bridge at 125 cents a 100 by Joe Meade and Drew Wallace. My partner and I end 4,900 points up, making a gain of $12.25. Cash! 'The Syonan Times' reports that there is no resistance in Northern Sumatra. In the newspaper, there is a remarkable similarity in the wording of the various official notices e.g. 'Those who do not comply will be severely punished.' Thus falls the British tyranny! I chat to the Dutch District Officer from Rhio. As he left, the Chinese were looting and murdering. There was no control; the military forces had gone. Altogether, he'd rather be here. Also, about 300 of our troops arrived in small batches. They all wanted help and small boats. There was no discipline. He also referred to Best's party – about 40 hours to the Indragiri River, then another 20 hours brings them to Rengat and a road. So they probably got there, but after that. At 7.30 p.m., I go to the St Patrick's Day celebration. There are a lot there, including the Governor. We are a queer race: we sang all the Irish songs with gusto, including 'Wearin O' the Green', to a fiddle and accordion (played by members of the Selangor Club Orchestra). The Governor says he has never spent St Patrick's Day in gaol before and the next one will be in happier circumstances; we shall have an 'ell of a time, or words to that effect.

18 March: At 7.15 a.m., I run six times round the concrete in the exercise yard with Jack – it opens the bellows. We try the showers; they are good, but you have to turn 50 on at once. It is rather a waste for two. Dick Hewitt, operating as camp policeman, tells us they are to be on only from 6 to 9 p.m. My throat is still sore – I decide there is to be no smoking today. I wash handkerchiefs etc. in the laundry. I actually get hot water. I observe a pillar of Singapore scrubbing his false teeth, using water out of an old soup tin and a floor scrubbing brush over a filthy grating in the concrete floor! I am put on a fatigue party cleaning the exercise yard – it is not very strenuous. I walk a long time with Murray Jack. He says the Aussies in the Chief Justice's house (Sir Percy McElwaine's) despoiled everything and actually defecated on the carpets. I have no rooted objection to beards as such, but these growths cannot be so described. The true beard is an aesthetic entity designed to enhance the beauty of the wearer. Its function is to conceal or subdue his less desirable facial features to throw into relief those best fitted to bear the light of day. But too many of the hairy outcrops in camp have no recognisable design or purpose. They are anarchic growths – uncontrolled, unlovely – indiscriminately obliterating the human visage until, in many instances, all that remains to us of the face of former friends or acquaintances is a scarred nose and a pair of eyes peering furtively from the tangled depths. Fifty of the engineers return! They had worked on one of our evacuation camps! Three thousand of our troops are there. I go to a meeting of the 'Changi Guardian' editors; they want help; I offer to assist. I go to bed with a stocking round my neck, wrapped in a sheet and wearing a sarong and a sweat shirt. They call us 'haughty, proud, arrogant, degenerate' – the latter description is definitely disproved by us! I firmly believe no other race could have 'taken it' as our 2,000 – it is such a change. 'The Syonan Times' reports that Eden, the Foreign Secretary, has spoken of the prisoners in Hong Kong and of their 'wonderful treatment' by the Japanese. There is no mention of Singapore and no Red Cross representative has been allowed in here so far. The rain sweeps right through these rooms with the wind, it will soak everything. Today, I have folded everything, beds etc., and put the lot on Jack's camp bed behind sandbags. We have eight new men in; they have been put in the storeroom with five Danes and Norwegians. It is a gloomy spot – about 42 feet by 9 feet. According to 'The Syonan Times', our and the Allies' naval losses are astronomical and the Nipponese microscopic. *(At this stage of the war, the newspaper reports are just about right. American and British setbacks at sea continued for some months after Pearl Harbor.)*

19 March: Fairy and the others never got their trestle beds – typical. At 7.15 a.m., in spite of my cold, Jack and I run seven times round the exercise yard, which is equivalent to 700 yards. I have now been constipated for four days, but this is common. All say it is the diet and there is nothing to worry about. Certainly, I don't feel stuffed. Hugh Bryson and L. Forbes come to our bed and chat. Hugh says the change of diet will in the long run lengthen our lives! I hope so. 'The Syonan Times' says that 11 ships have been sunk off Colombo, Rangoon and the Indian coast; also the Queen Mary with 10,000 troops in the South Atlantic. *(This report is false.)* The newspaper also warns the Asiatic population that the way to happiness etc. will be hard, but they must tread it for the sake of their children! The arrogant British then come in for more castigation. My cold is now in my head. I wash two handkerchiefs. The Nipponese have sent in a consignment of Irish stew; we haven't had it yet. I smoke a little today, but it is not very enjoyable and I don't like Frontier tobacco. I give L. Forbes a pipe full; he hasn't smoked a pipe for several days. The kitchen is giving us mead tomorrow – some genius has made yeast out of hops. There is a remarkable variety of snores in the night; one gentleman is like a kijang or barking deer; another is like a borer beetle. I hear an offer of $15 for a tin of cigarettes today.

20 March: Poor Dugan Hampshire died in hospital yesterday; he looked very fit when he came in. He was born in 1877 and came to Kuala Lumpur in 1902. He was buried at the hospital yesterday. I do not have a very good night, what with coughing etc., so I stay in bed till 8 a.m. I go to the dispensary at 10 a.m. I have been six days without going to the bathroom; Gibb holds the camp record – 23 days, he told me. They give me two pills and an aspirin for the cold. 'The Changi Guardian' alleges that this is the Governor's birthday, but Clem says it isn't; it's Hugh Fraser's *(the Acting Colonial Secretary).* Still, I send Sir Shenton Thomas my crossword number one. I play some bridge and sit in the sun for a bit. I sweat, but this flu makes me all rather weak and muzzy. A hoary-headed old reprobate who beds behind me thinks nothing of these spelling bees and quizzes after Lights Out. 'Why don't they get someone to tell smutty stories? I can tell a dozen!' I take a census of B-Block today: in the top row cells, of which there are 44, there are 132 persons. It is the same on the 2nd and 3rd rows. The centre space of the 3rd (1st floor) is full of folk, say 50. And there are 80 on the ground floor in Room 1, 110 in Room 2 (ours) and 50 in Room 3. And this is accommodation to house 132 convicted prisoners. A young Empress of Asia seaman trades in a four-ounce tin of 'No

Name' tobacco for one tin of condensed milk, three small packets of chocolate and a packet of cigarettes. They always brew tea in the yard and are presumably running short of milk! It is an appalling supper. It is called 'savoury rice' and is flavoured with ghee and a little soya bean sauce; it is horrible. There is also bread, butter and tea, but the bread is very sour. I get a library book, 'Dandelion Days.' Written on the back cover is an extraordinary message dated 15.1.42 at the General Hospital, thus: '23.25 – what the hell has the night sister done to me? Injection refused, but given some other awful stuff – made to feel like a drunk in five minutes – didn't ask for anything – or injection – God, she's a bitch. Evacuated from Penang and now a thorough defeatist – anti-everything. I feel stewed except the pain in my leg has not gone.' Signature illegible. There is a musical quiz after Lights Out. One of our older men knows the Belgian National Anthem, but cannot whistle it, because he has taken his teeth out.

21 March: My cold is much better, but I have to cancel a heavy sandbag fatigue. The Governor is put on a light fatigue cleaning the passage; so is Clem. Washing – we have used every bit of Sunlight soap, but we had a new issue yesterday – a piece one-inch by two-inch by two-inch. Jack trades 20 cigarettes for a cake of carbolic soap. There was a squad working in the women's section this morning. They say they all look well. They have much more room and are better fed than we. This is good. One man had a long chat with his wife. I have a haircut – Jack and I give the barber 150 cents each. The regular barbers are off work – whether because they aren't paid or what, I don't know. An ancient gentleman with a couch behind mine requests that I pull my tin box further in, as folk in the night stumble over it, then step on him. I am prepared to do what I can until he spoils his case by adding that I've got 20 feet, when actually I don't, so I take some umbrage. Second helpings are a feature of meal-times now. Each half of the room takes turns to go up first; there is usually only rice available. The community singing is very good. E.A. Brown knows his business. We are in four groups of about 15 each, with a large audience. We sing 'Three Blind Mice,' 'The Chestnut Tree' etc. The best is a combination of the chorus of 'Tipperary' and 'Pack Up Your Troubles' sung simultaneously; they harmonise beautifully. To bed – and a mosquito annoys me for the first time, but not for long. What a blessing – 100 nets in this room is unthinkable.

Sunday, 22 March: What a treat it will be to sit on a chair again. There is no rice today! I run eight times round the track at 7.15 a.m. I send a poem to 'The Changi Guardian'; they welcome it. It is entitled 'A Lament':

Some poet – I know not who –
(I'm sure he was no sage):
Stone walls do not a prison make

Nor iron bars a cage.
I wish he were in Changi now
His rash remarks to gauge.
In lieu of stew, he'd eat his words
And gnash his teeth with rage.

A.J. King is here. I see Blyth and others. Blyth thinks that the prospects of an exchange are hopeful. He says he has heard that Joan's lot left Cape Town in a 20-knot convoy; I don't know how he can have. I talk to R.K. Bell; he says Brian may be in Brazil now! He has a brother there; he told his wife to go to Brazil if Singapore fell! I bet she didn't. For lunch, there is good soup and macaroni – lots of it – but I refuse to overeat at any meal. One of the cooking difficulties has been that the ovens were run on diesel oil and have had to be converted to wood. Macnab has had a big hand in this; it was not easy, I gather. This morning, our representatives met the Garrison Commander. Officially, he is being replaced; he is going to a fighting area. There was a mutual exchange of compliments. He explained that the short rations were due to a food shortage. The Nipponese expect a long war. Nipponese soldiers go for a week without water, he said, and they fight to the last man; it is glorious to die for Nippon. He said there was no use dwelling on our good points, so he would mention others: some people show selfishness – their own wants. Only people with wives expect to have communication, Nipponese soldiers go for months and years without. Of course, we know nothing about this sort of thing. It is their duty to protect us, as internees, and they will continue to do so, but, if communication were allowed, he could not guarantee the soldiery would not get out of hand. Our representatives, asked, said they had no criticisms to make of our treatment. What about the overcrowding, the transfer to Changi, the walk carrying our luggage? 'The Syonan Times' announces with a flourish the resumption of the delivery of letters. It is marvellous value – only eight cents, the newspaper says. I wonder if the stamps are surcharged.

23 March: The number of women is 359, children 50 and infants nine, making a grand total of 2,553 (official). There are 44 in hospital; they are included. Clery goes to hospital with dysentery. I run eight times round the exercise yard. There is a complaint that our running (two people in tennis shoes!) makes a noise and disturbs sleepers! Our half of the room is spring-cleaned and the floor washed. I air my mattress; it is a fine, sunny day. Today, ten packets of cigarettes (100) are sold for $45 – disgusting profiteering. There is an appeal for money from the Bishop. He and two curates are carrying on the Cathedral services. They have no income – or very little – and are dependent on the Asiatic congregation for food. I give $5, so do a lot of others. A meeting is arranged with Lieutenant Chasaki, the new Garrison Commander, taking over from 2nd Lieutenant Sayka. His second-in-command is

2nd Lieutenant Tokuda; there are also Imura, Hayashi and Okamurah. They are all introduced to our representatives and, after a mutual exchange of courtesies, Lieutenant Chasaki says he is anxious to do his best, is willing to listen to any reasonable requests and asks for a list by tomorrow. There is to be an inspection at 3 p.m. I spend a fair night. Some people are either entirely selfish or entirely thoughtless. One dons a pair of boots or shoes at 5.30 a.m. (= 3.30 a.m.) and clumps out of the room on the concrete without the slightest attempt to tip-toe or anything – and over 100 others asleep in the room.

24 March: I hear the Javanese murderer of Charlton Maxwell and his wife has been set free from Taiping Gaol. He was awaiting hanging. It's a damned shame. My cold is gone, but the catarrh is still hanging around, as it used to do with Nora, but not with me. Can this change be due to taking no alcohol? Classes are going now. Jack is doing Dutch and shorthand. I would not mind Elementary French. Linehan wants to know if I can find someone to take Elementary Astronomy. I fear not. The stuff our surveyors do is not what they want. Jermyn is giving a talk on crocodiles soon! At the library, I chat to Middlebrook. He tells me that Rendle will know about the ship Nora went on. I locate Rendle in Block D, Floor 3, Room 29, with Joynt and Gorsuch, but he is out on a firewood squad. I talk to Gordon Lawes; he is convinced we'll be out before St Andrews Day *(30 November)*. He has accepted an invite to dinner! I put a shirt on, out of respect for the Nipponese High Command! King says the committee want uniformity in the measurements of every square foot of available space, so we see the other Blocks C and D and tell them what we did. We are inspected by the Nipponese at 3 p.m. They have no comments, except to ask what that is surrounded by sandbags? Squatpans! At 8 p.m., Lieutenant-Colonel Kato makes an inspection. Jack is on food fatigue at St Andrews School. He comes back with tins of jam and pineapples, bread, cheese and milk – all bought at the roadside. Marvellous! Victor gets a few too. This is fine; we divide the food among our four, of course. Jack also gets Pirate cigarettes for $5. Vic's lorry had a Punjabi driver. He knocked over a bucket passing a narrow barrier. He was made to stop and had his face smacked. He then had to refill the bucket. Good propaganda! Jack paid 50 cents a tin for the jam and traded 50 cigarettes for 2 oz of Capstan. He is very noble – he is going halves with me on this tobacco. I should have been on the fatigue, but he wanted to go. As I was just back, I let him. This was providential, as I am not in the same class as a scrounger as he is. There were a few shops open, but no stocks visible. The telegraph and trolley bus wires are still down. There are road barriers all over the place. Some trade in fresh fish is going on at Paya Lebar. There are new arrivals from Woodleigh Pumping Station; they have no news.

25 March: There are more new arrivals, I know not whence. The Committee have handed in suggestions to the new Garrison Commander: fresh meat is required (there are 2,900 tons in the Cold Storage) and vegetables. We need ground-nut oil in lieu of butter. We need more room for exercise. And a list of internees should be made for sending to our next-of-kin. I hope this is done. I wonder where Nora is. There is an appeal for turns for a variety concert in a fortnight or so and for 'After-Lights-Out' talks. I have a disturbed night. I go to the laundry three times and stub my big toe badly.

26 March: There are 2,585 of us now, including 354 women, 40 children and 9 infants. The resume of Colonel Kato's speech to our Committee on the 24th is very interesting: he said he had been away a few weeks. He asked if there were any Danes or Spaniards in the camp. The reply was one Spanish woman, two Danes. He said we would probably find life rather trying, but the Nipponese authorities had no intention of treating us harshly. 'We will treat you as the British authorities treated the Japanese internees here. All the internees were put into the prison some time ago, but we do not now know where they are or whether they are safe. Sumatra has been captured, but we do not know where the Japanese from there have been sent. The Japanese in Java were sent to Australia. The Japanese Army has captured Sumatra, Java, the Philippines, Celebes and New Guinea, but we have no informa-tion as to the safety of any Japanese internees.' He repeated that it is not the delib-erate policy of the Japanese authorities to treat us badly, but, when they consider the way in which the Japanese internees have been treated by the British authori-ties, they feel they cannot give us 'freedom, and an easy life.' They wished to be generous, but they must treat us on the same lines as the British did the Japanese. We undoubtedly found our life rather trying, but we must have patience and wait for the day when more concessions could be permitted. We must take particular care of our health. Asked about the supply of drugs for the hospital and if there were any urgent requests, our reply was that we had submitted them to the Garrison Commander that morning. We are not to smoke in the corridors and the camp divi-sions are to be 1,2,3,4,5 and not A,B,C,D,E, as already labelled. I have a quiet afternoon; I feel muzzy. I see Rendle – he knows nothing about ships on Friday, February 13th.

27 March: At 7.15 a.m., we do not go for a run as usual. Jack and I wash and shave, but we are both feeling rather muzzy. I have heard people speak of the same feeling that I get – you stand up and immediately go dizzy – due to general weak-ness, is it? Jack gets a hint of a possible fatigue party outside. There is a cigarette issue of five per man and we draw lots for 17 oz of tobacco amongst 105 people. I certainly have diarrhoea, but I don't think its dysentery. I can't remember when last I suffered from diarrhoea; it must be the diet. Drew says a visitor to Changi yester-day was horrified at the appalling conditions. Jack and I draw two ounces of to-bacco *(in the lottery to allocate the tobacco ration)*. Our fatigue involves a curious procedure: we are ordered to cut a brand-new lorry in two to provide a trailer for a firewood lorry! There is community singing again. My favourite song is Drink To Me Only. When shall I see the family again, I wonder? There are three further dysentery cases from this room today. Twenty-five more doctors came in yesterday, including specialists e.g. English – the gynaecologist. He will get a holiday here! Surely the Nipponese can't have enough professionally trained people to dispense with these? In the angle of the wall at the exercise ground, I see a gentleman today whispering, 'Jane! Jane!' But I doubt if the yard is open to them *(the women)*. I have seen or heard no signs. They have other open spaces. On the whole, I spend a good night, though all are disturbed by snores, eructation's and lazy people who WILL use the latrine a few feet away! I didn't get up at all.

28 March: I speak to a man from the Censor's Office who says he knew our son was in the Navy. He used to see his letters pass through. He has travelled on the Felix Roussel – a fine, big ship. He heard it went to South Africa. *(Tom thought Nora might be on it.)* This would be excellent. Perhaps Nora would take Brian home and then we could all settle down – all I ever want to do after this debacle. Drew went out yesterday with a fatigue party. He contacted a Chinese shop – nothing doing; some of our 'lower deck' had robbed his shop. But he then tried a Malayan. He was obviously takut *(afraid)*, but willing. He got 25 eggs and sundry tins. The sentry saw, but turned a blind eye. An egg WOULD be good. The Padre announced that there is to be no gambling in the camp of a nature which benefits an individual, such as Crown and Anchor or roulette. The weights of about 20 people are to be recorded for the information of the Nipponese to prove the diet is insufficient. I have mine; I appear to have lost eight pounds.

Sunday, 29 March: We have kanji for breakfast. How I loathe this rice; it is polished. If we go on at this rate, we shall all be as weak as kittens, if not actually developing beriberi. And we'll all get curvature of the spine, sitting on small boxes or on a mattress on the floor – with nothing to lean against! It is most uncomfortable for days on end. The vegetable garden is getting on nicely. A Hokkien nearby has contracted to supply fresh vegetables, but will the Nipponese agree? I hear again that the Duchess of Bedford – Joan's ship – reached home – splendid, if correct – and the passengers were given warm clothes and money, if required, in Cape Town. This is alleged to have been on the BBC news some time ago. *(The ship on which Joan escaped was, in fact, the Empress of Japan.)* There is a tobacco and cigarettes issue – 207 people on the ground floor of our block – three rooms – get 10 cigarettes each at 30 cents and 34 oz of tobacco at 75 cents to draw for. I'm not included, as I was a winner in the last draw. And there's a great shortage of matches! We are OK at present – about 10 boxes. And my tobacco will last, with care, till the end of May. But how annoying when I think of all the supplies of everything which Nora accumulated so well. I could have lived for six months and been short of nothing. Those big tins of Klim! How I could do with one! Folk with no money get a free issue out of camp funds. There is a rumour that we are all to be sent to Port Swettenham. Then we are told that the up-country people are to go there. It would be beastly – heat and mosquitoes. Carl Lawson's wife is removed from the camp today – for broadcasting, it is alleged. The rumour now changes to: the women are going to St John's and the men to Port Dickson. What a hope! But, if we were to go to Port Swettenham, we would have government-standard coolie accommodation. This is a cut above ours. Jack and I walk in the vegetable garden for about one-and-a-half miles. We take a good look at the gaol. The plan is simple when you know more about it, though confusing inside. There are just about 500 cells and punishment cells plus a European prison block.

30 March: Ah, sleep it is a wondrous thing, beloved from pole to pole – is that right for the morning? Anyway, I slept more than usual. My crosswords are a great soporific – I am composing a golf one; I went to bed trying to get a word beginning 'D' and ending 'P-R-'. I came to the conclusion that 'Dum Spiro' was the only phrase possible! So I had to change it. I jocularly discussed escape the other day. I said I would get as brown as possible, don a sarong and beard and, with my build, I'd pass as Malay. 'What. With those eyes?' Too true. I air my mattress after breakfast. It is mildewed below with damp coming up from the cement floor. I wash my shorts – which is difficult. I meet the Governor, Sir Shenton Thomas; there is no news. George P. came in yesterday; he said Singapore is being stripped – thousands of tons of flour etc. are being exported. Is the implication that they are not expected to hold long? The country cannot feed itself; our camp stocks will soon be finished. Then there will be rice only, but we can't live on that. Then, if you can't feed your internees, you should open negotiations for a swop. Who should? The Japanese, of course, said I. 'The Syonan Times' announces the resumption of the retail sale of sugar. And they are to reopen the schools soon. Jack is out with a firewood fatigue party. There is no lorry now – they push a truck. He does not manage to scrounge anything except coconuts. The neighbouring smallholdings are being devastated. High-ranking Japanese naval and military officers drop in to look at us in the afternoon, but it is not an inspection. At 7.45 p.m., Edmonds, our Block Commandant, gives an account of the position – a good one – I mean his account. We have asked for a Red Cross representative to visit and the Swiss consul (Arbenz), but so far without success. We have also asked that the Red Cross should pass on the list of internees – also to no avail so far. The reply is that the Japanese have received no list yet. The idea also appears to be that what rations the Japanese soldier has are sufficient for the European internee. Three doctors and two orderlies from our gaol hospital go to the other hospital with dysentery. There are some very stupid requests to the Japanese authorities: 'Will you stop people clumping about the corridors in heavy boots after 9 p.m.? Make them wear slippers.' The reply: 'They haven't got any slippers.' There is a snappy bit by the ventriloquist's doll at the Variety

Show in D-Block: 'An invisible man married an invisible woman and they had an invisible child. What did he do?' 'He joined the Air Force in Malaya.' The Governor has finished my cricket crossword. We discuss reasons for thinking that the Malaya Command had no idea that there would be a collapse. The Empress of Asia arrived on February 5th; six months' ration books were issued on February 10th; I was surveying a new cable line to the Naval Base as late as February 10th. General Percival arrived on February 7th *('arrived back' is probably what is meant)* and Paterson on February 9th.

31 March: There is an issue of sweets – two-and-a-half chocolates per man! The Japanese want an electrical engineer who can repair a dynamo. Which, we wonder? When we meet a Japanese officer in the corridor, we are to halt and pass on, but not bow. Lights Out will be 10 p.m. I see the Governor: he says conditions are very bad and that negotiations are well advanced for an exchange! Somehow, there is an atmosphere of cheerfulness about today. Is it the rumours? I have made a billycan out of a Brown and Polson's cornflour tin. It can hold all my tea ration and my mug won't. Hear we are to get bread daily. V.J. says that, when he gets out of this room, he will have to have a gramophone record with various noises to put him to sleep – snores, snorts, a chain being pulled and other noises which cannot be specified in a respectable diary. What a wonderful screed one could write on the lines of Nat Gubbins to his tummy. Ours must have been incredibly astonished during the last six weeks – never-ending rice and not one hard drink.

1 April 1942: I tell Hope that the Padre wants 12 copies of the House list – 200 names before tiffin! He swallows it. *(April Fool's Day joke).* Rumours – we are to be sent to a neutral country and interned – to wit, Goa! That would suit me. We block the port of St Nazaire with a concrete vessel, so submarines cannot get out. *(There was a successful raid on St Nazaire on 27 March.)* 70,000 Germans surrender at Kharkov. *(About this time, the Russians finally drove the Germans out of Kharkov. The camp rumours regarding world news are remarkably accurate. It looks as if somebody has a radio.)* Hope has made a grater to grate the coconut – out of a tin. He can't chew on account of his cracked dental plate and our dentists in camp have no equipment for a repair. The grater is excellent. Jack has grated a coconut and, mixed with molasses, it makes quite a good sweetmeat. I speak to Foston and hear about the latter's experience with the L.D.C., coming down the peninsula in touch with the Army. It is very interesting, but what a pathetic muddle. He agrees with our views on this so-called infiltration. It could have been done both ways. H. Fraser's account of the visit to the Nipponese High Command to surrender the city is also interesting, but very humiliating for us. And the only British soldier he met apparently was a sergeant who had had too much to drink – disgusting at such a time and typical of the whole campaign!

2 April: Abang alas is very ill, I hear. I take in the waist of my shorts four inches by the simple expedient of stitching a fold in the back. They are now much better to wear. From tomorrow, we can now bake four-ounce rolls; and we have made machinery for de-liming the rice. We are getting 50 frozen carcasses from the Japanese. Our tinsmith is making little lamps to save matches. It has been pointed out to the Nipponese that it's time bathing parties started, as it will take 25 days to get through the lot at 100 a time. I have been placed on the Games Committee. I receive a blow – I open a two-ounce tin of Raleigh cut plug and it is all mouldy. I must try drying it in the sun. 'The Syonan Times' reports that 200 mixed British and Dutch refugees have been rounded up in North Sumatra. They had fled there. I wonder – does this include Best and company?

3 April: The Nipponese issue us with 25,000 cigarettes – 10 each. Jack and I trade ours for one ounce of tobacco. I talk to G.W. Bryant and Dr Lawson. He was Medical Officer of the Gaol when the Nipponese internees came in – 1,700 of them. They were well fed. They were 18 days here and thanked him a lot when they left. I see A.E. Fawcett – he was out with a fatigue party the other day: he tried to buy tobacco and matches at an Indian shop nearby – they would not sell. Rumour: the U.S.A. bomb Japan from Vladivostok and the Nipponese have protested to the Russians and received no reply. What CAN one believe? *(The rumour probably refers to the Doolittle raid on Tokyo. The B-25 bombers took off from the U.S. carrier, Hornet, and, after bombing Tokyo, crash-landed in China.)* At a sports meeting, we elect representatives for soccer (young Empress of Asia men); basketball, baseball and deck tennis. I take cricket; it will be with a tennis ball – no running. The boundaries will be like deck cricket and 'Over the wall – out!' The long-expected meat is a great disappointment! The 50 carcasses from the Japanese turn out to be very dead! It is just a good thing that, for years now, I have eaten to live, not lived to eat. Belgrave points out that the area of our room is almost exactly that of a tennis court and 90 men eat, sleep, hang up washing – everything – in it!

4 April: Yesterday, I noticed that the Japanese flag on top of the gaol tower was so blown around the staff as to show white only. The keyhole in the door between B and A *(the women's)* Blocks now has a large piece of paper pasted over it, covered with Nipponese characters. Some folk are completely anti-social – they will not observe rules made for the good of the whole camp unless compelled; and, without being snobbish, it is a fact they nearly always hail from the less well-educated portion of the community. The yeast used in making our bread is our own culture from hops. We spring-clean half of the room, sweeping, applying disinfectant, but there is no floor-washing this time. It is a good day for airing mattresses etc. I see Commander Robinson, Master Attendant. He had lived in the Fullerton Building with his wife until two days ago. He had nothing to do. There is a marvellous variety of educational classes now – elementary French – Brothers Vincent and Charles; advanced French – G.S. Tostee; book-keeping – H.C. Allen;

elementary Russian – D. Konstantinoff; English composition – G.T. Gurney; drawing etc. – A.T. Greig; mathematics – R.L. Richards; German – K. Brooch, J.W.L. Kirkman and R. Eisinger; elementary German – Dr J. Moncur; Pitman's shorthand – C.S. Dant; Gregg's shorthand – Edmonds-Hill; Bible study – the Archdeacon; Bible sources – Dr Amstutz; Cantonese – J. Jeff; Mandarin – E.C.S. Adkins; Dutch – J. Heymans and E. Parlevliet; Malay – A. Hyde, E.N. Taylor, W.S. Ebden; colloquial Malay – J.M. Meade; elementary Hokkien – A.M. Oakeley; Tamil – Heywood-Waddington; physics – Professor Alexander; pastel drawing – J.R. Charton; male voice choir – J.L. Woods; physiology – Professor Scott-Macqueen; and Developments in English History, 1485 onwards – Professor W.E. Dyer. What a diversity of talent! The women internees' bows to the sentries are not sufficiently acceptable according to appointed standards. Today I have an egg for dinner! The best egg I have ever had. D-Block gives us a variety show after dinner – it is very good. And so to bed and an inter-squad quiz after Lights Out. It is quite good.

Sunday, 5 April: We don shirts for the church service. What a terrible waste of time an internee's life is – over 2,000 men, nearly all of whom were doing important work, are now obliged to spend day after day killing time – for that is what it amounts to. Our male voice choir functions well at the service and, at intervals during the day, we hear the women's choir – very pleasant. As some individuals won't play properly, we close the latrine in our room between 10.30 p.m. and 7.30 a.m. They sneak in and then don't pull the plug and the stench is abominable; and, if they pull it, it wakes everyone. It is only laziness, as there is one outside a few yards away.

6 April: Easter Monday – I rise at 7.15 a.m. and do nine rounds of the exercise yard. What a contrast to Easter Monday last year! Then we rose early too and Nora, Joan, Strachan and I climbed Gunong Pulai and got soaked, but we had a very good day. 874 mattresses are being made in town for us. There are 17 new arrivals in camp – I think they are from the Auxiliary Fire Service. Robinson thinks there has been much looting of personal property in the Fullerton Building. He says our machinery was smashed up. News has come in via the newcomers: there has been an air raid on Colombo and 47 Japanese planes were brought down. Flying Fortresses are operating and have bombed the Andamans. There has been a Nipponese landing west of Rangoon. The newcomers also say that the Raffles and Sea View Hotels have become brothels for officers and 'New World' men. They report, too, that the people of Singapore have only money and food for another month. Other items of information from the newcomers are: many Nipponese troops are leaving Singapore; and the Aussies are working on the docks at 10 cents a day and are looting and living like fighting cocks. How much of it can one believe? I go to the meeting of the Committee. Edmonds gives an account of the week's developments. The necessities we ordered are it seems, on the way. The Committee today met

Gian Singh and other merchants who have the lists and will get what they can; we pay. They are forming a central fund; we can deposit money in it if we have surplus money. We can hand in cash for the Central Camp Fund and it will be a first charge on the revenue of the Government later. The eggs we had cost 10 cents. The meat fiasco was a 'misunderstanding.' We have arranged for a supply of 800 pounds of fresh vegetables per day, but, so far, the Nipponese have not agreed. The reply is that their soldiers have not had them. The most interesting item is about the forms we filled in. They have four clerks working translating them into Nipponese. The interpreter, when asked, 'What for?', always replies, 'For purposes of exchange.' You can take that how you like! I also hear that a list of those over 45 has been handed to the Nipponese for the same purpose. So what? Someone asks if more notice can be given of the Nipponese inspections, as his room was not ready to receive them and, by his tone, he seems annoyed. The camp is told of 'Singapore foot', mostly got by paddling about in the laundry, I imagine.

7 April: We discuss our lot as internees. In some ways, it is worse than that of those interned by, say, the Germans. We have lost our homes and our property. Our families are scattered all over the globe (in many cases we have no idea where they are) and the simplest communications are out of the question. As for parcels, the situation is hopeless. I fix up the cricket for tomorrow. I draw up tentative rules, put up our eleven and, after talking to Johnny Foster, decide to have the pitch on the concrete in the middle of the ellipse. Over the wall – out! No runs. You score one for a hit which goes outside the concrete ellipse; two, if it reaches the drain or a wall, four if it hits the wall full pitch, but you can be caught out on the rebound. We have two county men – Johnny Foster and H.O. Hopkins. Wow! There is a draw for tobacco – 37 oz. There are 52 pipe-smokers on the ground floor of B-Block. $1.10 per ounce! So much for 'price control shall be severely implemented!' Our interned doctors – over 100 – have submitted a strong memo to the Nipponese High Command, emphasising the deficiencies in the present diet and pointing out the consequences if it is not improved. They also point out the inevitable deterioration of the Cold Store stocks if they are not used. Rumours: we are doing well in New Guinea, badly in Burma. Benghazi is surrounded. The Russians continue to advance. Beleaguered Germans are fighting desperately and being killed. Germany is being bombed with fury. Clery is back from Miyako Hospital after a bout of dysentery. There is one European doctor left there – Landor. The sisters are all Asiatic. Abang, alas, is in a very bad way; at times, he cannot recognise people. The Empress of Asia cooks are now helping in the kitchen and the food is certainly better. Washing my clothes today, I inadvertently soak four pieces of precious bumph in a pocket, but it dries out virginally in the sun – to my surprise.

8 April: I see Winter; he can take an order for shorts. He doesn't know when he can get it through to his cutter who is Russian and is still at work in Battery Road.

I see Dr G.V. Allen. He advises a visit to the dispensary. I see Caldwell there. McMullen tells me that the Nipponese wanted the lens of his camera in the Fullerton Building. They brought him here to see if anyone knew of its whereabouts. I am almost sure it has been destroyed. Jack has seen del Tufo. He says a man has just come in who was on a ship, which left Singapore on the Friday (February 13th). Would this have been Nora's? This ship was bombed and sunk. I wonder. But survivors are said to have been taken to India by the Navy. I must see del Tufo and find this man. I see Cherry. His wife was at the hospital and was presumably on Nora's ship. He has seen the rescued man and he says Mrs Cherry wasn't on his bombed ship. Also Cherry has heard that the ship had been signalled to the Navy as having arrived at Batavia. It was a hospital ship, so perhaps Nora is OK. There is an issue of Javanese tobacco from the Nipponese. I try one pipe – it's impossible. I get hiccups, just as I do if I eat very pungent curry.

9 April: I weigh 122 lbs. At 7.15 a.m., we do nine rounds of the exercise yard before washing. A gentleman complains of the noise of splashing (we bathe using a tin cup as a dipper) and also says that two blokes disturb his delicate sleep by running round the concrete at 7 every morning (we use tennis shoes). I express an opinion that he should be put down. The shop stuff has arrived – great news. I wonder how on earth they will distribute it. There is a call for volunteers for a special fatigue – I offer. It is stripping canvas blocks off the inside of a Dunlop lorry tyre to make soles for shoes. Never have I tried anything more fatuous. We have a pair of pliers and a knife. Dunlops are very strongly built. After two hours' hard work, we have separated – four of us – enough canvas to do at a maximum two pairs! Ridiculous! We have a lot of fatigues this morning. Every able-bodied man in the room is on one or other of them. Forbes comes to see me. He has had one operation in the Mental Hospital – varicose veins – and is due another. A curious thing about the rice diet is that I get so full, I can't eat any more. I hand it to Jack, then, two hours later; I'm hungry again. At 4 p.m., there's another fatigue – unloading lorries full of shop stuff. I notice shoes, broma, talcum powder, shirts, malt extract, toothpaste, toothbrushes, soap and enamel mugs and plates. I give my talk. There is a good crowd and it seems to go very well. At any rate, a number of people make a point of coming up and congratulating me on it. V.J. gives me a decent cigar – what a treat! Gibb says that the gentleman who complained about our splashing has asked him to speak to us. It really is absurd; the noise is tiny and never before 7.30 a.m., when lights have been out nine-and-a-half hours. Gibb says the dining room, where 40 of them sleep, is so very peaceful that there's not a sound from 10.15 p.m. to 8 a.m. No-one snores etc. – there is one inmate who occasionally talks in his sleep. Well, as they've got George, Cyril, Jos and Fairy in there, I know what they can do. They must have reformed!

10 April: Rice is now being ground to flour in the kitchen to mix with the porridge and ordinary flour for bread, as we are running short. A survey party – Hamilton, Bedlington, Sworder and I – survey the area of the whole of the ground floor, less fixtures, including refractory cells, punishment cells and part of the hospital, for the Committee to allocate accommodation. At present, when new people come in, every room says, 'We can't possibly take any more!' The number of available square feet plus population figures will enable the Committee to decide who is the most overcrowded. At 3 p.m., we have a great cricket match – Block B ground floor versus the upper floors. I skipper our team. We score 89 and 121 to 55 and 77. I make 24, retiring on the maximum, and take eight wickets in the first innings! Everyone is very keen. My old gold turnip watch is sent in from the Women's Section. I can't think – I suppose Katherine de Moubray had it. We did our tyre-stripping fatigue so well yesterday that the Arch-Stripper wants us to do it one day in every three and we will be excused all other fatigues. Nothing doing – it's a dreadful occupation. We have permission to get fresh vegetables twice a week. Geneva has told the Nipponese that their internees at New Delhi are OK. Abang Braddon died yesterday, aged 83. He was over 50 years in Malaya.

11 April: My razor blade is getting blunt; do not have a good shave today, though I go over it twice. Must try to make it last a month. This is the 23rd day. I do comparisons of the areas covered in yesterday's survey. We play bridge. We have not lost a rubber all through, but this morning is a tough battle. By the way – bathing this morning at 7.30 in the exercise yard au naturel with a mug and a bucket of water, I suddenly hear two female voices: 'You're up early this morning, dear!' 'Yes, I am.' I leap like a startled hog, as Joan would say. Of course, they are on the other side of the wall in A-Block, but I got a shock. The Nipponese flag flies, but it is now completely white. Dinner consists of rice pudding, a roll and butter, tea and an EGG! I keep mine for tomorrow. I speak to A.J. King. He was caught at Haad Yai, then he was taken to Singora and spent nearly three months in Saigon. There is a summary of information about the Kuala which left on February 13th and I don't know if Nora was on it or not. Briefly – this from Salmond, a survivor – he was on the Kuala: she was a small Straits Steamship boat. She was bombed on the morning of February 14th when at anchor off Pompong, a small island in the Rhio Archipelago. The casualties were not heavy, but a few people were carried away by a strong tide. She had on board nursing sisters from the General Hospital, Alexandra. The survivors were transported to the Indragiri River in Sumatra and Rangot with the help of the Malay headman of a neighbouring island and thence across Sumatra to Padang on the west coast. The survivors reached Padang on March 7th. The total number of refugees there was 1,050. These people are presumably still in Padang. Hundreds who reached Sumatra safely were taken to India by the British Navy or to Batavia by inter-island vessels. It was learned that the British Navy had removed 2 – 3,000 folk to India and the last boat called on March 2nd. (But Nora's name is given as having gone to India. How is this reconciled with Kuala survivors reaching Padang on March 7th?) There follows a brief list of folk Salmond can remember being in Padang on March 16th who were probably taken prisoner on the 18th. Salmond left in a small boat with officials and services and was captured by a Japanese tanker in the Indian Ocean and brought to Singapore. A.J. King had a thin time in Singora. He could not even get enough water to drink and drank washing-up water. RAF fellow-prisoners told appalling stories of incompetence at the outbreak. A.J. King says that the Nipponese told him we were destined for Saigon, but we are too many; they never expected such a crowd.

Sunday, 12 April: I go to see the Governor and spend most of the morning with him. I see Hopkins, a doctor, just in from being in charge at St John's Island, where the mental cases had been sent from the Mental Hospital, now being used as a general hospital. I receive a medical inspection. Molesworth takes me. He has a beard; I don't recognise him until he says, 'Oh, yes. I turned your daughter into a Giant Panda!' Dinner consists of rice pudding, a fifth of a tin of pineapple and tea. Rumour has it that the Nipponese say they can not feed us and have asked our government to send a ship to remove us! Quel espoir! We play bridge – the first round of the Block tourney. Drew Wallace and I versus Coles and V.J. It is a grim battle – we lose the first rubber and get the next two and end 660 up. But we play on a TABLE and sitting on boxes, which is much more comfortable than the usual floor – a most backbreaking business. We have suspected for some time that there is a black market. It appears to be via a Nipponese sentry and the Empress of Asia lads who are being supplied with cash. Goods, including tinned food – looted? – are being brought in. The rumours say that expert opinion has it that it is now or never for the Axis. In the next few months, if they can't win, it is fini. The U.S.A. production capacity is irresistible.

13 April: The camp shop appears to be about to be active. I acquire two yards of cloth; it will make a pillow-slip. Somehow the morning passes. I do not seem to do very much. I help Jack with the issue of shop articles; we get toilet-paper, mugs, enamel plates, blankets, sarongs, face-cloths – not enough to go round, though. I acquire a mug, a face cloth and toilet paper. I have a look at the cricket with a view to spotting talent for our block side. I see none! The Empress of Asia boys are very keen and noisy. Edmonds, the Block Commandant, gives his weekly report at 7.45 p.m. He is still pushing to have our names sent to relatives. There has been no connection made yet with the representative of the Geneva Red Cross. Dr Paris is now in charge of health, Bowyer on the medical side. Those with near ones on board can see the full Kuala report. I can't get this Kuala business out of my head. I wish I knew where Nora was and if safe. There is no chance of knowing, though. There is nothing about an exchange of internees except that the Nipponese have the matter 'always under consideration.' In connection with this, Drew Wallace says the doctors have instructions that there will be no operations unless absolutely essential, the inference being that they would be hard to move afterwards. This is the only LATRINOGRAM *(gossip)* I get today. I sleep fairly well. I find, if I think of something I want to remember, I never can, unless I write it down, so I'm getting used to writing in the dark.

14 April: We finish our last tin of pineapple, but Jack is out on a fatigue this morning and there are hopes. Now that I have a new mug, I can use it for drinking and confine the old one to shaving and bathing. While waiting for a haircut, I chat to Jenkins, an ex warder. He and his wife were going to catch a boat on January 30th (Joan's) when planes came overhead. They took cover in Caldbeck's, but were hit. He got a nasty one on the leg, his wife on her arm and they were taken to the General Hospital. She got away later. Their baggage was all on board the first ship. Jack returns; he was in town. He went to Ally's; there is very little in it. The town is fairly clean; people are lounging about aimlessly. A number of the shops are open and some have stocks. Everybody is very friendly. The trolleybuses are running to Geylang. He manages to replenish our tobacco stock. And – oh joy! – A box of cigars each – good 'uns from Ally's – $7.50 for 25. He got lots of tins too, but these were shared amongst the fatigue party, so our share is half a loaf, a roll, a large tin of jam (pineapple), two tins of sardines and a tin of date-nut bread. I acquire a Japanese one-dollar note. We play cricket versus the Ground Floor, Block D. We win 118 and 163, 120 and 116 – 517 runs in two-and-a-half hours! There is some good fun, including a very funny incident: the ball is rolling off a flat roof very slowly – the field can see it and are yelling to the expectant fieldsman, who cannot know where it is going to drop off, but it falls just out of his reach. The following deaths are reported: A.V.L. Davies, Mrs Woodhouse and Mrs Hannay. Reverting to town, there is no motor traffic and it looks very empty. The High Street and other main streets have no business going on and there are only small stocks in the shops, but there are hawkers in plenty. I talk to Ryrie – the Nipponese have surcharged the stamps. He has a set. The fatigue party were allowed to get 700 lbs. of meat, so we shall have over four ounces each! The Empress of Asia cooks are convinced we have facilities for baking bread daily. The gaol bakers say 'No.' the Empress of Asia bakers say they baked for 3,000 on the Asia with fewer ovens. So I think they are to be given a chance.

15 April: Jack does not run round with me this morning; he got a slight knee-sprain yesterday. I am worried about Nora's diet if she is interned; this incessant rice won't suit her at all. A sentry *(word in code)* says that England will win this war. An interpreter *(word also in code)* says we are interned, but 'not for long.' He blames the military for keeping educated and cultured people under such conditions. The death of Mrs Woodhouse is 'a great tragedy and entirely due to the conditions.' A woman went to town to buy necessities for the babies and children.

She went to a shop where she had had a previous account and the shopkeeper insisted on charging her purchases to her account. 'But you know where I am living now?' 'Oh yes, I know all about that, but we've learnt something this year.' And he insisted on a credit account. At 12.30 p.m., I have access to the full account of the Kuala sinking. It is very depressing news for me: only two ships left on February 13th and both were sunk at Pompong. The other was the Tien Kuang. (Both were flying the white ensign. Why? It seems suicidal.) So Nora was bombed and sunk and, if not killed or drowned, is either interned or got away. The suspense is appalling, but one can do nothing. The Kota Pinang took 206 wounded and women to Batavia and was reported as arriving there. Nora may have been on that – although that's not likely, I think. The survivors had a terrible time – there were no medical facilities and food was very scarce. Rice was so scarce that only children under 13 were allowed it. The adults had to eat sago. Tongue was killed while swimming to shore, so were others, by a bomb aimed at the Tien Kuang. Pompong is uninhabited, but there is water. They split into two parties. Gradually, they got to other islands in various boats and eventually to Padang. I shall never know what happened to Nora until all this bloody business is over. It is a most poignant account. How I hope Nora is home and OK. Enough – there is no more to be said. For lunch, there is rice and a real stew with fresh meat in it. Our first here. This afternoon, I meet a man who has to have the little finger of his left hand amputated. It was a scratch when he arrived, but it has gone septic. There are no medical facilities – at least they are locked up and we are not allowed access.

16 April: Jack again does not join me in my nine times round the exercise yard. Our accountants estimate that the total waist measurement of the camp has decreased by quarter of a mile. I see Winter; he can't take orders now; the Nipponese have closed his business down – why, we know not. I find where Salmond *(the Kuala survivor)* lives, but he is out. J.B. Daintry (just in) tells me that our troops were counter-attacking on February 11th. Some actually reached the Causeway, but the left wing let the Nipponese through (the Aussies and Indians.) The Nipponese are now letting Williamson do our eyes; spectacles can be got (perhaps). For lunch, we get rice, soup with 'vegetables' (alleged) in it. They seem to be green tops of something and leaves, but Jack gets two bits of what appear to be lalang. I go with a firewood fatigue party outside the camp and buy 600 cigarettes for $60! T. Parker has died of dysentery. It is Lights Out at 10 p.m. as usual. There is generally silence at 10.30 p.m., but the snorers are active this night.

17 April: Dusty can't eat rice or porridge; don't know how he exists. Fairy is offered a four-ounce tin of tobacco for $40 today; he offers $15, but is refused. I again fail to contact Salmond. Corner, Birtwhistle and N. Hunt are still outside the camp on duties and living together. There is quite a lot of cricket business to deal with; people are very keen. I see a very nice wooden cross made in gaol for T.

Parker and painted with the usual inscription by our Art master, Walker. The 12th annual meeting of the Senior Golfers' Society of Malaya is to be held on the 25th to elect officers etc. Dudley Parsons asks if I will be the representative for Singapore and Johore. I say, 'No – as soon as I can get out of here, I intend to beat it and find my wife and family!' I put a gusset (is that right?) in the back of my other pair of shorts – about four inches. We have an issue of sweets – two jujubes and three sweets per capita! We queue up for them with eagerness – I think everyone is feeling the absence of sugar. An internee was outside the camp yesterday getting petrol from an Army dump – a 65-gallon drum. A Sikh lieutenant ordered a Sikh private to get it – using a siphon and sucking to start it off. The private just took no notice and walked away. The officer did nothing; there is no discipline at all. And on the fatigue parties, the Sikh sentries who assist the Japanese are nothing like as amenable as the Japanese. Food – I notice that, when our squad is first, we grouse because the last squad get the best stuff, being at the bottom of the container; and, when we are last in, we say the first squad always gets a second helping. At 10.45 p.m., Jack turns his torch on for a few seconds to look at a crossword. A querulous gentleman five yards away gets out of bed and complains it is impossible to sleep owing to the reflection from the page! In the watches of the night, I finish cross-word number seven.

18 April: At 8.15 a.m., there is heavy rain., accompanied by a strong wind; it blows right through! We park what we can under the camp bed, groundsheet etc., but everything gets very wet. At last, I see Salmond and get very full details about the Kuala. It is certain that Nora was on it – all the women were. Poor girl – what an appalling time they had! The intention was to lie there all day *(in the lee of Pompong Island)* and sail at night. There were nine bombers. The first stick hit the Kuala and there were many casualties, but mostly from bomb splinters and, on the whole, they proved not very serious, although it looked dreadful. Of the swimmers for shore – 250 yards – some were washed onto nearby islands, but Salmond is almost certain he heard Nora's name as being on Pompong. He left early – after two to three days – to get help. Ultimately, he was established on Singkep Island and Nora did not pass through there. Therefore, unless she was killed, Nora either went to Batavia with the 200 on the Kota Pinang or to Padang with 500. The remainder of the survivors were taken up the Indragiri River in Sumatra to Rangat in four junks and overland to Padang – 450 miles – and ALL these were taken to India by the Navy. So the odds are she is safe, thank God. She is definitely not in Padang. He has the official list of all civilians from Malaya who were there when he left. Salmond himself, though very modest, obviously did marvellous work and he says the women were marvellous too. This news is a relief. I don't think Nora would be a casualty; she is a good swimmer. Casualties in the sea were largely caused by tummy blast from bombs – like a depth charge to a submarine. All the survivors from Pompong had been removed from Padang to India by the Navy before Salmond got there. He heard nothing of the Best and Goss bunch either. There were casualties amongst the passengers from the dock raid which we saw from the Union Building, but they were taken on board the Kuala. An internee buys one loaf, one jar of honey and one tin of jam for $65 on the camp black market! This racket should be stopped and we have a shrewd suspicion where the vendor gets his supplies. There is extra bread tonight – the result of 1,500 loaves from Gian Singh's. And a supply of vegetables twice a week has now been arranged with a Chinese dealer of Paya Lebar. We get four coconuts for the room (103 persons). They are drawn for. Birkinshaw gets one; Jack and I buy it from him for five cigarettes. An 'important memorandum relating to our future is being drawn up for presentation to the Nipponese.' Dinner comprises rice, one-fifth of a tin of pineapples, one-third of a loaf, butter and an EGG. A regular feast. B-Block give an excellent concert; I like the choir's sea shanties. In a quiz competition, our team score 47 and are in the final, but the questions are not very good, I think. The Padre announces that there is enough margarine from Gian Singh for two-and-a-half months and 2,500 tins of pineapple are to be sold at 30 cents each. We have also inquired about the possibility of using the camp's Girdle Road for exercise. And, if they can't feed us, will they approach our government about an exchange of internees? We now have a new machine for grinding rice and may expect daily bread. I'll go no more a-roaming when I get out!

Sunday, 19 April: Reverting to yesterday's chat with Salmond, he said the Nipponese Navy treated them marvellously and were very insistent that they were prisoners of the NAVY! What a time they had! The boat they used for their escape was a native sailing-craft 50-foot long. They decked her in and put a small shelter on top. The other nine crew members (all Service personnel) were selected for sailing experience. They started from a point well north of Padang – there was great excitement getting there; the Nipponese were all over the place. They called at sundry islands for vegetables, fruit etc. Their sails were rotten; they made new ones. They dodged one Nipponese ship by taking a risk over coral reefs (the boat drew about five feet). Salmond used to take the tiller dressed as a Malay with a big round hat and a sarong. When planes flew over them, the others disappeared and nothing ever happened. When they were finally captured 150 miles from Sumatra, the Nipponese captain was tickled to death at their temerity in trying to make Colombo in such a cockleshell, with only a school atlas as a chart, but was considerably surprised when they gave him their position and were only 35 miles out.

20 April: Hope is on an outside fatigue party today; we discuss what prices he should pay if he gets the chance of buying food or tobacco. We decide on $5 maximum for a four-ounce tin of tobacco. I acquire a packet of razor blades and a pack of cards out of the stock supplied via Jack's 'shop' and we draw lots when there is not enough to go round, due regard being made to especially urgent cases e.g. blokes without a towel or shoes. The Nipponese are very anxious to restart the Pk Hydro Electric Station, but the machinery is bust. There are intricate valves etc. and no designs available. A man interned here is asked, but he can't help. What a mess there is to be cleaned up when we resume! When? Not if, you note. I've never heard an 'if' yet. The fatigue parties pay 70 cents per packet of cigarettes. Hope returns with nothing; the only tins on offer were pineapples at $1. Dinner is a feast! Rice pudding, half a peach, a slice of fresh pineapple, one-third of a loaf, butter and tea! This has been altogether the most adequate day for food we've had. Edmonds makes his weekly report to the Block after dinner: the exchange of names will probably take place via Geneva. We have another form to fill in. It will be three months, I should think, before our people hear anything of us. The cigarette ration is 30. The Nipponese say it will probably get less. The soldiers only get 10. And our merchants' estimate of stocks of flour in Singapore is grossly exaggerated and the ration cannot be increased! Bong! There is the usual battery of foolish questions. Some people can't or won't think. The Nipponese agree to the use of the gaol's Girdle Road for exercise. They suggest it be used from 4.30 to 6 p.m. in parties of 50 at a time. There is to be no smoking during exercise.

21 April: Dusty leaves for Miyako Hospital. G.W. Lawes has also gone and C.V. Brandon returned. It is now strictly prohibited to look through the bars from Kitchen 2 into the courtyard! Jack has scrounged a semicircular sort of half-tub to poise it on a box to make a seat. I am trying soaking tennis balls in water for cricket; they are better – not so lively. Lunch consists of rice and soup with spinach leaves in it. I eat the meal with fortitude, remembering that Nora says spinach is good for me. Latest news – we are now allowed to sing the National Anthem! Several copies of 'The Syonan Times' arrive. The propaganda is so blatantly one-sided, one can't imagine it being swallowed – by anybody. The black market via the arch crook seems to be flourishing. There is talk of new elections: I am asked if I will stand. I say I will, if there is any suspicion as to the integrity of the administration, so to speak. Otherwise, I am satisfied with our room representative.

22 April: Some tempers are getting frayed. This morning, very early, one gentleman tells another he is using too much water for bathing. Before they finish, they go thoroughly into each other's ancestry, habits ('you only bathe in the dark because you're so b——y dirty') and morals. They get back to the Boer War and why they are not fighting in this. Breakfast: kanji. It needs sugar – most insipid. Our ration is less than one ounce of sugar per day. The Nipponese say they can't increase it. Is it usual when you overrun a country to change all the names immediately? The Nipponese appear to have done so in Singapore. The Victoria Theatre is now the Bazooka Gizaka or similar balderdash! Apparently, there is to be an election for Floor Representatives on May 1st. Several people want to know if I will stand. I don't want to. On the other hand, it is said it is my duty to do so if they want me. And undoubtedly one must in this prison life resist the tendency to get lazy and lethargic. So perhaps I may stand. Lunch – rice, vegetable stew, fruit juice. It is said to be meat and vegetable stew, but I see no meat, nor does anyone else I know. Now Seymour W., the ass, has been taken out by the Nipponese – for what object, we know not. He has a ladylove from Malacca and has been in the habit of snatching surreptitious or otherwise chats. But, after being warned, he has overdone it this morning. This has, as usual, repercussions on other people. The regulations have been tightened up and little privileges which were winked at and which allowed husbands to snatch a moment with their wives, are stopped. It is ever thus: how many times have I known a privilege stopped because one person abuses it? Dr Braine has been sent to Miyako Hospital with dysentery. A lot of new folk have come in – from Customs etc. Some are in our room. The gaol has reached saturation point and it is time the Nipponese were told so. For dinner, we have rice pudding, tea, one fifth of a tin of pineapple; there are great wails of hunger all round. Must admit I could eat more, even I. After a game of cricket against C-Block, which we win by one wicket, we barter 130 cigarettes for four ounces of Bruno Flake. A newcomer says they had passes and could go practically anywhere, doing no work. As usual, the pitch was spoilt. A Nipponese general arrived and there were orders to stand up etc. Some would not or didn't, so all were ordered in 'except those doing actual work.' The Anzac Club is a registration centre for folk who wish to register as anti-British! Churchill has received a report on the Malayan campaign. He says the time is not ripe to make it public. I should think not, unless indiscipline and cowardice are to be broadcast to the world.

23 April: There are 2,598 internees with 356 women, but 'The Changi Guardian' says over 70 came in yesterday. It's St George's Day; will we have a blow-out? There will be no roast beef and beer, that's certain. Breakfast consists of tea and watery ground rice – alleged to be porridge; it's the worst we've had. There is a baccy issue – 15 oz of Capstan for 20 pipe-smokers in this room, at $1.50 an oz. The balance get Java tobacco. I hear that the Danes are back on the coconut estates; they are getting to work again, producing copra. I find Fairy busy making cigarettes using toilet paper as wrapping. A vendor is offering two tins of bully beef; he wants $15. I still have mine, issued at Karikal when we came here! We receive an issue of sweets – 21 each for 20 cents. I help Jack with another 'shop' issue – big dishcloths, shorts, Quink, sandshoes, cards and medium towels. I put two boiled sweets in my cold tea preserved from breakfast; they improve it a lot. 15 people were put in the H.E. block above the kitchen yesterday. Lady Thomas, the Governor's wife, is back from Miyako Hospital after two months. Her husband is not allowed to visit. The spoilage of Singapore goes on – all refrigerators are being removed, for example. 'The Syonan Times' says that the Nipponese have given

Hong Kong internees money and cigarettes and they allow canteens where they can buy anything. Comforts have also been received. 'OK, what about us,' say our Committee. For dinner, we have rice pudding, a roll, margarine, an egg and tea. A feast! 'The Syonan Times' has announced that, by order, the first Nipponese public holiday is to be April 29th, the Emperor's birthday. The populace ('all families') will fly the Nipponese flag and will take care to see it is of the correct dimensions; these dimensions can be got from the Education Department. At 10 a.m., they will observe one minute's silence. The traffic will stop. The populace will turn to the north-east and spend that minute thinking of the gallant Nipponese who have given their lives to bring them peace and protection. At 8 p.m., there is a very good St George's Day concert by D-Block. They read extracts from the works of Shake-speare, Rupert Brooke and Kipling, as well as Noel Coward's 'Cavalcade'. It is very inspiring; it ends with 'God Save The King'. The fly in the ointment is the thought of the recent behaviour of some of our troops in Malaya! At 10 p.m., the Padre announces the resignation and elections on May 1st of the Floor and Room Representatives.

24 April: For breakfast, there is kanji and tea. I eat with relish my egg and half a roll I had saved. Hugh Bryson and Pendlebury go to hospital. *(Bryson survived the war and brought these diaries out for the Kitching family.)* Bidlake and Cuthbert Smith also go to hospital. I have seen the new stamps issued by the Nipponese – 2, 3, 4, 8 and 15. They have a curious red surcharge in Nipponese. D-room want me to stand as Floor Representative, but I see Jarrett; he will, so I won't. Now the Empress of Asia lads ask me to be Room Representative 'because we want a fair deal.' I find it hard to refuse that, yet I don't want the job. There appears to be no doubt about the result if I stand. For supper, we have rice, dried figs and tea. We draw for the last spoonful of jam in our tin. I win.

25 April: Lord, I don't know how many people have asked me to stand as Floor and Room Representative. I have agreed to both. I can't resist this pressure. Cedric Carver and McMichael go to hospital. There's a lot of bad Singapore foot about; Ryves has it now. We hold the annual meeting of the Senior Golfers' Society of Malaya – a remarkable affair, with about 50 present. D. St. L. Parsons, as honorary secretary and treasurer, gives a very detailed resume from memory (the records being in Kuala Lumpur) of the year's activities and balance sheet. We elect the Governor president, A.E. Fawcett captain, then the territorial representatives. The Governor makes a short speech of thanks and, inter alia, opines that this interim will not be of very long duration. There are two visitations in the afternoon. We stand to attention; there is a perambulation and a peering – bespectacled. Nothing ever happens as a result of these inspections, except that we continue to increase in numbers, but not prosperity! There are new rules regarding handing in scrounged (i.e. bought outside) tins, cigarettes etc., but no rules will make a man give up what he's bought – only compulsion. Then he won't scrounge, so where are we? After supper, there is room housey-housey; I win $3.50, but, on the whole, it depresses me. I cannot help being reminded of the last time I played – On the Sarpedon *(the ship which brought the Kitching family back to Malaya in 1940)* with Nora, Joan and Brian all there. Well, if there is any truth in the news we are getting, I may see them all sooner than we expected. The Padre addresses us for the last time; he says he has hopes! The main thing is stricter control of the stuff scrounged by outside fatigue parties, the abolition of Floor Representatives and the substitution of three Room Representatives; and an emphatic warning to conserve our money supplies by not buying at extortionate prices outside the camp and to deposit as much as possible with the Control Committee for food purchases. The Carpenter said nothing but 'Cut us another slice.'

Sunday, 26 April: I have $2,100 – I will deposit $500 at the moment. I learn that the five Danes and Norwegians in our room were in gaol before the capitulation. They were in as deserters. They have been offered liberty to work on Nipponese ships; they have refused. Our half-squad are on kitchen fatigue this morning; we fetch the stuff and clean up. I see the Governor; we discuss this and that – he is optimistic. He is darning a sock and making a very good job of it. A fatigue party returns from St Andrews with rice and other items. A number of Tamils came round selling tins etc., but the jagas *(guards)* were not complaisant. One Tamil was severely beaten up and tied to a fence. I do a spot of cricket umpiring in the afternoon. There is a small argument about the camp shop. They have been allowing certain folk to make individual purchases; obviously this is unfair. Two thousand people cannot do it. All should put down their needs and draw lots and take their chances. The stuff available now is: Vim, Listerine, hair stuff, cotton, Lux, pillowslips, syrup of figs, Beechams, various other laxatives, toilet soap and other items, but there is nothing like enough to supply demand.

27 April: The kitchen fatigue at 10.30 a.m. is cleaning-up, so is the room fatigue. The rice-grinding, wood-cutting and anti-malarial fatigue parties have just left. Folk are still buying individually in the central shop. Why shouldn't I try it? I walk in and get a bottle of Listerine for $1.50. The whole system is wrong. Victor returns from the wood fatigue with 150 cigarettes for $12.50 and one tin of condensed milk ($2.) One of our tea mugs has mysteriously gone since tiffin; I think one of Jack's shop clients has inadvertently picked it up. A serious loss! There has been a serious row in D-Block: a Nipponese sentry, probably making a bit of money for the holiday celebrations on the 29th, came in with four bottles of wine and cigarettes. This is the first time I've heard of booze coming in. He sold the wine at $20 a bottle. Someone tried to cheat over the cigarettes and got hit over the head with a bayonet and was bleeding. The Camp Commander had to be called up. It was altogether a hell of a shemozzle. I don't know the upshot of it all. No-one is to be allowed in the kitchen without a permit. 'The Syonan Times' says the scorched earth policy in Malaya was a failure – the rubber and tin are still there! H.W.H. Stevens died on St George's Day aged 91. He started the Cold Storage in Singapore and founded the Royal Singapore Yacht Club. W.J. Garcia, who was in the piano business, has also died.

28 April: The Nipponese have given permission to get coconuts for camp use as distinct from individual scrounging. A fatigue squad goes out; they also get some tins etc. Prices are a shade lower, as they are in a virgin area! Apparently, the owners get nothing for the coconuts; I don't know how they view this. I see one man composing music for a choir. I must find our sketcher and get him to do a sketch of our corner for me. Air the mattress etc. this morning. I talk to Jervis who came in only three days ago. He says they had quite a good time until the bombing of Tokyo, then there was a change. He used to go to a Chinese restaurant; it had very good food – pork chops, steak, fat prawns, it makes one's mouth water! He says it was the only one open. We have some green leaves as our vegetable with our lunch; nobody knows what they are – it is a lottery. I get a bit of sweet potato in my soup. Announcement (result of last night's fracas): nobody in camp is allowed to possess any alcoholic liquor. If they do, they will be punished with the severest camp penalties. The highest legal opinion in camp has been taken and it confirms that no civil action after release can succeed versus the camp authorities for taking this step. Whatever the truth of this may be, I don't agree with blokes buying from the sentries at $20 a bottle, but I don't see the validity of total prohibition. For supper, we have rice, one spoon of jam, tea and a slice of papaya. We are first, so our squad comes up first for seconds. We are in luck – there is more of jam and papaya, so we get extra of both until the papaya server realises it and, giving an agonised yell, says, 'They can't have both papaya and jam extra! They must say which!' However, by this time, Jack and I have got ours. And that papaya is good for the soul and body.

29 April: There are no fatigues today; it is the first Nipponese public holiday – the Emperor's birthday. The cash appeal has realised $38,000 so far; we need more. The vegetables cost $2,000 a week. (We seem to get very little for it.) And everything from Gian Singh's store has to be paid for via the Nipponese, even before we check it. There is a rake-off, no doubt. We institute an extra cricket rule: bails are intended to be a help to the umpire only. If he is satisfied that the ball has hit the wicket, the batsman is out, whether the bails fall off or not. (This is necessary because of the tennis ball!) I acquire a pillow slip for 80 cents and T.C.P. instead of Dettol for $1.95. If we get out before it is finished, I shall be only too pleased! There is a bottle of Optrex, which Nora would seize, but I'm too lazy to use it. Today's snappy bit – an internee was out with a fatigue party yesterday. A Nipponese sentry pressed two pieces of bumph on him as he retired to the rubber trees. Vic and I play bridge against Birkenshaw and Miles in the tourney in the morning, then I play cricket in the afternoon B-Block versus D-Block. They win by two wickets – our catching is bad. The cricket is getting very keen and we have quite a barracking crowd, what with the Empress of Asia lads and others. In fact, you can hardly get a seat at the arena side! For supper, I eat the cheese and other items from breakfast; the cheese is good. There is also rice pudding and a third of a tin of pineapples, the birthday gift of the Emperor. I play bridge with Forbes, Vic and G.D.B. On our return, we have to go right round by the laundry instead of past the kitchen – 150 yards detour. This is either an attempt to stop the black market or due to the sentry incident. I hear he is to be court-martialled. The general opinion is that the matter should have been kept quiet. Later, we take part in a quiz competition.

30 April: Yesterday's porridge – the best yet, is explained. It was the last, so they made it good. For breakfast, we have kanji made with pulut rice. The Malays use it, I think, on ceremonial occasions such as weddings. It is more expensive and contains glutin or something like that and is said to come from Patna. We also get coffee and six pounds of honey for 104 people. I am on hospital fatigue at 10.15 a.m. Jack is on wood fatigue outside; the squad goes armed with dollars and hope. My fatigue is not long, but rather smelly and dirty: cleaning out the hospital refuse-bins. It takes an hour, carrying them to the incinerator and the swill-pit for wet refuse. It is galling to see a large tin of margarine with enough waste on the sides to give us three rations; and two large uncut rolls wallowing in a mass of rice refuse. After this job, I need – and have – a bath. Jack and Vic return with 400 cigarettes – $40 – and five tins of condensed milk for $10. They refused jam at $2 for a small tin. The Chinese who sold these items said that rice in town is about $1.50 a gantang. In the afternoon, Drew and I play the winners of the Block Bridge Tourney. We finish plus 1,300 points. Our opponents, Van Hien and partner, actually have an electric kettle in their 'cabin.' They give me a cup of 'afternoon tea'. We are given an egg for dinner. Ah me, I never peel that hard-boiled egg without acute nostalgia. It reminds me of the many delectable picnics we have had. The good news is that we are to get a four-ounce roll daily in future. There was a row this afternoon over an outside fatigue party buying cigarettes and tins from the locals. The sentry butted in and hit one of ours across the back with a stick. The two Tamils and a Chinese were tied up, brought to the gaol and beaten severely. The purchases, I gather, were scattered to the four winds of heaven. Now, the Nipponese officer commanding the camp has issued an order that no purchases are to be made from locals, under pain of the severest penalties (obviously beatings). He says we have disobeyed orders, but I know of no such orders. He notes also that we are not paying sufficient respect to the Nipponese officers and this must be seen to. This seems to me nonsense as a general instruction; 99% do show respect and, if some individuals have transgressed, they should be told. We draw lots today for six empty honey jars (amongst 104-odd people), two packets of Bruno tobacco and seven coconuts; I am not lucky. The quiz final takes place in the evening. We do rather well with 23 points out of 100.

1 May 1942: The first of May dawns on just about the bloodiest world it can ever have seen. We are on kitchen fatigue at lunchtime. There is a lot of rice left over; it tastes OK to me. There is considerable excitement at 6 p.m. when we start the voting for Room Representative; there are two candidates Burnham and myself. He gets in by 50 to 49. I do not vote! The possible votes are 102; that is a pretty good turnout. Jacko tells me that one old gentleman voted the wrong way – he was so confused – and some of the Empress of Asia boys succumbed to recent blandishments. But I am very pleased. I didn't want the job and have done my bit by standing. Anyway, the new restrictions on outside fatigues will stop a lot of the rackets and the grouses that the Room Representative was not distributing outside fatigues fairly. And the outside fatigue squads were not playing the game. They spent the time hanging about for scrounges and did not do the work. Firewood in particular is short; we want reserves and have been unable to build up stocks for that reason. Hope is toothless. His denture has been sent to Singapore for repair. The real latrinogram – Nippon has offered peace terms, to wit, she keeps Java and Singapore is to be an international port run by the Nipponese. Quel espoir! I go to sleep feeling the war is almost won.

2 May: Mosquitoes were in evidence last night; I was bitten several times. I don't see what can be done. You can't very well have a hundred nets in a room the size of a tennis court, even if you had them. Celebrations of the Emperor's birthday included cinema performances at various cinemas, all renamed; the Cathay is the Dai Towa Theatre. There is also a public notice saying that anyone who 'deposits or causes to be deposited a corpse in a public place shall be severely punished.' Sign of the times? The sugar position is better. So, I hear, was the Nipponese attitude at the meeting this morning. Again, they promised fresh meat, more sugar etc. Bathing will be arranged as soon as possible and we will be able to buy outside the camp with the sentry's permission. I understand that Lady Hopkins, the Women's Representative, put up a very spirited protest about the slapping of a female internee's face by a sentry. I presume she had not bowed properly. I gather this rather took them aback and is a good line to take. Or is it the international situation or just the milk of human kindness? I meet F.M. Still outside the library. He says that he and Key think that most of his family was shot and that there was an attempt to rape his daughter. I also meet Wig; he is keeping a diary too. There is an issue of fruit cordials at $1.20 a bottle – two-and-a-half bottles per squad. Nine out of 13 in our squad don't want it, so we get more than half a bottle each – incredible. We play bridge with Housey-Housey going on simultaneously. It is difficult to concentrate with loud cries of 'clicketyclick – 66', 'all the eights – 88' and 'by itself, number four.' More details about the meeting with the Nipponese: meat and vegetables will be supplied AND PAID FOR by the Nipponese Army. Also there is no more milk available except for the sick, the aged and the children. The Nipponese say, 'We cannot eat rubber and tin and you know Singapore does not produce food.' But they admit that Europeans need more food than Asiatics – which is sensible. 'Some, no doubt,' say the Nipponese, 'will get beriberi and scurvy, but we will supply all the drugs and medicines we can.' Our list of names has now been delivered to the Nipponese authorities, so something may be done about letting our wives and other relatives know.

Sunday, 3 May: Robinson tells me we now have about $60,000 in the Camp Fund plus about $40,000 from before, so we should be in order for some time. At breakfast, Vic spills half his rice over the mattress, so, as I burnt a large hole in it last night, we patch and air it. I come across a very good poem by Kempas on the use of bad language in camp, not reproducible in full, unfortunately:

Verse 1:
To preserve his finer feelings, with some measure of urbanity,
In other words, to keep within the pale
In a concentrated atmosphere of masculine humanity
Is the duty of the self-respecting male.
He should guard against unpardonable lapses from propriety,
Which at present may be neither here nor there,
But will hardly be acceptable if uttered in society,
Or if practised in the presence of the fair.

Then the last four lines of verse 4 are:
But if, when we get out again, oracular sanguinity,
Engendered in this atmosphere of crime,
Should overturn the apple-cart twixt you and your affinity,
Don't say I didn't warn you at the time.

4 May: Pretty goes to hospital. The Dutch from the Kariman Islands were visited and the place taken over; they were given official papers to carry on at their posts. Then the second contingent of Nipponese arrived three weeks later and said that their papers were all tripe and tore them up. And here they are. They were about one month in Singapore and saw some harrowing treatment of the Chinese. I am now on Capstan Navy Cut, but I am still holding on to my last four ounces of J.C. I am on the wood-piling fatigue. I report to the courtyard in charge of a squad of 10. There are 52 of us in all. Our 10 push a wooden cart out of the main gate. I get my first glimpse of the great big world since March 6th and it looks good. Pengerang in Johore attracts the eye. I recall 1933 when I climbed it with Nora, in connection with reciprocal vertical angles for artillery fire from Singapore Island. A fat lot of use that was. There are two Nipponese sentries; they don't bother us. Our lumbermen are doing very stout work felling rubber. One tall French Canadian is very expert. We load our cart and the other squads two more and push them back and round the Girdle Road to the laundry. Here, another squad takes over and stacks the wood. We return for another load. The sentry, speaking laborious English, says: 'Must be finish half-past 3 o'clock we want go to Singapore.' So we get one more load only. I much enjoy the brief change, but there is no chance of buying. There was another row this morning: a fatigue party bought one packet of cigarettes each with the connivance of the sentry, then produced them as they came in at the gate. It was no good. The cigarettes were confiscated and, as punishment, our coconut fatigue was cancelled. Out of 103 in our room, only 37 are on the 'fit for heavy fatigue' list. I was amused when our squad paraded and the elderly men were picked out for filling sacks with chips. Several were younger than I. Edmonds' resume is very good and interesting this week, as usual. Our names, occupations and family details have all been beautifully bound in book form and sent by air (to Tokyo, one presumes) for transmission to the British Government. How? Via Russia? Our town fatigue party which went to the godowns has brought five tons and sundry bags of sugar. There are 37,000 tons of flour in town; much as been shipped. The rest is going rapidly. There are 50 tons of dried milk in 40-pound drums. We know how to reconstitute it; they don't. We have asked for this. One drum is sufficient for the camp for one day. The actual rations supplied by the Nipponese to Changi to date work out per head per day: rice – 21 to 26 oz; cooking salt – 0.27 oz; flour – 2.5 oz; sugar – 0.77 oz; milk (evaporated) – 0.93 oz; corned beef – 0.59 oz; tea – 0.09 oz; lard –0.15 oz – and that's all. We have some unfortunates in the Mental Hospital; their plight is dreadful – they have no care and no amenities. They are all mixed in with Asiatics. We are voting money from the camp funds to improve their lot. There is to be a bathing parade at 1.30 p.m. tomorrow for the whole of B-Block. The engineers outside are living in the residential quarter and get 50 cents a day for reconstructing houses. The labour is military.

5 May: At lunch, the vegetables consist of tapioca tops and leaves; they are nauseous, but they are no doubt full of some vitamin or other. The bathing parade will involve 50 minutes walk each way; only 33 in our room feel fit or willing to do it. The Block parades 265 out of about 680. We move off in column of fours at 1.40 p.m. I observe that the coat of arms and 'Dieu et mon Droit, 1936' is still over the main gaol entrance. I'm surprised the Nipponese have not removed it. The decrepit plank Chinese shop apparently flies the Nipponese flag, but there is no sign of life. Nor is there on the main road. We march along that, shepherded by a few sentries, turn left along a private road, past Dr Hunter's house, then 40 minutes to a good, sandy beach fringed with houses occupied by Nipponese. The tide is excellent. We bathe; it is not so good; sea-lice nip and there are jellyfish. But the garden is excellent. We lie in the sun and shade for over an hour, then march back by a short cut in 20 minutes. We pass a few Malays and Chinese. All look listless in the extreme and are doing nothing. It is very hot, of course – it was noon by the sun when we started. How those sentries sweated! And one got covered with kerenggas *(weaver ants)*; something new had swum into his ken. His face was a picture as he savagely slashed the offending shrub with a bayonet, which had a knife-edge. It was a very pleasant change. Yet, to see Singapore in this state had a depressing effect on me. McHardy and Drew go to Singapore on a ration party. There is no buying, but they have a good feed – and Tiger beer! Food is still being shipped away. 'The Syonan Times' says the lack of food grown in Malaya is due to the deliberate policy of the British Government, who thought of nothing but wealth for their merchant princes. And there are fewer motor accidents in Singapore now. This is due to the imposition of a 30 m.p.h. limit and the superior driving of the Nipponese. There is an excellent variety concert from 7.45 to 9.15 p.m.

6 May: Some tobacco has come in from Gian Singh's store. I am lucky and draw one ounce of Garrick for $1.60 – the price of four ounces six months ago! I see Alexander. He has a marvellous fungus now – it extends right round his face and is rich auburn. There is a very keenly-fought cricket match between the Rest of B-Block and the Empress of Asia – 'Gents versus Players', an Empress of Asia wag alters it to. The lads are very anxious to win, but we have the batting. I lose the toss, they score 130 (four wickets fall to me); we score 165. There is excellent fielding on both sides. The most amusing incident is when a lofty hit lodges on a concrete ledge above the third floor and rolls about, with the expectant fielders gathered en masse below. In due course, it rolls off and pursues a devious route, bouncing off corners and angles, but is duly caught – four and out! Hugh Bryson comes round to see me; he too has a feeling that the Nipponese are anxious to get us out of their way. Supper is a feast – vegetable stew with definitely some fresh meat in it and, at one moment (fleeting), I actually get a taste of onion. We got the Cold Storage meat yesterday. It is grand to eat something solid again. It is our food fatigue. I find cleaning the very greasy tin containers (converted petrol tins) which held the stew very dirty and difficult. And what a day for baccy. There is a free issue of 13 cigarettes each from the Nipponese and 15 small local cheroots for 65 cents. A whole lot of stuff has come in from Gian Singh's. There are matches in quantity, sardines, (real) cheeses, cream, Christmas puddings. I don't know what else. It looks like lashings, but, when you divide any individual article by 2,700, you realise there ain't much for you!

7 May: Gray and Wyld both have dysentery; there were four cases in this block yesterday. I do my washing-up; I do a spring-clean of all my utensils, using Vim and Dettol. The Governor has been moved to much better accommodation at the main gate. The reason why is not known – one can only guess. Is there a visit from the Red Cross imminent? Perchance from Adolf? The popular theory is that it is window-dressing. For lunch today, we have rice, vegetable soup and meat. Yesterday, the meat was in the soup, so the dip was a lottery. Jack got seven pieces in his half-mug; I got only two. Today, they have the meat separated, so the distribution is more equitable. I am on a fatigue party at 3 p.m.; nine of us stack wood on carts and take it to the kitchen boilers. It is only for an hour and is not very strenuous. It is good for the body. There is good news: the Nipponese have now agreed that we can buy fresh fish twice a week. Our representative left this morning to arrange this with the Changi fishermen. The Nipponese regret they can't pay for it, as they are paying for the fruit and vegetables as from next week. Recent supplies are 2,205 lbs of tinned onions, 3,150 lbs of flour, 30,016 lbs of rice, 250 lbs of tea, 224 lbs of salt, 350 lbs of ghee, eight cases of soap and 35,000 cigarettes. Things are looking up! And 'The Changi Guardian' says in the 'Do You Know?' pages: 'That each dawn is now broken by the patter of running feet – two enthusiasts etc.'! The editors must have been a long time waking up, as this is our 50th successive day running round the exercise yard in the morning. Walker, the Art Master, has just painted a church notice: 'Holy Communion at 8 a.m. daily; Evening Prayer at 7.45 p.m. on Saturday.' I hear that the Governor may be in solitary confinement. At a meeting with our Camp Committee today, when asked why the Governor had been moved, the Nipponese said it was by order of the Nipponese High Command. There was nothing more forthcoming, so the committee walked out.

8 May: I awake at 7.10 a.m. and fall asleep, so I oversleep by 10 minutes and we are late for all our morning operations. That isn't so good, so I shave in daylight – the first time for many weeks. The coconut fatigue was suspended for only one afternoon. The Eurasians are parading at the Main Gate; is this preparatory to release? At supper, being heartily fed up with rice, I open my Karikal tin of bully beef, eat it with my roll and butter and thoroughly enjoy it. In view of the dysentery all around us, I carefully cover the bully beef left for tomorrow with a clean hanky – precious, but worth it. After Lights Out, Bayley reads a poem – anonymous. 'J'y suis, j'y reste' about the war in Malaya. It is good and comprehensive. I disagree with the part, which mentions rape and looting by our troops. I have never heard of rape by them, but looting – ye gods – they were past masters. More comic little local cheroots are issued. There are 25 each for 60 cents, about 20 sweets for 30 cents, four boxes of matches at 20 cents and Polar Bear toothpaste made in Shanghai. I don't use it. The boast on the packet says: 'So, so audible, yet no harm to the enamel possible.' Nobody can fathom this. A curious note: the verb to 'bisseker', meaning 'to make a getaway when you should have stayed' is in common use in camp. Bisseker was number two to Brigadier Symonds in charge of Civil Defence,

I believe. There is a very strong rumour that the Nipponese have lost two cruisers, one destroyer and some transports off New Guinea. *(The Battle of the Coral Sea, to which this rumour no doubt refers, took place on 7 - 9 May.)*

9 May: I sew buttons on my shirts. How these women manage to hit the holes in a button, from the hidden side, so to speak, 'no feller can understand.' Fifteen pillows and one mattress arrive from Gian Singh's – this for distribution among over 200 on this floor. There will be fierce competition and lots will be drawn! Many have still got neither and the cement floor is hard and cold. At breakfast, the tea has a most curious and rather unpleasant taste. Some say it is paint, others mouldy tea. The Camp Committee assures us it is natural, but the brand has changed. I suppose we shall get used to it. I put two boiled sweets in to neutralise it. There is a rumour that Corregidor has fallen. *(It fell on 29 April, thus completing the Japanese conquest of Luzon and the Philippines.)* The Nipponese committee refused to meet ours this morning. A rumour also states that we got a big convoy through to Murmansk, but lost the cruiser Edinburgh, two destroyers and three transports in the process, Colin would not be on the Edinburgh now, I think. I wonder where he is. *(The Murmansk convoy arrived at the end of March. Colin was fortunately transferred from the Edinburgh some time before.)* At supper, the tea has the same flavour, but I guess I'm beginning to get used to it. Pringle had his face smacked for smoking! *(Tom writes this in code.)* The three big banks – the Chartered, the Hong Kong and the Mercantile – announce they will redeem the official government receipts for money lent to camp funds when we get out. This solves a problem, which has been bothering us. It is all very well if you have some spare cash to let them have it now, but we will all want it when we get out. Poor Vic has dropped his watch and the spring is gone. He's had it since 1920. There are several repairers here, but no spare parts or tools.

Sunday, 10 May: I notice that, even at 8 a.m., with bustle all around, some people are still sleeping like babes. There are strange variations of the human condition; I could not possibly sleep through it. Fairy's scalp has gone all pink with brilliantine; it won't come off! A quaint sight! I did a big wash yesterday – a sheet and a sarong, a towel and two handkerchiefs, but it's a problem – the oftener you wash, the quicker your wardrobe will wear out. There is bully beef stew for lunch today. The Nipponese gave half a tin of bully beef to each member of the rice unloading squad last night – a pleasant gesture. How they fluctuate! An internee who has liaison with the black market via the sentries offers me one ounce of Log Cabin tobacco (free comforts for the troops stuff) for $2.50 – nothing doing. The Nipponese are making two large war memorials to their dead – one six miles from Bukit Timah. According to 'The Syonan Times', 10,000 prisoners are working on it. A 'Lisbon cable' published in the same newspaper says that Sir Anthony Eden, the Foreign Secretary, has told the House of Commons that conditions in prisoner-of-war camps in Singapore and Hong Kong are good and the food is enough. Cricket days are to be restricted to four a week, ostensibly so that there may be two days for deck tennis and badminton. And Sunday is a day of 'rest' – ye gods. But the real reason is that certain tired young gentlemen must have their afternoon siesta and the Empress of Asia youths are enthusiastic and noisy.

11 May: It was a very hot night. This room will be very smelly with stale sweat and humans and dirty clothes. When playing cricket, all around is festooned with clothes, clothes-lines and props. When the ball hits obstructions, the umpire decides what, in his opinion, its ultimate destination would have been and calls out the number of runs to be booked. Mattresses on the grass are also obstacles to the ball and fielders. And there are two sides to the question: should the batsman get four for a hit reaching the wall and being caught on the rebound? I say 'Yes.' We now have a tablecloth – two dishcloths stitched together. Jack and I spread it over our aerated water-box, which is poised on another box, and it is much cleaner and hygienic. Farrer is now in hospital with beriberi. It's early for that to develop. That is three empty sleeping places opposite us; I can't call them beds. There is a curiously optimistic feeling in the camp. Chat to H.B. Clifton and A.J. King (he is 68 and already arranging how he will restart his firm's tin mines in Southern Siam.) Both say in effect, 'Good Lord! Exchange? We'll be out of here and back on the job long before an exchange can be arranged – July at latest!' There is an issue of goods to the room. Three bottles of Worcester sauce and 14 packets of jelly crystals are drawn for. I get shaving soap and five Blue Gillette blades for $1.65! They cost 45 cents pre-Changi. At 3 p.m., I am on a fatigue party, taking logs from the laundry to the kitchen. We form a human chain from the cart up the steps to the kitchen. It's quite hard work passing them along. I can give anyone in the squad 10 years. Edmonds gives his report at 7.45 p.m. He states the attitude of the committee to the removal of the Governor. It is correct that the reply to their question 'Why?' only got the answer 'By order of the Nipponese High Command.' Edmonds says that they as representatives feel it is not good enough 'if the Nipponese are to be allowed to remove any of us and put us in solitary confinement (which he confirms) and give no reason.' So they bowed and walked out and, up to now, there have been no further relations with the Nipponese. We all endorse their action. Edmonds says they are trying to get Field Service postcards for us to communicate with. Fresh fish has not been arranged yet. We have tried Changi and Tanah Merah, but there is only small stuff there – no good for a large camp. They are also trying to get the Nipponese to agree to a banana supply, which we can arrange. 'The matter is under consideration.' He warns that we must economise on water. It has all to be pumped up to tanks on the roof. The pumps are feeling the strain of 2,700 folk instead of 600! And if we all pull the plug every time, thousands of gallons go west. Our squad draws for eight jars of potted meat among 13. We are lucky. Jack, Vic, Hope and I get one each. Mine is Brand's bloater paste – it will go well on the roll.

12 May: There is fierce controversy in this room; should we close our latrines or not? I say, 'No. If we do, there are over 200 for two outside. The congestion would be too much.' So we agree to join the squad for keeping the two in our room clean. The Camp Committee meet the Nipponese today, so the breach is healed! We also hear that the Governor was seen returning from somewhere outside to his solitary confinement – thumbs-up was the sign he gave. It may mean something or nothing. Our Committee's 'Askings' are to be resumed but are to be in writing in future. For supper, we get plum pudding and custard. The plum pudding is very good – alleged to be three ounces – and a dessertspoonful of custard. Vic gets a little silver bell in his; he was grousing away beforehand about finding a bit of cloth in his pudding! G.C. Irving and Carter go to hospital. Our empty sleeping-places are increasing.

13 May: The one certain thing is that we are a day nearer release. 'The Syonan Times' confirms rumours that Corregidor has fallen and that MacArthur said he would be back. Beattie tries to get a bottle of cod liver oil emulsion out of Jack. He says he is lacking in proteins! As if we were not all in the same boat! I see G.C. Irving in hospital; he has fever and a wild attack of dysentery; he looks very thin. Lunch is so poor – questionable stew and an unknown variety of green leaves – that we open our last tin of fish and it makes all the difference. Dr Wallace gets stamps for me, surcharged by the Nipponese. There are five – one, two, three, eight and fifteen cents – and it is incomparably the worst surcharge I have ever seen. Rumour has it that Churchill has told the Nipponese they cannot stand losses on the scale of Colombo, Trincomalee and the Battle of the Coral Sea. 'We are too strong for you,' he said. 'Get back to Nippon and await your fate.'

14 May: It is still rather hot at night; perspire on to my pillow, which makes it stink. I am put on a fatigue party at 10.30 a.m. We proceed to the back of Girdle Road. Here we are shown three bags of broken cargo rice. Our job, we are told, is to clean it i.e. get out the maggots and weevils. So we turn it out onto the concrete road in the brilliant sunshine and spread it out. This exposes a number of the creepy-crawlies, which we pick out and throw to the sparrows, while others of the squad sieve the rice with two very inefficient sieves. This gets rid of the cocoons which consist of grains of rice hanging together sausage-like. Then we handpick; the maggots are caterpillar-like creatures half-an-inch long; the weevils are smaller and blacker insects. Lastly, we sweep up the rice from the road with brooms, shovel it back into the bags and take it to the store. We have walked on it and sweated on it and the road is continually being used by firewood fatigue parties, but the rice will be washed and cooked in the kitchen before we eat it, so tidapa *(never mind)*. It's hot and sweaty work and a strain on the eyes, with all those white grains in the sun. Cargo rice, I learn, is usually for export only and is used at home largely for by-products. Nipponese officers inspect. We stand to attention in the room. Suddenly, one seizes a dishcloth from the food table by the door (breakfast is just over) and, for no apparent reason, hurls it with ill temper into the room. It falls harmlessly to the floor. Next, he strides in; we follow his movements and espy Ridgwell SITTING in complete oblivion in a corner reading a book. The Nipponese officer raps him sharply on the knees with his sword-scabbard, whereupon he awakes and leaps up, exclaiming, 'Sorry!' There is another inspection in the afternoon by a large personally conducted party. These are mostly privates. The guard, we hear, is to be doubled. The innards of the gaol are evidently being explained to the newcomers. Doctors Braine and C.S. Wilson are back from Miyako Hospital where they've been patients. Then comes a bombshell – the Nipponese order a permanent black-out from 8.30 p.m. to 7.30 a.m. No torches or lit matches allowed outside. The same applies in town. There will be an inspection by a Nipponese officer tonight. The blackout will make our nights long and tedious, but who cares? It can only mean that Singapore is again vulnerable to our attack. And so to bed at 6.30 p.m. by the sun.

15 May: Heard in the yard at 8.30 a.m. from two Empress of Asia lads: 'Black pudders from Rochdale on a Saturday night – Ah could do six easy.' 'Eh, give me pig's ears; there's not much of 'em, but they're sweet.' There are all sorts of people interned here who never should be. Why on earth they aren't taken out when we are so grossly overcrowded beats me. They are mostly Eurasians who are just the same as thousands outside, but by misfortune or circumstance happen to be inside. I make a curious discovery – my mug had the flavour of Dettol in it. I put Eno's in and the result tasted like lemonade. They say the Nipponese now have fire-watchers on duty in Singapore. Morale in town is said to be very low. There is much trouble up-country. A Turk is said to have come in yesterday. Why? New orders: there are to be no outside fires later than 8 p.m. or earlier than 7.30 a.m. We experience a curious example of a dream coming true. D Block run a daily tote on the 'ship's run.' It starts at 380 represented by the ace of clubs. The cards go on in bridge order, with numbers allocated to certain cards. Last night, von Hagt of this floor dreamt that 415 won. He dashed along early, bought 30 tickets on 415 at 10 cents each. Nobody else was on 415. It won, paid 56 to 1 and he scooped $168. The main gate is closed tonight for the first time; no-one knows why. There is a very persistent rumour that our troops are being sent to Indo-China. The wood party today had it from the Chinese outside. The ration party in town do very well today and, at the end, are turned loose and do very successful individual shopping. So much for the 'inflexible regulations'! We receive 3,000 lbs of Cold Storage meat, salt and cigarettes from the Nipponese today.

16 May: During the morning run, I have the wind, but my legs won't respond to a sprint in the last round – caused by the diet, I presume. The deaths are reported of T. Rogers and W.W. Redfearn, the trainer; his wife is interned here. D-Block have a 'Freedom Sweep' on the date we get out. Dates start May 1st and end August 29th. Each person has a date between those limits and all dates are booked. The exact supplies from the Nipponese yesterday were: meat 3,000 lbs, sugar – five bags; salt – $1^1/_3$ bags; flour 21 bags; ghee – four cases; soap – eight cases; and 35,000 cigarettes. Parry got a permit to see Dusty at Miyako Hospital without any trouble at all! A strange race! We have asked the Nipponese High Command to say under what conditions the Governor is confined. The Bishop has presented us with a piano. We have asked permission to bring it in. We receive an issue of 24 sweets each for 33 cents and one-and-a-half ounces of various tobacco at $1.60 per oz. I get Garrick and Log Cabin. There is also a free issue of 13 cigarettes. V.J. is now 15 stones 1 lb.; he has lost 5 stones 13 lbs. in three months! I lend Hugh Bryson $50. He is thin and he says I am also! Parry returns from Miyako; he says Dusty is seriously ill; he can't keep food down. Wyld is poor too. Gray, Ryves and A.H. Miles are all improving. A concert is held in the evening; it is good; I like the choir. They sing old English melodies. 'Rule Britannia' is fine and very appropriate, in view of the recent news. I meet a tin-miner, Jones. He says, 'I haven't seen you since 1922. We played rugger for Perak at Taiping.' So we reminisce. He says A.J. King has gone to hospital with a tummy upset, probably from eating coconuts.

Sunday, 17 May: There are 2,680 internees, with 361 women. It is rather curious not having seen oneself for three months, except an ugly face in the shaving mirror. Breakfast is late, because there is no water; no-one knows why. At 12.30 p.m., there is still no water and therefore no lunch. Jack and I open a tin of Karikal celery soup and share that. It is very good. We also eat our rolls and cheese. The water comes on at 1.15 p.m. E.A. Brown asks: will I organise the entertainment's for Block B? I will consider. A fatigue party goes out this morning. The Nipponese specially ask for 20 young and strong men. They move furniture out of bungs outside the gaol and it goes Changi-wards. The Nipponese give them lots of tins of various food – there are lashings of it in the houses. They say that 3,000 Aussies have gone. They were issued with heavy raincoats. Are they going to Formosa? The 'Lost' notices on the Camp Police board include 'one set of false teeth, full upper plate.' There are fair-sized pieces of steak for supper. It is good to get one's teeth into some meat again. There is also a banana. Salt is still lacking in the food. There is news that the Nipponese have agreed to the fatigue parties collecting bananas as well as coconuts. I have a long talk with Van Hien. I finally agree somewhat dubiously to taking on the entertainment organisation for the whole block. I don't particularly want it, but, again, I think it is up to each individual to do what he can for the welfare of the community. The Bishop's piano has arrived and the women have pinched it, so how do we get it back? Lights out at 8.30 p.m. It makes a most protracted night and you can't talk all day and all night. I talk to Jackson, the artist:

he will do a sketch of our corner for me.

18 May: Waiting in the courtyard for the firewood fatigue party to move off, I see a number of the women; some I know. They all look quite bright. They bow to the sentry every time they pass over the threshold. Ugh! It's ridiculous. *(When Tom makes remarks like that about the Japanese, he generally, as now, puts them in code.)* The fatigue is quite a pleasant change – not too hard work. Three cartloads are filled and pushed. There is no trading allowed. Small boys offer two ounces of Raleigh tobacco for $6 and 10 cigarettes for 90 cents. A Sikh outside the shop opposite Gaol Road indicates beer for sale. I would have relished some. I go to C and D-Blocks with Van Hien and Beale, the honorary secretary. I meet John L. Woods, Block C, and Folliot, Block D, the respective block entertainment chairmen. I am fixed to give a concert on May 26th –'Over the Garden Wall', so to speak, for the women. Today's true yarn: daily, the interpreter takes Lang, our communications officer, to the Women's Block, where he sees Mrs Gregory-Jones and Mrs Hopkins to find out if they have any requirements. After the interpreter has had a few words with them, he turns to Lang and says, 'You can now have a short connection with these ladies. (Gregory-Jones told this himself, so presumably she told him.) At 4.30 p.m., the Head Commandant and the Commandant of the Women's Block are called to the office of the Nipponese Commander and informed that Lieutenant Okasaki will replace Lieutenant Tokuda 'for the time being.' The Nipponese Commander says there are many points about the camp, which require improvement. Lieutenant Okasaki will try to improve matters, which are still unsatisfactory. 'If you have any suggestions for improvement,' the Commander says, 'especially as regards accommodation, you will be able to ask Lieutenant Okasaki... Lieutenant Okasaki understands you are suffering much inconvenience in the camp. He will try to make every possible arrangement for your life to be made more comfortable in every possible way. For this purpose, Lieutenant Okasaki will be here. You can make your requests to him and he will try to do everything possible.' The interpreter adds that the first thing Lieutenant Okasaki can do is present a piano and this has been done plus two tins of biscuits for the children in the Women's Block. He ends by saying that, while Lieutenant Tokuda has been strict, Lieutenant Okasaki is a stricter officer! 9.30 am. daily is fixed for the 'askings'. I see Dawson, the Defence Secretary, this morning. He spoke to the Governor yesterday. He is OK, but really this solitary confinement is cruel. In England, the most hardened lag never gets more than seven days at a time, then a break.

19 May: When running this morning, I hit my shin a hell of a crack on the concrete edge of a drain and receive a very nasty gash. I disinfect it with fullstrength T.C.P. and put an elastoplast cover on. I hope for the best. It is right on the bone. My wrist is thinner by about three-eighths of an inch. I can tell by my metal wristwatch clasp. I have a very quiet day, resting my leg which is painful and waiting for it to stop bleeding. Supper is to be from 5.30 to 6 p.m. to enable the kitchen staff to clean up before Lights Out. The Nipponese refuse to increase the salt ration which is five grams per day, but they may agree to fatigue parties fetching seawater to boil the rice in! Ye gods! They will not agree to our contacting fish merchants in town and are unable to give any information about the visit of Red Cross representatives. We are to pay all the funeral expenses for Miyako Hospital internees. I move only when necessary. I grate coconut to mix with the rice pudding; it improves it a lot. Everyone has made a grater out of old tins etc., but we find the Malay claw-type the most effective. Some put the results into a handkerchief (NOT a sock), squeeze, extract the juice and make a paste-like concoction. Judges of the High Court, British Residents and merchant princes – all get down to it. We have quite a hoo-ha about a visit of high officers today, including very high civilian officials, but we do not see them.

20 May: I do not run on account of my leg. I see that, in reply to our request that Europeans working outside should be put on our register of names to be communicated to next-of-kin, the Nipponese say there is no need for this. Now, what is the inference? – 1) They are bats; 2) sheer disregard of humanity; 3) no real intention of getting the list through; 4) knowledge that they will be out before it can be got through! I rather favour 3 or 4. We receive an issue of Brazil and hazel nuts, doubtless left-over Christmas stock, but I'm sure they are full of vitamin something. There is an issue of chewing gum! I take some; it is not one of my vices, but in here – yes! Balfour Ross is dead. Fairy has gone to hospital – due mostly to weakness perhaps because he does not eat rice. We receive a visit from Nipponese officers. These are decent. We stand to attention and they salute and even smile. There is a cricket match between B and C-Blocks. We win 264 to 169. I do not play, as I am giving the leg a chance to heal. There is no sign of its going bad yet, but this place is dreadful for healing – weeks and weeks for most folk. Jack and I have supper about 10 p.m. We have extra kedgeree parked in the so-useful B & P tins and a bottle of Penang sauce bought from Bayley who drew it and doesn't want it. We have a night-light – a candle inside a large tin suitably perforated and perched on our box-table. It is a most excellent repast. The pipes afterwards are much more soothing with the little light to illuminate the blue fumes. I go out to the exercise yard to clean my teeth with Dettol and so to bed at 10.30 p.m.

21 May: I go to the dispensary and get a raspberry. The doctor says that T.C.P. at full strength would burn the wound and it has. He puts lint on. I have to go again tomorrow. I should have been on a wood fatigue inside the camp today. I see Keet who has just come in. He has brought a mattress, bedding, a full kit bag, two very large suitcases and two boxes – luxury compared with the poor waifs who came in at the start. I'm sure now that I could have stayed out a considerable time, yet I don't know that I regret it. I have seen the whole thing through anyway. At the library, I meet surveyors Deshing and George Sava. Deshing, who is working for the Nipponese fixing up radios in the gaolers' quarters, says he can get developer and other such materials. The shops in town are doing very little business. In Battery Road, there are only Allys and Gian Singh and they have practically no stocks. The Singapore Photo Company is bare. Chris Mustard arrives with white zinc and linseed oil wrested from the store. With much toil, we make a white mixture and I mark the creases and a block for cricket. Coconuts are issued – five per squad. At 5.15 p.m., there is a meeting of chairmen of the block entertainment committees to decide certain details i.e. the allotment and custody of the piano and progress for the concert for the women on Tuesday. We decide to allow lessons to continue for small boys, if they have attained some proficiency, but not if they are just thumpers.

22 May: We shall have a spring-clean tomorrow, everything, inside and out, with disinfectant. Many 'cabins' are getting buggy. I've not seen any in our room yet. When washing up, I pick up the dishcloth, as I suppose, and dry our dishes with it. Then I find it is Jack's sweat-rag, which is a converted dishcloth. However, little things like that don't bother one here. Innes Miller and Beattie of our room have gone to hospital and Mrs Grist is back from Miyako. Yesterday's wood fatigue party was searched. They had to turn their pockets out and were given a thorough search. Luckily, nothing was discovered. Drew had four packets of cigarettes. I hear internees in Penang were very badly treated in gaol. They were given rice and salt only. Van Geyzel didn't want the pickles he got in the draw yesterday; he handed them over to me. They were cucumbers pickled whole and produced by Del Monte. I got about half a cucumber. My leg is swollen a bit. Walker, the ex-art master, has drawn a very good picture of the Birth for the altar *(This painting is now in the collection of the Singapore Art Museum)*. He will colour it under difficulties. They are a versatile crowd in this gaol. Templeton, our Scots engineer, is making a trolley wherewith to bring the rice and container which is very heavy for two to carry normally. Now the Nipponese officers are doing the rounds, but they are pleasant and polite. I hear North Hunt died very suddenly; he has been helping Corner in Raffles Library.

23 May: The number of internees is now 2,685, with 362 women. At 4 a.m., I was going out to the exercise yard and thinking about the crossword I am compiling. In the blackout, I overshot the right turn and walked into someone's camp bed in the passage. He must have subconsciously heard the faint slip-slop of my rubber sandals approaching and, absolutely simultaneously with me contacting his camp bed with my leg, he shouted, 'Bang!', which I thought an interesting reaction. Apart from the usual kanji, tea, roll and margarine, there is cucumber with vinegar for breakfast. Everyone says, 'What the hell! Cucumber and vinegar for breakfast!', so we offer to eat the lot, but there are no takers. I can now sympathise with and understand the hearty eructation's of Malays at banquets, having recently eaten large quantities of rice. Last night, our saxophone trio performed in the courtyard. Okasaki asked for 'Blue Heaven' and 'Auld Lang Syne' and thanked them very prettily when they finished. It is a strange world; he is a Presbyterian. In Karikal, a miscellaneous lot of clothes from the Fullerton Building was brought in by the communications officer. I distributed them and one man who was sleeping on the concrete was most grateful that I gave him a greatcoat to sleep on. Yesterday, the recipient, Doscas, saw on a line a coat, which looked like his. He inspected it, but the name had been cut out. He awaited the owner. It turned out to be Doscas's coat, the one I handed out, and, as Doscas is now sleeping on concrete again and the other has got a bed, he gave it back. Thus is justice done at times. I go to the dispensary. My leg is still not quite clean. Three doctors work there in a store-room about 12 feet by 16. Miller and March from our room have gone to hospital with suspected dysentery. Gilmour gets a Gillette razor from the camp shop – $5; the normal price was about $1. In future, the camp store is to supply goods on indent only; there is to be no more indiscriminate buying. It will be essentials only. We must preserve the camp's diminishing cash resources. The Nipponese have agreed to our representatives contacting fishermen in Bedok for fresh fish. Hope says the experts are very surprised by the survival of our diabetics. Many here were expected to die. The rice diet has dissipated the diabetes and they are quite fit! What is not known is – will it return? Doscas brings me developer, but no hypo. More people have come in from Customs and Food Control. L.A. Allen and his wife, seven Frenchmen and a Frenchwoman. They were in gaol for weeks with no change of clothes and all mixed up with Asiatics. A large score against the Nipponese is piling up.

Sunday, 24 May: It is Whitsunday and Empire Day. I hope never to spend another like it. Story from D-Block: Question – if an internee were given two hours leave in London and five bob, what would he do? Answer: He would go to the Regent Palace Hotel, sit down in the lounge, take off his boots and scratch his feet. Then he would go out to the back and wash his shirt in the fire-bucket. He would then go to the dining room and cut up his meat with a spoon. He would last be seen walking out of the front door with a carpet, having spent his five bob on a packet of cigarettes. It is curious how food increases in importance when it is inadequate. I have never heard so much chat about it in my life and I certainly think more about it than I've done for 30 years or more. The menu today is'orrible. There are loud groans about the breakfast for a start. The doctor says my leg is going well; it is still quite painful. A fatigue party goes to the Cold Storage in Orchard Road. They say our troops are walking about without guards! I fail to understand this. Why are they so strict with us? Johnny Baumann, who is about 5'3, and used to weigh 14 stone 5 lbs., has dropped to 10 stone 2 lbs. and is much fitter. He is 67! We are told a man died in the gaol hospital due to congestion of rice and coconut in his stomach. I don't know if this is true. I put up the notice concerning the week's program of entertainment's from Monday, May 25th to Saturday, May 30th. The program includes: 'Backs to the Audience' (concert for the ladies); a talk on Famagusta, Cyprus by Murray M. Jack; a debate on 'The Sword Is Mightier Than The Pen'; a talk on 'British Christians'; 'Vaudeville' by Block D artistes; a talk on Mount Everest by E.O. Shebbeare; a classical gramophone concert presented by R. Eisinger; a Mock Trial arranged by Adrian Clark; a talk on Madagascar by F. Middleton and an address by the Commandant.

25 May: There are crashes like bombing in the night. We all awaken hopefully, but it is only remarkably loud thunder. Luckily, this is proved beyond doubt by the lightning or else we would have had a plethora of rumours. Jack runs; I can't yet. The fatigue party which went out yesterday had a conversation with some Northumberland Fusiliers who one fine morning awoke to find they had no sentries! Now they and the Aussies are allowed to wander round the town without let or hindrance. Yet, simultaneously, the French, the padres and what not are being thrust in here and we have no freedom at all. Can you beat it? Why? I go to the dispensary; my leg has improved. I think I'll risk cricket. It is certainly my one and only chance of playing in the Federation of Malayan States versus the Colony match! The Governor has been let out again, with no explanation. He is now in the Hudson's Bay section as an ordinary internee. The cricket match between F.M.S. and the Colony turns out to be a grand game before a large, keen crowd. I take a wicket first ball to huge delight. Our fielding is excellent. The result for the first day is F.M.S. – 321, Colony - 110 for 2. I had two tennis balls painted red. A curious effect is they do not bounce higher than a cricket ball and are less lively altogether. So it is a great improvement, but the fly in the turps is the turps in the paint. It seems to cause the balls to split and both, though brand new, were split at the end of play.

26 May: The doctor says that, if the cricket is rained off today, I should rest my leg; the exercise has done it no good. 'The Syonan Times' has a headline: 'European War Decided In Two Months,' but I cannot get near enough to see which way! And, as usual, the paper vanishes in the night. Some swine does it systematically. There is no rice for lunch today! Instead, we have a very good mince with vegetables and one small potato boiled in its jacket. We also receive an issue of sweets – $1 per bottle. We get a quarter of a bottle of barley sugar each – four-and-a-half small sticks. So gradually the tissues are restored. We actually get some cheese as part of our supper! The cricket continues. We – the Colony team – collapse and are all out for 214. It is an excellent game. The concert for the ladies is in the main courtyard and is a howling success. The Nipponese Commander says, 'Sing "God Save The King" and as loudly as you like.' Jack and I sup at 9.30 p.m. – cheese and biscuits. A pint of bitter would complete the glorious picture. A large mosquito is after me during the night. He is so attentive I actually get him imprisoned under the sheet when I put the sheet over my head to get rid of him.

27 May: I have now been interned 100 days. If we don't have more than another 100, I can take it! I am busy all morning writing and doing work for the cricket and the entertainment committee. One of the internees of my acquaintance called Pop has lost three-and-a-half stones. Ferguson is in now. He was shot in the bottom at Bakri in Johore. He took refuge in the jungle and an old Malay looked after him. A Javanese gang of robbers were in the vicinity. They had to keep moving and lived in pondoks *(huts)* on rice and salt. The wound went septic, but the old man cured it. After seven weeks, hearing that Singapore had capitulated, Ferguson gave himself up to the Nipponese. He was given the choice of work or imprisonment and became batman to a Nipponese general living in Hamilton's bungalow at Batu Pahat. He was very well treated. Then the Nipponese general departed, so he was bunged in here. The cricket ends; the Colony loses by 63. I make four, Mac bowls me with a real snorter. The game is unanimously voted a great success. The French who were brought in a few days ago had been perfectly free until then. Suddenly, they were interrogated and quickly deposited here. The theory is that this is the result of the Dakar news *(rumours of French co-operation with the Allies in Africa),* yet we have had no confirmation. The French group is highly optimistic. Lewis S. D. and company are allowed out today to their godown. It was intact 10 days ago, but has now been ransacked by the Nipponese. But he gets $1^{1}/_{2}$ tons of salt, 60 cases of tinned fish and some dried milk.

28 May: M. Farr and Beavis have been taken to hospital. Two hundred more are coming in, some say from Padang and Sumatra, which I don't believe. Others say they are odd-bods from all over the place. They are to go into the Women's Hospital. The women don't like this, but they are nothing like as overcrowded as we are. I take the chance of a leisurely read of 'The Syonan Times' of May 18th. The headlines include: 'Decline Of British Empire Inevitable'; and 'Shaping Of Future Destiny Of World In Nippon's Hands'. After attending a talk on 'Everest' by Shebbeare, I go back to my room at 8.15 p.m. and find many people have been sick – the meat was tainted. The camp police and the doctors are to be on duty all night. In the evening, I sally forth among the milling mob in the exercise yard; there is a lovely moon. I clean my teeth and resist the temptation for a final pipe. I hope a lot of people are not going to be sick in the latrines; several have already. It is said that the names of internees are to be broadcast from Tokyo. I can scarcely believe it.

29 May: When I go out at 7.15 a.m., the moon is shining brightly. Is any sight more ridiculous than men pulling on their trousers? Especially in mass formation, so to speak. Reports of Winston Churchill's speech on May 10th are going the rounds. As usual, every word is a gem: 'The end is near' is what we like best. It is remarkable how unanimous everyone is about Churchill – if he says it, it must be so. There is some controversy now: did he say, 'The end is near' or 'The end is clear'? We say 'near', being optimists. At 4 p.m., there is a race meeting in the exercise yard, with six horses and two dice as on board ship. I am much reminded of Joan on the Sarpedon. How she enjoyed her wins at the races! I am very lucky this time; I am $24 up. Then down comes the rain. 5 p.m. – people are still asleep and have been since lunch. How do they do it? Van Geyzel has been released. Half the squad is to be released with 35 other Eurasians. Van Geyzel says that some don't want to go; their families are away, their homes destroyed and they have no work. A.B.C. Ramsay gives an interesting talk on Trengganu. He is willing to try 'The Green Eye of the Little Yellow God', if we can reconstruct it. The Nipponese have told the Camp Police they are not wanted at the Main Gate after 8 p.m., thus leaving the coast clear for black-market transactions via the sentries! – And consequent rake-offs. Jack has an incipient cold, alas, and Hope's poisoned leg is still bad.

30 May: A.N. Wyld died in Miyako Hospital on May 27th. He was a Johore planter; his bed was just opposite. J.B. Kinsey, an electrical engineer from Kuala Lumpur, has also died. His wife is interned. And Denison Smith, a young police officer, has lost his reason and has gone to the mental hospital, which is a dreadful fate these days. I go to have my leg dressed. It is a deep wound, but it's OK now. The doctor says to come back in two days. Neilson bought 1,400 Chinese cigarettes for $15, among them a Nipponese dollar. The sentry was very indignant; he did not want to take it. We discuss another 'Over the Wall' concert for the ladies. Someone says that some of the items may not be quite – well, in order. 'Doesn't matter,' says someone. 'Those who don't like that sort of thing won't understand and those who understand will like them.' Brigadier Newbigging has asked us to give $100,000 to buy absolute necessities for the sick and convalescent and supplementary diets for the hospitals in the prisoners-of-war camps. I don't see how we can do it; we are said to be running short ourselves. Surely it is the duty of the Nipponese. We have suggested a meeting. I hear that looting in the Fullerton Building was done by order of the Officer Commanding, Royal Army Medical Corps. He told his men to rifle everything for cutlery and sheets for the hospital in the building. If so, there is not much chance of seeing my canteen of cutlery again! I umpire a cricket match between Block B and the Kitchen. I also work on the entertainment program for June. And for to-night's variety concert, we produce the piano from the laundry and construct a stage from two laundry tables. But, of course, at the last minute, have I got the black sheet for the back of the stage? And three chairs and two boxes for the artistes to climb on and off the stage? And a policeman to stop people coming past during the turns? However, I produce them all and all is well and the show is very good. There are at least 700 there from 7 to 8.30 p.m. Gray is dead. There are now two empty spaces six feet from us – Gray's and Wyld's. Burney goes to hospital. There has been more face-slapping by a Nipponese sentry. A husband and wife were passing the time of day in the courtyard. Jack and I, after supping off bread and cheese, cold tea AND A BANANA EACH, swop reminiscences about our jobs until 11 p.m., then I go to bed pondering about a word for my latest crossword puzzle.

Sunday, 31 May: It is 29 years today since I sailed from Tilbury for Singapore in the old Maloja, aged 23. Mother and Mrs Nickal came out on the tender and saw me off. I'll go no more a-roving! 'They didn't win this campaign,' says Hope. 'We lost it.' Very true. Mrs del Tufo has been taken to hospital. Dusty is reported to be better. Our team lose a cricket match – I am not playing yet. K.L.B. and Miller MacKay are to be seen sitting on a camp bed under a large gay golf umbrella – a sight for the gods. All bedding becomes wet with the rain blowing in. We can't do anything to stop it, except sit on the mattress and keep it as dry as possible. I chat to Dant. He says Joan was doing very well at Pitman's. Jack and I take the plunge and buy four ounces of Barney's tobacco on the black market or via the sentries for $13. I inspect 'The Syonan Times' from May 23rd to 28th: the usual unadulterated propaganda – in such mass and so blatant you would expect it to stultify itself completely. The highlight is: 'Our treatment of the prisoners-of-war is such as to win the admiration of the world and the chivalry of our army is a by-word.' Headlines include: 'Day of Reckoning At Hand For Britain'; 'Spectre Of Revolution And Famine Stalks Through The Land'; 'Britain And U.S. Reduced To Third-Rate Naval Powers' (by the 'smashing victory' in the Coral Sea). I deal with cricket fixtures in June and various entertainment matters. Today's rumours are that the women are all to be released; and we are not to be allowed to buy any more supplies, in bulk or individually. It is just as well there were three lorries in today with two tons of cheese and 225 cases of sardines.

1 June: Will we get flat-footed with wearing nothing but sandals for months on end? Or drop our arches. Vic goes outside the camp with the firewood fatigue party. Before they leave, they receive a harangue about not buying anything. So, when they are outside, although there are swarms of children offering tins of condensed milk and jam, among other delicacies, and although the sentry gives them carte blanche to buy, they obey instructions and buy nothing. And there is no search on their return to camp! It is all most annoying. We buy three tins of meat and vegetables for $4.50 on the black market! We get Rusk, an Empress of Asia lad, to cut our mattress in two and give him $1. Now Vic and I each boast a mattress 2' 3" by 6' 6", which we can use lengthwise for sleeping on. When Vic was out with the fatigue party, he talked to a Chinese who said we shall all be released in two weeks. I'm glad they take it that way – that it's only a matter of time. Two of our old men,

Naughton and Manassela, go to better quarters in the isolation hospital. Darland has died and A.J. King is seriously ill in Miyako Hospital. I have sent a hand-written request to be allowed to go and see him. He has four daughters, all married. They are not in Malaya now, nor are any of the sons-in-law – Goss, Lindsay, Forbes and Milne. Apart from certain items, the food position is good in the sense that rations on the present scale can be maintained for a few months. We spend $18,000 per month on food. We can't give $100,000 to the Army. We could give a cheque if the Nipponese would give cash for it. As the black-out has been lifted in Singapore, we ask this morning for Lights Out to be at 10 p.m. again and the Nipponese agree. A camp post-office has been suggested. Private lotteries must be approved by the camp authorities. There was a case of a man who raffled an ordinary charpoy for $180! Malaria control continues outside the camp for a radius of quarter of a mile – a mosquito-breeding spot. A warning bell for rain is being considered i.e. to warn people to bring clothes in. Trafficking with sentries is heavier and more open than ever. They are in the kitchen at 11.30 a.m. selling tobacco. We can't stop it. Vacci-nation and inoculation against typhoid have been recommended for those who have not had it done recently. There is no more about our lists being sent to next-of-kin. We can only hope they've been sent. The interpreter says that they have. And there is nothing about the Red Cross visit. Is the representative too pro-British? There is an issue of 15 chocolates for 30 cents. They are very good – and that means 40,000 chocolates to supply the whole camp. There is also an issue of one seventh of a tin (two pounds) of Jacob biscuits per man – $3.50 per tin – a welcome addition to the diet.

2 June: I spend most of the morning seeing people about the June entertain-ments and the cricket program. Tiny went to his office in Singapore yesterday. The jaga *(guard)* burst into tears and prostrated himself at his feet – which was embar-rassing in front of the Nipponese. Our first real criminal has been sentenced by the Camp Disciplinary Committee. He is to be posted on all notice boards and has to dig cesspits for two hours each morning and afternoon for seven days. This is for trying to cheat the Tote by altering the figures on a ticket and sending another gentleman to collect the $24.50. I win $24 on the last race and finish about $4 up. The Free List is difficult; it includes probably all the Empress of Asia crowd and others, as their money is exhausted. It is a large and increasing number. The Com-mittee rightly say that chocolates, biscuits and luxuries must be paid for. Some don't see this! But the Committee must recoup some of their outlay. It bristles with difficulties. Twenty-five per cent of people in this room are now on the Free List. We have a feast at 9.30 p.m. We finish a tin of meat and vegetables, then we have butter and cheese and cold tea, finishing up with chocolates in very good condition and a final pipe.

3 June: Today is Derby Day; we hope to be in England for it next year and all wars over. The black-out is back to 8.30 p.m. again. What is the implication? Six engineers go out at the request of the Nipponese for what work I know not. Yesterday, I won $1 at bridge. The loser proffered a $5 Japanese note. I gave him four Singapore dollars in exchange – probably a loss, but I wanted it as a curio!

4 June: Cyril R. is back after five weeks in Miyako Hospital. He looks very fit. A.J. King was very bad, but is now improved. He sent me a message to that effect. The following are still in hospital: Dusty, Lord (of the Salvation Army), Lawes, Miles, Middlebrook and Corbett. The nurses are all Asiatic and are very good. Dr Landor is still there. You can buy lots of tinned luxuries at less than half black market prices in hospital. The cobbler's shop is in a small room off the laundry. Here they work from 10 a.m. to 5 p.m. with an hour for lunch, clad in striped overalls made out of old mattress covers and surrounded by leather and bits of old car tyres. They say the women's shoes come in a much worse state of repair than the men's and that the shoes generally are deteriorating badly. They advise us not to use them unduly, as replacement is impossible. My only pair are hanging from the roof awaiting the day of freedom. I send A.J. King $30 to help his diet; I know he has none. Corbett says he put up a marvellous fight. He was almost gone. He's a tough egg; he is 68. The Nipponese are turning down requests to visit people in hospital. A husband whose wife has had a stroke had his visit postponed for a fortnight. Garcia's son is not allowed to see his mother in hospital. No reasons are given. As for me, the doctor says my leg is now quite clean. Drew is on firewood fatigue outside the camp today. There are dozens of kids selling goods and there is open encouragement from the Nipponese sentries for the internees to buy. They have been warned about possible problems with the sentries coming back in. However, they buy just enough to conceal easily on their persons.

5 June: The two batteries in my torch are marvellous. They are of Fullerton Building vintage and I use the torch a lot, jotting down brainwaves in the night and so forth. What a mess many people's affairs must be in e.g. Dugan H. who had property and papers all over the place is now dead. At a meeting of the Leisure House Committee at 11 a.m., everyone resigns, but we all decide to carry on; it's only internitis! But organising concerts is not my forte and I say so. I acquire a very posh thermos for $13.50. It has three tiers inside and will be useful for keeping the food clean and the tea hot. I put some tea in the thermos for supper. I start making star charts and revising my geographical knowledge generally with the aid of a very good atlas – the Oxford Advanced – borrowed from Bayley. Among the rumours, the Niponese are said to have bombed Midway Island, but we have the initiative in the South-West Pacific. The coconuts often have a shoot inside when we open them. We eat it and sometimes it is very good. Today's is large, spongy and dry, but it has sweetness in it when chewed. The bananas are ripening at last; they are five cents each though and Jack has a hell of a job distributing them to the other internees.

6 June: Jack runs again at 7.15 a.m. Denison Smith, the young police officer, is dead. It is just as well perhaps, since his reason was gone. Gilham Browne and Dr Lawrie go to hospital. G.W. Lawes is out. R. Don has died. Our memo about overcrowding has gone to the Nipponese and they have promised to give it 'close consideration.' Dant offers shorthand lessons to anyone who wants to start again. We receive a tobacco issue at $1.60 an ounce. I get an ounce of Temple Bar and an ounce of Bird's Eye. I haven't seen it for decades. As soon as we open the tin, I recognise it. When I was a boy, it was kept in large tins in tobacco shops and the smell is distinctive too. Vaux, who has smoked Bird's Eye for 37 years, swops for his ounce of Frontier, so we are both satisfied. I get things arranged for the concert – laundry tables for the stage, a piano, three chairs, a small table, a box as a step – it all takes time. There has been more scrounging trouble: on the wood fatigue, one sentry let the internees scrounge, but the other disagreed, so some stuff was kicked into the ditch. Later, the co-operative sentry explained it was no use scrounging unless both sentries were of the same mind, like Billy Dibbs and his wife. The concert is very good; it lasts from 7.45 to 9.15 p.m. A sketch with two men dressed as women discussing the effects of internment on their husbands and another about the menu for dinner with Seymour Williams as a Chinese cook are very funny. I liked the trio singing 'Faint heart never won' from 'Iolanthe' and the choir singing folk songs such as 'Summer is coming in.' I spend a large part of the evening shining a torch on the piano. The official Nipponese scale of rations for British internees per man per day: rice – 500 grams; flour – 50 grams; milk – 15 grams; sugar – 20 grams; tea – 5 grams; and salt – 5 grams. As available, fresh meat – 40 grams; tinned meat – 10 grams; and vegetables – 100 grams. We are also supposed to get cooking oil and 40 cigarettes per man per month. Comment is superfluous.

V

MIDWAY, THE END IN SIGHT?

Sunday, 7 June 1942: The tea in the thermos last night, as expected, is just warm, but the milk has gone sour, so that is that. I am lucky. I acquire a spare pair of tennis shoes so small that no one else can get them on.

C.S.K. Bovell and W. Cherry go to hospital. I send chocolates to Nic in the Women's Block. I see Dr McMahon; he will see what can be done about films. The Nipponese want the names of all those over 60. They also want details of anyone who has lived in India for a 'considerable period', which we interpret as six months or more. Why? We had our first birth in the camp a day or two ago – a Mrs Clark, I think. The child died of diarrhoea. I hear a rumour that the Nipponese lost, sunk or damaged, off Midway Island two aircraft carriers and 10 other warships. This may be connected with a rumour of the 5th about a battle at the approaches to Midway Island. *(At the Battle of Midway a powerful Japanese fleet, sent against the U.S. base on Midway Island, was heavily defeated by American aircraft. It was a turning point in the Pacific war.)*

8 June: I have a look at the rooms newly opened for the old men and others. They have more room and a bathroom and other facilities. It was the women's hospital originally, adjoining the other. It was quite unnecessary to keep it empty so long. There is a class of small boys using it at the moment – rather pathetic – five of them, aged 10 to 12, I suppose. I should have been on rice-grinding fatigue this afternoon, but they asked me to arrange cricket versus the Empress of Asia team, which I did with alacrity. Rice grinding is a monotonous fatigue. The Asia boys field and bowl well, but they can't bat. We beat them 178 to 84. I make 14. Jack was on firewood fatigue this morning and got, among other things, 50 cigarettes and two ounces of tobacco for $5. At Commandant Edmonds' weekly meeting at 5 p.m., we are short of milk and flour. We have indicated exactly where the stocks are and have asked the Nipponese if we can get them. The results so far have been negative. The Diet Committee says peanuts contain a very high percentage of vitamin B, so we must eat them and the supply will be increased. Palm oil, of which we have a stock, is valuable food, so we will take one teaspoonful per man per day. It may be unpalatable – n'importe. Coconuts and bananas will be free in future. We hope to get dried fish and are still angling for supplies of fresh. We tried making a vegetable out of tapioca leaves. The results were horrible. We are now experimenting with sweet potato leaves. A thousand books for the library have been supplied via Brigadier Lord of the Salvation Army. Chinese ladies collected them on our behalf – nice of them. Bathing – the tides in the near future may be very favourable, say the Nipponese! The committee have no idea why the lists of ex-residents of India are wanted, nor has anybody else. You can make up your own theories. If we are moved, wherever it may be – Formosa or Lourenco Marques – we shall want to carry food, so iron ration bags are being made up for each man. The black-out continues in town. If and when it is lifted, ours will 'receive consideration' too. The Southern Irish need not be classified as neutral unless they want to be. (Many don't). It has been decided not to ask for the internees in Penang, Malacca and Kuala Lumpur to be sent here. They may be better off where they are. Anyhow, it is inconsistent with our congestion. The rumours are that the Midway Island affair was an attempted landing. It was repulsed by planes, submarines and shore batteries.

9 June: Early to bed, early to rise, makes a man healthy, wealthy and wise – well, we should be all of these by now. It is a sunny morning; I air pillows and other things. I receive a message at 4 p.m.; I am wanted at the gate. I go – the Nipponese want two land surveyors. They will be engaged in repair work e.g. Government House and godowns. The pay was 50 cents a day, but has been reduced to 35 cents! I don't think the prospect will allure any of my people, but, anyhow, two mining surveyors arrive. They decide to go and are given half an hour to get ready. It is just as well, as I ascertain none of mine wants to go. The men who do decide to do this work are taken in lorries to work and back, but are not allowed to wander about. Of course, they can get anything they want – if they have the money.

10 June: A notice is read out today: 'All internees under the age of 60 who consider themselves medically unfit to remain in Changi are to give their names in.' This is no doubt to relieve congestion. A parcel arrives for me from A.J. King in Miyako Hospital. It contains two tins of condensed milk, two of jam and one of pineapple. The parcel is very welcome. We also have an issue of H. and P. biscuits, a sixth of a tin each; 60 cents for about 20 biscuits. We also get bottled cordials, of which I get half a bottle. For lunch, we have rice, curried bully beef stew, fruit juice and a third of a fresh pineapple each, so we are doing well today in the food line, although our pineapple is overripe. We should be able to get them; there were thousands of acres of them in Singapore and Southern Johore. I hand films for developing to Dr McMahon, but they will not go off until Saturday now. We hold our first big boxing tournament – mostly Asia lads – with one-and-a-half-minute rounds. Two Nipponese officers and a sentry are in the very large crowd. I have a chat with an engineer who was employed making cars fit for the road again. A Nipponese officer took him round Holland Road and showed him European houses all smashed and looted. 'Your Army!' the officer said. It is quite true. The engineers went on a binge after two Nipponese officers took them out one night. About 10 p.m., they said, 'Go home now', but the engineers went off and stayed on the bust for 48 hours. When he went back to work, the engineer, Coltman, reported to a Nipponese officer and got solitary confinement for one week on rice and salt. But the sentries were very good and gave him tea and cigarettes. When it was over, the Nipponese said, 'You've served your sentence – back to work.' But their team refused to have 'em – they had, I gather, done it before – so here they are.

11 June: I am out in the exercise yard at 3 a.m. There is not a decent constellation in sight. Since I looked up astronomy in the books, the stars have all disappeared. I go for a dressing every second day now – a slow, but quite a clean healing is the verdict. Our foraging squad yesterday got 17,000 pieces of gula malacca – good. We are given a special lunch for the King's Birthday – a sausage each, rice and soup with vegetables. We play an interesting cricket match – Non-Benders versus the Malayan Police. We have a good eleven – Johnny Foster, captain; H.O Hopkins, S. Bayley, Saunders, Stiven, A. Mustard, Cochran, Steele, Sir Shenton Thomas (the Governor), Riches and myself. They score 247 and we 184. I go in last and make 37. Heavy rain causes the Kitchen Block concert to be moved from D exercise yard to the laundry. It is excellent. A trio of violin, saxophone and piano accordion – run through the gamut of selected tunes popular during the King's lifetime, from 1895 on. They start with 'Soldiers of the Queen' and 'Goodbye, Dolly Gray' and I observe that, the more recent the tunes get, the fewer I know. And this applies to the majority of the audience; the volume of choruses grows less and less as the songs become newer. This is because of the high average age. Then there follows a Kipling poem, extracts from Shakespeare's 'Henry Vth' (including 'St Crispin's Day'), appropriate solos, then finally a choir. Their 'Rule Britannia' is magnificent. The concert finishes at 9.15 p.m., just in time for me to lay out my bed. I am all clean – clean sheet I tuck in under mattress which is on a ground sheet; clean pillow slips; and clean sarong. Barron says that the tops of 10 thermos flasks in his room in the Union Building all blew off when a bomb burst, but the flasks were intact. Why?

12 June: At 7.15 a.m., I run nine times round the exercise yard after a gap of 23 days. I take it quite well; my bellows are as before. Jack's bananas are roundly condemned this morning. Dickson bumps his head against a bunch as he is going into the latrines. It is early and he must have a liver. The bananas are misbegotten and addicted to all the vices, judging by the adjectives. I am amused by the expression of mild surprise on Gray (senior's) face at the explosion. The camp atmosphere is one of extreme optimism. Fairy and others under 60, but medically unfit have filled in forms for going out, in his case to Port Dickson; can he live there; cash etc. There will probably be gang robberies all over the place, but we think the Europeans will not be molested. The Chinese will be so pleased to have us back. We are offered 20 tins of jam today on the black market for $50; we consider the price too high. They are 11-lb tins. They sell for $48, so we miss it. There was ack-

ack practice yesterday and today. There were warnings in 'The Syonan Times'. It is a clear case of cause and effect – we get the rumour that U.S. reconnaissance planes were over. A food fatigue party go to the town and meet some Army volunteers who say they get fresh meat every other day and have much more freedom. It seems to be a Nipponese trait to abuse civilians and treat the Army well. The dangerous internees can't go to bathe or use the Girdle Road! There is an issue of Mackintosh's toffee – two-and-a-half sweets per head for 10 cents! And there is a draw for tinned chicken curry made in Penang and for tinned tomatoes. I get curry. We eat it for supper. Whew! It is hot! We also have savoury rice and tea.

13 June: James Carbry dies in the camp hospital – at the age of 25. He was an engineer on the S.S. Largs. Our stock of flour is finished. We have only the Nipponese ration. This is sufficient for only one three-ounce roll on alternate days. The Camp Post Office is progressing. We may even have registered packets and a Changi stamp for these! Black-out has been re-imposed in Singapore, because we bombed Alor Star and Penang. A Nipponese officer told Fisher this when he was on yesterday's food fatigue. He also said that the Nipponese would take Midway Island in 10 days and India in a month. Which raises the question – how much do the Nipponese here know? On a fatigue party outside camp this afternoon, a sentry gave two internees three strokes each on the bottom with a big stick. They had gone scrounging for three-quarters of an hour and the sentry had had to wait for them! And they did no work. I meet a bloke who had a wonderful scrounge in Singapore. He had gone to hospital for X-ray. He finished at 11.30 a.m. and was told to scram until 6 p.m. He bought lashings of food. He also saw his contractors and his coolies – all bursting for THE DAY. In fact, about 20 coolies followed him round the town and carried things for him. He says there's lots of food in the shops and prices are reasonable. The administration is a comic opera – in fact, non-existent.

Sunday, 14 June: A very wet day; at 6.30 a.m., the rain is blowing in and beds and blankets are getting wet. We huddle in blankets (if you have one; I haven't). But they are worse off in the cells. The rain runs down the walls and floods the floors. The banana fatigue party is offered cigarettes by a Malayan youth. He will not take money. 'Orang kaki pendek *(literally,the men with short legs, meaning the Japanese)* will be out of Singapore in a month,' says he. I pick a Camp cricket team with Hopkins. He insists I play; he says my bowling is quite difficult and gets a wicket when others can't. We get a parcel from A.J. King – two tins of jam and two of milk – bless him! I meet Gilham Browne; he has 'The Fortress' from the library and on the flyleaf is 'To Nora from Tommy, 24.11.32'. This gives me an acute attack of Noraphily; it was a birthday present. Brian was 19 days old. I have a presentiment from this that Nora is OK. In a cell today I see the occupant washing his face in the squatpan. One knows it is perfectly clean – and yet. Lieutenant Okasaki took a party of officers round. Now there is a notice that he observed

139

cigarette ends in the passages and on the floors. The camp was dirty. Men were playing cards and dropping ash on the floor – this must cease. We riposte with an order for large quantities of brushes, dustpans and cleaning materials to be supplied by the Nipponese. The black market is to stop and we are to be given facilities to buy fairly. I wonder, I wonder. Anyway, that's what we have wanted all along. Who wants to pay $7.20 for two ounces of Barneys tobacco and find it mouldy when it is opened, as we did yesterday? There is no late supper – we have nowt!

15 June: We are asked to give again to camp funds. The first appeal realised $125,000 from 450. We spend $18,000 per month or 22 cents per head per day on extra rations. We have $72,000 in stock and $9,000 in cash. This will take us to the end of October. They are asking for $50,000 to secure the position until the end of December 1942. One ration of meat, cheese and egg costs $2.80, milk 80 cents and margarine 62 cents. At 10.30 a.m., I am put on a fatigue party washing the dirty clothes, sheets and other linen from the hospital. It is not a nice fatigue and I'm sure we are most inefficient, although we do our best. The squad consists of Dr McNab, Perrin, Darge and the Jew, Elias. The Nipponese supply soap and scrubbing brushes, but I'm sure the things need boiling and not washing in cold water. I win $3 at the races. I see Cherry, the printer. He will try to get cards for my cricket telegraph. The difficulty is to get anything past the sentries, whose actions are totally incomprehensible. He took his shoes in one day, wearing sandals, and it was three days before he was allowed to carry them out again, although the sentry saw him take them in. An Empress of Asia man who has been a prisoner-of-war with the Army has come in. He says some troops are being sent to Formosa. Edmonds, reports at 7.30 p.m. that there is nothing further about next-of-kin being informed or about communication by letter. With regard to the shortage of flour, the Nipponese have given permission for us to buy bread in Bedok village. Ha, ha, the 'controlled' price of a loaf in Singapore is eight cents; the price of the flour in it is 16 cents. 'Nuff said.' We get 712 pounds of green-leaf vegetables from the gaol garden this morning. From Wednesday, June 17th, we are to get one-and-a-half ounces of bread daily, because there is plenty of margarine in stock. We are exhorted to take the spoonful of palm oil daily. Edmonds appeals very strongly for more funds – we must buy NOW before stocks of what we want vanish. We have spent up to the end of May: food – $55,000; hospital – $9,800; camp equipment – $4,000; cobblers – $1,800; and vegetables – $2,400. Since then, we have spent another $43,000 on tinned food and so forth. Edmonds says bathing 'is being arranged' by Tokuda.

16 June: Hope finds a bed bug this morning. We knew they were in the room. They say the library books, inter alia, are stiff with them. The sentries are still at the black-marketeering, selling cigarettes in spite of horrific threats from the Nipponese Commander. I lend Sofeldt $10 'until we get out.' Today's 'Syonan Times' brought in by Miller from Miyako Hospital provides interesting information if you probe it. The newspaper states: 'The U.S. Navy Department again repeated fantastic reports of alleged losses inflicted on our warships.... If the Aleutian landings develop, ... the Nipponese losses in the Midway operations are more than compensated.' I change the torch batteries at last; they have lasted four months. It is a lean day for food.

17 June: The buying party in town yesterday reported that, of 10 bakeries visited, none has been working for 10 days; they have no flour. The cricket match against the Police is completed with a win for us. It is a very good, keen match. I take three wickets for 53. I fix up the Magic Show in the laundry owing to the very heavy rain. I pay $50 to the new appeal for the camp funds. I manage to get a bottle of cod liver oil out of the shop for $3; it is absolutely lousy with vitamins A and D, I believe.

18 June: I am on a fatigue at 2.30 p.m., carting rubber firewood from the back of the laundry to the kitchen. It's quite hard work, especially the human chain part, passing the logs hand to hand up the steps and to the pile. However, it lasts only an hour. At 7.30 p.m., I listen to E. N. Taylor on the custodianship of enemy property: preservation, not confiscation, is the principle. He says that the Nipponese authority dealing with the problem in Malaya has a Herculean task here and has no staff and no local knowledge. In fact, it is impossible, but he believes they are working on the same principles as the British. Land is not sold. Personal effects, WHEN STORABLE, (and not looted!) will probably be returned, but he does not hold out much hope as regards anything else. The question is all tied up with peace, postwar conditions and reparations, which no one can foresee. Tiny is in town again today buying, but he has been told to settle all outstanding accounts and cancel all orders. This gives rise to the rumour that we are going to Formosa. I shall believe it when we are on board a transport! Hopkins brings his gramophone and gives a recital from 9.30 to 10 p.m.

19 June: There is great news this morning – we can send a field postcard to next-of-kin. I don't suppose I can say, 'Nora left on the 13th on the Kuala. I don't know what happened to her, but her ship was sunk.' Details of what we can say on the postcards are: information of safety, health and happiness. Use block letters and we are allowed 10 lines. There has to be no politics, no business, trading, or mention of location of the camp or that we are in Singapore; there is to be no mention of the Nipponese military, naval and air forces. The popular sign for kisses – xx – is allowed. Then we are to sign and add our full name in block letters. You can say that a friend or relative has been seen. A Nipponese matron and 15 sisters have arrived at Miyako Hospital, we hear. A.B.C. Ramsay comes to see me. I agree to perform 'The Green Eye of the Little Yellow God'. He is asking N. Rees instead of Alexander. The latter has such a prodigious hairy growth that Ramsay thinks he can't possibly be a 'pukka sahib.' I buy more black market tins of jam and milk for

$6 – a colossal price, but one must eat and keep fit. 'The Syonan Times' says very naively that the essay competition on Nipponese culture was very disappointing. There were only 45 entries; no first and second prizes will be awarded. The population of Syonan don't seem to have realised that Nipponese culture is the finest in the world, especially in science and engineering. This is proved by the fact that her inventions have been adopted all over the world.

20 June: I have my first spoonful of unrefined palm oil. I eat it with a spot of rice and it's just tolerable. We have a very small issue of local tobacco and are told it's the last we get. I smoke a pipe of it and am still alive, but it's poor stuff. Thane knows his wife and daughter are interned in Palembang, so is Mrs Gilmour. They left on February 12th or 13th, but not when Nora did. There is no chance of her being there. Somehow, I have a conviction she is all right. I can't contemplate any other possibility anyway. We have asked the Nipponese to send the Palembang inmates here; the French are being sent to Saigon. I see H.K.B. 'cabin'. On the door is 'Hongkong and Shanghai Banking Corporation (incarcerated in Changi), Syonan Sub-agency; W.T. Yoxall, sub-agent; H.E.D. Davies, sub-orned; EM. Moffatt, sub-ordinate.'

I write my postcard. Expressions like 'Keep your chin up' are inadvisable, the interpreter says. They may be suspect to the censor. Mine is very simple. I take no risks – the object is to get the postcard through! There is an inspection by two Nipponese officers. The corridor is dirty, they say! Eight hundred use it constantly. We light our pink brilliantine – it is excellent used as a nightlight – while we have a final pipe. I never thought I'd smoke in bed.

Sunday, 21 June: There was a most obnoxious mosquito buzzing round my head in the night. I enveloped myself in my sheet, so that he would go away and bite someone else. At the second attempt, he did. Was this a selfish act? We hand in our postcards for sending to next-of-kin. Vic raises a storm by saying that he could not put much more in if he were given a free hand, except that he would say how thoroughly he enjoys his rice! The longest day – it's time we started in Europe. *(Tom's choice of phrase 'the longest day' in juxtaposition with his musing about the Second Front in Europe is a remarkable coincidence as the phrase is the title of the famous film about D-Day.)* The doctor says I can dispense with a dressing on my shin and use Mercurochrome. The healing has taken 34 days, but they say it has done extremely well to fill up in that time. I read 'North to the Orient' by Anne Lindbergh. I imagined they had flown over the top of the world! But actually it was via North Canada, Alaska, Kamchatka and the Kurile Isles to Tokyo and Hunkow. The Nipponese were kindness itself. I don't think they met the Nipponese High Command. There is an appendix case today. The patient has to go to Miyako Hospital. He walks to the ambulance. A Nipponese sees him – he can't go; he's obviously not sakit *(sick)*. He returns on a stretcher – all is well.

22 June: I am outside on the wood fatigue at 2 p.m.; this time, I get on the 'chips and compost' – the old men's fatigue. We are six; our duties are to fill four sacks with chips and one with leaves from the felled trees, for compost. It is all done in 15 minutes. We wander round, as do the sentries and the Chinese. The sentries' attitude is non-committal. The Chinese are scared stiff if one is about. There are women and babies. I eventually get two tins of condensed milk for $3. Others get more – or less – but all is done in a semi-secret atmosphere among the rubber trees and we push the swag into the sacks of chips and leaves. The fatigue is over by 3.30 p.m. Lots of our prisoners-of-war pass in lorries, all looking fit and cheerful. I am also on a chassis-pushing fatigue today. We get 16 pikuls of vegetables; the Nipponese will pay for 10. The Commandant (Edmonds) reports that the new appeal for the Central Fund totalled $9,000. This Block gave $6,000 of this.

23 June: There is cheese for breakfast. This is said to be the last issue of cheese – alas – it's the best food we get. There is salmon kedgeree for lunch; I cannot see the fish, so we open a tin. We are in the Block's bridge tournament semi-final, after beating Carter and Morgan. Rain starts again at 2.30 p.m. Cricket is abandoned for the day. We have two good sides. Spectators and players are astonishingly keen and I must say that, although I invented it, it is a remarkably good game and a good imitation of cricket. A ration party goes out in the morning. It is time I had a turn. What a gamble. One lorry goes to St Andrews School and gets flour and other items. The flour is very weevily now. There is no scrounging because there is nothing to scrounge. The other lorry goes to the Cold Storage in Orchard Road for meat. They get 17 carcasses. The party goes into the market, but most of the shops are shut – no stocks, I suppose. Where can they get stocks from? There are no imports. The whole thing is one ghastly mess. This party gets a fair number of tins once the market folk tumble to who they are. We find the best way to eat our palm-oil, which is waxy and apt to stay with you a long time, is to mix it with two to three spoons of rice at the beginning, then to cover the lot up with the rest of your meal. Our medico-chemical expert, Byron, assures us it is full of carotine which, when absorbed into the torso, converts to millions of globules of vitamin A. At 8.45 p.m., there is a sudden order from the Nipponese for a blackout. It is not known why, but we hope. I am out cleaning my teeth at 10.30 p.m.; there is a lovely moon. There are groups of Empress of Asia youths about. I am not squeamish, but every other word is a swear, a particularly objectionable swear too. It is so unnecessary to such an extent. Two internees have arrived from Kelantan – Dr W.J. Geale, aged 67, and J. Baker, aged 73. They came via Siam by rail. They started last Thursday. Both went straight to hospital!

24 June: The cricket scoreboard is ready. The cricket is very good indeed. Singapore Cricket Club score 260 and the Selangor Club 140 for 8. I bowl three overs but get no wickets. The order goes out that Lights Out will be from 8.30 p.m.

to 8.30 a.m. until further notice. It was 7.45 a.m. before –why? I have a chat with a warder. He describes all the suspensions *(hangings)* he has assisted at. The formula is 1,000 divided by the weight in pounds equals the height of drop in feet. The conversation being thus nicely on hanging, Kayn tells of a Tamil employee on his estate who hanged himself in a cattle-shed. He was of high caste and the general regret was not at his tragic decease, but that he should lose caste by hanging himself in a cattle shed! The women have a concert. The singing sounds are very sweet. A-Block – where the women are – is very close to us.

25 June: G. Wiseman and Dave Anderson go to Miyako Hospital. Wiseman is 56 and I thought he looked very fit. 'The Syonan Times' reports that Mrs Arbenz, wife of the Swiss consul, has been killed in a motor accident. Joan knew the daughters well. 'The Syonan Times' leader complains bitterly that the population of Syonan-To are just waiting. They don't learn Nippon-Go *(Japanese language),* they don't take off their coats and work; and they shamelessly let their sisters (to whom 'The Syonan Times' takes off its hat) go out and earn money as waitresses (?) to keep the family in idleness. 1,034 pineapples and 2,584 pounds of flour (less than usual) were obtained by the ration party yesterday. The Free French give $90 and 15 guilders to the Camp Fund in recognition of the kindness they have received here. The Nipponese announce that interviews between husband and wife will be granted only in really exceptional circumstances in future. Wedding anniversaries are not in this class!

26 June: It is exactly 29 years since I landed in Penang from the old Empress of China. I stayed a night at the E. and O. Hotel. I got into a Siam jar for my bath and had great difficulty getting out of it. In the Block Bridge tournament semi-final, Drew and I beat Curtin and Crichton (winners of the last tourney). After lunch, I get the reward of virtue. While Jack, Vic and Hope are having their siesta, my stern sense of duty leads me to search for a cricket ball hit over the top of the gaol yesterday. I have an idea it might have trickled down the opposite side of the roof and lodged in an area between our barred passage and the high wall which separates us from the European block, where the women are. So I get a special key from the kitchen, open the formidable door and go in. It is about five yards wide and the grass is rather lush now. It runs the whole length of B-Block and a bit beyond. I am prowling along it; head bent, and have reached the far end. Suddenly, there are loud cries, 'Tommy! Tommy!' and there, if you please, behind THEIR bars in A-Block's extreme low end are Nic and I.G. We have quite a chat and shake hands through the bars. Nic insists on giving me a tin of milk. I then have to beat it. A sentry, I gather, is in the offing, which seems very wrong in the female quarters at 2.30 p.m. It is very interesting and pleasant to speak to women friends after 130 days of exclusively male society. I should have done a coconut fatigue; it is a coveted one. You can get into kampongs and it is always good for scrounging. But I had cricket, so I handed the fatigue over to Jack – and it turned out to be oakum picking at the back of the laundry! There is a concert in B-Block. It is very good.

27 June: At 7.15 a.m., I run 10 times round the yard and I take them a bit quicker. I am quite puffed at the end. I open the $13 tin of Garrick – it is mouldy. I dry it in the sun – it is just smokable. We win the Block Bridge tournament final against Van Hien and Llewellyn. The prize is $4 of goods each at the Camp Shop – very useful. Our committee has again asked about bathing. The official reply is 'there is a suspected case of cholera on a ship in Singapore, so you cannot bathe or be allowed to purchase fish!' I hope the Marines hear of this. The blackout in Singapore originally said to be a practice for seven days is now until further notice. A notice in 'The Syonan Times' asks the public to cooperate in measures for the suppression of mosquitoes. There weren't any in town before. It is interesting that these notices are all signed by the Mayor now, not the Military Administration Department, as previously. We win our cricket match by 30 runs. I catch the last man at mid-on from a very low, hard hit and am considerably congratulated all round, including by the Governor. Walker is given a permit to be out all day. He meets lots of staff, all bursting to have us back and very optimistic. A high Nipponese officer and about 20 lesser officers inspect us. He is said to be a cousin of the Japanese Emperor and is wearing British decorations. At any rate, he acknowledges our standing to attention by a salute. And they have pinched our orchestra from the concert to play for him tonight. I suppose he wants to hear the barbaric English music. It is a glorious night – the moon is almost full. I emerge with Hope and Jack and identify the Southern Cross, Scorpio and the Plough. 'The Syonan Times' naively says to learn Nippon-Go now –'you will never have another chance!'

Sunday, 28 June: We collect the bridge prize. We each get one-and-a-half tins of Mackintosh's toffee, a tin of pineapple and papaya jam and a bottle of Symington's coffee essence – Grand! 'The Syonan Times' gives full details of an exchange of diplomats and others from the U.S., Canada and South America and the names of ships involved. They will meet in Lourenco Marques for picking up and include Hong Kong and Saigon, but not Singapore. A second exchange is being arranged, also Americans. However, this shows it can be done. I shall ask tomorrow: 'Have the Committee asked what stage the arrangements for an exchange have reached?' Walker was in town yesterday. He lunched at the Cathay. The waitress was one of his education staff; she burst into tears. 'The Syonan Times' reports that the Governor of Malacca has been touring and inspecting the rubber estates at Jasin. The men now plant vegetables and the women tap for rubber. They receive no wages, just free rice. We have another shot at making a cake – rice, grated coconut, lots of margarine, a tablespoon of condensed milk – but it is not very successful.

29 June: I was pooping around all morning on entertainment arrangements. The films are not yet developed – they are awaiting a reliable worker, I am told.

There are some questionable garden leaves as the vegetable for lunch. They may be spinach; I eat them anyway. Being on food fatigue, I clean up the serving table and the floor afterwards. I meet Kundy; he remembers meeting me at K. Intan in 1932. Jack and Vic are on wood fatigue and get 16 packets of dates for 50 cents each, four tins of milk for $1.50 and two tins of jam. At his meeting, Edmonds, the Commandant, says the reports around camp that 40% of the postcards have been rejected are sheer fabrication. The interpreter says the cards are of a very good standard. There have been no root vegetables from the Nipponese since June 2nd and no explanation, therefore the vegetable position is very difficult and disturbing. A lorry went to town two days ago. The internees on it were impressed with the fact that there was no food and no milk to be bought. Today, the Nipponese take away 300 bags of rice from our stock. Bathing is off. The Nipponese explain that there was a cholera case on a ship, he may have been sick over the side and a fish may have eaten it, so all bathing, fishing and the sale of fish in Singapore are prohibited. You can draw your own conclusions. To bed. I dream about Colin, Joan and Brian, all dead in an epidemic. The dream is probably a sequel to all the talk about cholera.

30 June: I am on a coconut and banana fatigue outside the camp at 10.10 a.m. There are about 10 of us with one sentry. We have to push a tricycle and a cart to a Chinese hut a few hundred yards away. Here, the coconuts and bananas are assembled. There are also some Malays, Sikhs and Klings eager to sell tins, but the Japanese in command of the party is vicious, as is the sentry, slashing them with the scabbard of his bayonet. Still, we do some dealing. From a Kling, I get tobacco ($2.50 an ounce), dates, cheroots, sweets and chocolate biscuits. We are just concluding the deal when the sentry arrives. He chases the Kling, draws his bayonet and hurls it after the retreating trader; he just misses. I chat to the Malays; they say there is no work. One was a cook-boy to a tuan now in gaol, another a prison employee earning $51 a month. He says, 'Kerja tiada tuan *(there is no work sir)* – how can there be work when you are all away?' I reply, 'Sementara' *(for the time being)* and we leave it at that. The fatigue is quite a spot of work. We load 700-plus bananas and return at midday. There is some doubt about the sentry who has looked and knows where the scrounged goods are in the cart, but all is well. There is a fatigue party again at 2 p.m. This time we expect much because the sentries collude. We get tins of cheese, milk and jam in due course. I incur the sentries' wrath by buying seven tins of milk ($10) and 100 biscuits ($1) from Sikhs. If we want, we are each allowed to buy one tin of cheese, four tins of milk and two tins of jam. We eventually load another 700 bananas and we are back in camp at 3.30 p.m. We halt under the office windows, but all is well. We celebrate my record scrounge which is shared with Hope, Victor and Jack, of course, with two spoons of condensed milk and one of jam with our supper.

1 July: I have now been interned 135 days. I notice that the premium is due on the Prudential Insurance policy on Brian. On a fatigue party, Alan meets H.L.W. He sends me a chit to say that he is fit and well, also Gray. In town are Neil, Billing, Nelson, Watson, Jerram Booth, Billy Farrington, Cameron, Bruce, Spinks, Griffin, Greig, Benham, Moule, McVilly, Gibson, Stubbs, Homer, Walker, Taylor, Himely and Cooper. There is no word of Pearson. The Nipponese are now interrogating the Chief Engineer. The coconut fatigue party this morning is not so lucky. The sentry gets peeved and sticks his bayonet through the tins they have bought. All the French, including the Free French, have now gone. Parry is to see Dusty who is very seriously ill. He has dysentery as well as tuberculosis. King is hanging on well. I discuss the life of a safety-razor blade with another internee. Mostly, mine lasts only 14 days. 'Ah,' says he, 'but you shave in semi darkness every morning.' I still don't see how this affects the life of a blade. Jack has been cooking again and this time the result is good – four small cakes. The ingredients are, dates, milk, ground rice, grated coconut and dripping. Kayn says we should try Eno's for baking powder. The continual drain of dollar notes is a serious problem now and will get worse. None of the casuals we buy from outside ever has change, so everything is paid for in single dollar notes and none comes back.

2 July: I go to the camp shop and buy a tin of sweets for $1.50 and send them to Nic in the women's camp. I would have sent another to Katherine, but two are not allowed. At 2.15 p.m., I am on a fatigue stacking timber. It turns out that we have to go to a workshop in A-Block and remove and sort timber. It is quite a heavy job, but I am very interested to see the conditions. Of course, the women have far more room than we. We carry a particularly heavy table to a dormitory by request of a female officer wearing an armband. The dormitory is the same size as our room, but has about 30 beds as opposed to our 100. In fact, it is quite like a dormitory in a school. At 4 p.m., the women queue for tea, so, being thereabouts and the sentry complaisant, we have tea and Bridget Hegarty gives us a biscuit. I meet Katherine, Nic, Miss Tonkin, Miss Pratt and many others. Katherine says, 'I hear you are doing crosswords. I remember your saying that, if ever you went into internment, that's what you would do.' She is very surprised I didn't bring a dictionary in, but she doesn't know I would have had to carry it! Katherine asks if there is any truth in the rumour that Churchill has gone to meet Roosevelt to discuss peace terms – which shows the difference in rumours. No one on our side has thought of that one. We have half-an-hour – a very pleasant interlude. All I speak to seem fit and, like Billy Dibbs, a't same mind *(of the same mind)* – if it don't go on too long, we can take it. The Nipponese say that flour is very scarce in Singapore. The price is controlled and you can't buy it, but, if we care to buy at black market prices, we can! If we can get any! And we are also to get 16 cwt of vegetables twice a week. And they are going to let us have rice polishings, for which we have asked for weeks. It increases the nutritive value of the rice. Okasaki says he has seen letters in which a Nipponese internee in Singapore complains of ill-treatment. This signifies nothing. Could we not write in a similar strain, if allowed? Nattrass goes to hospital.

3 July: Kerr Bovell goes on a ration fatigue party . He says there are lots of kids with tins for sale and the prices are much decreased. This is probably because our people simply haven't got the money. Morgan of the Empress of Asia gets us two tins of milk, two of pilchards, one of bully beef and one of jam for less than $7. Black market prices are therefore also down. In Kerr's fatigue party, two are late returning from a scrounge. This angers the Japanese in charge who orders the guard to give them two strokes, which he does. (They had kept the lorry waiting.) I chat to C.S. Clerk. He says the streets are full of aimless strollers. Motor-traffic, except for the military, is non-existent. Now we hear that the ban on our shopping at G. Singh has been lifted and scrounging on all fatigues is completely open. The bugs are approaching our area. They have been found in quantity in the next row and Smith's camp bed is lousy with them. In the room below are Nic, Mrs Grist, Mrs W. Hunt, Miss Nela Macdonald, Judy Good, Barbara Walker, Irene Whitehead, Joan Boston, Helen Latta and G. Tompkins. The night before last, there was another burglary on the kitchen store. They smashed cases through a grille and stole 56 tins of bacon, sausages and other foodstuffs. One would think it could be traced within these walls. If caught, they should be dealt with most severely. I regard this as much worse than an ordinary burglary outside.

4 July: It's American Independence Day; will the Americans in camp stage something? It's Ethne's 21st birthday party. Kerr is throwing a tea party and V. of course is going. The cricket match between blocks ends with a win for us. I was skipper, of course. It is a good win, as the kitchen refused to allow their men to play in our team. It is said that there is a death penalty in Singapore for listening to the radio! Shock – Dr McMahon says that my baby powder box which held my films is empty. It cannot be unless they've been stolen. The Post Office is open again. Mrs S.J. Vincent has died. D-Block stage a concert in B-Block; it is good. I go inside to listen after ascertaining that arrangements are OK.

Sunday, 5 July: I run nine times round the yard at 7.15 a.m. It is astonishing what a lot of folk seem to think I am endangering my life by running half-a-mile every morning. They say the heart will go etc. I know that, if I hadn't, I would not be able to do it at all now. Cobden says we are to perform *('The Green Eye of the Little Yellow God.')* next Friday. We haven't got the script yet. Jack has made quite eatable cakes with crushed rice, grated coconut, sweet potato from lunch, palm oil, butter, dates, a dab of jam on top and cooked on my tin plate on the Dover stove in the exercise yard. Official: our postcards leave tomorrow by the Conte Verde which is taking interneees to Lourenco Marques for an exchange – lucy devils. With luck, my family should get mine in, say, eight weeks. To give the de'il his due, I must say

I hear that the death penalty connected with wireless is for the possession of a transmitter. This is more reasonable.

6 July: We were supposed to have moved about 400 sandbags from around the latrine to the vegetable garden. It is about 250 yards there and back and there were only 12 of us. I said yesterday it would be impossible without carts to transport the bags. It was found to be so and the fatigue was postponed until tomorrow. Vic and Jack go out of camp on firewood fatigue. Their scrounge is very good and, with the sentries actively assisting, they get 10 tins of milk, four of jam, one of butter, 12 of dates and – joy! – A packet of salt from Middlewich – about 1lb. in good condition. In his report, Edmonds, says our cold storage experts have rigged up a refrigeration plant, largely with the aid of coconut husk. They hope to be able to keep meat for eight days. He also reports that the Nipponese have admitted a mistake over the vegetable supply. They did the sum the wrong way round in changing kilos to pounds. But we shan't get as much as promised. We are not leading a sufficiently active life to need it! The morning roll yesterday was our first using rice polishings from the mills. We thought it was fusty. Personally, it reminded me of the smell of an old barn – fowls, feathers, hay and other aromas all mixed. Now it appears that this is a quality which appertains to Java rice polishings and we expect it permanently. Mrs Mather is to see Dusty. She knew him well as kids. He is very bad. She thinks he cannot live long. What a miserable end for poor old Dusty. I put my name down for astronomy classes.

7 July: I am on a heavy and messy fatigue today, moving sandbags from our room to the vegetable garden. They are full of laterite. We have more light and air round our bed space, though. The firewood fatigue has trouble this morning. The sentries have gone very strict again. A Chinese trader is very severely beaten, his hands tied up and left. This is no doubt due to trouble yesterday, when one internee strayed a little from the firewood fatigue and was found by a Nipponese patrol. He has been beaten and is in solitary confinement. $200 reward is offered by the committee for information about the kitchen burglary. Over 100 tins were stolen. Official: all our postcards have been passed for sending on. The yeast grown in the camp which we use for raising bread is now standard and called Changi Culture or Callanan C. It has been grown by Callanan and Doctors Byron and Field. I see Donald Grant. I give him a note from Isobel. I also receive one for her. He sits next to a man newly back from Miyako Hospital who confirms that the Nipponese in Java only occupy the ports. Anywhere inland is controlled by the guerrillas. This is the heaviest day yet. What with running, one fatigue, cricket, bowling, I retire quite tired. In the night, I hear a steamer hooting. Can it be the Conte Verde? She would not be allowed in port, of course.

8 July: I send a tin of toffees to Katherine de Moubray. This is just as well, as I hear all parcels from outside and between camps have been stopped. In fact, this is a day of oriental contradictions. Long is taken off in an ambulance. An Indian driver takes over and Dr Lowther is told not to accompany him. Miyako Hospital is to be taken over by Nipponese patients. The civilian patients are to be moved to Tan Tok Seng, doubtless dispatching a few in the process, as before. The compost fatigue party is scrounging (which has gone unchecked and winked at for days.) The sentry suddenly goes berserk and ties the Kling vendor to a tree for two hours. He gives the fatigue party six tins and retains two and the balance of the money they had given the vendor! Yet, another fatigue party waltzes in with a whole case of condensed milk! And the Governor received a gift of much beer, sherry and butter from some lofty source 'with felicitations.' So, I ask you, what? There is great excitement at 11 a.m. – a formation of 27 plus 21 bombers and 12 fighters fly over heading eastwards and, at 11.30 a.m., there are many bangs and anti-aircraft bursts. Is it a practice or not? G. Brown has died. Money, money.... More folk are spent up. The results are that black market prices are down. I get five tins of milk at $2, jam for $2.25 and cheese for $2.50. I rehearse 'The Green Eye.' The Post Office works very successfully. In view of the stoppage of parcels ordered by the Nipponese, the Post Office is even more useful. Jack cooked cakes. We sent one to the Women's Section. They say it was delightful! The ingredients were: sweet potato, pounded rice from lunch, palm oil, margarine, jam, condensed milk, dates, coconut, apricot juice and Eno's. At 7 p.m., we hear that Dusty died on Monday, so he will be buried now. It is very sad – he was a grand player of cricket and hockey and a splendid fellow. I've played with and against him since 1913. Lining our narrow gangway when they herded 100 of us into this tennis court room on March 6th were Van Geyzel, Parry, Rhodes, S.P.K. Snoxhill, Miles, Elias, Wyld, Gray, myself and two others – eleven of us. Three are now dead.

9 July: I am on firewood fatigue at 10 a.m. I am on chips, but there aren't any. I fill only half a sack in two hours. The scrounge is peculiar. The sentry's attitude is uncertain, but, eventually, a trader arrives on a bike with the stuff and sells bully beef for $1 a tin and Ogden's Guinea Gold cigarettes at 75 cents for 10! I get 100, two tins of milk for $3, two tins of Chinese biscuits for $8 and 10 local cheroots for 50 cents. They go in with my wood chips in the bag and all is well. J.G. Wylde, the Malay Regiment adjutant, has died. I knew him well. Greetham, who worked with a mining company, has also died – of dysentery. I receive a note from Ward. I must find out how to get one back. They – the Forces – get an amenity grant. The officers receive $7.50 a month, the N.C.Os $4.50 and the privates $3, so they can afford more. The weekly meetings of surveyors have collected information about records and other matters. Neil is at the racecourse making hay! And Billing is in the R.V. Road camp, working on the roads. 'You are at present Surveyor General, of course, and, unless you want to rush away when we get free, you should remain.' Ward writes. The camp team win the cricket match against the police team. Something must be done about the ball. Johnny speaks a few words about Dusty and we stand silent for a minute before play begins. We rehearse *(The Green Eye)* at 5 p.m. It is about time A.B.C. and Alex stopped altering their parts! Elias offers five eight-ounce tins of Walls beef sausages at $2.25 each. We refuse – we wonder if they are part of the theft. I see Beck; he is making buttons and a buckle for his wife out of coconut husk; a lot of patience is needed. Local news: eight Malays have been beheaded for rice stealing. The heads have been exhibited at the G.P.O., Cavanagh Bridge and Raffles Place, among other locations. Kultur! Nine bombers left Singapore a few days ago. Three returned in a battered condition. There are also two aircraft carriers in the harbour – damaged.

10 July: Birkin shows a note from Cobly; he is fit and well, but short of money. He hears that our camp is rolling in it! We rehearse at 11 a.m.; it is a bit better. Fairy had a remarkably vivid dream about Nora and he would not know her now if he saw her! She rang him up: 'this is Nora Kitching. Can you tell me who was elected Room Representative for Tommy's room?' He told her that it was Belgrave. 'Oh, I'm so pleased – now Tommy will be Block Commandant!' Now how can one explain a dream like that? Anyhow, perhaps it means she's alive. I umpire a cricket match between blocks. We try a tennis ball with a string cover. It is good, but the string wears out. I change into grey flannels (I have to use pyjama cord to keep them up), plain shirt, sweat-rag, socks and shoes. It feels quite strange! The final rehearsal at 7.15 p.m. is very good. The concert is in C-Block at 7.45 p.m. We are the fifth turn; there must have been 1,000 there; ours goes down excellently. A senior police officer is convinced we'll be out on an exchange in a few weeks. The Nipponese want to get rid of us and want theirs back, particularly as they let them down by attacking on the 8th, whereas they had been told the 20th and were packing for that date. They told the police this when they were interned. Forty-two men and two women move in today! They are from the municipal administration and elsewhere. Where they will put them, God knows. I am offered two eight ounce bottles of Marmite for $25. Nothing doing, but I'd love it. At 9.30 p.m., I make coffee out of essence, enough for our four. It is very good and Jack and I sup from it, plus biscuits cheese and butter.

11 July: 60% of the flour obtained by the last ration party is in such bad condition its useless. We uproot most of our belongings this morning and have a cockroach hunt. One chirped in my ear most of last night. I chat for most of the morning to A.E. Fawcett, Dr Lawson and Gilham Browne. What is the disease cockroaches are said to convey? A report from Miyako Hospital says Mr C. Kitching has malaria. That's the first time I've seen my name in Malaya except for my own family – it can't be Colin! Lieutenant-General Yamashita, has presented 30 cases of tinned pineapples to the camp. An internee has asked permission for a photographer to visit the camp. He wants to insert himself into one of the pictures, so that he will have proof of his extraordinary state of thinness for his wife, who will otherwise never believe it. Sad to say, the committee has refused this request. The performance in D-Block is an improvement on last night.

Sunday, 12 July: I buy two eight-ounce bottles of Marmite for $23. Most of the tea offered for sale at $4.80 a pound is returned to the camp store. People won't buy it. So now reduced to $2.20. Arthur Sleep goes to hospital. A memorial service is held for Dusty (Vernon E.H.R.). He was only 48. He came out here very young in 1911. He was made to walk to Changi by the Japanese and never really got over it. He had a bad heart and tuberculosis. Transport was promised, but did not turn up. It is a good service; there are about 100 there. Johnny F. does the reading and H.M. Parry speaks about Dusty. The Governor attends, as do, I notice, all the Negri Sembilan rubber planters.

13 July: When we do our run nine times round the yard at 7.15 a.m., there is much cursing from two Empress of Asia lads sleeping on the concrete about the noise we are making, the usual adjective. I am on a fatigue at 10 a.m. At the Fatigue Office, it turns out to be cleaning corridors and other parts which are designated as camp areas i.e. not appertaining to any particular block. Kennedy and I, armed with stiff brooms, dustpan and container proceed to clean from the entrance to the laundry. It is hot work. It takes one hour and is complicated by the feet of the library queue, but we finish the job satisfactorily. I am back on the same fatigue at 2.15 p.m., but, owing to our energetic morning work, it takes only half-an-hour. Nevertheless, it is very heating. An internee had a wonderful scrounge this morning. He got more than he could deal with, so we bought four tins of milk for $1.70, four tins of bully beef for $1.60, four tins of cheese for $8, two tins of jam for $1.60, one tin of sausages for $2 and, from Elias, a small tin of cream crackers for $2.50 and gula malacca (just like fudge) for $1. Marmite added to the mince we got today was a great improvement. At the Camp Commandant's (Edmonds') meeting, there is some doubt as to whether our postcards to next-of-kin have gone. The Nipponese have been asked, without result. Our cold storage experts' cold room is now OK, so the meat will keep and we shall have four issues of three ounces instead of three issues of four ounces. Last week might be described as 'withdrawal of privileges week.' No reason is given. Getting eggs is difficult – the sphere of collection is restricted. Rice polishings were delivered only once, although they were promised regularly. We have again asked permission to exercise in Girdle Road from 8 a.m. to 8 p.m. There are more complaints about noise after Lights Out. I say the situation is much improved and this is greeted with loud applause. Some folks' susceptibility is absurd. But I must say that the new Nipponese gong which strikes the hours all day and night is trying. (It's the gaol clock they have got going again.)

14 July: A bombshell is dropped today with the fatigue parties. When they get to the gate, they are told they are not allowed to take any money out, so they have to return and leave it. Is this another effort to stop scrounging? But it has been encouraged lately, as far as one can judge. We spring-clean our sideboard, disturbing large bodies of small cockroaches. And a large contingent of Nipponese would choose the moment when we have stacked everything on the floor and the place is looking most untidy to inspect. I cover everything up with a sarong. Many people, including perfect strangers, continue to pop up and congratulate me on my 'Green Eye' performance. The latest is in the laundry today; he has seen it in town too. With the Post Office in operation, Jack makes a cheese cake and we send a bit of it to our friends. We eat the rest for supper, plus a cold sausage each. I try to get hot water for the coffee, fail and mix the stuff cold in a thermos and stir the mixture. Bang goes the thermos. I think I must have set up a vibration in the glass, as I was very careful with the stirring. Fairy has it on 'unimpeachable authority' that there were 49,000 maximum of our troops here as prisoners-of-war. Now there are only 20,000. The rest have been sent north – to Jitra or Siam.

15 July: There are 2,710 in the camp, with 363 females and 50 children. A notice is read out, summoning all engineers and those with engineering experience to attend at the laundry at 12. When they assemble, a notice is read: 'Who is willing to go to Nippon?' They will be 'considerably' well treated. The meeting breaks up with roars of laughter and no volunteers. Quel mentality! Our carpenters (B-Block only) are still on strike. They threw down their tools in dudgeon on account of their complaints to Edmonds about the noise in the afternoon, to which he referred somewhat jocularly on Monday. So strikes are not confined to – shall I say? – The 'lower strata.' H.R.W. Lobb has died. The ban on fishing and bathing has been repealed as from July 11th.

16 July: The fatigue parties are still being searched for money. The Nipponese found $3 on a doctor who was going on the firewood fatigue, so he was fallen out for a further search and was thereby enabled to pass $30 which was in his cigarette case to somebody already searched. There are lots of stores outside, but there is no business, of course. The sentries are doing it. An internee says two or three people who have been in hiding have arrived in the camp. They were beaten up and those responsible for helping them decapitated. I don't know if it is true. Vic, contemplating a spindle-shanked biped in shorts, says: 'Some people have sedentary legs.' Hope: 'What do you mean – sedentary legs?' Vic: 'Well, I mean legs which you can see have spent their lives sitting under an office table – legs that have not done any manual labour.' Shrieks of delight. At lunch, we get greens from the garden – nauseous, but doubtless good for us. The Camp Committee report: 'we (the Committee) have made an emphatic protest about the withdrawal of privileges one by one. Our discipline has been extremely good; orders have been carried out.' Examples of privileges stopped: books and parcels from Miyako Hospital and the carrying-out of work in the printing shop. The replies to our questions are: 'Have the postcards gone?' Answer. 'It is unnecessary to answer.' 'A visit from the Red Cross Commissioner?' Answer: 'No directions have been received from the High Command.' 'The use of Girdle Road for exercise?' Answer: 'We will consider this.' Concerning the appeal for engineers willing to work in Japan the official reply given by General Macrae to the Nipponese was: 'I have the honour to inform you that no internee is willing to go to Japan for the purpose specified.' The death has been announced of Weir of Muar, who was well-known as an amateur photographer. At 4 p.m., I attend a lecture on astronomy by Professor Alexander. It is concentrated, but it is what I want. I can't remember taking notes at a lecture since 1913. I hear that our Post Office officials are in at last. Some have been helping with the Camp Post Office. An internee had his face slapped by a sentry today. Our Commandant, Edmonds, insists that the sentry be reported. Pop Wiseman is back from Miyako Hospital. C. Kitching is an old bird who lived in a Penang hotel. He is a damned nuisance, says Pop, so I shall not pursue the matter further.

17 July: We run nine times round the yard at 7.15 a.m. The massed Empress of Asia forms appear to be trying to push us off the concrete. J.G. Wood, C.V. Brandon and G.B. Kellacher go to hospital. I eat some gula Malacca which I bought – 10 bits for 50 cents. It is just like fudge. Who would believe it is lime and toddy? I have never seen anything less like the result of such a union. All fatigue parties are searched again. On the firewood fatigue, a sentry tells an internee where to stand so as to evade the search, helps him to buy when he is out of the camp and, at the end, says, 'I don't like to see you without enough food. In three months, we may be in and you may be out.' An internee is accused of giving false information to the Camp Police. He accused a fellow internee of stealing from the kitchen. When called upon, he was totally unable to substantiate the charge. He has all privileges of 'free issues' withdrawn (cigarettes and so on) and he is given heavy fatigues for 14 days – and another 14 days for refusing to do a fatigue. Another citizen is given 14 days extra fatigues for using abusive language to a policeman. And it really was bad – the favourite adjective plus another more unusual noun.

18 July: The morning's bright remark by a merchant prince sweeping the corridor: 'If my parents weren't founder members of this club, I'd resign.' Eisinger, who is Swiss, was sent for yesterday and told to go out. He said he didn't want to. Why? He had no money, nowhere to go and no work. The Nipponese told him: 'well, you'll have to make up your mind before August 16th. The British are going to be changed.' Speculations are is it true? If so, what does changed mean – exchanged or moved? The Central Committee met Okasaki yesterday. They were told supplies of wheat were negligible. Any bread in future should be reserved entirely for women, children and the sick. All other internees must learn to live on rice, as there will be no further supplies 'until we take Australia!' He also said that the camp diet supplied by the Nipponese was much better than that given by us to

Nipponese internees. This being not only impossible, but directly contradictory to irrefutable written and printed evidence, led to a heated discussion. Anyway, they have agreed to let us have rice polishings in lieu. Parcels to the Women's Camp have been resumed. Katherine was very pleased with hers. R. Scott and K.S. Morgan who were brought from Palembang are in solitary confinement and the Committee can get no satisfaction. They arrived on Wednesday. Weisberg has come into Changi at last. Sennett isn't in yet, nor, or course, are Birtwhiste and Corner. The Committee say that fraternising in any form with the Nipponese is to be 'severely discouraged!' Hear, hear! I do a fatigue unloading two lorries full of miscellaneous goods purchased from Gian Singh – mostly tinned food. Current story: this morning, two internees were on a fatigue near a Nipponese bungalow close to the gaol. They heard a radio and listened. 'The Russians are advancing on all fronts', the announcer said. Then they were discovered, the radio was switched off and they were sent away. An inmate who was in town today says that the Chinese are very jubilant and highly optimistic – a marked change from last time. 'The Band Wagon', a very good concert with an orchestra, is presented in camp.

Sunday, 19 July: What induces otherwise normal citizens to grow these beards? On the Equator, too, with the heat and sweat. I surmise it is vanity; he's always had a sneaking idea that a beard would fit his manly form and seized this unparalleled opportunity. Now they've seen the result, many of the beards are coming off again. In some cases, it's laziness, of course. The exchange of parcels with the Women's Camp was stopped because of unauthorised meetings – of husbands and wives! I hear that the Governor, General Macrae and three judges – Trusted, Howell and McElwaine – are to go on Wednesday. The camp is agog with speculation – and there is a mighty laugh when we learn that their instructions say they are not to take forged money or pornographic literature or postcards. I don't know if I have chronicled it before, but many say the Nipponese were scandalised at the Governor meeting them in shorts and shirt at the capitulation – hence, partly, their treatment now. For lunch, we have rice, a vegetable, bully beef stew and fruit juice – one of the best meals we've had. The Camp Supervisor – the new title for Lieutenant Okasaki – complains that the internees are not showing proper respect to the sentries. When we pass, we must take off our hats and bow. Thank heaven I ain't got no hat. H.R.W. Lobb, who died recently, was a past president of the Singapore Swimming Club and, as his obituary notice says, 'one of the fast-diminishing band of pre-1914 stalwarts' – of whom I am a member.

20 July: The latest motto, I hear, is the kitchen staff's – 'We can take it.' In view of their known habits, it is very good. I see the Governor packing; he is very cut up. He hates leaving. He says no reason has been given, but it's obvious – they will be hostages. I say that, in that case, I don't understand the choice e.g. why Macrae? To which he replies, 'Oh well, nobody knows.' Lady Thomas, the Governor's wife, is not going at present, anyhow. The Governor and I shake hands and he thanks me very much for all I've done. I change a book at the library. En route, I observe two judges cleaning up the refuse yard rather incompetently! I send a note to Katherine. At 2 p.m., I am on firewood fatigue. We are lined up to be searched for money. I have none, but I'm not turning out my pockets like the rest, unless I'm told to. I merely say, 'No money,' and the searcher takes my word for it. We march out. I am on chips. I wander around with the Dutch district officer, picking 'em up. In due course, a Chinese arrives with two bags of tins. The district officer buys two tins of milk for $3. A sentry arrives and takes the lot from the Chinese. The sentry sells the tins to the firewood squad, some of whom, of course, have concealed dollars on their person. Whether the sentry just pinched the stuff, I cannot say. It looked very much like it and the Chinese dared not protest. At 3.30 p.m., it is very hot; the time is really 1.30 p.m. I join the 'regulars' (woodcutters) under a spreading rubber tree. I drink tea, eat three rambutans and a Chinese sweetmeat they give me – all very pleasant. We are back at 4 p.m., having filled one sack of chips and one of leaves, which they use for protecting young shoots in the vegetable garden. On the way back, I talk to a municipal officer. He came in last week; he was working in the power station. He is glad to be in. Things were getting very unpleasant for them.

21 July: Drew and I beat Crichton and Cutler in the Block Bridge Tourney. I skipper a B-Block team against Perak in a cricket match. We try dipping a tennis ball in melted candle wax. The result looks very good. I must try it on Friday. There is a great shemozzle on the outside fatigues. The Nipponese Commander reports four men, two for being found possessing money when searched and two for bringing in tinned goods. He directs that disciplinary action be taken against these four. In addition, unauthorised goods – cigarettes and tins of food – are found in a vehicle. We are warned that, if members of outside fatigue parties are found in possession of money or unauthorised goods, the whole camp will be penalised by: a) confiscation of all money in the possession of internees; b) the camp shop will be closed immediately and the goods returned to Gian Singh; c) no further goods will be allowed in. All fatigue parties and vehicles will be searched. (The fatigue parties were searched today and money found in boots, hats and other hiding-places.) Of course, the answer is that, if they had let us establish a proper camp shop where we could buy, as requested five months ago, this would never have happened. However, we MUST obey this now. A.T. Spitz, Governor of Sumatra, who has been in solitary confinement here for four months, is to go to Japan with the Governor and the others. It is by order of the Imperial General Staff, Tokyo. Holgate and R.P. Bingham go to hospital. G. Walker has died. In reply to an inquiry about the reasons for their solitary confinement, Okasaki says that Morgan and Scott are not internees. At a concert given as a farewell to the Governor, he makes a speech. He defends his decision not to allow all Europeans to leave the country in the lurch. If he had to do it again, he would make the same decision. Although our position here seems quite useless, I must say I think he was right. The Governor says: 'When a man from home goes out to a colony to live and work among backward people, he takes on himself, whether he likes it or not, his share of the responsibility for the good name of Great Britain.' One opposite us taking the place of Wyld (deceased) removes his artificial leg – a gruesome sight. He has a double hernia and can't see much. He has an ulcerated tummy and no false teeth. He stepped on them in the blackout.

22 July: I receive as part of my breakfast an egg which is doubtful, but I eat it. I chat to an internee who tells me lurid stories of more heads on poles, riots and the invasion of Australia. I conclude he is a hot-air merchant. I send parcels from the shop to Kath and Nic – a tin of Ovaltine rusks and a pot of marmalade each. At cricket, we get Perak out for 230 and go for runs quickly. I declare at 166 for 10, giving an hour for them to get 236. The last wicket falls five minutes before time at 222 – an excellent game. From Axel Munthe's 'San Michele': 'Imprisoned monkeys, so long as they are in company, live on the whole a supportable life. They are so busy finding out all that is going on inside and outside their cage, so full of intrigue and gossip, that they hardly have time to be unhappy.'

23 July: At 10 a.m., I lead a fatigue party of six to the main exercise yard. We proceed to the store, collect four bamboo brooms, two baskets, and a bucket of disinfectant, hooks and pricker with long handles, then report to A.M. Pilter. I remind him that last time I did that was just before the Singapore Mutiny in 1915 at the M.S.V.R. camp. He was corporal of our section! He explains our duties – to clean the drains, sweep up generally, scrub the seats of the latrines which are over the main drain and flush the said drain, among other things. We allocate duties: I get the spike and spend the next hour spearing debris and putting it into the basket. I have often watched our Kebun *(gardener)*. There's quite a knack in it. You must spear hard when the ground is hard. Eventually, we complete our various tasks satisfactorily and return. An astonishing number of people remarked they'd like to take a movie and send it to my family. The same thought seemed to strike them all. Weisy has arrived, stiff with luggage. The new Head Commandant is to be chosen by camp election. A hundred names are required in a candidate's support. Camp rumours say that, up-country, there are heads on poles all over the place. The Governor has to go to hospital with dysentery, so he may not go to Japan. It is well timed; he is very pleased. It must be almost the first time on record that anyone was pleased to get dysentery.

24 July: There are now 2,737 inmates, with 363 women and 50 children. For breakfast, we have kanji, tea, margarine and rice cake. The latter is most irritating – dry crumbs stick in the throat. At 10 a.m., I am leader of a fatigue party detailed to collect vegetables. We fall in in the courtyard, lined up – there are 10 from our room, and 30 altogether. We are asked by our own fatigue officer if we have any money. The answer is 'None.' We take a huge wagon with a steering wheel – a five-ton lorry with everything stripped bar the chassis. We push it a mile along the road to Singapore; we meet the Chinese contractor. We have two sentries. Jones of the Agriculture Department is in charge. The sentries exchange playfulnesses with the Chinese – a hint of the iron fist in the velvet glove, nonetheless. One sentry gives Jack and me a packet of Woodbines. Perhaps he likes our faces. The vegetables are weighed when possible and generally appraised. There is an argument about a sack of monkey nuts. The sentry says it has to go. Jones says Tokuda said no – it goes on the cart anyhow. Gus books his orders for the black market quite openly with a sentry. He will bring the goods in and they will be paid for inside – simple. The Chinese tell us the rice ration is two grams per man. We return at noon. Lots of our troops pass in lorries. They look very fit, but I hear there has been a lot of dysentery. It has been a very pleasant outing. At cricket, we try a new ball, treated with paraffin wax – it seems good. The rations brought in yesterday were much as usual – 17 carcasses of 3,116 lbs. gross. This has to make five meals for 2,734 people i.e. three of mince and two of stew. We also receieved 1,822 lbs. of sugar, 600 lbs of salt and 805 lbs of ghee.

25 July: At 8.30 a.m., Fairy has just soaped the whole of his body, prior to taking a shower, when the water goes off. A present from the Nipponese arrives – eight reams of paper for our room. It turns out to be Chinese toilet paper. We distribute one per squad! During breakfast, a Nipponese sentry arrives. He argues with Gus about the prices of yesterday's order. There is no bowing in this – not even standing! A parcel arrives from Katherine – a pair of Chinese trousers and a razor blade – very nice of her. The Governor has 'acute bacillary dysentery,' our doctors report. The Nipponese don't accept it; they send their own doctors to confirm or otherwise. Several sentries come into our room today on black market business; it is a curious state of affairs. I hear they are going back to Japan soon on leave and want money. At 7.30 p.m., there is a concert by the Empress of Asia lads; there is a big crowd – over 1,000. The concert is quite good. Bones Kirby is the star. It is a strange contrast – 8.30 on a tropical night; 1,000 Europeans are squatting in the exercise yard; a man is singing 'Somewhere a Voice is Calling', there is not another sound. Suddenly, out of the sky, there is a drone of five Nipponese flying boats passing low over us. If thoughts could be translated into actions! This afternoon, I am doing a crossword. Young Rusk says, 'Ah, Mr Kitching. My father would be doing them with you if you were at home.' 'Oh,' I say. 'Is he keen on them?' 'Yes, crossword puzzles and theatres; that's all he thinks about. Do you remember when that feller acted at Bootle – you know, that barber feller?' 'No, I don't remember; I expect you mean Sweeny Todd.' 'Yes, that's him. Well, my father took my mother to Bootle to the theatre to see him. At ten o'clock, he says, I'll just go round to the back of the stage and have a word with him. So off he goes. She never sees him again and he comes home drunk at 3 in the morning and brings the feller with him. Yes (with a slight sigh), you and me father would be just suited with each other if you was at 'ome.'

Sunday, 26 July: At 7.15 a.m., we run our usual nine times round the exercise yard. The course is lengthened by sleepers right across the concrete. We run round them, but the end man still disapproves and, on the third round, we find a ladder stretched along the last six feet, so Jack picks it up and throws it away with a loud noise! The place is lousy with Nipponese soldiers settling up with the black marketeers; it's a curious business. I negotiate for a 2-lb. tin of Lyle's Golden Syrup for $10. I think I shall take it. Money is running frightfully short now. About half of our room is on the 'free list'. Goods which can be drawn by such are specified – necessities only. Many of our troops have been moved from Singapore, whither we know not. *(Presumably to work on the infamous railway.)* Three of the kitchen staff are charged with pinching cooked meat! The crime is probably worth the punishment – a reprimand and a suspension of free issues for 14 days. Another gentleman, for attempting to take money out on an outside fatigue, is sentenced to 'no outside fatigues for 14 days.' Our only candidates for Camp Commandant to replace Macrae are Dr Johns (senior surgeon, Singapore) and Adrian Clark (judge).

27 July: Last night, Hope was not sleeping. He saw two figures steal out of our room. He followed and saw the black market in full swing in the wood yard behind the laundry. Bargaining takes place under the door, and then the goods are pushed under! The parties cannot see each other. I see Weisberg; he has no news. He was doing nothing until the last few weeks. He was in the Raffles Library; he is glad to be in. He is not fit, however; he has arthritis now. Our room invalid goes to Miyako Hospital. It is high time. The loose leg is horrid in the early morning and he has added piles to his list of disabilities. I read 'My Greatest Adventure' by Malcolm Campbell. While treasure hunting on the Cocos, he mentions as typical of the hardships they had to endure the fact that he had to eat a boiled egg without a spoon. This makes us laugh like drains. We have a discussion – some hang their wives' photos on their walls. I haven't one, but wouldn't if I had. Our circle agrees. We are buying the rice polishings. They provide the vitamins we are most deficient in, says the doctor. So he stresses the necessity of eating them. We have put various remedies to the Nipponese to relieve the financial strain: an advance from the Nipponese High Command, the International Red Cross, our bank accounts etc. I didn't know we even have to buy electric bulbs, all brushes and other gaol-cleaning equipment, and these so-and-so's have the sauce to say the place is not clean enough. More water economy is necessary: we have used 43 gallons per head per day for the last 55 days.

28 July: I am on a fatigue party cleaning B exercise yard. Hamilton and I do the latrines and refuse bins, the other two drains and sweeping. Hall and Cheeseman go to hospital. I chronicle only those I know; there are lots of others. The Nipponese are said to be offering $25,000 for information leading to the discovery of a secret transmitter, because the Singapore news is known in London in 24 hours. The figures for the election of Camp Commandant were: Johns 1,515, Clark 683. The Governor's transfer to Miyako Hospital has been held up by order of the Nipponese. I get goods from the shop for a bridge prize I won; very useful – real sardines, tinned vegetables, marmalade and Vienna sausages. There will be no bread tomorrow. The bakers are said to be on strike because their pals were sacked for pilfering beefsteaks. The real reason, I believe, is that they were sentenced by our Judicial Tribunal: then, on later information, the Tribunal increased the sentence. But the reason for no bread is no yeast, because the yeast expert is one of the sackees.

29 July: A.H. Dickinson returns from Miyako Hospital. In bed, I ruminate over my pots *(trophies)* which, presumably, are gone for ever. On the whole, I think I regret most the fine one given me by the Sultan of Trengganu for winning the Royal Trengganu Golf Club competition in honour of his birthday. It was a peach. Then my first pot – of all things – for winning the long jump at Peterhouse Sports! There was a solitary one for the S.U. Club billiards and lots for golf and tennis, with the men's foursomes at the S.E.L.G.C. with J.S. Aitken being a particularly nice one of beaten silver. And there were over a dozen tankards. Ah well; there are bigger things to think of. The only trophy I've kept is a set of evening dress studs and buttons, won at the annual meeting of the Senior Golfers. I shoved it in my case at the last moment. It takes up no room.

30 July: I collect a parcel from Nic – a jar of dripping. Holgate and G.G. Templeton go to Miyako Hospital. Three babies have been born at Kadang Kerbau – a curious coincidence – Sagar, Scott and Sleigh. How aggravating to produce a baby under these conditions. I am on rice-grinding fatigue from 2 to 4 p.m. There are six machines – only coffee machines – and the rice has to be ground four times before it's fine enough. It is monotonous and heating, but four to a machine gives us plenty of rest. I hand in my crossword 'Changi Compost' to the Exhibition of Arts and Crafts. I go to the exhibition at 7 p.m.; I cannot get near it, of course. I go again at 8.20 p.m. and get in to retrieve my exhibit. It is a pity that longer hours are impossible. There is a remarkable collection and no time to see it. I note a lovely set of buttons and a buckle, chessmen, box and board, a clock with date, a smoker's compendium, a great variety of chairs and pictures and sketches galore. 50% of some Indian regiments have gone over to the Nipponese, one hears, but the Gurkhas are steadfast. They are having a thin time of it. The women have been asked by the Japanese to put up typical pre-war menus – 30 women, 10 days' menus each! What can be the object? At 2 a.m., Jack wakes me. We watch for half-an-hour continuous flashes low down on the horizon due south. It looks like lightning, but I've never seen lightning so continuous for so long in exactly the same place. There are about eight flashes per minute. We surmise gunfire, hopefully. We scarcely believe it, but what the hell is it?

31 July: At breakfast, the new bakers' first rolls are quite good. In 'Guns and Butter' by Bruce-Lockhart (written October 1938), he says: 'To anyone who knows the East, it was already clear that, whoever won the war between Japan and China, the white races have already lost it.' It is probably true in the long run, but, now that the East has seen, the time may be postponed. At noon, I have a meeting with J.L. Woods, Van Hein and Gurney on the question of a permanent stage in the main exercise yard and the organisation of future concerts. These are not to be on a Block basis. We have planted 1,000 papaya trees within the precincts and fervently hope we never harvest the crop. They are four-foot high now. A few mattresses arrive; they cost $7.50 each. They are of poor quality and measure only six-foot by two-and-a-quarter foot. I lend Fendall $10 to buy one. Lots of people are still without – it is scandalous. At 10 p.m., we open a tin of real sardines and have a feast. I receive a letter from Katherine: she is very bucked with a parcel I sent her.

1 August: I put up the August entertainment's list for B-Block. I already have 18 evenings out of 31 filled with talks, concerts and other events. And I put up the August cricket fixtures list. Standing in queues for the library and other things which I won't detail takes a lot of time. Macrae and company have not gone yet! Today's cricket is first class. It is the first day of a three-day match between the Government and the Rest. The Rest for whom I play – score 218. The Government gets 156 for 4. I get four good wickets for 48. The new ball, waxed, is pronounced a success. The women are to be allowed to send a concert party across soon to entertain us, but the Nipponese instructions are that no 'passionate' dances are to be given! Cor! The orchestra has been ordered over to play to Oke *(Lieutenant Okasaki)*. We think it is a farewell.

Sunday, 2 August: The *(non-European)* Survey staff is said to be mostly back at work on 80% of their salary and with no allowances. There is no revenue except what is squeezed out of the public; the cost of living is up 100%. A prominent police officer was found in possession of $2.10 *(presumably to take outside the prison)* concealed in the collar of his shirt by our Camp Police, luckily. He was found guilty. His sentence – no outside fatigues for one month from August 1st; loss of privileges for one month from August 1st and of free issues of cigarettes and purchases from the camp shop; stoppage of credit, if any; and extra camp fatigues for 14 days from August 1st. (As this mean 14 days' cleaning up at the Wailing Wall, it is distinctly unpleasant.) Forbes goes to hospital for an operation on his varicose veins.

3 August: I use a new blade this morning. Exuberance always causes me to make long, dashing sweeps over the wide, stubbly spaces, as with the old blade. There is then invariably a cut, as this morning. It's the August Bank Holiday! Were it not for Hitler, I should be spending it at Old Trafford. On the last August Bank Holiday in England, I was on the Prom at Morecambe watching the Punch and Judy show with Brian. Its loudspeaker was blaring out 'Run, Rabbit, Run' – shall I ever forget that tune? How Brian loved the Punch and Judy show! The ration party yesterday got only 1,000 lbs. of meat. They had to go to Kranji and saw the Causeway. They also got 1,840 lbs. of sugar, 650 lbs. of salt, 630 lbs. of ghee, 300 lbs. of tea, 2,988 lbs. of flour and 50,688 lbs. of rice. The rice was very bad. We sup sumptuously off apricots and cream, topped by my last cigar. And so to bed. I dream I am running in a mile race, which I win in 5 minutes 25 seconds. The winner, an Asiatic, is disqualified for holding me back by the shirt-collar in the last lap.

4 August: The roll for breakfast is better than ever before and 'The Honest Bakery' have christened it 'Hovis.' I buy a second-hand Bible for $1. I always said that, if wrecked on a desert island, I would take a Bible, a dictionary and 'Shakespeare', but I didn't bargain for having to carry them six miles on the Equator, with all my other worldly possessions on my back. On the last day of the cricket match between the Government and the Rest, I have to go in for the Rest and make 5 to win. I do it and we win by one wicket amid terrific excitement, whoops, hoots and cheers!

5 August: Two months ago, the Women's Camp were given an order to embroider 5,000 badges for soldiers. They made it clear that they did not desire any personal reward. On Saturday, five cases of butter and 10 of milk were delivered 'as compensation for the work done.' The women are adhering to their decision and passing the goods to the Camp Finance Committee as a loan earmarked for charity. They will be sold in the camp shop. We have a bathing parade at 2.30 p.m. As before, about 350 out of 600 of us go out by the short path. I do not bathe. The water is very shallow. What a quaint sight – hundreds of men, stark naked, wading out, their bodies chocolate-brown to the waist, white to halfway down their thighs, then chocolate again! I chat to a Malay: 'Are things good?' 'How can they be, tuan? No work and no money until you return. And everyone steals. Someone steals my property and so I go and steal someone else's. And we can't buy fish without a pass.' All those pleasant seaside houses are stripped bare, completely looted. And it maddens me to see the marvellous fortifications stretching the whole length of the Singapore coastline – machine-gun posts, barbed wire – and not a shot ever fired, while the Nipponese came in at the wide-open back door, which hadn't anything. Thirty-four merchant seamen arrive. It's ludicrous how they crowd everyone in here. They were on the Hauraki which left Freemantle for Colombo on July 4th with a cargo of lead, wool and 1,500 cases of Australian whisky. They were captured by two cruisers returning from Madagascar. They got the ship and its cargo. The crew is mostly from New Zealand and Australia. They are as fat as butter and have been well treated. I fail to understand why they allowed the vessel and cargo to be taken intact. The reasons given are a) it was 10 p.m.! b) The Nipponese had their guns trained on her and threatened to blow them out of the water. What of it? These are the usual tactics. What else do you expect? 'Don't sink your ship, please. We'd rather have it.' The engineers, the captain and some others are still on board. They have to sail her to Japan. They were eight days out when taken. The Nipponese commander told them they were being brought here prior to repatriation about the end of September. The boilers are being cleaned, so we have tea, of a quarter of a tin of pork, beans and fruit juice.

6 August: On my morning run of nine times round the exercise yard, I note that the throng of al fresco sleeper's increases. One has to thread one's way delicately through the recumbent forms. We are 2,773 now. We have sent a memo, to the Nipponese, a strong protest. Cooking facilities are strained to the utmost, water and sanitary installations are overloaded, the danger of infectious diseases is always present. Many suggestions have been made to relieve the situation and none has been approved. One hundred and seventy-three internees have wives and children in gaol and, since internment six months ago, have not been allowed to speak. 'The Changi Guardian', in its cricket report, says: 'Kitching fought the vigorous attack amid rising excitement and, when the final two came just before time, there was wild cheering.' Firewood fatigue is quite a long walk now and a certain amount of hard work loading and pushing. I estimate that the double trip is three miles. Note: if you drop a coconut onto concrete, so that the side hits it, it breaks perfectly all round and in the proportion of one-third to two-thirds, so that Vic gets one-third and Jack and I get two-thirds. This apparently natural law is very convenient.

7 August: I do not go for a run at 7.15 a.m. Ill-fitting tennis shoes (size seven instead of five-and-a-half) chafed my heel on Wednesday. Farrer, Fatty King, Pretty and Maysar go to Miyako Hospital. Now Dalton has gone to hospital to have his broken leg dressed. I get 'Lorna Doone.' It is a good book so far. An author is the best profession for an internee! There is plenty of time. All you need is a pencil, paper and brains of the right type. Ay! There's the rub – I couldn't write a readable book to save my life. A fence is being put across the grass strip outside the corridor to enable the idle rich to lounge and read without seeing into the crypt. The interpreter originally suggested boarding up the crypt, but the women recalled the Black Hole of Calcutta and I should jolly well think so. What mentality!

8 August: The women go bathing today. Says Nic, 'I don't know whether they think they have interned a lot of Russians.' This is the result of the fiat, which has been issued by the Nipponese: 'Costumes must be worn.' I have a bad egg for breakfast. After smelling it, I cannot face another, so I don't return it to the kitchen.

You have to get a chit and produce the offender and mine is in small pieces. Practise my golf swing in the yard with a paper ball. Am not as stiff as I expected. The Nipponese send for three engineers. On learning they are to be employed making underground oil tanks (which the Nipponese didn't intend us to know), the Central Committee refuse to let them go. We await developments. There is a carnival from 4.30 p.m. onwards in aid of camp funds; it is a very good effort. There is a fortune-teller. He tells me that I am one of a large family and that I had a serious illness a few years ago – it was touch and go. He also says that I am going on a long journey shortly! There are hoop-la, coconut shies, crown and anchor, raffles and a band, among other attractions. The organisers capture the real atmosphere and the touts are as good as touts at home. There is even a wood-chopping and sawing competition; someone cut through a 20-inch diameter rubber tree in 96 seconds. C.V. Miles has been taken to hospital with some kind of fever. I meet a man who has been out here for 23 years and has just got benign tertian malaria for the first time, so there must be carriers about.

Sunday, 9 August: Nic and Isobel send lots of cream crackers to Donald and me, about 100 each – marvellous. Where did they get them? Wanted: internees with knowledge of Assam. There has been trouble in A-Block. Correspondence and an indiscreet diary have been found, as the story reaches me. A female internee has been taken to Singapore. 'The Syonan Times' of August 7th says: 'Grow more food. It is essential. It is to be planted on enemy-owned rubber plantations. The shortage is the result of bad administration by the British, but the Malayans must take their share of the blame, as there is responsibility both as government and governed.' It sounds OK, but the soil won't respond.

10 August: When is this hot, dry spell going to end? There are bugs in the mattresses all round. We take the mattresses out and deal with the bugs. The ants like 'em and the bugs have no defence. At his weekly meeting, Edmonds tells us that a second batch of postcards is to go off by the exchange ship, Tatuta Maru, due in now. These include those who did not send postcards before i.e. those from Miyako Hospital which was forgotten (!) and those from new inmates. There is a visitation from a large gang of Japanese former internees from the exchange ships bound for Japan from Lourenco Marques, along with some staff officers and others. We wonder what they think of Changi and our conditions compared with what theirs have been. Their manner as they file down the passage is not jaunty.

11 August: At 8 a.m., we discover that Birnie's mattress on the concrete is alive with bugs. We shall have to get it fumigated. Since his beating, it is difficult to get him to do anything. Cricket today is a curious match. Our team loses Jimmy Crick; he was seized with vomiting during the night and has been taken to hospital. We also lose Joe Ferrie; he has been a bad lad and cheeked a camp policeman. He is up before the Disciplinary Board. So we only have nine men to bat, yet we win. Hope and George Irving are sent for today. They are asked: 'Where are the plates and fair sheets of the topographical and other maps?' All have either been taken away or destroyed is the correct answer. There is someone on the Japanese side who is knowledgeable. We speculate whether the maps are wanted for development or defence! One of the most trying things over a long period is the complete impossibility of getting away from crowds and noise, even in the WC someone is waiting in the queue. The woman internee taken away on August 9th has still not returned. She was arrested by the Military Police and, as she had only returned from the Mental Hospital 10 days before, it is all very worrying. Her husband is in the camp for prisoners-of-war.

12 August: This camp is a living example of the falsity of the saying, 'There is no smoke without fire.' But, if these exchange stories are all bunkum, then the limit has indeed been transcended. Yet we have nothing official. The interpreter definitely tells Edmonds today that an exchange is afoot.

13 August: Laville, L. Forbes, C.V. Miles and Parnell record messages for their wives and families. I wish I could, but our wives may not be safe. Anyhow, Margie was on the same boat as my daughter, Joan, so I know Joan's safe. The Camp Committee informs us that the Japanese camp authorities take strong exception to forwarding messages to the Japanese High Command. But we point out that it is inherent in British principles of justice that there must be a right of appeal to higher authority. It is no reflection on them. The matter ends without their saying yea or nay. There are many rumours about what Admiral Namura and the ambassadors, our visitors on Monday, had to say about our disgusting conditions and food, but all seem to boil down to a Japanese officer who was detained longer than he expected. He asked for tiffin and got the same as we did and he didn't like it. We also have a rumour that we asked the ambassadors to stay for tiffin and they did. They asked where the meat, fish and vegetables were. They were terribly shocked when told that was all we got. So we see how things are embellished. The lights fail while we are playing bridge. We hope it is a blackout, in view of rumours of bombing raids, but it is only the main fuse blowing.

14 August: I see a list of names of those in Padang. Nora is not on it. In fact, there are very few I know, Mrs Harding, Boiler Brown, G.R. Percy, Wynne Dalley, D. Farquharson, G.B.W. Gray, S.A. Mountain, M.L. Phillips and Scobie Nicolson who left with the same batch as Nora. How did he get there? I have a meeting at noon with J.L. Woods to arrange final dates for concerts and other social events. Stuart opposite gets six weeks extra fatigues for pinching a pair of sandals in the laundry. We suspect he is a deserter. How hopeless I am at describing people. I am caught out in this camp over and over again. 'What is he like?' I haven't the foggiest idea how to begin to describe people.

15 August: Coles has gone to hospital with bronchitis and Brigadier Lord of the Salvation Army and C.V. Brandon have come in from the hospital. They are both very confident about an exchange. There is to be a section for beards at the next camp show! 'The Syonan Times' says there is to be a public holiday today for the half-anniversary of the New Birth of Malaya. On August 12th, a huge mass meeting of Indians in Farrer Park protested against the arrest of Gandhi. Gandhi had given a very anti-British speech. He was at college with me, damn him.

Sunday, 16 August: I have a clear space for my nine times round the exercise yard at 7.15 a.m. At last, the sleepers have been cleared off by the rain. They were there at 2 a.m., when I went out. I play bridge morning and afternoon. The Governor of Malaya and company leave this morning. I hear that they are kept hanging around the docks until 5 p.m., then they embark on a freighter with 1,400 of our troops. They have 21 days' iron rations; there is to be no cooking. The Governor is mixed up in the hold with all the others, I am told on unimpeachable authority. Although General Percival protests, it is useless. Nic has fallen into a drain and sprained an ankle.

17 August: There were a lot of bugs about the beds last night and this morning. We must air and search the beds as soon as I get back from my fatigue. We go out on a firewood fatigue at 10 a.m. This time, six of us have our own cart and six sacks which it is our job to fill – one each – with chips. We then have to load them on a cart and shove it back. It is quite pleasant. There is heavy rain and we get wet through. I sit in the Malay coolie line and talk to one. Their attitude is entirely 'wait and see'; this is a disagreeable interlude for them, but, of course, they can't do owt about it. Coming out of the gaol and proceeding along the road, the whole fatigue party of about 30 stops because we suddenly find we have no sentry. A concert is held in the main yard; I see half of it – it is very good. There is a skit on a quiz contest.

18 August: There are now 2,800 in Changi with 367 women and 49 children. Eighteen more arrive before breakfast! Where, oh where are we going to put them? They are from Taiping, I hear, and include an American missionary, miners, plumbers, an artist and a policeman The only one I know is E.V. Peters, the miner from South Siam. There are four Norwegians off a ship, the Hafthor. We also have a full-blooded Maori off the New Zealand ship. He is named Papua and is as broad and thick as he is long. The Governor has left a farewell message. It ends: 'I ask one thing of you: when the time comes, do what you can for the people of Malaya.' Eight regulars and volunteers made a daring escape from Pudu Gaol on the night of August 13th. I am told they got a duplicate gate key. Two British sergeants were recaptured quickly and were sentenced to be shot, but the order was suspended. At large are Macdonald, Bill Harvey and Vourerein. I am on a very heavy fatigue. We unload 320 bags of rice from eight lorries. Each bag weighs 224 lbs. A remarkable number of people can carry them on their back; I can't. The work is completed by

2.50 p.m., with all the bags stacked in the store – damn good. In the store are 6,000 lbs. of maize flour marked 'a/c Red Cross from Johannesburg'.

19 August: The finding of the Camp Police Officer on the theft from the kitchen case is that 'there is not sufficient evidence to justify the prosecution of the person or persons suspected', which is what we expected! We asked the Japanese for a conference between the camp medical officer and the prisoners-of-war medical officer, but it was refused – no communication is allowed between us and the prisoners-of-war. We asked for a list of local volunteer soldiers among the prisoners-of-war. They said, 'There is no need for an answer.' The camp is seething today. A Roman Catholic, a Church of England and a Salvation Army padre arrived from Malacca. They were told they were going straight onto an exchange ship, but after one night in the Southern hotel, they were sent here. During the night, I hear a ship apparantly hooting in distress.

20 August: I have had a letter from the Block Commandant asking if we will defer our run until 8 a.m. for the benefit of the sleepers-out! This throws our morning completely out of gear and we don't propose to do so. We run in tennis shoes and the noise is infinitesimal. The reply to the Committee who pointed out that the recent arrivals have been told they are intended for inclusion in an exchange is: 'Lieutenant Okasaki and Lieutenant Tokuda have no knowledge of any negotiations for an exchange.' My tummy is out of order, although there is no discomfort. The deaths in six months in the Men's Camp total 26, giving an approximate rate of 25 per 1,000 per annum. Weisberg goes to hospital with sciatica.

21 August: Paley borrows $200 for a day or two – the sentries are leaving and have to be paid up! I go on a fatigue with Macnab, sweeping B yard and cleaning the drains. It is quite strenuous and the water being turned off doesn't help. There is a meeting at noon of the entertainment's representatives for B, C and D Blocks. We fix dates. Johns, the new Camp Commandant, issues a statement about our attitude to outside fatigues for the Japanese quarters and related duties. It says: 'The conditions under which we are interned are unjustifiable, possibly unprecedented.' But we must walk warily for fear of reprisals. There are many women and aged here. He disapproves of our cleaning the houses of the Japanese, cleaning fish for their meals (!) and serving meals to them, but it can hardly be called 'aiding the Japanese war effort', so we will take no action at present. But anyone who strongly objects can say so and an effort will be made not to put him on such fatigues. It is very anger making, I think. I haven't been on one, luckily. I believe Bags was on such a fatigue – fish-cleaning and waiting! Pamadasa, who was teaching outside, boggled at teaching his pupils to salute the Nipponese flag three times a day. He lost his job, but hats off to him. We have received from the South African Red Cross 3,648 lbs. of jam, 2,150 lbs. of soup and 640 lbs. of sweets (vitamins A and C). I am planning our next concert, but Buster has gone to hospital with a hernia and Osborne is contemplating the same. That seems to bust our organisation from B-Block for some time. Belgrave goes to hospital. Neilson of our squad is already there. I finish 'Accident' by Arnold Bennett, write up my diary and so to bed.

August 22nd: After breakfast, I spring-clean. I wash my groundsheet, debug my mattress and find a small pocket of about six bugs. I clean and polish the haversack. I air the contents of my suitcase. A Sikh guard contingent begins to take over from the Japanese. Are they ex-police? And is the reason infinitely complex on account of the size or are all the troops needed, or both? I understand the black market was handed over last night! Okasaki is going to be the adjutant to the Officer Commanding in the Changi area. Nattrass is an ingenious old man. He has made a frying-pan using an old iron, a bit of the top of a car and a specially-adapted old kerosene tin stove. A Sikh sentry on duty for the first time sees a police officer who was his superior formerly and says, 'Tabek, tuan.' *(Greetings, sir)* He is overheard and gets his face slapped. I go to a talk by Edwards of the Forests Department on a trip to Tasek Bera; it is interesting. I've always wished I'd gone there when I surveyed Pahang. I could easily have got Sakai guides. *(Native jungle inhabitants).* Jack fries Walls tinned sausages and two duck eggs for supper in Nattrass's frying-pan – a veritable feast.

Sunday, 23 August: A notice appears on the board: 'The Indian policemen on duty are Japanese subjects' (I thought Asia was being freed and particularly India) 'and you must obey them as you do the Japanese sentries. If internees do not bow to Indian policemen sentries, they will be severely punished.' Bow-wow. I play bridge in the morning and afternoon.

24 August: We hear another 100 are coming in. It's incredible. Where CAN we put them? Well, if true, it must be a gathering of the clans for the exchange, not that the Japanese could visualise it otherwise. Every nook and cranny of this gaol is occupied. But later we hear that the aged and infirm are going to the Alexandra Barracks to make room, that we are ALL going to the Alexandra Barracks; that the Major-General now in charge told Dalton there was no arrangement yet with the British Government; that Churchill has broken off negotiations as a result of the removal of the Governor and company; and that Kayn saw in 'The SyonanTimes' that 907 British internees are being brought from Hong Kong on the next exchange ship. So you pays your money and you takes your choice. I chat to Ferguson about earlier in the war in the Johore jungle. After capture, he was batman to a Japanese. He says that 3,000 troops defending at Muar retreated because 150 Japanese in boats got between them and Singapore. In the area where he was later, there were a small number of Aussies sniping and the guerrilla stuff gave an infinity of trouble. This confirms my view that, if we'd split into small units harassing the Japanese all over, we'd be fighting yet. Such units are immensely difficult to deal with in the jungle. Edmonds, with reference to the Sikh police, now our guards, says not to prejudge; they are acting under orders and probably find it more distasteful than we do.

25 August: I win first prize in a 'Changi Guardian' competition with a glossary I have compiled. The prize is a packet of cheroots and a packet of Chinese cigarettes. The Camp Committee have pointed out to the Japanese that they are a bit premature in saying that the Sikhs are Japanese subjects! They are not – until the conclusion of peace at any rate. Nic is out of hospital. The rumour there is that all fat internees are to be taken to Tokyo, so that the Japanese can see how well we have been fed. Rice tummies are being ruefully looked at, says Nic. Kayn tells us of a man who had cancer of the throat. He used to breathe through a hole below his neck and was at times in great pain. He used to drink whole bottles of neat whisky and could not get drunk no how. Why? Pop Wiseman and C.C. Brown go to hospital. We buy a 2-lb tin of Lyle's golden syrup for $10 and eight ounces of Marmite for $9 on the black market.

26 August: I witness more face-slapping of a Sikh sentry for not saluting properly the way the Japanese like it. The B-Block strip of grass between the high wall and the passage is now open. It is to be a haven of peace for readers and others. There is to be no talking. So there is a notice: 'B Sanctuary. Do not pluck the flowers or disturb the wild life. You may sleep, but do not snore. Keep your B-trap shut. Silence is golden. Gather riches here.'

27 August: An early rumour: the Duke of Kent has been killed when flying over Britain. *(The camp telegraph is again fast and accurate. The Duke of Kent was killed on August 24th in a plane crash in Scotland on his way to Iceland.)* 'The Syonan Times' says that, in spite of the 'evil scorched-earth policy' of the British, the hydro-electric installations are now in working order, also 70% of the tin mines. I go out on the wood fatigue at 2 p.m. I am on chippings. We now have a chipping cart. Six of us each fill a sack and we push the cart back at our leisure. It is really quite a pleasant outing from 2 to 4 p.m., with a little gentle exercise, stooping and walking. I talk to Barraclough. He got an urgent cable to return and got back from Australia on the Gorgon, the last ship, a fortnight before the capitulation. How very annoying! A man in our gang meets several Malayan and Tamil employees. How pleased they are to see us! He also observes a Chinese cyclist go up to a barrier on the road, with tins piled up high behind. He gets off, approaches the sentry deferentially and produces a pass. The sentry speaks; he replies. Obviously, neither understands a word of the other. A couple of face-slaps are obviously necessary, after which and more unintelligible altercation, the Chinese is allowed to proceed. And Don tells me of two more face-slaps of Sikhs today. Don also asks, 'Do you know a man named Ewens of the Electric Company?' 'I think I do, but very slightly. Why?' 'Well, he came to me this morning, quite shaken, and asked, is Tom Kitching in here or in the military camp?' 'Here, why?' 'Oh, I had the most realistic dream. He was in a coffin awaiting burial and I saw his eyes open and knew he wasn't dead and I was rushing around looking for a doctor and couldn't find one.' I have a lot of congratulations on the Glossary.

28 August: I get busy on my pre-internment diary. The proprietor of the Sun Studio in Kuala Lumpur is a big noise there now; it's the same with certain people in Malacca and other places. R.K. Bell went out to the hospital to give a pint of blood to Lady Heath. He had a good day! Lots to eat and drink. I meet an Indian when out on a fatigue party. He hopes the English do not think they are doing nothing because they like the Nipponese. He is very abusive about them.

29 August: The secret of making this life tolerable is to have something to do that you are really absorbed in, like my diaries – if only I had them here. Even the 1942 pre-capitulation is helping to pass the time very well. A coincidence! Morris, who, reminds me muchly of Harry Baxter, hails from Carnforth. His father was stationmaster there. He has relatives in Kellet called Fell. His mother's name is Postlethwaite and she comes from Cumberland 'somewhere Millom way'! *(These places are close to Tom's Home territory. Nora had Postlethwaite relatives.)* Our memo to His Excellency, the Commander-in-Chief of the Nipponese Army, Malaya, points out that 'the men and women interned at Changi are neither combatants nor criminals, but peaceful civilians who, like every one else in the world, owe loyalty to the country to which they belong.... Many of them at the time of the capitulation were in Malaya solely for the purpose of carrying on the essential services and assisting the local inhabitants. For more than six months nearly 2,800 civilian internees, including women and children, have been living in a prison built to accommodate 600 convicts.... Relief in these urgent matters of accommodation has repeatedly been promised, but, instead, additional parties of internees have been continually added, with the result that the position has become an almost desperate one. There has been no Red Cross visit, no financial assistance. Nothing has been provided – no cleaning materials, no bedding, and no medical supplies. We have had to find our own and pay for them. We have been constantly ordered to keep all parts of the prison clean, but nothing whatever has been provided for us to do so. Many are still without beds, pillows, mattresses, blankets and chairs. There are no facilities whatever for recreation, except for two short visits to the sea beach. There has been no communication between husbands and wives and children. A comparison with other internees culled from The Syonan Times: Manila, S. Tomas University – 3,200 internees in 64 acres, Changi – 2,800 in less than 11 acres. In Hong Kong, they are in villas. In Peking, they are in their own houses. There have been no parcels and only one postcard in six months.' An appendix gives a comparison of the Nipponese scale of rations to us and ours to Nipponese internees. I am to get my films at last! There are many mosquitoes. I am bitten a lot. I hope they are not anopheles.

Sunday, 30 August: We decide to rest on Sundays and don't go for a run. The new Japanese Commandant, I am told, is Oxford-educated and named after the beer Asahi. The cricket meeting fixes up a Changi Cricket League with seven teams. There will be 65 minutes of batting. There were scenes reminiscent of Whipsnade this morning. The Nipponese drill the Sikh sentries here. They goosestep, turn and halt with many barks and growls, neither side being able to understand the other. One sentry cannot get the idea at all. He is completely unbalanced. This is not surprising, as he is poised on the wrong foot with the wrong arm stuck out behind, so to speak. I inspect my films properly. It's a pity. They would have been most interesting. One lot is completely ruined. However, I'm lucky to get any, I suppose. My right big toenail seems to have another growing under it. Men and their hair – why is it so many seem to be so vain about it? All over the room, you see them spending far more time over hair than the rest of their toilet and even those who never appear to wash or look after their personal appearance at all will value their 'quiff' highly. The barber can't touch it and they may be without trousers, but never minus brush and comb. An orchestral concert is held in the Big Yard.

31 August: The Dutch are celebrating their Queen's birthday. She has reigned since 1898. 'Je Maintiendrai' is the motto of the House of Orange – and a very good one too, I say to Parlevliet who is looking for cardboard to mount the motto on. I arrange all the fixtures for the cricket league – seven teams – two from each block and one from the kitchen. I also arrange the entertainment's diary; B-Block's turn is fixed for September. Thomas and Joseph from the Education Department were sent for yesterday and asked to write propaganda! There was nothing doing, of course. I hear that the new Japanese Commandant has agreed to 1,400 books being transferred from the Raffles Library. I pick our cricket side for the away game. I skipper B-Block. I ask Gick to tell Butler. Says he, 'Oh, he won't play.' 'Why not?' 'He's got a bit of Chinese stuff over the other side.' The shopkeepers are said to be increasingly reluctant to take Syonan money. I go to the Dutch concert at 8 p.m. They have taken infinite trouble. There are only about 27 Dutch in camp. Yet they have decorated the stage with greenery and a small windmill left and a boat right. There is a huge audience of over 2,000, I'd say. Parlevliet speaks in Dutch and English. Johns speaks very well and we give three lusty cheers for William of Orange. There are orchestral and other items. Van Hien reads a passage from Morley's 'Rise of the Dutch Republic' on the siege of Leyden. I hear that, as a result of our memo, we are asked to send a deputation to the Nipponese High Command to expound the Geneva Convention as it relates to internees. There are mosquitoes late at night – and we have no nets. They seem to go for one's hands and feet. Perhaps our hides are too much for them now? The rumour is that, when the United States bombed Tokyo, the shadow of a plane passed over the Imperial Palace and this was so heinous that it caused a crisis in the Cabinet and the two highest A.R.P. officials committed hara-kiri. And the bombing occurred, curiously, just as Tokyo Radio was blaring forth that it never could happen. *(American B-25's, led by General James Doolittle, flew off from the aircraft carrier Hornet and bombed Tokyo on 18 April. Tom Kitching and his fellow internees are as always remarkably au fait with world events. They seem to lean one way, then the other, as far as their own fate is concerned, particularly as regards the possibility of repatriation on an exchange basis with Japanese internees in Allied hands, but this is probably quite deliberate manipulation by their captors, in the hope of keeping the internees confused and docile – almost like a Chinese torture.)*

– VI –

FAIR WINDS AND FOREBODING

Starting with the Battle of the Coral Sea in May, then advancing ever more strongly with the Battle of Midway in June, the tide of war in the Pacific was already on the turn. On 7 August the U.S. landed on Guadalcanal where the Japanese were building an airfield. Battles here and in Papua-New Guinea seriously challenged the myth of the Japanese infantry's invincibility. Tom Kitching and his friends in the overcrowded misery, disease and suffering of Changi Prison sensed some of what was going on in the world outside, but it was difficult for them to sift the facts from the dross of all the information and rumours flying round the camp.

1 September 1942: I have increasing difficulty in swallowing anything above the size of a pea. I ought to see a doctor. A Sikh sentry hits one of a fatigue party, so all refuse to go out. Apparently, the situation arose because we have never been numbered off, but, this morning, they were. One group did, but the second group stuck at an Irishman. The Sikh ordered him to number. He didn't. The Sikh referred him to the Japanese n.c.o. who apparently said, 'Make him.' The Sikh said, 'Number' and, when the Irishman did not, he was struck. Whereupon, the fatigue parties all came back in. There was an inquiry with no officer present, as far as I can gather. The Sikh was alleged to have been called a black bastard. His word was taken and the Irishman, Fitzpatrick, was beaten with a strap. Johns, our representative, went to protest and was locked in the lavatory. All this was without the knowledge of Asahi, the Japanese Commandant, who arrived later when Johns was being searched for! Nobody knew where he was. Then Asahi went away and the Nipponese let Johns out. Asahi came back unexpectedly and saw Johns, but apparently thought he was the culprit and gave him a few words of advice. Johns later had handed to him a letter explaining what had occurred. In another incident, when Dr Evans went into the offices on business, he was ordered to wash an n.c.o.'s cups and plates. When the doctor told others that he had been told to wash them, Ewart took them to the kitchen and left them. An Indian orderly was sent to find out what had happened. He told somebody in the kitchen to wash the n.c.o.'s dishes and was promptly told what to do with himself. So we shall have to wait and see, but it is intolerable if any Tom, Dick or Harry of a sentry is to be allowed to strike internees or order them to do menial duties. And the outrage to Johns is indefensible. But, in a way, it is encouraging. All the Anglo-Saxon traits are showing up. If so, the others will follow when the test comes. The Nipponese have tried to get schoolmasters and journalists to do propaganda; the orchestra to go out and play; and certain women to sing, do shorthand and other duties. In all cases the reply to the invitations (which carried a hint of freedom) was 'Sorry, no.' I have a busy morning on the entertainment's program. We play cricket in the afternoon – our first league match!

Elections: I am asked to stand as Block Commander, but I won't. The camp is now under the control of the Military Administration Department (which is really as 'civil' as anything in Singapore.) Mr Asahi, who is the equivalent of a Lieutenant Colonel, is Custodian of Enemy Civilians in Malaya and Sumatra. W.E. Jenkins has died, aged 48. We now have six lorries and an ambulance; they ask for the names of two ambulance drivers, 14 lorry drivers and five mechanics for servicing. I don't know yet what the idea is.

2 September: The fatigue parties go out – all is quiet on the Changi front today, outwardly, at any rate. A.J. King sends news via Bruce who has just come out of hospital. King is progressing, but he will be in hospital another month. He can now walk a few paces. He sends me one dozen duck eggs, one container of salt and four tins of milk. I do my diary in the morning. In the afternoon, I watch the second cricket league match between C-Block's first and second eleven's. A returned engineer tells of a Tommy being nagged by Nipponese sentries. He eventually KO'ed one. He was punished by being locked up jammed standing up, and kept without food and water. Then there was a further period with water only. Then there was rice and water for a longer period. When the engineer returned here, the Tommy was still in prison.

3 September: In the main yard, I watch the Sikhs change guard. Alas for our once smart Sikh police. They are so confused with the changed drill and the barked instructions in Japanese that they don't know their right from their left. And the bowing! 'The Changi Guardian' reports: 'The Changi Cricket League, long expected, is now in being, thanks to the untiring energy of Mr Tom Kitching.' Mrs James has died in Miyako Hospital. Her husband is here in Changi; he was chief electrician for the Raffles Hotel. We agree to some women working for Asahi – in the Fullerton Building, I believe. He assures us that it is in no way connected with the war effort. It is the collection of information regarding enemy civilians under the Hague Convention. 'The Syonan Times' informs us that one Nipponese is worth at least six white soldiers, because he fights for ideals and for love of country, but the whites are materialistic and fight only under the influence of rum and drugs. At 4.30 p.m., the whole camp is in a ferment and all because a paragraph in 'The Syonan Times' about an interview with an official in Lourenco Marques. He is alleged to have said: 'Arrangements will be made as soon as possible for the repatriation of about 4,000 British subjects remaining in East Asia.' 'So that's it,' say the optimists, and proceed to put initials on their bags and so on. 'No, it isn't,' say the pessimists. 'It's Shanghai and the rest. We're not in East Asia and it's all lies anyway and the official never said it.' Personally, I think it does mean us, Hong Kong and the Dutch East Indies; we may get away in two months or so. Johns has had a talk with Asahi. I don't know the gist, but Asahi certainly said we would get enough cleaning materials for two months. At 7.30 p.m., there is a United Service of Intercession in the Big Yard on the occasion of the third anniversary of the outbreak of World War II. All are there except the Roman Catholics. There is a big congregation and it is an impressive service. I rather take exception, however, to the prayer for the rulers of ALL nations – why should I pray for Hitler, Mussolini and Hirohito? And there is no prayer for victory.

4 September: On our 7.15 a.m. run, we discover that the sleepers have purposely stymied us, but we run 11 times round the minor axis of an ellipse – half a mile – thereby pattering past much more frequently. My throat obstruction is very bad. I must see a doctor, but first I will stop smoking for two days and see if it is due to that. According to 'The Syonan Times', the Government of Malaya says that the Nipponese will educate the youth of Malaya properly. We only did it intellectually. They will educate them intellectually, spiritually and physically. The reaction of people to rumour is very interesting: some are up like a rocket and down like a burst balloon. Some (like myself) are very bucked to hear good, but not down and out when the rumours are knocked on the head or when the news is bad. And the third category takes absolutely no notice of any rumours, which may be strong and silent, but causes them to miss a lot of excitement! Asahi wants particulars of the money we brought in, what has been spent, who guarantees the loan if we get it, and so on. Then he will pass the information on to Tokyo, but we can't possibly hear before mid-October. H.H. Bell goes to Miyako Hospital.

5 September: I go to the dispensary and see the doctor about my throat. Naturally, he cannot diagnose. It may only be a spasm, he says. It possibly may be a growth, but not likely, as there are no other symptoms. Am I worrying? I am not. I don't believe in worrying when it's entirely useless. I am to see the specialist on Monday. Meanwhile, I am to take the medicine and I am not to smoke. A Chinese is brought in. He has been punished outside. I don't know what his offence was. We believe in corporal punishment after a fair trial with strict control, but Johns issues a notice: 'I have again been given instructions by Mr Toyoda, the Camp Commander, in connection with bowing to sentries on duty 1) at the main gate, 2) at the entrance to the Women's Camp, and 3) in front of the guardroom. If two sentries are posted, internees must bow to both. Mr Toyoda is not yet satisfied with the manner in which the bowing is being carried out and has stated that he will punish internees who do not give this salutation properly. The bow is a slight flexion of the whole body from the hips and should be given while at the position of attention, facing the sentry. Individuals or parties of two or three should all bow. In larger parties, the leader only should bow. I am instructed that this matter is to be treated seriously and that any internee who gives the impression that he is treating these instructions frivolously will be punished.' Nora comes to me in a dream this night. We have a long, intimate talk. I feel sure she is all right.

Sunday, 6 September: We are to have a course entitled 'A Study of British Malaya.' The course will study 'The Growth and Development of British Malaya.' The lectures will be from 12 to 12.45 p.m. every Monday and Friday after September 27th. The following are the lectures:

1. Historical Survey – J.B. Neilson;
2. Constitution and Administration – Adrian Clark;
3. Geographical Survey – T.J. Thomas;
4. The Malayan Budget – H. Weisberg;
5. The Trade of Malaya: a) The Rubber Industry – R.O. Jenkins, R.J. Chittenden; b) Mining – H.A. Coates; c) Agriculture – W.N.C. Belgrave; d) Forestry – J.G. Watson; e) Commerce – E.C.H. Charlwood;
6. Health and Medical Services – R.B. Macgregor;
7. Education – H.R. Cheeseman;
8. The Principal Races in Malaya: a) Chinese – A.B. Jordan; b) Malay – W. Linehan; c) South Indian – Their Background and Culture – A. Heywood-Waddington; d) Eurasian – Trevor Hughes; e) Europeans – A.N. Kenion;
9. Labour: a) Chinese – W.L. Blythe; b) Indian – H.T. Haswell;
10. Law and Order: a) Law and Justice – N.A. Worley; b) Police – A.H. Dickinson;
11. Municipal Administration – R.J. Fatten; Development of Surveying in Malaya – T. Kitching;
12. Transport and Communications: a) Road and Rail – A.L. Stallworthy; b) Postal and Telecommunications – W.R. Dowse;
13. Flora and Fauna: a) Flora – J.N. Milsum and J.G. Watson; b) Fauna – E.O. Shebbeare;
14. The Co-operative Movement – R. Boyd;
15. The Press – W.A. Wilson;
16. The Social Services and Youth Movement – H.A. Lord;
17. Symposium of Sports Talks, including reminiscences on soccer, cricket, rugger, hockey, tennis, badminton, athletics, the Turf and swimming;
18. Social Life and Entertainment – E.A. Brown.

There is a remarkable display of talent, industry and patience at the camp exhibition. The pictures are excellent. There are articles carved out of coconut shells –

ornamental and ingenious – brooches, buckles, buttons and ashtrays. There is a pack of cards made from cigarette cartons! There are pipes of rubber-tree wood. There are models of ships – the Mauritania, the Hood, the Empress of Asia and a very well finished speedboat. There is an evening dress made of bits of everything and, mounted on a frame, it looked just the stuff. There are clay models of heads, life-size. There is a competition for the best beard grown in Changi. I don't know if Mr Kra won. He should have – he is just like the monkey who blows his cheeks out, seen from behind. And, talking of behinds, I wonder if our gent who has an eye tattooed on each cheek of his behind won the tattoo competition? Basil O'Connell wins the beard competition. Among the contributions from A-Block are three quilts worked for presenting to the Red Cross. Each patch was sewn by a different individual – most amusing. The bookbinders have a good exhibition; one book 61 years old has every page hinged to its fellows by paper strips. The whole was re-sewn and a new cover was made from the lining of a dinner jacket.

7 September: Following doctor's orders, I do not go for a morning run. I should have been on wood fatigue, but Jack goes instead (by choice). I see the doctor at 10.45 a.m. Heron takes me to see Cameron. The laryngoscope reveals nothing. My throat is certainly a shade better than on Friday and Saturday, though it is still very annoying when I swallow. The final advice is that I may be worrying unconsciously. I should smoke less, take it easy and continue the medicine (which contains bromide.) I am to come back in a fortnight. 'The Syonan Times' says that M. Egle, the Red Cross representative, entertained to dinner by the Nipponese in Shanghai, said, 'Your kindness (to the prisoners-of-war) has been just wonderful.' Short-wave wireless is strictly prohibited; the penalty is severe punishment under military law. The reason, the newspaper leader says gravely, is the poisonous British propaganda. In his weekly report, Edmonds says we have asked if we can send postcards on the next ship (with the exchange). There has been no reply. Did any letters come for us on the last ship? The sentries now in charge seem to be looking for trouble. Last night, they stalked into the Fatigues Office where the band was rehearsing. They came in out of the dark and fussed because the band had not stood up. Why were they playing there? Who gave permission for a concert? Some ass has pushed a pencil through the Nipponese paper seal over the keyhole of the door to A-Block (the Women's Block). We have ordered 40 mattresses for the most urgent cases among the aged. The others have never arrived. All dogs are to be destroyed, except Scottie who is in a class by himself, says Edmonds. Is this racial discrimination? Anyhow, he belongs to the Women's Block and only comes over here when he wants a night out. Asahi has asked if we would like a radio (yes!) and a cinema (yes!), but we don't want Nipponese propaganda films. 1,400 books have arrived from the Raffles Library. Another letter about the 'noise' we make on our morning run mentions 'justifiable homicide'! Asahi says this is the Changi Enemy Civilians

Internment Camp and is not to be referred to as a prison. The name 'Singapore' is not to be used in correspondence. It is 'Syonan.'

8 September: Jack takes his run. A shower of rain in the small hours removed the sleepers to our shaving and bathing pitch, so we have to move to the tap. And they made a hell of a row moving, but that, of course, is NOT selfish! I hadn't realised that the doctor is one of the principal objectors, so no wonder he put a ban on my running! There is an amusing scene in the courtyard. Just outside the entrance to the Women's Camp is a husband, armed with the most decrepit broom possible. It has about one bristle and he is sweeping the drain. His wife emerges with him, goes back, then appears again. He sweeps one way, then back again – and so it continues. She has to bow to the sentry each time, of course. I air the mattress and bedding and find only one bug. He has led a blameless life; he is not gorged with blood. A ration party goes into town; I should have been on it, but refrained. They are allowed to take 50 cents for tiffin. They bring no meat, I hear. The meat supplied was bad. So are many of the cigarettes!

9 September: I write to the Commandant of B-Block, saying Jack and I are prepared to postpone our run to 7.30 a.m. Fairweather, Selby and Stallworthy all go to hospital. The number of people with bandaged limbs and extremities is still extraordinary. Is it my imagination or am I really hairier than when I came in, due to 205 days of wearing nothing at all except a pair of shorts? There is a tobacco and cigarette famine. The Sikhs cannot touch tobacco or even its container. Anyway, Rodyk says the black market is dead, at present, as the Sikh sentries are not playing. In the election for Block Commander, Edmonds receives 506 votes and Mr Justice Aitken 204.

10 September: In the semi-final of the Block Bridge Tournament, my partner and I beat Hassack and Latham, but only just! A review of six months of classes shows that there are 64 classes in 37 subjects – Malay, Book-keeping, French, Chinese, German, Choir-singing, Sight-reading, Pitman's shorthand, Gregg's shorthand, Bible study, Welsh, Russian, Siamese, Physiology, Biochemistry, Physics, History, Political thought, Malaya, Gardening, Swedish, Portuguese, Hindustani, Arabic, Japanese, Modern and Ancient Greek, Latin and Navigation. The Boys School must be a world record with seven pupils aged nine to 14 with a headmaster and eight masters – all professionals except two. 'The Syonan Times' says that the Raffles statue is being moved to a museum. You'd think they could have left THAT alone. Raffles found Singapore a malarious mangrove swamp, crocodile-haunted, almost uninhabited – and saw its possibilities. All this sort of thing looks as if the Nipponese have no idea they may ever be booted out. Curious! The newspaper says, 'The territory the Nipponese have occupied is greater than the British Empire.' I eat too much today, lashings of leaves from the garden at tiffin and a big helping of bully stew. I am just recovering at tea, then I get a much bigger helping of prunes than usual and eat them because they're good for me. It is too much. But there are nine stones, so she still loves me! The Commandant forbids bathing in the exercise yard before 8 a.m., so we can run, but not bathe. It's comic.

11 September: The Chief of Labour Control says: 'In the British regime, labourers were regarded as nothing but tools – with no facilities accorded to them as human beings! Now they are to be properly looked after as regards their health, food and other facilities.' (They were better housed and fed than we are now, anyhow!) The 'gigantic' war shrine on Bukit Batok was unveiled yesterday. (The above extracts are all from 'The Syonan Times' of September 10th.) Ledoux goes to Miyako Hospital with suspected dysentery. And Bayley is not too good. That lad Stewart has been convicted of theft again. He has admitted he is a deserter from the R.A.M.C. I go to the Beachcombers' concert given by the Empress of Asia men in the main yard, designated for the performance of 'Coonville'. They are all got up as coons. The stage is well done and the performance is amusing in parts. There is heavy rain in the night. The sleepers are outside. They make SOME row rushing inside.

12 September: I dream of Nora again, good. Parker, who goes to Johore Bahru for rice polishings, chats to the interpreter on the lorry. Parker asks: 'How long is this so-and-so war going to last?' 'Five years', says the interpreter. 'What? Are we going to be in this bloody hole five years?' 'Oh no. You are next on the list for exchange.' I see Dr Heron. Nattrass, Bayley, Ledoux – all have dysentery. They are all within ten feet of my bed; so is the latrine. This may be cause and effect. And Stewart, the deserter, who is also within ten feet, is sent to the military camp. We are to get meat every five days, hence the short supply. This is sensible, as there is no proper refrigerator here. 'The Syonan Times' refers to 'the miserable hordes of distressed humanity who were barely able to eke out an existence on the borderline of starvation in British times and who are now on top of the world! There is a lovely view from Bukit Batok where the Japanese shrine has been built. Nora and I have often walked to the top. The shrine gives rise to a discussion: is a shrine of this kind to be respected afterwards? Some say yes. 'The Syonan Times' supplies the information that Rommel is retreating. You can get a lot from reading between the lines. Sometimes we wonder if this is done purposely by the pro-British on the newspaper staff. I attend the lecture on the aborigines of Malaya. It is interesting.

Sunday, 13 September: How are the mighty fallen! The black market king has no condensed milk. Can I swop one for Symington's coffee essence and meat and vegetable? So I do! It seems that the Sikhs won't play. I expect they're too frightened. I play bridge all day and finish 63 up. Byron is going to Singapore tomorrow to draw up a dietary chart for Europeans for the use of the Nipponese. Why, no one knows. Still living in Singapore, to my knowledge, are Corner, Birtwhistle, Sennett and Dr Canton of the municipality. There is an orchestral concert in the main yard. It is very good. We now have a platform there. Puasa *(Muslim fasting month)* started yesterday. The Nipponese are going to honour it as if it were their own, with their usual solicitude for races previously oppressed by the British and their regard for the customs of all races, vide 'The Syonan Times'. They are a curious mixture. They have erected a shrine to our dead also on Bukit Batok. Some of our people were there to see the unveiling. They propose to scatter wreaths over the spot where the Prince of Wales and the Repulse went down.

14 September: There is no run for me at 7.30 a.m. I had better obey doctor's orders, although I'm sure it doesn't harm my swallow. The exchange baraometer is feverish; there is still no reason. It's to be next week! My foot! And there is a rumour that all those over 50 are going on Saturday! There are six cases of dysentery on one floor in C-Block. All go immediately to Miyako Hospital now by order of the Nipponese. Forty engineers are said to be coming into Changi soon. Will I put up a room layout scheme? There will be a subcommittee of Franklin, Bedlington, another and myself. I will take part. The point is that we may HAVE to find room for some and a rearrangement may be the only way. I hear that our electrical engineers are busy in town helping convert wireless sets to medium wave, so that they can only get Syonan. Isn't this helping the war effort? Don Grist tells a tale of marrows. He looked in his compost heap and found about 30 lbs. of them. They were perfectly good, yet had been thrown away by the kitchen. He took them out, distributed them to his pals and informed the authorities of the wastage. The kitchen representative said it was an error of judgement. They were soft, so they thought they were rotten and threw them away. 'If Grist finds any more, will he bring them back and will he take on the job of looking for them?' 'I will not,' said Grist. 'Oh well, if that's the spirit – no co-operation – I throw my hand in,' says the kitchen representative. When obviously what he should do is so to organise the kitchen that it doesn't happen!

15 September: There is unconscious humour in 'The Syonan Times'. Two headlines state: 'NEW ORDER SIMPLIFIES CHINESE FUNERALS' and 'NIPPON CULTURE – WHY DOES THE WEST FAIL TO UNDERSTAND IT?' The new census of Penang shows 66 Europeans as opposed to 2,500 pre-war. The newspaper says it is doubtful if 20% of the 100,000 men are in fixed jobs. But this doesn't matter – the balance earn their living as petition writers, running errands, pushing tricycle rickshaws and so forth. Burnham has gone for X-ray. The plates are running out, but they can throw it onto a screen, I believe. I suppose the Nipponese make X-ray plates? But we don't get them. We play bridge after dinner. Nobody plays bridge for cash now. Wins and losses are entered in a book to be paid on emergence from gaol. Very few people have any cash left. I still have about $300. Out of 100 people in this room, 75 are on the Free List. I have a meeting with the survey committee. We agree to redistribute the space in the middle of the room first, if necessary, and they accept my plan. The organisers of 'A Study of British Malaya' want a map enlargement. I undertake to get it done – India to Polynesia; Indo-China to Australia; 40 by 24. Five men have left to work in Asahi's office in the Chartered Bank; they live in the Customs House.

16 September: For the maps for the Malaya course, Walker has paper 40 by 24; Coates is supplying a board; so we progress. I try to get hold of an annual report on surveys for any pre-war year; it's no bloody good, naturally, so I will have to concoct my lecture out of my head. Nick Burnham had a 'marvellous day' in Singapore after his X-ray. He shopped in perfect freedom – dispensaries, haberdashery, Bata shoes, Aurora. He had lunch at the Rising Sun Cafe – tomato soup, fried fish, fillet steak, peas and brinjals, beer and stout. Today, 'The Syonan Times' has the speech of welcome given by the Mayor to Nipponese internees who have arrived on the Tatuta Maru from India and Great Britain. Those from India are going back to their old jobs in this country – planters, miners, doctor's etc. – And will be most useful, the Mayor says. Surely our Government is not so criminal as to let them come back, unless we are being exchanged too? Kelly and Walsh's has been reopened as a Nipponese book-shop.

17 September: All but 100 of 1,400 books from Raffles Library have been passed by the Nipponese for our reading! What on earth! We have mutton stew for lunch. Again I have to disgorge food which has not gone down. Something is definitely wrong. I am umpiring cricket when sent for to go to the Commandant's office. The Nipponese want the areas in square metres of various parts of the gaol e.g. the vegetable garden, the hospital doctors' accommodation and the exercise yards. They also want copies of the gaol plan. I inspect them and, after seeing Johns, tell them we can't do the work here. There are no facilities, material or, for that matter, draughtsmen. 'The Syonan Times' says that the evil influences of the British education system are to be swept away completely and replaced by an education in which the mainspring is faith in universal brotherhood. Floreat! Our half-squad were on lunch fatigue today, reduced to four members, Ledoux being in hospital and Victor somewhat incapacitated by a wound on the ankle which had gone a bit septic. So Jack and I took the two kerosene tins which had held the mutton stew for 100 and a giddy time we had getting the grease out of them.

18 September: We play in the Block Bridge Tournament Final against Gibb and Gibson and lose. We receive a letter from Edmonds – there is to be no running before 8 a.m. We feel very bolshie. Our Block plays a most exciting game of cricket against Block C's 2nd eleven. The game ends in a tie. Discussing food, one school argue that, as long as we are fools enough to provide the bulk of our own rations, the Nipponese will continue to let us do so and give us inadequate supplies. I am not of this opinion. I think we would have fared very badly without our own supplements.

19 September: Pendlebury, Preedy, Imrie, Johnny Papua and Sandy Simpson go to hospital. R.C. Weston has died at the age of 59. The schedule of education classes now includes (in addition to those previously noted): Tiu Chiu, elementary Spanish and Italian, magnetism and electricity, pastel drawing and applied mechanics. 'The Syonan Times' of September 17th contains an account by a Chinese nurse who, I think, must have been on Nora's ship. She left on a steamer for Java on February 13th. It had two direct hits from bombs. About 500 swam to a small uninhabited island (Pompong?). They spent three days and two nights there. They had two meals a day (half a cup of water, one piece of dog biscuit and one tin of milk among 12). On February 17th, a Dutch relief ship took her away. The next night, it was shelled and sank in 50 minutes, 'many going down with it.' She was on a raft with others. The majority died. She was finally picked up by a Nipponese ship and taken to Banka. Now, could Nora have been on that ship? The story is remarkably like the one Salmond told me on April 18th, but he was very definite that the Kota Pinang reached Batavia. They had a message to that effect. I cannot consult Salmond, as he is working in town for Asahi. There is a very late story at 10.30 p.m.: forms are in camp now with details of repatriation – the numbers in each batch, the particulars as to luggage and what not – all highly circumstantial. It is something to sleep on anyway.

Sunday, 20 September: We play bridge after debugging. What a turnout! All squads have regular dates for debugging now – not before time. I killed a few crawling on me just last night. Eveson says they are quite like the home bug, but the bite doesn't bother you. Certainly, I have never noticed bites, but the bugs are full of blood nonetheless. I cop seven on my mattress and a few in the crevices in our sideboard and wooden boxes. Last night's repatriation story is now entirely denied. Cherry was the alleged author, yet he had never heard of any forms. Who in the name of Heaven starts these things? The Nipponese, with their usual clemency to internees, are to allow fathers to see their children of under 15 years for 15 minutes once a week in the 'rose garden' in A-Block. 'The Syonan Times' is running heavy propaganda for people to learn Japanese. They say people evidently don't like it. The following yarn comes from the engineers: a party of Nipponese conduct a house-to-house search. The engineers surmise they are looking for a radio. The engineers lower their radio in a biscuit tin to one of their colleagues waiting at the back of the house. A sentry at the gate looks in the tin, says nothing and accompanies the engineer to a garage where another engineer lives. He sits on the tin. The search party arrives, turn the place upside down and find nothing. It transpires they are looking for stolen tobacco. The engineers are very relieved.

21 September: There are now 2,830 inmates, with 367 women, 55 children and six infants. The measuring in square metres of various parts of the camp has been completed, except for A-Block. So I go to the office. Dr Hopkins (Mrs.) introduces me to Mr Nakajima who is in charge. She deputes Miss de Cruz as chaperone and George and I are just ready to go in when there's a great to-do. Barrel Roberts was copped outside last night and the whole camp has to return to their cells for roll call. So done, I go up to the Nipponese office again, I shove my head through the swing doors and call for Miss de Cruz. I hope it's polite. Off we go, past the Sikhs. Her password is 'itu orang boleh masak, yah?' *(This person can cook, yes?)* We get the measurements for the vegetable garden, the hospital, the living and sleeping accommodation and so on. I see Mrs Thompson, Mortimer of the Censorship Office, Elkins and others. Nic says I'm getting thinner, but I'm nine pounds heavier than my lowest. I don't measure the crypt – fool that I am. A notice appears: duck eggs eaten raw have caused disease in Europe, so we are advised not to do it. This is a pity – I was going to beat them up with Klim *(powdered milk)*. This is officially to be referred to as Changi Internment Camp. Johns and Dr Hopkins are men's and women's representatives respectively. It transpires that Barrel was out on a beat-up with X and Y and was getting back over the gaol wall when the rope broke. He was last and decided to chance coming in by the main gate. He as a police inspector knows the Sikhs, but they daren't take a chance and he was handed over. He was tied up, as usual, and taken to the vegetable garden this afternoon to show how he got out. He is now being 'tried.' Rumour has it that he has already been beaten up. It was a very foolish risk just for a spree and it may have repercussions on all of us e.g. the use of Girdle Road we've asked for months. Now, if it had been an escape.... The immediate results are: more attention is paid to roll call. We are not to speak to the local inhabitants (as a result of a civilian giving cigarettes to an internee out with a fatigue party). The civilian has been 'severely punished.' George has lost his wallet containing $20, his sole remaining cash. It fell out of his pocket while he was squatting at the Wailing Wall. So I give him $10 and Fendall $10; he is broke too. I have a queer dream in a restless night, involving Nora, Kath and A.B. Cross. We are all interned together.

22 September: The morning passes rapidly, although I appear to do nothing. I hand in the area measurements. They are (in square metres): Girdle Road = 5,515; the vegetable gardens, men's = 7,323; women's = 30; exercise yards = 15,400 and 6,500; corridors = 2,036 and 382; offices (internees) = 78; kitchen = 1,158; stores = 488; laundry = 546; library = 40; carpenters' and cobblers' areas = 90; motor mechanics area = 20; doctors area = 174; dentists' area = 31; hospitals = 290 and 177; living and sleeping accommodation = 3,688; (B gate = 134 for 36 men, Labrador = 72 for 16 men, Victory = 290 for 61). Barrel is still tied up and now Dumbleton also. Kling, who gave the cigarettes, is released today. The ration party got 28 carcasses, 1,710 lbs. of mutton yesterday. The most expensive purchase I've heard of yet is a flint for a cigarette lighter bought in town by Dalton for $5. The dogs are again reprieved. Among them is Susie, a black and tan terrier belonging to Captain Anderson. She was born in Singapore in 1933. She was given him when a few weeks old and has never left the ship and rarely the bridge deck ever since – until last December, when he was taken by the Nipponese. Then the dog walked 34 miles to Singora and was with her master in the internment camps – Alor Star one night, Taiping five months, Kuala Lumpur six weeks and now Changi.

23 September: The maize flour is running out. Our daily roll now weighs two ounces. At 11 a.m., Cameron examines my throat again and says it is perfect. There is nothing to worry about. He is convinced it is something to do with the nerves of the swallowing mechanism (nothing neurotic). It may come and go. When we get out of internment, it would be advisable to let the doctors look at it properly with the proper equipment. But, if it was something serious, it would be bound to show up in the throat. We have asked for a permit to go to town to get valuable documents in safes and offices. There were a lot of mosquitoes last night. I was bitten quite a bit. Many places are worse than our room. If the mosquitoes are malaria carrying, an outbreak is only a matter of time, especially as our general condition is not getting any better. 'The Syonan Times' says the Tatuta Maru brought parcels for the prisoners-of-war 'direct from their kith and kin.' So we have asked if there were any for the 'poor bloody infantry'. And the newspaper says there are more supplies from the Red Cross. In my first spoonful of rice and stew at tiffin, something gets lodged in my swallowing apparatus and I have a most distressing time. I take no more tiffin. I cannot swallow. Even my own saliva will not go down. I try washing it down with water, but the water simply piles up and comes back again. I try to spew it up and it will not come, but, after half an hour with determined sticking of the fingers down my throat, up she comes – a small piece of mutton about a half-inch by a half-inch by a quarter-inch thick. So I show Cameron and, if they have the equipment at Miyako Hospital, he will arrange an examination there. I had a nasty hour and a half with it. 'The Syonan Times' says the goals of this war are a triumphal entry into London and a Naval Review off New York by Axis forces. And one of the newly-returned engineers, who has had much to do with the Nipponese socially and otherwise, says their idea is that Germany will deal with Russia, then the Axis will defeat the British Empire. The Nipponese will deal with the U.S.A. via Canada, which will let them in perforce, and about three years hence will come the final struggle for world supremacy between Japan and Germany. And the Japanese have their own view of the end of that! I finish reading 'The Vicar of Wakefield.' The world has changed more in the last 30 years than in the previous 150. The camp is stiff with stories of the fate of Barrel and the others in custody for the over-the-wall episode. They say they have given away the location of the place they went to.

24 September: It is very wet today and all fatigue parties are cancelled. Barrel and his three companions have been released, I hear. They are in hospital; they are apparently baddish. The bug which infests us is cimex rotundatus. The textbook says: 'By a wise provision of nature, the young bedbugs are sexless until they reach years of discretion, thus saving themselves from those scandals that can so disturb our family life. The young bedbugs or nymphs have five moults and it takes them some 24 days to reach maturity – but then, O boy! The female lays eight eggs a day, which is eight times better than the Buff Orpington can do. What's more, it can keep it up for months. Like the camel, it can go for weeks without a drink and, like the pigeon, it has a strong homing instinct, making for the same crevice that it feels it owns – altogether a most versatile creature.'

25 September: An official notice says that the four internees who were detained by the Nipponese authorities have returned to the camp. We are warned that, if there are any future attempts, the culprits and 'others' will be 'severely punished.' Fairy goes to Miyako Hospital, but I don't think its dysentery. Our books are full of small bugs. One does not know what to do about them. I suppose you can't cook books to 230 degrees as we did the mattress.

SONG OF THE RUMOUR-MONGERS
We are the workers of rumour,
The heralds of counterfeit hope;
From gossamer threads of a murmur
We fashion a perilous rope.
Before the beginning of daylight,
Around the war-world we have sped.
Like witches' dark runes in the grey light,
Our whispers awaken the dead.
We speak, and a city of ages
Is ringed with a terrible flame;
We dream, and the enemy's rages
Are stilled to vainglory and shame.

Guerrillas hold out in the highlands,
With banners of freedom unfurled.
Commandos recapture the islands,
Ill-lost to the civilised world.
We scorn the cool laughter of reason;
We mock at the mildness of fact,
For truth is the stronghold of treason,
When faith is besieged and attacked;
For we are the workers of rumour
The heralds of ———

(Tom gives no source for this song.)

26 September: I debug at 8 a.m. and find three large and a few small bugs in the mattress. Our next bathing parade will be on Wednesday and names are to be in by tomorrow! I shan't go. It irks to be chaperoned by Sikh soldiers and I'm not so keen on sea-bathing in any case. In a bridge league match versus C-Block's first team, Falconer and I win by 4,030 points. 'The Syonan Times' reports that, 'owing to unavoidable circumstances, the Malayan-Chinese Goodwill Mission's visit to Japan is postponed.' The Malayan dollar and the guilder exchange is to be stabilised at par. This applies to the Syonan dollar, the Nipponese military dollar and the guilder.

Sunday, 27 September: In his sermon today, the Archdeacon says 'thanks for the imminent victory of the forces of Right.' The Sultan of Trengganu is dead at the age of 53, alas. He was quiet and unassuming. This upset must have been a sore blow to him. Here is 'Roei No Uta' ('The Song of the Camp'), translated by T. Fujimori:

Having once left the native country with a brave determination
                                                towards victory,
How can one be killed without achieving brave deeds,
Every time on hearing a marching bugle,
Flash the remembrances of the waves of crowded flags through the mind!

Through endless soils of plain with graves and fires burning,
Marching flags of sunrise with soldiers in helmets,
How can anyone advancing on horseback expect life even tomorrow!

In a dream in slumber in the camp amidst shells, tanks and bayonets,
Appears father encouraging with the words 'Return having been killed,'
On wakening from slumber, dare to glare against the sky of enemy front.

How can one forget the last voice of comrade
'Tenno-haika banzai' shouted in today's battle,
When he died in blood with a smile.

Having determined to sacrifice life for country,
Don't chirp, crickets in a bush,
As never think of life more valuable than the peace of the Orient.

28 September: I pack my bag for Miyako Hospital. We have to take our own towel, toilet paper, soap, knife, fork and spoon. I have to be aboard the ambulance at 1.30 p.m., so I open a tin of Vienna sausages and have that with cream crackers for tiffin. The ambulance has eight dysentery cases, including J.A.P. Cameron and M. Baker looking like the wild man from Borneo. We travel 10 miles via Tampines to Yio Chu Kang. I see one car and one bus during the whole journey. I arrive and am told there is no laryngoscope, so I will just return at 4.30 p.m. Meantime, I chat to G.C. Bedington; he has been in hospital for five months with tuberculosis. Also speak to W.J. Mayson, then Bowyer takes me to the 'shop', a place in the hospital run by a Chinese employee and his wife, both very nice. A sentry comes up too with a Jap-Malay dictionary. He speaks scarcely at all, but we sit down at the same table – Bowyer, Spragg, the ambulance driver, Elizabeth, the wife, and myself. I have two Tiger beers (aha! at last!), soup, omelette, pork and beans. I can't pay, but they absolutely refuse any payment in any case. I buy 2 lbs. of honey in a bottle for $2, a packet of Chivers jelly and suet. Spragg's first job this morning was to collect a Eurasian woman and eight children in town. Her husband, a European, is interned. When he got there, the baby of two months was dead, so he brought the rest and left the relatives to deal with the dead baby. The woman has asked to come into Changi; she has no money, of course. Dr Elliott (Miss) of the Orthopaedic Hospital and Sister Grant arrive and have food and beer too. Grant asks me: 'Was it your wife who was at the General Hospital in Dr Cameron's house?' 'Yes.' 'Oh, she was such a dear. She did look after us well. I was one who persuaded her to make her decision to go on the Friday morning.' So we return, with the Jap, the two women and six cured dysentery cases including Ledoux and Sandy Simpson. At his weekly reporting session, Edmonds says parole is under consideration, but the Block Commanders know nothing. Rations from the Nipponese today are all much less e.g. 366 lbs. of salt compared with the previous 652; and ghee, tea, sugar and soap are all reduced in proportion. There is also an unidentified kind of flour and we are told there will be no flour at all and no cigarettes after October 8th. Our own supplies are running low and can't be renewed. Edmonds says the Governor arrived in Formosa on August 31st. Nothing more is known of his whereabouts.

29 September: The ladies' bathing parade takes place today; it is quaint to see them escorted by Sikhs! The fatigue party out fetching food bring back coconuts and bananas, but no eggs. There is not so much bombast in the latest 'Syonan Times' report on the war: 'Our nation remains determined ... to achieve ultimate victory.' There are sundry interviews with returning Japanese internees arrived in Japan. There are the usual complaints: Mr Zenammi, a chick-sexing expert from Great Britain, was interned, then released for four months, then reinterned. During the four months, 'we could not get a room in the hotel we had been staying at and, when we would go into a restaurant, people would shout, 'kick them out!' Dreadful!

30 September 30th: Keith White, whom I met in Kulim, was on a fatigue sweeping the courtyard. A Sikh sentry orders him to sweep the guardroom. He points out politely that his fatigue is not that and refers the Sikh to the Fatigues Officer. Tendang *(kick)* and, when the Nipponese in charge is referred to, more tendang. He receives many bruises. This is intolerable. Are we to take any order from any Sikh? If so, how can we organise our camp work?

1 October: There are planes overhead at 4 a.m., 7.30 and 8.30 a.m. I am told that troops passing Sikh soldiers in lorries invariably make the Victory sign. *(Tom reports what he hears with little comment. Perhaps the troops know something he doesn't, that the news on the war front is gradually looking better for the Allies.)* I have an idea about my swallowing problem: might it be caused by too much strong tea? I drink it far more than ever before and usually minus milk. I will try no tea for a day or two. I talk to R.J.H. Sidney about diaries. He is very complimentary about mine from 1.1.42 to 18.2.42. He offers to help in publishing them. He has much experience. Someone suggests 'Thirty Thirsty Years' as a good title! And I might; it's arresting! There is a competition for the best translation of a Malay poem. The winner is:

The limpid moon swims through the sky,
Its rays of hope through crannies shine.
When tide is full, our ship will ply,
Borne westwards by a breeze divine.

2 October: I've noticed for some time now that my fingers are quite numb when I awake and today I hear that 'concrete rheumatism' is the name for it. There have been many cases caused by our sleeping on concrete for so long. I've never had any rheumatism symptoms before. We purchase four new tennis balls for cricket – $8! The other day, C-Block Police played the Old Men's XI, the over-sixties. The first arrangement was that they were to give one run of a start for each year of difference in the combined ages, but this came to over 300, So they compromised on 200. The Old Men won by four runs! 'The Syonan Times' announces postal services are resumed to Burma, Borneo, Hong Kong, the Philippines, Formosa and China as from October 1st. So what? Complaints from returned Nipponese internees include: 'We only got the SAME FOOD as the convicts in Pudu Gaol'! And 'Women on St John's Island had to wash their own bed-boards'

3 October: From the Red Cross, we have received inter alia 5,000 lbs. of sugar, 2,100 lbs. of flour, lentils, ghee and 100,000 cigarettes (in cartons decorated with a large V for victory!)

Sunday, 4 October: At 8 a.m., while cleaning and sweeping up round my living space, I get a most violent pain in my right side. I cannot move. I am taken to the camp hospital on a stretcher. There is the usual routine – blood test and so on. They decide to send me to Miyako Hospital for an immediate operation, so Jack gets my things, then Cameron comes and says that a mistake has been made with the blood test. They diagnosed acute appendix or a stone in a kidney and had made all the arrangements then found they had made a mistake, but now I may have a holiday, as Cameron puts it. So I am carried to the ambulance, then to Miyako – a bumpy drive! It was formerly the Mental Hospital. Now it is the General Hospital, Singapore. We put a lot of mental patients on St. John's Island when the bombing was on, but there are cases still here. I am in Ward 27, bed 7. There are 36 beds. It is a treat to be on a bed again, but I don't like hospitals. There is a service at 7.30 p.m., conducted by the Rev. R.K.S. Adams. Lights Out is at 10.30 p.m. The verdict now is renal colic. A morphia injection (my first ever) gives me much-needed sleep.

5 October: The pain is much less. I can walk to the bathroom. Lights go on at 6.30 am! The patients are washed and attended to by Chinese boys. The nurses are Chinese and Indian; they are good and sympathetic. The doctors' names are Balhatchet, Chitty and Landor. I am not allowed to bath myself. I am washed by an Indian 'boy' and don't like it. There are hawkers constantly prowling round selling eggs (for 11 cents each), bananas, biscuits, Chinese cigarettes, cheroots and tinned stuff. They are continually being chased away by the Indian guard, but they return as soon as his back is turned. I buy cheroots for $1.80; and bananas and biscuits for 59 cents. I am to go to Kadang Kerbau on Thursday for an X-ray examination. I chat to G.C. Bedington again.

6 October: A Nipponese matron just arrived, addresses Nipponese nurses, stressing that Japan's is a just cause: 'I think you are inclined to be doubtful about it.' And, in the category of things that might have been better expressed, she mentions 'Penang, the first major Malayan town to feel the impact of Nipponese culture.' I buy a 2 lb. tin of Lyle's golden syrup for $3.80, eight ounces of vegemite for $2.40 and salt for 80 cents. On the question of repatriation, Dr Wallace asked Asahi when he could expect to get Lady Heath away to a temperate climate. 'How long can you keep her alive here?' 'A month or two by blood transfusion.' Asahi: 'It's all finished – a wash-out.' (Lady Heath had a caesarean operation and has been very ill ever since.) I stroll on the small lawn outside the ward in the evening. H.W. Evans is now very pessimistic. Does Asahi's comment quoted above squash all hope of an exchange? I think not. I can't believe our Government would not get us out, if possible. Why should we always swallow what the Nipponese say, if bad, and not if good? I feel certain that the women and children will not be left here indefinitely and, until they go, we don't. I remain optimistic. We may have a thin time if left. How will the Nipponese react to real bomb havoc in their homeland, which will come – and before long? Of course, early reconquest is not impossible, but I have never been optimistic about this. On my right is a very fat Dutchman called Hoope.

He is only my height, but weighs 14½ stones; he was 17! There is something wrong with his legs and his teeth are to come out. His Chinese wife brings provisions and sees him daily. Opposite is Sam Fortune of the Chartered Bank with gangrene in his leg. He has been sent here to have it amputated, but I think his leg will be saved. And N. Sullivan's mastoid was opened up this morning. He has been in pain and vomiting all day. On my left is an Australian – Passfield. He has been operated on for an appendix. He has a wonderful flow of strong language.

7 October: The Syonan Times has a headline right across the page: 'BRITISH MALTREATMENT OF NIPPONESE INTERNEES.' Mr Hon, spokesman of the Board of Information, cites six 'typical cases of enemy atrocities'. For instance, the Singapore Consul General was locked up in a criminal's cell at Changi! Another example given is that 3,000 were herded into 400 dilapidated tents at New Delhi. Only THIN blankets were provided (we haven't any); food was insufficient and frequently spoiled. (So they didn't have to cook it themselves!) A leader, headed 'FUTURE OF MALAYANS DEPENDS ON THEMSELVES' says, 'The local people who are working are working merely for their material benefit, for what they get out of it... The mere fact that those who are now employed are full of complaints instead of gratitude... constantly grumbling of the hardships they say they now undergo, is conclusive proof that they utterly fail to appreciate the realities of the freedom, happiness and prosperity they now enjoy....' The leader continues: 'They have been so used to whining and groaning as slaves dependent upon the favours of their former bureaucratic rulers that they are unable to understand that they owe it entirely to the enlightenment and benevolence of the Nipponese people and our Imperial Government that they are not working in chain gangs, herded in internment camps like cattle, with their womenfolk used as mediums for the amusement of their new rulers and their soldiers, which is the fate of conquered peoples in certain parts of the "enlightened" world of today...' I buy a folding chair for $3.50, a one-pound tin of butter for $2.20, milk for $1.50 and one kati of sugar for 60 cents.

8 October: The deterrent to taking infinite pains with this diary is that always at the back of one's mind is the thought that one may never be able to preserve it. At 10.30 a.m., I am taken by ambulance to the Kadang Kerbau hospital. There are a Nipponese matron and some Nipponese nurses there. Winchester examines me; he says the equipment is very poor and there are no X-ray plates and no barium sulphate. I swallow another barium compound (nitrate). He uses a screen. Verdict: 'there is no evidence of any oesophageal obstruction such as cancer or an oesophageal pouch. Both emulsion and paste passed down the oesophagus normally. There is no renal calculus visible.' Horace and I sally forth into Bukit Timah Road. We pass a number of the Nipponese army in the street and ignore each other. We enter the Colonial Bar. There is nothing available except Tiger stout and local brandy. I try one of each – not so bad! They have no matches. We have tiffin in the hospital with the doctor, Miss Elliott, and three other females. We see the Bishop of Singapore looking as prosperous as ever. *(The Bishop was later tortured by the Japanese.)* We have vegetable soup, fried fish and peas. Dr Wallace who lunches with E.J.H. Corner, will ask about my suitcase, but, as Wallace is now living at the hospital, I may not see him for ages. At 3 p.m., I return in the ambulance. We have a puncture on the Yio Chu Kang road. There is no spare. While waiting, three of us have coffee in a Chinese coffee shop. They have neither milk nor matches. 'The Syonan Times' reports that the register of unemployed in Singapore shows a total of 9,433! Firms have to state how many they can employ and, if they don't, they will be told how many they HAVE to employ!

9 October: I am to return to Changi on Monday. On the whole, I am not sorry, although a bed is a great asset here and I'm glad to have seen the hospital. There are six tuberculosis cases permanently on the verandah. When it rains they and their beds and everything gets soaked. That can't be good, one thinks. Passfield, the miner on my left, has been in Malaya, Siam, Burma and New Guinea. All these mines are now finished; the dredges were destroyed by us. The old gentleman who was operated on for prostate looks bad. I met him yesterday in the lavatory. He told me he had been warned he might die. He looks like a retired clerk, but is actually manager and part owner of a gold mine in wild Kelantan! Appearances are always deceptive and never more so than in this camp. Further examination of my throat shows a very small cyst at the back of my tongue – nothing to worry about. It may be causing the swallowing difficulty. The doctors can't tell. Miyako patients used to get 50 cents from the Camp Fund. It is now reduced to 20. The Aussie on my left is talking about a miraculous native cure for an incredible number of carbuncles he once had which had defied all civilised remedies: 'I had a f....carbuncle on my f....nose and it shoved my f.....face all f.... sideways and my b....f...ear.'

10 October: I buy five eggs for 55 cents. 'The Syonan Times' carries a report about Miss Estrop, a Eurasian from Kuala Lumpur. She was bombed on the Kuala, then was adrift on a raft and was rescued by two Chinese fishermen. As I read the report, I think that it increases the chances of Nora having been saved in one way or another. I have taken no rice since I have been here – a pleasant change – but how the food is thrown at one! N.J.A. Foster arrives, suffering from malaria. There are now many cases in Changi. As I remarked a long time ago, it was bound to happen. There are no nets and the anti-malaria work was stopped by the Nipponese. Now they are allowing the work to go ahead again. *(Clearing away areas of stagnant pools and other places where mosquitoes breed.)* It is curious – out of about 30 in this ward there are five from Seremban *(where Tom lived from 1913 to 1922)*. They are Foster, Evans, Bedington, N.B. Frazer and myself. It is hot as hell and a new order forbids us to sit on the tiny lawn outside the ward. The order is ludicrous and without reason.

Sunday, 11 October: A quotation from a book I am reading says: 'The only way to waste time is not to enjoy it.' How one realises that as an internee! The surgeon, Mr Chitty, thinks nothing more can be done for me. My swallowing difficulty may be due to the cyst. His assistant, who saw it says it is so small and thin it will burst of itself. I ask if this could cause the swallowing difficulty and he says it may do; the mechanism is so complex. My own opinion is that the cyst has nothing to do with my swallowing problem. I can only go on being careful and hoping it will disappear when I get normal food. I meet R. Verghese; he used to be my second clerk. It is curious – I saw his name in 'The Syonan Times' two days ago. I note that people at liberty have not adopted Tokyo time anything like as thoroughly as we. They speak of 'time' and 'clock time.' Today, bugs infest my bed – little, round, red and bloody. I think they have come out of my book. Padre Adams takes a service in the ward at 7.30 p.m. We each have a hymn book and a prayer book and sing fairly lustily, but oh – what voices! I sleep well, despite periodic terrific eructating of the baser sort on my right and an irregular, but constant piping whoop from the prostate case.

12 October: I awake in hospital. My pillow, bought for $1.50, will be very useful in Changi. I pack up. I get an issue of half a pound of cocoa from the Red Cross. I hang around most of the day. At 4 p.m., eleven of us plus luggage squeeze into an ambulance. What a squash! So I return to Changi; a lot of friends express pleasure that I have not left bits of my anatomy behind at Miyako. At 7.30 p.m., I go to the first lecture on 'The History of British Malaya.' The lecturer takes us from pre-history to the Portuguese occupation of Malacca – interesting. On the whole, I am glad to be out of hospital, but I appreciated the change.

13 October: I am back to the old routine – up at 7.30 a.m., shaving and so on, but I watch my side carefully when bending. On the ship that brought the Red Cross comforts were letters for internees, posted in Lourenco Marques via the Red Cross. I wish I had one! The comforts brought were: 750 lbs. of caramels, 2,560 lbs. of biscuits, 2,290 lbs. of cocoa, 2,500 lbs. of dried fruits, 750 lbs. of soup-mix, 24,000 tins of condensed milk, 720 lbs. of cornflour, 864 lbs. of jam, 473 quart bottles of lime juice, 224 lbs. of barley, 9,824 tins of vegetables, 3,600 tins of corned beef, 1,140 lbs. of hospital stores and invalid and infant food, 2,160 jars of Marmite and 268 tins of essence of chicken. I find Thursfield and give him the message that his wife produced a daughter on October 9th; the baby weighed four-and-a-half pounds and both are well. I don't know; I suspect it was not the first time; the father took the news very composedly. Rusk is making me a coconut ring for a souvenir. I shall present it to Nora. Husbands and wives and engaged couples in the camp can now exchange letters once a week but they still can't see each other. The last Nipponese rations supplied were very much less than normal. Was this because of the Red Cross supplies? If so, this is not the game at all. Edmonds resigns. He hints he doesn't think we'll be here long. He has his own affairs to attend to. And the District Officer from Victoria Point has arrived from Bangkok by rail. He was told he would be in Changi only a short time before the exchange. He took two-and-a-half days to arrive. So the exchange stock is up again. Another fool was locked up today. When on a fatigue party, he told the sentry that we were attacking in Burma. The sentry reported him. Now, I am told, the Nipponese want to know where he got his 'news.' Graham and three others who escaped from Pudu Camp were recaptured, then shot. Their effects have arrived here. That is the story. They had escaped before and had been warned. There are many mosquitoes this night and I am much bitten. The ban on smoking in the corridors is lifted!

14 October: We receive an egg for breakfast this morning, but mine is bad. We do breakfast fatigue. I see A.J. King; he is much wasted, but fit after four-and-a-half months in hospital. A lady supervisor is slapped; I don't know why. I have a long talk with Sidney about his 'Saga'. The bit I like best is Sunday, February 15th, 9 p.m. and the announcement of the capitulation:

Syrens wailing, wailing, wailing,
Broke the still, uneasy silence,
Woke up many weary people,
Quivered, faltering, through the darkness.
These were not the normal syrens.
These vibrations seemed to quaver.
What their message to the people,
Many had not the least suspicion,
Thought it might mean further bombing,
Did not truly care about it,
Felt endurance had reached limit.
Others, though, knew all about it:
Knew that this was grand finale –
Wondered gravely of the morrow.
What will be our fate? they wondered
Is there still a hope of fleeing?
Fleeing quickly in the darkness?
There are still three hours to midnight.
Ere the daylight we might journey
Far away to other islands.

Arthur heard the syrens wailing;
Was quite certain of their meaning,

Of this all clear that was sounding;
Sensed in it a note of anguish,
As it had been human voices
Crying loudly through the city:
Singapore the Great has fallen!
Fallen to the Nippon foeman!
Singapore the Great has fallen!
Fallen! Fallen! Fallen! Fallen!

I go to the second instalment of the 'History of British Malaya' lectures; it is good.

15 October: A fund has been opened for the relief of the distressed in Singapore. Our camp fund has subscribed $100. A list is posted of 91 internees for whom parcels await. I am not one, alas, nor any of our group. Heaven knows when we will get them. I expect they are all from South Africa, though A.E. Fawcett receives one and I think his wife is in Great Britain. There are also 300 letters. There is a lot of chat about this parole we are to be compelled to sign on Saturday. We will know more about it later. The Lady Supervisor was slapped because she said, 'I don't know about that; you'll have to ask the Commandant.' And Asahi has admitted that it is contrary to Nipponese chivalry, but she was slapped only once! So the story goes.

16 October: I find it most difficult to swallow anything solid. What to do about it, I don't know. I will see Macintyre who is an osteopath. After a bridge session, I have a meeting of the subcommittee at noon to draw up room rules about the regulation of noises – McNab, Jackson, another (V.J.) and myself. We decide on a minimum of restrictions; we leave it to the squad leaders as much as possible. At 7.30 p.m., Edmonds, the Block Commandant, explains what we have to sign. It is an undertaking not to try to escape and to obey the camp rules. If we refuse, we'll be 'imprisoned'! The Camp Committee have told the Japanese that it's signed under duress and is therefore not binding, so I see no harm in signing, but it's going to be a long job. The whole camp will parade in Girdle Road at 9.30 a.m. in alphabetical order; the women are also to report in their section. Edmonds also reads the parole oath; this is for folk allowed to reside outside and is very reasonable, but won't affect the likes of me, I fear. I'm told that Seife's wife was on the Kuala. He got a wireless announcement that she was OK. I wish I could, but Nora came to see me in a dream again tonight and I'm convinced she is alive.

17 October: Breakfast is early today – at 8.30 a.m. Then we assemble in the yard at 9.30 a.m. and proceed from there to the Girdle Road inside the gaol. The whole camp is there, excluding the Women's Block, who, of course, are not allowed to mingle. We move up slowly and sign on the dotted line – a pure farce. I don't see what point there is in forcing us to sign. Two internees, I hear, refuse to sign. I reach the head of the queue at noon. The Nipponese sitting at tables when we sign seem bored by the whole proceeding. I play a bridge league match with Falconer versus Moore and Beasley. We finish 1,500 points up. Moore is a miner from Siam. He left Kg Tok with another man on the outbreak of war and went 80 miles through the jungle to the vicinity of Betong. The Japs were there. They then went over the Siam-Kedah watershed and emerged near Sik. From there, they went to Kg Pan at the roadhead, where Malays, treacherous swine, seized them and were taking them by car to Baling ten miles away, when they managed to escape into the jungle again. (I know this country; I walked to Sik once.) They eventually crossed and re-crossed the Baling-Padang Serai road four times, owing to the proximity of the Japanese, and so on to Kulim. They passed close to Selama, then over the Bintang Range to Lenggong in Upper Perak. Here, they came in contact with Malays, who came in the small hours, held them up and handed them over to the Nipponese. So they were cast into Taiping Gaol after ten weeks wandering, in which the Chinese were uniformly good and the Malays uniformly bad. When we retake Malaya, the Malayans have forfeited all claims to be the owners of the country by heritage. They have done all they can to assist a Nipponese conquest of their own country. Moore went from there to Pudu and finally arrived here. The Nipponese want a list of the over-60's, with a view to their release, if they can be looked after by relatives or friends outside. This doesn't sound like an imminent exchange, but it may be a gesture. Anyway, none of these lists has ever led to anything yet. Regarding the 'list of internees of higher social rank' which the Nipponese requested, the Camp Committee have replied that, since the Governor and his party left, we don't consider we have any of higher social rank here. The Committee ask for what purpose the list is required, in order to facilitate its preparation.

Sunday, 18 October: Perhaps owing to a brew of coffee at 10 last night, I lay awake until 1 a.m. Nothing would send me to sleep; I tried crosswords and thought of my past, present and future. I also thought of the family (not that that helps at all.) I reviewed every leave – 1919, 1923, 1928, 1931, 1934, 1937 and 1939 and the ships we sailed on – all to no purpose. 'The Syonan Times' leader says: 'today, hundreds of thousands of people in Malaya are suffering severely from insufficient food, not because there is a shortage of food, but because they have no money.' The paper also says that Nipponese soldiers interviewed wish that Malayans would fraternise more – and quote a case where Malays stood and watched them work without offering to help! I fear they will have to get used to this, from what I know of Malays! Nora used to be very insistent that servants washed milk receptacles very thoroughly. I have proof of the wisdom of this today. I mix Klim milk powder in a Dunlop tennis ball tin, which I can't clean properly. It went sour in three hours. I sleep much better tonight. I make cocoa from the Red Cross supply. It is very good with cold water. But I wish I could get my bed off the concrete.

19 October: I am working on my address on 'The Development of Surveying in Malaya.' It is not easy with no data available. I hear that the two who refused to sign on Saturday did so after seeing the Venerable Archdeacon sign. So what was good enough for his conscience was for theirs. The women are incensed at our signing; it gave them no option, they say! I go to the second lecture on Malaya by Adrian Clark – interesting. I sleep fairly well. I dream of Nora again – all smiles, very pleasant – a very vivid dream.

20 October: It is my intention to write up Changi cricket. The home papers would take it, I feel sure. I would start with the cricket section of Father's library: 'Kings of Cricket' by R. Daft. And Brenda's *(Tom's sister)* comment: 'They certainly are.' And daftness would seem to reach its zenith here. Eleven men on the Equator, wearing only shorts and bathing trunks, using a tennis ball, playing on a strip of concrete and so forth. And yet we are keen as mustard. Another internee remarked to me: 'It is astonishing how often you are in the limelight' – and, looking back on it, it is. The wave of malaria continues and there is much dysentery. We are warned against handling food when we have recently returned from hospital. A military party with high officers visits. One tells Johns that a second exchange is being negotiated at Geneva and he thinks we will be included. The camp becomes very excited over this. They also send for a representative of each nationality and ask if there are any complaints (only one each!). They name overcrowding, no communication with their families by letter nor between husband and wife in camp and so on. Nic says the women were called for too – English, Irish, Scots, Welsh, Russians, French, Belgians and Dutch – for the same purpose, but, by the time they were assembled, the Army officers had gone. Asahi is surprised that our letters and parcels have not been handed out yet. It appears that the interpreter is sitting on them. Tiffin is dreadful today. My oesophagus rejects it – it all comes back!

21 October: It is debugging day for us today – there are not many. I win $2 in cash at bridge today. I don't agree with playing for cash now. Both Wallace and Davis, against whom Falconer and I played, are on the Free List and are supposed to have no money. Hope now goes out daily on an anti-malaria topographical survey, escorted by a Sikh! The Sikh starts by being merely a sentry (he gets a different one each day), then proceeds by increasing stages of curiosity – 'what on earth can it all be about?' – and ends by being quite human. THERE IS A LETTER FOR ME! It is from South Africa, addressed to Tom Kitching, Chief Surveyor, Singapore, but Heaven knows when I may get it. I wonder if it's from Nora or has news of her safety. That would be worth 100 parcels. Well, I must possess my soul in patience till it pleases the Nipponese to release it. I go to Adrian Clark's lecture on 'Constitution and Administration'. It is very good and, of course, being Legal Adviser to the Malayan States, he is able to give real examples to illustrate his points. The women had a tea party yesterday, charging 30 cents a head. They got coffee, cake and sweets and the proceeds are to buy sheets for the women's hospital. This should not be necessary. The Nipponese should provide. The women have little enough cash left.

22 October: There are rumours of food riots which took place in Orchard Road in Singapore. There were casualties, including Nipponese *(in code)*. In 'The Syonan Times', there is a very anti-British speech by S.C. Goho – the Indians are not supporting the Indian Independence League. Could there be a finer example of biting the hand that fed you? He was up at Cambridge with me in the same college. He takes all he can. He comes to Malaya, he makes a very comfortable living and a small fortune, and now...! There are hints of an offensive in Burma. 'The Syonan Times' says the sea route is too dangerous because the Nipponese hold Singapore and an attack overland is 'virtually unthinkable' – two well-chosen words, methinks. The newspaper quotes Mr Hon, the Government Information Officer, as saying that this will be 'a long-term war.' The tone is changing; not many weeks ago, the Allies were finished, according to the newspaper. This swallowing is a menace. Every tiffin is a nightmare, although I usually manage to get it down without having to fetch some back again, owing to a food blockage in the oesophagus. I see Dick Hewitt; he tried to find out who my letter was from, but failed. From the description of the writing, I think it may be Nora. They are to be delivered on Tuesday. What suspense!

23 October: The parcels are released this afternoon; they seem to be clothing. In an amusing cricket match, the 'Owners, Trainers and Jockeys' take on the 'Over-60s'. I talk to Hadcup who saw his brother off with me from Singapore when we went home to join up in 1918.

24 October: 'The Syonan Times' has more about the wonderful conditions of prisoners-of-war and internees in Hong Kong and Shanghai, but nothing about us! The newspaper also says, 'The majority of private individuals who own cars in these days are Nipponese...' Nuff sed. Is the leopard assuming our spots?

Sunday, 25 October: I receive fruit and vegetables from the Women's Camp through the Camp Post Office – two mangoes, four oranges, three small tomatoes, cucumber and spring onions – a very pleasant change. The women had a 'market' yesterday and were able to buy the produce in gaol. Seabridge, who has a job on a newspaper in Durban, has written to several internees here. He gives much news of who got away, casualties and so on, but I hear nothing of Nora. There is a black-out practice in Singapore. Our signal is beating a gong (which nobody can hear) on the kitchen roof, but, as we have no shelters and I hear the Nipponese have refused to let us dig trenches either in or out of gaol, it does not seem to be a matter of grave importance whether we hear the gong or not. A mock parliament was mooted; it was going strong, with three parties – Constitutional, Commonwealth and Independent (led by an Irishman, of course!). But the Nipponese heard of it; the word 'parliament' obviously stirred some chord of memory and the verdict came: 'No politics allowed.' We point out that this is not politics, but only in effect an amusement, a means of passing the tedious hours of internment. They graciously consent, on condition that they get verbatim reports of every speech. Our Committee point out that this would be far too tedious. Will it not be sufficient to indicate the subject? There it rests.

26 October: There are now 2,809 internees, with 362 women, 60 children and six infants. How can I write something worthy of being written every day? It can't be done. But, if I were a journalist – and I've always had hankerings in that direction – I'd have to write something interesting every day. Yes, but then I'd be outside and would have something to write about – not cooped up in this lousy gaol. Do you mean to tell me that, with 3,000 internees – all different, like a stamp collection – you can't find something interesting each day? Nonsense. Yes, I suppose that's correct. Anybody with a flair for observation – and able to write about it – must be able to find something. Here's an example to hand: Hope in my room is rolling a cigarette; ingredients: Sikh's whiskers – which is the name we give to a local tobacco; a bit of an exercise book for paper; and Brylcream to stick it down. Yet he smokes it with the appearance of enjoyment. I meet the Block Committee at 4.30 p.m. to discuss the cricket. They propose three days a week from 3.30 to 5.30 p.m., on account of the noise. I say four days from 3 to 5.15 p.m. as at present. They decide on a referendum of the ground floor only and I have little doubt that the result will be against us. So many here are now in the frame of mind to vote against anything. And floors II, III and IV are not consulted.

27 October: 'The Syonan Times' reports that a week's holiday starts in Japan and elsewhere on December 5th at the end of a year's successful warfare. The first three days will be devoted to reflection on the past year's achievements and the last three to a renewal of the determination to prosecute the war to a successful conclusion. A new note is struck by 'the rise and fall of the Empire is at stake.' Only a few letters are released today, but not mine. Some give many details about people, but I get nothing about Nora. Mrs Cheny, who was on the same ship, is dead. There is a bathing parade for our block, but I do not go. The results of the vote on cricket: our room votes 61 to 30 in favour of a 3 p.m. start (versus 3.30 p.m.) and by 52 to 39 for four days, not three. This agitation is caused by people who object to the 'noise'. My own view is that cricket has done a great deal of good – exercise for some and interest for many. Barron has some mouldy tea. Numerous pundits tell him how to make it drinkable. He tries about six ways – all no good. He meets another internee with the same trouble. They compare notes. He has found no solution either. 'So what do you do with it?' says Barron. 'Oh! Quite easy. We smoke it!'

28 October: Colin is 22 years old; I wonder where he is. He may be in the

Indian Ocean with our new fleet. My letter still does not emerge from the fastness of the Nipponese office; and Nakajima, who is in charge, has gone to town and won't be back, so there'll be no progress today. It's maddening. If only I knew who it is from. If it were Nora, I could wait. Hope caught a snake in the corridor last night – quite harmless and unharmed. The cat had it. And a small black cobra was killed in Hudson's Bay. It is remarkable how they get in – through the drains, I suppose. I see Macintyre about my swallowing problem. What is his speciality – is it bloodless surgery or osteopathy? He thinks it is a paralysis of the nerves operating the rings of the oesophagus. I shall see him again on Saturday. He certainly impresses. There is a colossal number of bowel complaint cases and we have new regulations about sterilising food containers. Hugh Bryson and Arthur Worley are in hospital. Nic sends me about two pounds of potatoes – very nice of her.

29 October: Bailey on cricket: 'It has given more pleasure to internees than anything else in the camp and we voted solidly for it. What on earth do people want to sleep from 2 to 4 p.m. for anyway?' I am offered a new pipe for $5. It is worth it, but I have little tobacco left and I can't smoke the local stuff, so what's the use? An internee out with a fatigue party sees Dutch troops from Sumatra going to Changi. They de-lorry near the gaol, line up and a Nipponese for no reason slaps one of them on the face three times *(in code)*.

30 October: There is very heavy rain again; my pillow, sheet and mattress are very damp with the spray. 'The Syonan Times' has an amusing error in its leader today. The Chief of the Military Propaganda Department has been saying that there is more chance of snow covering Malaya or the sun ceasing to shine than there is of the Allies retaking Malaya. Says the leader: 'If there are people in Malaya who still entertain hopes of a British or American attempt to recapture Malaya, let them ESCHEW the words of the Chief of our Military Propaganda Department.' One of our men dies very suddenly this afternoon. It is heart failure. A motor mechanic, he is working when he collapses. The permission to send a postcard has had a most depressing effect on the repatriation market. Even Fairy is downcast for the first time. I can't see any reason for it. We asked permission to send a postcard weeks ago and we've got it.

31 October: My letter is from Brian. I have not got it yet, so I have to write a postcard with no news of Nora. Instructions vary from the morning: mention nothing except health and kindred matters; we are not to say where we are and on no account that we are interned and with a large number of people. By the evening, we get instructions in driblets that the position is that we can put Changi I.C., Syonan and we can say anything we like bar military affairs. This, of course, could not be strictly interpreted, otherwise we would a tale unfold whose lightest word would harrow up thy soul. What caused this complete volte-face? It is in honour of the birthday of the 'greatest of all Nipponese Emperors', Meizi, hence the relaxation of restrictions. On my postcard, I quote Genesis, Chapter 39, verse 20 *(refers to the imprisonment of Joseph)* and refer to little Mac and Anne. *(The Malay word for food is* makan.*)* I trust they don't think I'm bats. Nora will see it if she's at home. And I think she is. I see Macintyre; he is practically certain he has diagnosed my swallowing trouble, not only by my description, but by palpation. He eventually gives me a couple of sharp tweaks in the neck and I am to go again on Monday. Tiffin seems easier already, but I get very little solid and no meat in the dip, as it happens. A coincidence of the most remarkable kind occurs: one of our engineers buys 'nut toffee' locally made and brought in by a fatigue party. It is wrapped in his own diploma! Doubtless looted. After much cogitation, I buy three four-ounce packets of Punchbowl tobacco for $25 – my last fling, I fear.

Sunday, 1 November: The chlorination of Singapore's water supply is being discontinued. We are running steam pipes into a tank for sterilising the water for dishwashing and other kitchen uses. The Nipponese say there will be no chlorination for two months until they can make chlorine locally. We are also warned that there are no more electric light bulbs of our type available, either here or in the whole of Malaya. This is a most astounding day for rumours. If they were all true, the war would be over! I can't attempt to remember them. One report says that Admiral Cunningham caught the retreating Japanese fleet in the Solomons and sank the lot! All Nipponese ships south of Formosa have been recalled. Rumour also says that 20,000 Nipponese have been taken prisoner by the Australians in Buna, New Guinea. Timor is said to be practically in our hands. Akyab and Rangoon have been bombed and captured. Penang has been heavily bombed. The Germans have suffered heavy losses in a tank battle in Libya; they are short of petrol; we have complete air superiority. Timoshenko is advancing near Stalingrad and the Germans have asked for an armistice to bury their dead. There are lots more, but I really can't remember them. Where on earth do they come from? Anyhow, it doesn't matter. It is as well for the truth, if any, to be mixed up with a farrago of nonsense, as the Nipponese had Johns up and asked how many wirelesses there were in camp and where do we get our news? The answer is none and, like Topsy, it just grows and we get a lot out of 'The Syonan Times' and, from that, fantastic stories are built up and circulated. Oh, and add to the rumours that two repatriation ships are en route from Japan. *(During October, the Americans beat back the Japanese attacks on their newly-occupied defences on Guadalcanal, with heavy losses to the Japanese. Advances were also made by the Australians, who had been steadily driving back the Japanese in Papua New Guinea. The Germans had met their 'Verdun on the Volga' with their ill-starred siege of Stalingrad. And in North Africa, the British Eighth Army had begun a big offensive at El Alamein which would eventually drive the Germans and Italians out of Africa altogether.)*

The Committee decide we can have 20% of our deposits back in cash. Good –

I get $110. The boiled water ration is served out at 4 p.m. – a quarter of a pint per person. We sit playing bridge in the gloom, with only half of the room lights on, as a measure of bulb conservation, but no other room is doing it. It is most depressing; are they Foolish Virgins or are we Dismal Jimmies?

2 November: I have Brian's letter. The opening words are: 'Dear Mum and Dad, I hope you are all right.' This fills me with gloom. It can only mean they have heard nothing of Nora. The conclusion is that Nora is interned or a casualty. And I fear very few of the Kuala survivors are interned. I await Bell's letter from his wife. Brian, at any rate is fine. There is no mention of Joan. They *(Brian and the Bell family)* are living at Stellenbosch. He says, 'The room I sleep in has a lot of nice books, including some encyclopaedias which I am reading through.' I expect he thought that would strike the right note, bless him! They built a tank out of planks and boxes. Dammit, I was doing the same (but not tanks) at the same age during the Boer War. Happy is the country that has no history? His writing and spelling are much improved. Brian writes: 'We have a libbery that we pay 6d a term for and eurythmics.' *(Mrs Bell, in a letter to her husband, who was interned with Tom, writes: 'I wonder if you ever see Brian's Daddy. Tell him he is very happy and doing extremely well at school. Joan is safe in England. Tell him I am doing the best I can for Brian. Our children adore him. He has had all his teeth seen to. The money arrives for him regularly. It is more than enough. I save what I can for our fares home.')* So this is excellent as regards Brian. It is most curious there is no mention whatever of Nora, if Mrs Bell thinks Nora is interned with me. From Brian's letter, Mrs Bell would appear to think so. She has certainly seen the letter, as she wrote the address at the head of it. I will write to the Camp Committee tomorrow morning, asking them to press for a list of internees in the Dutch East Indies. Hope and Sworder go to hospital with dysentery. The Committee have written very strongly to the Camp Supervisor about Nipponese interference with Red Cross parcels. Many articles were missing or spoilt. The abstraction of medical supplies served very little purpose, as most of them were intended to meet the idiosyncrasies of the addressees. Met D. St. L.P. who had an interview in town with Asahi. In the interview, Asahi agreed to his going to live in his Kuala Lumpur house. This doesn't mean the permit is in his pocket. That is a matter for higher authority – a different kettle of fish. Asahi asked: 'And what are your views on this war?' Internee: 'I hold very strong views, which it would be inadvisable to express here. But I can say that I am extremely disappointed to find, at this juncture, Japan, one of our staunchest allies in the last war, fighting against us; and the bombing of Singapore before any declaration of war was inexcusable.' Asahi: 'I quite agree with you.' He says Asahi is pro-American and anti-Gestapo. I go to Weisberg's lecture on the Malayan Budget, then I chat to James Bell about Helen's letter and about Nora. He will alter his postcard to let his wife know the position.

3 November: The following sums up my thoughts about Nora's fate: I am almost certain she was not in the Padang crowd, otherwise she would be away with the rest. Therefore she was either a casualty on the Kuala or in the sea or she got to Pompong Island. If the latter, she must have gone on the Kota Pinang headed for Batavia and the report of the Chinese nurse of September 19th indicated that that ship was sunk with many casualties, though Salmond was confident she reached Batavia. I fear he was wrong. So Nora was either a casualty on that ship, or not. If the latter, she is interned in the Dutch East Indies. Finally, there is just the faint possibility that Nora got through and reached Australia, but so far has not contacted Mrs Bell in South Africa, having forgotten the address. A curious situation has been created by our Committee writing to the Nipponese, asking for a deputation of ex-servicemen to be allowed to visit the Cenotaph on the 11th. Considering that they were our Allies then and that the Committee presumably mean to honour their dead too, it will be interesting to see how they will react. They are mad on shrines, so I expect they will agree. They also like (at present) to exhibit themselves to the populace as magnanimous. The Bishop of Singapore came in for confirmation services yesterday. The story is that, mixed up with the blessings, he mumbled: 'Two battleships, five cruisers' and other snippets of news. It is no doubt untrue, but it is a good yarn. 'The Syonan Times' really is astounding – they must think their readers have no intelligence whatsoever. Sunday's leader, after cursing the population roundly for non-co-operation, as recorded previously, says: 'So far, the people of Malaya have shown the utmost zeal in co-operating with the (Nipponese) authorities...' And it continually gibes at the U.S. for tardy revelation of their naval losses, yet, according to the newspaper, the Nipponese Navy have not lost a ship yet! There is an article in 'The Syonan Times' by Charles Nell about Malayan Shylocks: 'Do they tell Mr Office Assistant that he will be given his old job back by the British.... And also give him the latest BBC and U.S.A. news which they receive either from their own wireless sets or from highly placed friends? Do they, deep down in their hearts and in the sanctuary of their temples and mosques, pray for the return of their British benefactors?' I should say the answer to all these rhetorical questions is 'Yes!'

4 November: An internee tells me that a Sikh sentry said he is very disappointed with the microscopic pay; the food allowance, too, is very meagre. His family are all semi-starved. We are treated to a comic opera in the form of an A.R.P. practice. It is farcical in the extreme. First, we are given a notice: 8 p.m. – stand-by; 8.30 p.m. – brown-out; 9 p.m. – black-out; 9.20 p.m. – brown-out; 9.40 p.m. – all clear. This, of course, is not adhered to in the smallest particular. The signals are supposed to be the ringing of sundry telephone bells and the beating of gongs. The brownout beats 11-11-11; the black-out – 1-1111-1-1111; brown-out after black-out – 1-11-1-11; all clear – 111111111. What use all this can be to us, when we have no protection at all, is not explained. Anyhow, long after 8.30 p.m., all the lights go out without the slightest warning. Tin cans are being beaten in the gaol, outside the gaol and in the kampongs round about. No human being can possibly tell whether the beats are 2-2-2 or 1-4-1-4 or anything else. It is just a noise, like Chinatown makes when there is an eclipse, and the din is intensified by people shouting, 'Brown-out! Blackout! Put these bloody lights on!' and so forth on all sides. And someone creates a fitting climax by falling over the refuse bins and knocking all the lids off. In the pitch blackness, the noise reverberates down the corridors and drowns the tin cans and 102 voices in our room raise a mighty shout of laughter. This sort of thing goes on at intervals until 11 p.m. I suppose it is the Nipponese idea of protecting the populace in country districts.

5 November: So Brian is 10 today. We had planned never to separate from him in childhood, as we had for Colin and Joan. Alas! We have sardines for tiffin again; there is no meat. The ration party went to get it yesterday, but our little friends were on holiday, so the poor bloody infantry got none. I discuss last night's farce with a stranger while waiting in the latrine queue. He says: It's just the same when a ship arrives in Yokohama, as a rule the first port in Japan for western ships. There are about 40 of them there, all very busy and, as a friend of mine put it: 'The most efficient people at being inefficient I've ever seen!' Which is all very encouraging when one thinks of future operations. An internee had a letter from Palembang. His wife was in the water for 19 hours clinging to a raft. She was not on the Kuala; she left Singapore on the Thursday *(12 February 1942)*. I talk to A.J. King. He is interesting on the subject of the Budak tin ramp. Orton, his winchman, used to salt the mine. He describes the trip up the Moda River with Honest John who was sent from Australia to report on the mine. He had been stuffed by Orton with stories of tigers and crocodiles. Every time he dozed off in the Malay sampan, he was awakened by bang, bang! Orton had saved his life from a crocodile or tiger! The same thing happened when the inspector was watching boring at the mine. A coolie would make noises in the jungle like a tiger, the staff would bolt and so did Honest John. Then Orton salted the bores. So Honest John's report would have given even bigger values per cubic yard than Orton's. Notice: the Nipponese authorities are seriously annoyed; the camp did not take last night's A.R.P. practice seriously; there was too much noise. There will be no singing or gramophone records tonight! The joke of last night: our Block Commandant was in the yard towards the end of the exercise. A Nipponese in the tower directing operations shouted at him, 'Clear out!' 'I don't understand,' the Commandant shouts. The Nipponese shouts rather more angrily: 'Clear out!' The Commandant is still non-plussed, but, after one or two repetitions, he understood. The Nipponese meant 'All clear' He got confused because of the other instructions, 'Brownout' and 'Black-out.' The air-raid practice is much better today. We have signals by siren, but what a gloomy evening! There is a black-out from 8.30 p.m.. We have asked for the camp to be clearly marked for aircraft day and night. This request is refused. There are no slit trenches either inside or outside. But dispersal outside may be permitted under certain conditions. Query: how can we get out 3,000 people and one narrow exit?

6 November: I spend a bad night, being on the receiving end of many bites, whether mosquitoes or bugs, I know not, but I find about 20 bugs on my mattress this morning. I see Seabridge's letter from South Africa; it is very interesting. There are details about many people who escaped and about the casualties. G.L. Peet is missing. Seabridge writes: 'and yet, mentally, I am not always as comfortable as I would like to be. It may make you grin or cuss. I can't guess... but there are moments when I wish I had seen it out... Such news as has been published regarding the manner in which you are faring has been reassuring and we all hope that it will not be long before we can receive confirmation direct from you.' This makes me boil. It is proof that the Japs have been spreading lies to the world about the way we are being treated. 'The Syonan Times' gives it away: 'The English who formerly lived like kings are now sighing in Changi Prison.' The score mounts. An internee saw a Chinese being tied to a lamp post and beaten because he failed to bow in a manner satisfactory to a Nipponese.

7 November: I go to Macintyre; he does not give my neck any manipulation. He is satisfied with my progress. There is a misplacement of the bones of my neck – due to rugger, perhaps? But there is an improvement. A new notice appears: 'Nowadays, some of the internees are not showing any sign by bowing and standing to attention of respect towards the Nipponese officers and the members of the Changi staff (who wear a red and white ribbon on the upper left arm) whenever they see them. So, if we find such an internee (or internees), we shall give a strict warning to him (or her) on the spot, or reprimand, if necessary. So we shall give this previous notice for your information. S. Nakajima.' We win our cricket match versus D-Block. I come across a curious example of perverted reasoning: an internee, who is one of the world's worst grousers, objects to the noise of people clapping at cricket. Says he, 'The b-s go out there and play cricket and somebody makes a catch – that's what he's there for – and the b-s all clap, as if he'd done something b.... clever.'

Sunday, 8 November: I spend an awful night – bugs cubed! So we have the boxes, bags and beds out again and get hundreds of them. I was bitten to bits during the night on the hands and arms. Dear Joan is 20 today. I do hope we shall be together soon. I wonder what she's doing with herself. At 3.15 p.m., I can hear the women singing 'O God our help'; it sounds good. The Nipponese are round with cameras today, taking photos of the female hospital, but Nic, who is on duty, walks out and they don't get a sister on duty 'with a veil', which disappoints them.

9 November: There are now 2,799 internees in Changi. Morgan, who has been in close confinement along with Scott for many months, is seriously ill. No wonder! Later I hear he has been yanked out of hospital. I go to Macintyre at 11.45 a.m. He now wants me to try to bring my swallowing nerves into proper use. Reading at meals may help – Nora would not like this! Parry goes out collecting stag moss for wreaths for the Cenotaph. There are two major events: Sheppard is detected in the act of passing notes to a prisoner-of-war in a matchbox. He is beaten, but allowed dinner, then he is locked up. And some fatuous individuals put notes in parcels to A-Block *(the Women's Block)* and are detected, so the parcel service is stopped. We are also not allowed to bring anything from Miyako Hospital and no smoking is allowed in the ambulance. The latter rule is reasonable.

10 November: Nic is getting Klim for me at $4.50 a pound and eggs are now 14 cents each – 13 cents outside. 'The Syonan Times' announces that there is to be a songwriting contest, with prizes of $100, $30 and $10. 'The songs must be easy to sing and should reflect a strong determination, besides containing noble ideas about the founding of the Greater East Asia Co-operation Sphere.' The songs are to be in Malay, Indian or Chinese.

11 November: I go to the Armistice Service in the main yard. There is a big attendance. We have a painted Cenotaph on the stage and painted flags – an impressive service and two minutes silence. All denominations attend bar the Roman Catholics who had theirs at 7.30 a.m. 'Contakion' in the announced program puzzles us, but it is the 'Russian Contakion of the Departed' and the choir sing it beautifully at the end of the service. The Nipponese refused our request for ex-servicemen to lay wreaths at the Cenotaph proper. It is just as well, as they would have taken photographs and made propaganda out of it.

12 November: Shepherd is still in confinement and I hear he has been given six weeks confinement in addition to a thrashing. Another internee, Mather, is now in the toils of Nipponese punishment. They are using the usual tactics of corporal punishment first and enquiring after. There is to be an air-raid practice all day today and tomorrow. We are not allowed lights at all tonight, so I go to bed at dusk and cogitate over a crossword I am compiling, but I have a very disturbed night with bugs.

13 November: I rise at dawn – and out with my mattress, pillow and all other possible bug-harbourers. I bag about 15 and air everything, as it is a sunny morning. I play bridge for part of the day and cricket later. The repatrition baraometer has slumped heavily. The utmost optimists are depressed. Personally, I see no reason to alter my opinion that it is being arranged. Reasons: 1) the principle has been accepted; 2) Craigie saw that the arrangements for the remaining 4000 were going on as rapidly as possible; 3) I don't think the Niponese would keep us in this goal, if they were expecting us to be here for the duration. Sheppard and Mather have been removed to Singapore.

14 November: I fill the crevices on the outside of the small case with soap. I find a few bugs. There are still half a dozen bugs in the mattress! The repatriation rumours are strong. There is no particular reason; someone says we shall go on December 12th. The Nipponese conduct very keen searches nowadays. A nursing sister arrives and shows some natural reluctance to have everything looked at. Suspicion is aroused; they turn everything out, including a packet of Jeyes toilet paper. In this they find the usual printed notice warning: 'Only 20 pieces left.' Aha! They impound it with glee. (They could not read English.) A few days ago, our little friends staged photos of children playing outside the gaol, no doubt for propaganda purposes. The Camp Committee, doubtless with tongue in cheek, are now asking that the children be allowed to play outside, lest a false impression be conveyed by these photos.

Sunday, 15 November: After tea, we play in the bridge league versus Mann and Hawley. All our other matches are finished and we have to end 2,240 to win for our team. We fail by 350 only.

16 November: Breakfast is enlivened by a discussion between Jack and Victor on the relative merits of different kinds of toilet paper as cigarette papers. Bromo is too porous; Jeyes has a chemical taste; Vic's 'fluted' variety (not named) is voted the best. There are more repatriation rumours – ships have left Great Britain for Australia and India! And now the best jest so far in Changi: the editors of 'The Changi Guardian' suddenly have their cells turned inside out this morning. They are sent for. We all wonder what the offence is. It is in Saturday's 'Changi Guardian': 'SAD DEMISE OF SABBATH PAPER' – 'With mixed feelings, we announce that, owing to shortage of newsprint, publication of the 'Changi Chimes' ceased on Saturday last.... From all parts of the world we have received messages of sympathy and condolence and, from these, we append the following extracts: 'your ... little journal' ('The Feathered World'); 'the originality of the contents never failed to surprise us' ('The Dredgemaster's Weekly'); 'we think this paper is run on.... Lines... it has points' ('The Railway Magazine'); 'its value as an authoritative work would be increased by the addition of an index' ('The Times Literary Supplement'); 'it is ...that this paper should be a success' ('The Financier'). The Japanese open the proceedings by asking how we got these papers into the camp. (They were looking for them, hence the ransacking of the cells). And, after the most painstaking explanations, the editors are reluctantly released. The matter is not understood at all and no explanation can explain away all those dots, which must be a cipher on the analogy of the Morse code, I presume. I go to the Malayan lecture on 'Rubber' by R.O. Jenkins. It is interesting; he has clear diction and chooses the right word. Hope comes back from Miyako Hospital.

17 November: Once upon a time, there was an old lady who got mixed up in a war and got interned with a lot of other women in a prison. And they all got rather bored with life, so the old lady, being very clever at Italian, gave lessons in it to the other ladies and they all learned how to talk Italian, which was very nice and they were all not so bored as before. Then one day, the old lady thought she would send some dog-biscuits for her son to eat, because he was in the same prison, but separated by very high walls, because it would not do for sons to see their mothers or husbands their wives, but they all liked eating dog biscuits. So the old lady wrapped the dog biscuits in some handy bits of paper and sent the parcel to her son, because their so kind captors would allow you to send parcels, but not letters. And the so kind captors opened the parcel and found the wrapping-paper was covered with writing in a strange language which they could not decipher; so, immediately, their minds became full of suspicions and they ordered that the old lady be produced before them and that right speedily. And she was so produced and they said unto her, 'What is this strange writing that thou art sending to thy son? Verily, it is a plot and ye shall all get it where the rabbit got it.' But she made reply, saying, 'It is only some old notes of my Italian lessons,' and, though they were loth to believe her, they let her go. But privily they said unto themselves, 'It is a plot to undo the Italians,' and sent the strange writings to a far town, where dwelt one who could read all things, yea, even unto the Italian language. But he made reply, 'what is all this ye send me: Have you the pen of my gardener's daughter? No, but my aunt has a piano?' And he waxed exceeding wroth. So the kind captors also were enraged and the dog biscuits were never seen again. And the old lady wept because her son was an-hungered.

18 November: I hear that Sheppard is back, whether permanently or not, I don't know. If permanently, he is in hospital. The report says he looks much the worse for wear. These doings sometimes make me doubt that there will be an exchange. Could the Nipponese so behave, if we were going to be at large before the end of the war? Hope is back on the anti-malaria survey.

19 November: The balance of Europeans from the Fire Brigade arrive in Changi – Shaw and Buckeridge among them. What a contrast! They have brought large trucks full of clothes, food and other useful items. And we've done nine months on what we could carry! Clothes for 10 days, ye gods! They have no news; they have been segregated for a week. The Nipponese are taking so much trouble keeping the news from us that it rather points to there being something worth suppressing. And even our 'Changi Guardian' has to have the censor chop on it now, before it can be posted up – due, no doubt, to the lamentable affair of last Monday! We have been experimenting in the kitchen with sago flour and have been successful in producing a reasonable bun out of it.

20 November: BUGS! BUGS! There was quite a lot of nibbling last night. I now find my tin box harbouring them. It was previously immune. I suppose they went there faute de mieux, when I got rid of the wooden box. There are masses of them in my grey flannel bags, in my blazer and in the folds of a face towel. I try soaping the edges. Hope, out on his survey, passes a guard post on Tampines Road. The sentry searches him – not gently. He is considerably peeved.

21 November: I hear that instructions have been given to the Camp Committee that no further outbursts of cheering are to be allowed, unless previous notice has been given, as it upsets the Sikhs! There was some at the lectures on Malaya recently. I buy eggs at 14 cents each; we now buy through the Nipponese. What about the much vaunted price control? The Sikhs come round looking for wireless aerials and sets. As we haven't any, we view the proceedings with interest and amusement. They also go on the roof and inspect all clotheslines, including those in the Women's Camp. I attend a concert entitled 'The Gay Nineties'. It is good. The players include Levy, Eugene Stratton, Charles Cobon and George Grossmith and the acts include Can-Can girls – very funny.

Sunday, 22 November: Our Sikhs are still prowling, on the lookout for radios. Today, they penetrate to the kitchen store. At last, they find what they are looking for – a case marked 'Radio Malt'. There is great excitement, until it is opened up, then excitement subsides and disappointment supervenes. The Nipponese still have trouble with the flags over our gaol. They get blown to bits by the gentle tropic breezes and the rain washes the red colour completely out, thus we had a white flag waving proudly from the tower – which will never, never do. So, after a period with no flag, they produced a brand-new one yet again a week ago, but now it has gone the way of all its forerunners. Ye Mariners of England! 'The Flag that braved 1,000 years and the breeze' is not yet challenged by the Nipponese!

23 November: 'The Jap Times and Advertiser' held a slogan competition. The winners were. 'Nippon Action Spells Construction, Enemy Action Spells Destruction,' 'America and Britain Dig Their Graves, Greater East Asia Builds Paradise.' 'The Longer the War, the Stronger the Co-Prosperity Sphere.' Wonderful! Yesterday, we de-bugged as a squad. Jack and I got a few, but in our sideboard – a box surmounted by an aerated water box we evicted a large number of absolutely prize cockroaches. Camp tradition has it that they eat bugs, but I don't believe it. I fancy they are vegetarians. I go to the Malaya series lecture by Coates on 'The Mining Industry'. He draws a very gloomy picture of post-war conditions – no money, no market, no power, no machinery, no dredges, no prestige, no food and constant rioting. The Sikhs are still around, in all the blocks, looking for non-existent wirelesses. It gives you a very comfy feeling when you know there isn't one. *(Tom was probably wrong about this.)*

24 November: Nora is 45 today. Is there anything in dreams? Last night, I knew that, if alive, her thoughts must turn to me. (This is her 24th birthday since our wedding and I have never forgotten one). So I went to bed trying to induce a dreamy contact – and succeeded. We were at a dance and dancing together. It was very pleasant; though, as the band was not playing the only tune I can dance to – 'Tea For Two' – I was distinctly clumsy, but she put up with it, in spite of determined efforts by other people to bag her as a partner. Then I awoke at 3 a.m. and I wonder if she is interned somewhere in the Dutch East Indies. How long will it be before I know? I filled in a form with details two days ago, but, with the Nipponese, forms appear to be made for the sole purpose of filing. There is a bathing parade today; I shan't go. Macintyre now has his little room and table. He extended me on this today and gives my spine some jerks. Afterwards, I open a Canterbury cake and we hold high feast in honour of Nora's birthday. Coconuts are up to eight cents and peanut toffee to 35 cents a packet. It is 10 cents in town. The Nipponese seem to have well developed business instincts. December 8th being the anniversary of the start of the Greater East Asia War, Nipponese stamps will be on sale in Malaya – at three, five, eight and 25 sen – and in Sumatra – at three, five, ten and 25 sen.

25 November: Bang! goes the gong in the exercise yard – the signal for rain – and out rush hundreds of men to collect their clothes and bedding hanging all over the place. A paragraph has been cut out of 'The Syonan Times'; internees are not allowed to see it, but, with the usual efficiency, enough of the tops of the letters in the headline are left to enable one to read it: 'ALLIED AIRMEN BOMB CIVILIANS'. I am amused by a purchase I make today: it is toilet paper and on the wrapper it says in large letters, obviously as a guarantee of excellence: 'BRITISH PRODUCT. MADE IN SYONAN-TO.' We give a concert in the courtyard for the ladies. They enjoy it a lot. Of course, no one but the performers is allowed in. Husbands sneak up the passage and try to get glimpses of their wives through the bars. I go into the Birdcage; it is full of Empress of Asia lads. They are now keen on soccer. They ask, 'Can you get us a football?' I listen to an amusing talk by Adrian Clark on 'The Lighter Side of the Law.'

26 November: The orchestra is busy practising for St Andrews Day. We receive 26 carcasses today. This works out at approximately one carcass for over 1,000 people for five days! So the amount of meat we get can be gauged.

27 November: 'The Syonan Times' is again full of articles putting the blame for the war on the Allies. A headline right across the front page says: 'ANGLO-AMERICAN IMPERIALISM MADE WAR INEVITABLE. TREACHEROUS ATTACK ACCUSATION NOTHING BUT SOPHISTRY.' This is a quotation from a speech by Kururu who was negotiating in the U.S.A. when the attack was made. I think the impending war anniversary, at a time when things are not going well for the Axis, is responsible for this spate of excuses. The points made in the newspaper are as follows: on 20.11.41, Japan presented the following five reasonable proposals to the U.S.A.: 1) Japan to keep her military advance into the South Pacific area and South China, excluding French Indo-China; 2) the two governments to co-operate in the acquisition of necessary materials in the Dutch East Indies; 3) Japan and the U.S. to return to the commercial relations existing prior to the freezing of assets; 4) the U.S. not to hinder Japan's peace efforts in China; 5) withdrawal of troops from the southern part of French Indochina. And the U.S. note of 26.11.41, which they say was tantamount to a declaration of war, postulated the withdrawal of the Japanese from China and French Indo-China; non-recognition of the Nanking Government; reconstruction of the Washington Conference structure; and virtual withdrawal from the Tripartite Pact. So, you see, the attack of 8.12.41 was not treacherous.

28 November: There are still many bowel complaints about; 16 went to hospital yesterday. Macintyre gives my spine another tweak, but this time the effect does not seem good. The first swallow of kedgeree sticks will not be forced down, so I have to fetch is back again. This is always easy, though embarassing in a crowded room. The latest 'Syonan Times' is again mutilated for our benefit by the gaol censor. Patients returned from Miyako Hospital, who bought the newspaper from a common or garden newsboy, tell us the offending paragraph referred to the 'wholly unjustifiable' Allied bombing of Rangoon. I go to the St Andrew's concert in the main yard; there is a large audience and I enjoy it. Scottish music always stirs me, but the crowd doesn't get worked up. I think the mournful comparison with previous St Andrew's Days affects their spirits. And the Rest beat Scotland at seven-a-side six to one on our diminutive football pitch. At midnight, I remonstrate in the yard with two Empress of Asia lads who are making the night hideous and am told 'to keep a civil tongue in your 'ead!' Me, from them? But they desist, so the object is achieved.

Sunday, 29 November: My watch is out of order; modern wrist watches are not made with an eye to the conditions of internment. It could be repaired in five minutes, but our skilled watch-repairer can't open the back; it needs a special spanner. What a nuisance! At 9 p.m., I have an egg with Worcester sauce. It's an excellent way of disposing of a doubtful egg, which this certainly was – and one can't afford to throw them away. The Archdeacon preaches a brave sermon tonight. He believes we are the race chosen to maintain truth and equity and our struggles are just beginning to bear fruit. Thoughts on propaganda course through my brain in the night. The world is not what it was. Now no credit is given to the foe; he is cowardly, mean and despicable in every way. Or is it just the Nipponese and Axis propaganda that takes this attitude? Is it more unfair and vituperative than ours? Certainly, we need to be capable of giving credit to a brave foe – the Fuzzie-Wuzzies and the Boers are cases in point.

30 November: Bugs, bugs again – I bag about 30, mostly from the tin box and the grey flannels, and a lot of bugs' eggs. The repatriation rumours are very strong for mid-December. How we hope they are true! Nine months in gaol, dreadfully overcrowded and on an inferior diet are telling on the best of us. The women are wonderful. They were a fine sight at the concert, all spick and span, with hair waved and rouge and lipstick judiciously applied. As our 'Changi Guardian' put it, they must be famished for the sight of men. Or are we being conceited? On a dull, wet afternoon, I cast my eye along our half-squad as we squat or lie on our apologies for beds on the floor: Ledoux, over 60, a proprietary planter, came out in 1906; Parry, over 50, planter in Negri Sembilan; Sworder – in charge of Topographical Surveys, Malaya – aged 55; Perrin, planter, aged 54, came out in 1910; myself, 52, came out in 1913; and Snoxhill, planter, aged 41. Considering our age, we are a tough lot, taking what are real hardships jolly well. We have practically no clothes, no bedding and we have inadequate food of no variety; we do our own washing and all other domestic tasks bar cooking; and we perform various distasteful and sometimes arduous fatigues. Think it most remarkable the adaptability that has been shown by men who have been waited on hand and foot for so many years. Lady Heath is much as before. Asahi has offered to send her to the Cameron Highlands or somewhere just as suitable with a suitable cohort of blood donors, but she has no money and it is impossible to accept, as the Nipponese would give no allowance. Part of the repatriation story has been blown sky-high. Wade in Asaki's office was said to have sent a message saying that an exchange was imminent, but he never sent any such message! Who invents these stories? But the other source (high Niponese officer to Padre) remains. Some are very opimistic; I know of one $500 bet that we shall be out by December 20th. I ruminate over the difference in mentality between the Nipponese and us – or is it more generally between Europeans and Asiatics? We are told: 'I have nothing to offer but blood, sweat and tears.' The Nipponese tell their people: 'The war is practically won; an eclipsed British Empire and a moribund U.S.A. may struggle in their death throes for a few months yet, but it is all over bar the shouting.' Which is better? Ours, I'm sure – but then that's in our temperament. I go to the lecture on 'Agriculture' by Belgrave. It is excellent; he gravely doubts if Malaya will ever be self-supporting in rice, but the Nipponese know better.

1 December: Typical of the Changi mentality is an early morning incident: Victor, in passing, knocks over the soapbox at the foot of my bed, which is my seat. Nine months ago, he would infallibly have picked it up and replaced it. Now, he gives it a look and passes on. Later, two step over it, but can't be bothered to move it. Someone passed me this morning and, without even looking, I knew who it was. This prompts the reflection on how nine months intimate contact with 100 others, sleeping, eating, washing, everything, causes one to recognise them by their voice, gait, characteristic movements of arms; I even think I know every pair of legs. They all file past three times a day for food, as the foot of my eight by three is on the route to the grub table. Anyhow, I can definitely recognise anybody in the room out of the corner of my eye as he walks past, without looking at him. There is a rumour that Tokyo and other Japanese cities have been heavily bombed – I do not credit it *(in code)*. Carr, who was in town yesterday with a fatigue party, says that the Singapore citizens driving Nipponese cars made encouraging signs. The whole atmosphere was optimistic, but the best part was an old Chinese cripple who called, 'Tuan, tuan!' *(Sir, sir!)* Carr waved him away rather regretfully, thinking he was begging and Carr had no money. But the Chinaman persisted, 'Tuan, tuan!' So Carr spoke a word or two in Malay and it turned out that the Chinaman wanted him to wait a moment. He put down his crutch, put a hand in his pocket and produced a box of matches to give to Carr. I am touched by this incident. And an internee, back from Miyako Hospital, tells me that the price of matches is $2.50 per carton of 10 boxes – and inferior Siamese matches at that. I live some cricket over again with 'A Cricketer's Book' by Neville Cardus. It is a very pleasant change to forget this blasted gaol and our captors and to be back to the music of bat and ball. 'The Syonan Times' advertises a movie at the Capitol, now disguised as Kyo-El-Gekizyo: 'Love finds Andy Hardy.' Mather and Sheppard return today, but they are segregated; they have been in the hands of the Military Police since November 13th. I don't know yet what has been done to them, but I do know that Mather hasn't had a bath, change or shave during that period – disgusting anywhere, but incredibly bestial in this climate. Our Committee wrote weeks ago, asking what the charge was, but there was no reply. When the request was renewed verbally, they were told Sheppard had been charged with delivering letters, Mather with sending one, but they had not been tried yet. According to the Nipponese, their stories did not agree and they were 'waiting' until they did!

THE BEGINNING OF THE END

2 December 1942: The repatriation rumours increase in detail: two ships have left Japan for Hong Kong. They will fill up here after taking on the poor bloody infantry of Hong Kong, then two more will arrive and take the rest of us! A message has been received in Changi: 'Repatriation is imminent and you'll get very little notice!' The only fact that I am quite sure about is that it's high time we were all got out of this. I hear that church bells were rung in England for the first time since the invasion scare of 1940 for the North African success. *(The bell ringing was ordered to celebrate the defeat of the German forces at the battle of El Alamein. In a speech to the House of Commons on 10 November, Winston Churchill growled the portentous words: 'It is not the end. It is not even the beginning of the end. But it is perhaps the end of the beginning.')* The upheaval is taking a sad toll of Malaya's veterans, whose experiences, if told, would have put on record a chapter of Malayan development probably now for ever lost. The latest is William Sasse. He was operated on when I was in hospital. He had been mining in Siam, Pahang and Kelantan since 1907, So must have had many interesting and strange tales to tell.

3 December: It starts raining this morning when Hope is out on his now daily inspection of mosquito-breeding sites. He shelters outside a Chinese hut. The woman occupant comes out, is startled to see him, recovers and asks in Malay where he has come from. He answers, 'The gaol.' The Sikh sentry arrives and talk ceases. The sentry goes into the hut to see what he can scrounge, no doubt. The Chinese woman emerges and furtively passes to Hope a packet of cigarettes. At the same time, she tells Hope that the Indians are no bloody good. Later, the Sikh sentry softens; Hope is allowed to enter the hut and receives coffee and biscuits. On later examination, the cigarette packet is found to contain a message from a prisoner-of-war to an internee. There is no doubt here on which side the population's sympathies lie. A paragraph in 'The Syonan Times' rather braces me, indicating that an exchange is still on the cards: the Tokyo Cabinet has approved the establishment of an Officer for the Management of Internees' Affairs, which will function immediately. It will deal with the protection of Nipponese property in hostile countries, the improvement in the livelihood of Nipponese internees and the exchange of internees through the good offices of the International Red Cross. I talk to another internee: he says he's always held the view that the Eastern war can't end before the end of 1944. All Nipponese prefer death or hara-kiri rather than betray their Emperor. And look what miracles they have performed already. I query the first statement; a certain class may prefer death, but the rank and file? And I ask, 'What miracles?' Whereupon he prates feebly of the Russo-Japanese War, but admits that wasn't much. China – well – yes, that's not much of an advertisement. And Malaysia – there was nothing to beat. So he withdraws the miracles theory.

4 December: Once upon a time, the brutal and arrogant British ruled in Malaya. (according to 'The Syonan Times'.) And they lumped all Asiatics into one category which they described as 'Bloody Asiatics' and treated them all with the utmost harshness. So much so, that in 1936 they built a large gaol at a place called Changi on Singapore Island and it was so big that it was able to accommodate no fewer than 600 bloody Asiatics in the conditions which they were called upon to endure under the tyranny of the British. Now it came to pass that, on a certain day, the Japanese descended on Malaya purely in order to free the bloody Asiatics from the tyrannous British yoke and with no thought whatever for their own benefit. For a space, they succeeded. Now the British citizens which were left were in number 2,800 and they were taken prisoner. And the Japanese looked about the land, saying: 'Where can we put these 2,800, so that they shall be harmless?' And one spake and said, 'There is a large prison at Changi wherein they can be cast and there will be plenty of room for them all, yea, even up to 11 acres! And it was so and they were cast therein and the Japanese broadcast and told the world how good and kind they were to their British internees. But one still, small voice spake up and said, 'How can it be that what was harshness for 600 bloody Asiatics is kindly for 2,800 Europeans?' And the Japanese did not like this still, small voice, so they silenced it forever in the usual efficient manner. I think the palm for hard lying must be given to the man who sleeps every night on a 15-inch concrete ledge outside our barred wall – and never falls off; and he has only a blanket.

5 December: There was an almighty clatter as Victor came to bed last night at 11. He was crouching on his mattress on the floor in the dark with a number of tintinnabulary objects spread out in front of him. 'Do you want a light, Victor?' No thanks, I'm only winding up my watch,' replies Victor. The watch is secreted behind all his domestic tins. I hear that our Committee asked for special rations at Christmas as a change, including beef, flour and suet; the Nipponese said, 'No.'

Sunday, 6 December: What a day! It pours all day and night – real, northeast monsoon rain. What a mess – 2,800 people cooped up all day and this gaol is of such poor workmanship that it leaks all over. An internee was in town on a fatigue party yesterday. The guard got tight and lost our supply of 'Syonan Times' from December 4th and 5th. He allowed the party to shop, but they had little money. The internee bought some sugar, but the shopkeeper would not let him pay.

7 December: The blue flag for an alert still flies from the clock tower. Of course, it's a wet day, so you can't expect the Nipponese to get wet taking it down.

It may as well stay there until the next alert. We must have efficiency! I am wrong – at 3 p.m. a notice goes up: 'A state of emergency exists and may continue to exist for some days. Lights out from 8 p.m. to 8 a.m.' What does it all mean – a state of emergency? Are they expecting retaliations for their criminal aggression of a year ago tonight? It is an appalling day, real Trengganu monsoon weather – but I manage a sharp two-mile walk round and round the exercise yard. And we have just had a good laugh at a Nipponese gentleman trying to reach the blue kerchief. The stick has broken and the drapery now adheres to the wireless directional outfit. And it ain't arf raining.

8 December: The great anniversary dawns to a cheerless sky, but it is not actually raining. Today, flags will fly (by order) from all public buildings and the whole population will celebrate (by order) the Nipponese onslaught, which started the Greater East Asia Co-operation Sphere and has reduced them to poverty and starvation. Rise up, O ye Malayans, and call them blessed. To quote 'The Syonan Times', 'All houses will hoist the Rising Sun Flag.' And, to add to the rejoicings, a ship has arrived with goods from Japan – the first. It brings enamel ironware, medicines, toys, pumps and accessories, electric fittings and spare parts, sulphuric acid, bleaching powder, formic acid and toothbrushes. This will be a great relief to the hungry population... Cyril asks if I'll join a poker school. I won't; it's all on the book and I've no desire to go out of here winning or losing large sums. More people have come into Changi – they are engineers; two are allocated to this room. So tomorrow my town-planning scheme, advocated eight months ago, is to be carried out. The Nipponese order that there are to be no concerts or gramophones on the 8th and 9th out of respect for the dead.

9 December: I spend the morning marking out on the floor our eight by three, then all move in. Hamilton goes to hospital with dysentery. Miller MacKay is back. The sick rate is terrific when you work it out. It is certainly not less than 40 per week going to hospital which equals 2,100 per annum i.e. 75% of the prison population per annum. What else can be expected in such appalling conditions of overcrowding, poor diet and little exercise? If we get a real epidemic, it will sweep the place! Sheppard and Mather were not beaten up after they left here, but it was a studied degradation to confine Sheppard in a cell with a Tamil coolie – without any trial, I gather. However, the coolie chatted to Sheppard: he was from the Rim Estate in Malacca. He had been working for a Nipponese officer who was in on some ramp about concrete, so the Tamil was naturally in on it too and, when it was discovered, he was clapped in gaol.

10 December: There was more rain all night and again today. Our clothes won't dry; everything is mouldy. I walk a pre-breakfast mile rapidly, then down comes the rain. It's terrific. Asahi's car stops in the middle of a flood on the road this afternoon. Our fatigue party has to get him out. They are very well treated again in town. They buy things at an Indian shop. The shopkeeper will not let them pay; they insist and finally he takes it, wraps up the goods and, as they are going out, shoves the money back on them. At lunch, I make a determined effort to eat the bully beef. I take it very slowly and masticate every particle, but it is no use. My swallow refuses to work and it all comes back. It is most distressing and annoying. Visits between relatives which were suspended owing to diphtheria in the Women's Camp will now be resumed in the Saturday schedule. They are allocated half-an-hour each and the visits are for fathers and children, sons and sons-in-law, fathers and daughters and brothers and brothers-in-law. Wives and husbands be it noted, are still not allowed to catch a glimpse of each other. Why, only God and the Nipponese know. Nic sends me some liquid gula malacca; it goes well with kanji. But she does not send a message.

11 December: Fine weather at last – at 11 a.m., the sun is shining. The yard is a sight for the gods – beds, mattresses, bedding, clothes, soapboxes – everything is being aired and dried and all the world, but not his wife, are basking. Oh for my camera! I try rice at tiffin and get it down with care, also a few beans. Sidney and I have agreed to swop diaries at the end of the year for two days, the object being mutual improvement – of diaries, I mean! I hear a man consulting a lawyer about making a will. He says that he was making about $12,000 a month. Now he is on the Free List and gets goods to the value of $4 a month. The summary of information gleaned from letters received so far is that up to July 27th no news of the safety of Singapore internees had been received. Two letters indicate the belief that we are living normal lives in our own homes. A writer of June 30th had cabled Malaya House and got the reply: 'No news.' The Colonial Office promised news 'as soon as possible.' Up to July 27th, our postcards had not been received. Our old man, Phillips, wished on us because he has a weak heart and can't climb stairs, is a liability. He snores dreadfully. He got up five times last night and used the inside latrine by special dispensation, because of his frailty, pulled the plug each time and woke us up. He got onto Carter's mattress by mistake (Carter was out) and was settling down there until I put him right. How anyone in his senses could do that, I don't know. The surroundings – and his bed – are entirely different. He stuffs a broom, doubtless buggy, under Jack's bed. He should go to Labrador, the old men's refuge!

12 December: Eight hundred and sixty-eight letters have arrived via the Red Cross from Great Britain and South Africa; they were written in June, early July and early August from South Africa – none for me, I'm told. Obviously, they don't know at home. On the brighter side, an internee has seen Corner and reports that my case with records, diaries and photos is safe in Raffles Library. And Corner also collected other property from my office, excellent. We now have a football league – seven-a-side – and an appalling pitch. Teams have to call themselves after home clubs and the first out of the hat is Liverpool versus Everton! With a strong flavour of Empress of Asia lads from Liverpool in both sides, this should be amusing. Some bright brain suggests there will soon be a transfer market – you trade your centre forward and a goalkeeper for, say, a tin of condensed milk. A discussion of the relative merits of mattresses and camp beds: mattress – can't break; rolls up; gives space in your eight foot by three; bugs are easily spotted; but does it give you rheumatism, as it is laid directly on concrete? Camp bed: fragile; harbours bugs; gives extra room – you can store underneath it; it is off the floor, therefore no rheumatics.

Sunday, 13 December: 300 bloody days in internment! And not a letter from home and no Red Cross visit. The list is out; there is no letter for me. It is therefore certain that, for some reason, those at home have been told there is no use writing – or the letters have gone astray. The Camp Committee have sent a strong protest about the treatment of Scott and Morgan. They are still in solitary confinement and have received no Red Cross visit. Aha! The transformed newspaper is an accomplished fact. The issue of December 12th carries its new name of 'Syonan Sinbun' but this is number five. Where are one, two, three and four? There is not a scrap of news in it. It's full of banquets and mutual admiration society meetings of the Axis partners here and there, telling each other the war is won, what fine fellows are they and how noble their motives. There is not one word about Europe or Africa or the war in the East. But Malaya is now Malai and so is the Malay language. Hooray! Poor Malaya! There is a notice offering rewards for producing weapons to the Nipponese, from $5 for a revolver to 50 cents for a cannonball. If they will let me out, I'll turn an honest dollar or two by pointing out some cannonballs in Malacca, relics of the Dutch wars. There are also rewards for giving information leading to the discovery of arms in a person's possession e.g. $10 for a revolver. This is very dangerous; it's worth twice as much if you plant it on somebody instead of giving it up! Edlin, the silly ass, reported to the Nipponese that he was being persecuted. On his kanji arriving this morning, he said it was poisoned. So the man who delivered it was sent for and made to eat some, which he did cheerfully. I now hear that Edlin has been beaten up and has been sent to Miyako Hospital for observation. He's certainly been a nuisance ever since he was put in our room. There is a rumour that the Russians are doing very well. *(So they were; they had encircled the German Sixth Army at Stalingrad and several thousand Germans in the bag were doomed.)*

14 December: Yesterday, four Norwegians arrived. They were in a small coasting vessel, the Woolgar, (4 to 500 tons) of the type that trades in rice, dried fish and the like, and they were sailing from Colombo to Java with a cargo of munitions when, on March 7th, they were attacked and the ship blown up by Nipponese bombers somewhere north of Java. There was a total crew of 48. There was a British gunner – a man called Whitehouse from Bromley in Kent. Five Norwegian officers and 20 Chinese crew got away in a boat. Their voyage in an open boat ranks with that of the Bounty's and the Trevessa's. The lifeboat was 26 feet in length; it had a mainsail and a jib, compass, sextant, chart, 100 lbs. of ship's biscuits, 12 tins of evaporated milk, 50 small tins of bully beef, 10 tins of fiskeballer, 10 tins of sweet biscuits, five tins of vegetable soup, 10 lbs. of chocolate, three bottles of coconut oil, 50 gallons of water, a small Primus stove, three gallons of kerosene, two bottles of methylated spirits and 20 sets of oilskins in bad condition. The rations at first were a gill of water and one biscuit or one-sixth of a tin of bully-beef on alternate days. After 10 days, this was halved. When the biscuits and the bully beef gave out, they had one dessertspoonful of fiskeballer. The water ration was 50 grams for 40 rainless days, then came the wet Southwest monsoon and they got extra in a sail. They caught occasional seagulls, drank the blood, then boiled and ate them. They also ate flying fish raw. An Estonian, picked up after the bombing with a fractured thigh, died after 70 days in the bottom of the boat. The Chinese were difficult to control. They would not help in working the boat or keeping to the water ration. Many started to drink seawater and went raving mad. Others lost all interest in life and appeared to make up their minds to die. All the Chinese did die. Eventually they lay for several days in an absolute calm, broken by a south-west monsoon which carried them north-east until they sighted land which they thought was Ceylon. Sailing through a strait, they saw a harbour and made for a pier. Behind this was a ship. Seeing a patch of red at her stern, they thought with joy – 'The Red Ensign'. A moment later, a puff of wind unfurled the Nipponese flag. They tried to row to the pier, but had to be towed – they were too weak. It was the month of June; they had arrived in the Andamans after spending 88 days in an open boat at the mercy of the wind and the currents. One Norwegian officer died on landing. The others have been sent here with a British internee and his wife and child, the last Europeans in the Andamans. One incident impressed the Norwegian seamen: as the stricken Woolgar plunged bow first and her stern stuck upwards, the Norwegian flag, which had been hanging limp at the stern, was caught by a rush of air and, as if pulled by an invisible cord, straightened out in a proud gesture of defiance. So she disappeared with her colours flying and that is their last memory of their ship, which they treasure. I have these details from Sofeldt who speaks Scandinavian languages and has talked to one of the Norwegians. The other man from the Andamans is Deakes, aged 72, with a wife and a son, aged nine. He took up 125 acres on Aberdeen, the largest island, 1,200 feet up. He called it Mount Harriet and planted coconuts and vegetables. His wife was the only woman among 23 Europeans when the Japs landed.

'The Syonan Sinbun' says that Chinese leaders in Singapore have expressed whole-hearted co-operation with the Government. One said: 'The Chinese people here are mostly merchants knowing nothing about politics.' He said that 'the people should strictly obey the instructions of the Japanese officials.' Very wholehearted. In the event of air raids, telephone messages will be sent in Chinese, Malay and Hindustani. This will no doubt help to increase the confusion, since English is not to be used. The newspaper also reports that in the Naval Base, working efficiency has trebled since the days of the British and already the number of vessels entering Syonan Harbour exceeds that of pre-war days! What an obvious whopper! I had a nightmare last night. *(Tom describes a nightmare about a fire.)* They told me Nora had sent a message that she would be arriving soon. A great wave of relief swept over me. 'So she is safe, then?' 'Of course, she is.' I had a fearful thirst after the fire episode and woke with my tongue cleaving to the roof of my mouth and convinced that I had shouted in my sleep, but Victor and Jack said 'No' and they should know. I go to the lecture by Watson on 'The Development of the Forest Department.' Halfway, it is rained off.

15 December: Well, if dreams – or telepathy – are any criterion, Nora must be safe and sound somewhere; we met again, in the watches of the night. This morning, our new-formed poker school meets for the first time – Forbes, Barron, Ivery, Laville and myself. It passes the time quickly and pleasantly – a change, too, from bridge. I have not played for over 20 years. C.N. Leembruggen, who was the temporary editor of 'The Syonan Sinbun', has gone. He wrote some anti-British articles under the pseudonym Charles Nell, which were pure vitriol. On the other hand, there are those who say he purposely used to give information 'between the lines'; I doubt this. The latest captive prisoner in close confinement is Dr Winchester. I hear that he was locked in the lavatory for some hours for the heinous offence, reported by the Nipponese matron at the hospital, of drinking beer there! At Christmas, A-Block *(women's section)* is to be allowed to visit us for two hours.

16 December: Hope's Sikh today is very young and an ex-scout. He is English-speaking. He went to Australia for the Jamboree. He accuses the Nipponese of beating people without trial *(in code)*. Nat, a fellow internee, has heard from his son-in-law; he is with the Volunteers. He is 50 miles northwest of Bangkok, making a tunnel through the mountains to join the Siam-Burma Railway. This is taking a long view! It will take five years to build, I should say. The food is poor and there are many deaths from dysentery.

17 December: The menus for the last three days indicate that the meat shortage prophesied is now upon us. I am on a fatigue party in the afternoon, unloading a lorry full of sacks of rice polishings. They are 'wick', as we say in Morecambe, with grubs and small, black creepies, but, as some one remarked, when cooked they will give us much needed proteins. There are two parcels from Nic – a tin of condensed milk costing $2 and a bottle of tomato ketchup locally made. Parry has a seizure at noon and is carried to hospital.

18 December: Helen Bell's letter from South Africa to James is like a breath of fresh spring air in this lousy gaol. They have moved to a cottage in farming country five miles from Stellenbosch. It stands on a hill with a view of mountains all round. God! What would I not give if Nora were there too – not to say myself as well! Attached to the house are acres of vineyards, apple, plum and apricot trees and a vegetable garden. There are lots of nice farmer neighbours and lashings of milk free. An evacuee from Malta shares the house with Helen Bell; she has two children. Brian, Tony *(Helen's elder son)* and Stuart go to school daily in a car belonging to a farmer neighbour – a five-mile trip. They have lunch there and return at 3.20 p.m. On Sundays, Brian and Tony bike to the farm and get the milk. The letter dated August 15th says they still have no news of us: 'we heard that you were being well treated; I hope it's true. Last week, it was announced that parcels of clothing could be sent. (James Bell got his.) I am getting half your salary.' Nora would love this farm; she's always wanted that for the children. Asahi has agreed to give a list of the women in Padang, but he refuses a list of men. Why on earth? On the subject of overcrowding, he says we are well off with permanent buildings and water sanitation, better than the other 20 internment camps he has visited. Several attempts have been made to move us; it is due to him that they have not been carried out. We open a tin of sardines tonight and I eat them with biscuits with little inconvenience. I buy four ounces of Bruno Flake from the shop for $10.

19 December: There is liver in the soup at lunch. I get most of it down, but one swallowful comes back. Some fine toys have been made for the kiddies' Christmas, including a fleet of yachts I saw being painted at the tin-smiths. 'The Syonan Sinbun' publish a long interview given by the Bishop of Singapore a few days ago, which is entirely fictitious! The Europeans from the Post Office arrive in Changi, including Coe, Gilliam, McLennan and Gurr; there are about ten of them. I chat to Gurr and ask what his general impression was and he says the Japs are grossly inefficient. What about the postal services being restored to New Guinea, Borneo and Celebes? He replies: 'There ain't no such animal.' I had wondered.

Sunday, 20 December: The arts and crafts exhibition is excellent. I marvel at the ingenuity some people have with their hands. I have none, nor the patience – yet I can spend hours manufacturing a crossword puzzle. There is a wonderful doll's house complete with furniture. It has been presented to St Andrew's Home. There are full-rigged ships and the most ingenious lighters. And the drawings and paintings are excellent. Helen Beck's poem I like immensely:

O lovely Dawn when this long night is over
And free winds sweep through open ports at sea.
When down the Channel loom the cliffs of Dover
And England takes the homesick heart of me!

O Lovely Dawn when, through the wide-flung casement,
I see the rolling downland, clean and sweet,
And all the spectres of this strange abasement
Are but as shadows passing in the street.
O lovely Dawn, when every man shall labour
In quietude beneath his spreading vine,
When he can plan ahead and trust his neighbour
And even humble hearts are honour's shrine.
O lovely Dawn, when dear ones walk beside us,
And we are free to wander where we will,
When none need pity and none dare deride us,
But we may go o'er moorland, vale and hill,
When homely speech and homely figures greet us,
And scent of roses drifts across the lawn,
When day's realities no longer cheat us
Of dreamland's rhapsodies – O lovely Dawn!

21 December: I go on a firewood fatigue; it is very pleasant. The distance we have to go is getting on for a mile now; there are Sikh sentries on guard. I take a walk along a cart track over a hill – how easy it would be to disappear! But you would not be free for long. In a deserted spot, I come across a looted cabin trunk with the name Coxon on it. It is empty except for ants and a brilliantly coloured land-snail shell. The only speech I have is with a Chinese woman and a small boy: 'Tabek, tuan' *(Greetings, sir)* and I suitably respond, 'Tabek. Apa Khabar?' *(Greetings, How are you?)* and she gives me a long look which spoke volumes. A.W. Brisk has died, aged 62. Saccharin is available at $5.50 an ounce. I should like to try some, but cash is getting short. Johnny (Dr J.) tells me he had five letters from Bunny up to the end of August. She had had absolutely no news of him; she heard we were being well treated and hoped it was true. She is living near Durban. McLennan, who was in Kuala Lumpur Post Office until September, says that the Eurasians and the Ceylonese were very good. The Malays were NOT helpful and were trying to arrogate his position. I go to the lecture on forests by Watson; it is very interesting. I miss the first football league match. Liverpool (our Empress of Asia lads) beat Everton by one goal to nil. Their football shirts were made in gaol. Johns kicks off. The crowd duly boos the referee and is complete with rattles and rosettes! The real atmosphere! Instructions have been issued for our mingling with the Women's Camp on December 25th. Of course, at the end, Mr Nakajima has to put his spoke in: 'Mr Nakajima states that everyone must be punctual and behave in an orderly manner.' Oh, go and boil your head. 'The Syonan Sinbun' of December 19th just about bears away the bell for sheer unadulterated tripe mingled with onions.

22 December: My day out! I win $33 at poker. There is a bathing parade, but I do not go. Dear, dear – another defeat: 'The Syonan Sinbun' headline on December 18th: 'TOKYO WINS WAR OF RADIO WAVES.' The newspaper lauds the superiority of Japanese broadcasts over those of the Allies, then says: 'why not let Malaya listen?' *(to the Allied broadcasts)*. Because they lie, my son. There is food available from the Camp Shop, but few have money to buy now; I still have a little. I get two tins of soup and a bottle of vinegar, local make, for $1.10. I hear that the lorry mechanics have communicated with Morgan, who is still in solitary confinement. They work under his window; it is too high for him to see through, but sound can penetrate. First, they sang to some well-known tune: 'Cough if you can hear.' He coughed loudly. Then they sang the news! And they do this fairly regularly now, when the coast is clear. And the news is good. *(The Allies have gone over to the offensive in Stalingrad, North Africa and Burma.)* Thinking things over, there is no doubt that Nakajima, the photographer, was a spy. I don't know if our gaoler is a relative. And we fostered Nakajima and treated him very well for 46 years. When I arrived in Singapore in 1913, the railway coaches were plastered with his pictures and very good photographs they were. He must have made thousands of dollars out of that. Looking back at my trip to St John's Island, when I took photos of the liner, the Ile de France, in harbour, Nakajima developed these and, when I went for them, the films (a pack of three) were blank! Obviously, I had forgotten to pull the slide out, but I knew I hadn't! He had kept them. And, of course, on November 26th, Nakajima sent bills and asked to be paid in cash, not cheque. How blind we were! The Nipponese are a curious mixture of savagery and elements of decency. I hear that the wives here are to be allowed to see their husbands (soldiers from the military camp) on Christmas Day too. And fathers are to be allowed to see their sons.

23 December: Padre Thomson arrives with a Christmas present of five packets of Davios from M. George, which I think is an extraordinarily nice gesture. I saw the padre in the Cathedral. The Waifs sing carols in B-Block yard at 8 p.m. It is very pleasant. Here is a summary of information from recent letters, inter alia: the food position in Britain is good; on July 1st, the Post Office issued a notice that it will be possible to write to Singapore and to write weekly while present arrangements last; the mail from Singapore on February 9th arrived safely in Britain, so my books should be OK; on July 4th, all recent letters were returned marked 'NO SERVICE'; the Red Cross said we were well-treated and allowed to live in our homes!

24 December: I receive Christmas presents from Kath (cocoa and a tin of condensed milk) and Nic (cheroots and tinned peas.) It's very nice of them. Hope has received three letters from his wife in Britain written in the first half of July. They were told on July 7th that communication was possible. My family and Brenda are sure to have written – so many letters must have gone astray. I am on a fatigue party supplying wood for the kitchen – six loads, specially for the Christmas cooking. I believe every man in the camp has had a Christmas present from the Women's Camp, a very stout effort. The clever Nipponese scientists have discovered a substitute for milk, which will build bonny babies and make mothers rejoice. It is a rice gruel made from rice polishings, red palm oil and fruit juices. There is an excellent performance of 'Scrooge' in the main yard. I walk there about 8.30 p.m. A lovely moon is shining, with 2,000 men bare to the waist listening to 'Scrooge' and the voices of the women floating over the wall, singing carols very sweetly. What a world! There is a special Christmas message from the Canadian Prime Minister to Canadians here, delivered by Asahi at 5.15 p.m. The Canadian internees are very much in their thoughts and so forth. I hope we are too and with a view to an exchange!

25 December: We are to have special food today. I have a curious sort of frog in my throat and it coincides with what seems like an improvement in my swallow. For breakfast, we have kanji porridge, prunes and coffee with sugar and milk in it – but you'd hardly notice it! For tiffin, there is tinned pork with a vegetable and applesauce, very good soup and an enormous slice of Christmas pudding. I eat it all carefully, but with little or no difficulty. As the great day dawns, we all don our best – in my case a blue sweat rag, khaki shorts and sandals – and, at 10 a.m., we are admitted to the holy of holies, A-Block, by invite only. Spend an hour in the Crypt with Nic, Mrs Grist and others, accompanied by Wakefield and another internee, Johnny (Dr J.), then they come over to us. The Crypt looks very nice – a carpet, rugs and beds. Of course, if we had it, there would be 25 men packed in. I must say the women are taking it marvellously; they look quite chic and how pleasant to chat to women again. The band is there too and there is dancing and lots of hors d'oeuvres – all very pleasant indeed. I wish Nora were here, or even if I knew she was safe. Before breakfast, Jack and I make coffee and put it in a thermos, so that we can give the ladies a drink. Vic is used to putting tea in Jack's thermos after breakfast, so he takes it and pours all the coffee away, alas. Then he discovers his mistake. For tea, we have rice pudding with sugar and milk (!), one-fifth of a tin of peaches, a large sardine, a roll and dripping, with tea to drink. A visit to the big yard for an orchestral concert and carols by the choir rounds off as satisfactory a Christmas Day as possible in the conditions. I particularly enjoy Wenceslas and the Hallelujah Chorus. And so to bed wrestling in thought with a crossword where I am involved in a particularly nasty corner.

26 December: It is a fine, bright day. I air my mattress and have a bug hunt; there aren't many. Rodyk tells me the exchange rate in town is now $110 Nipponese for $100 Straits!! This must be very galling for the Nipponese. And it is $40 for £1 gold. If this is true, it is very much a sign of the times and the news! In a message from Nic, she says: 'It made my heart ache to see how crowded you were, but, in spite of that, you were so clean and tidy.' High praise from a woman! I saw 'Scrooge' right through yesterday. It was a very fine effort and the scenery, made from nothing, was incredibly good. The youngsters in A-Block were having a marvellous time; we could hear them yelling their heads off. A chatty Nipponese sentry out with a fatigue party was blowing or shooting his neck off about the wonderful scope of Jap bombing: 'Darwin? Boom, boom, boom. Port Moresby? Boom, boom, boom. Colombo? Boom, boom, boom.' 'London?' says one of the party facetiously. 'London – boom, boom, boom.' 'Oh, bullshit,' says another. 'Bullshit, boom, boom, boom.' An engineer newly in tells me he noticed a marked increase in tension amongst the Japs in the last few weeks. He says you were much more liable to get your face slapped for nothing.

Sunday, 27 December: There's a lot of light 'flu about. I hope I escape. I see Davies from Hutterbach, Kulim; he has just come in with 15 other engineers. We are now 2,820! He says that whisky on Christmas Day cost $90 a bottle. An internee who was a male nurse in the Mental Hospital and was therefore captured on Wednesday, February 11th, says the Nipponese 'ran like hell' when our shells came anywhere near. Personally, from my own observation, I should say they are no braver than the average Asiatic when it comes to it.

28 December: I am on an outside firewood fatigue at 10 a.m. The Sikh sentry wishes to restrain parties from returning piecemeal, but he evidently does not like giving orders and asks me in Malay to do it, calling me 'tuan'. And Hope's sentry tells him everything is 'senang' *(easy)* now. Asked why, he says, 'Because the British and Indian governments have signed an agreement and the Indians will now fight like tigers for Britain.' A curious situation, Hope and the sentry – Gilbertonian, in fact. And when I return from my fatigue, I find there is a rumour that the Indian Congress has agreed to our terms of settlement. It was a pleasant fatigue, but it always gets my goat to see bloody-minded little yellow devils lording it in our cars and thinking they are God Almighty – the real truth being that they are utterly unfitted to rule. We passed one in a car – a swinish, bestial face. I can write freely in this diary now, as it will be put to bed in a few days. The death of J.M. Jansen is announced; he was on the Rural Board with me. British Army captains working for the Nipponese were told the pay was $120 per month. Of this, $60 was deducted for maintenance, $30 was 'banked' for dependants, $10 for hospital contingencies, leaving $20 which has never been paid.

29 December: There are eggs for sale at 17 cents each; I get six. Eggs are a typical example of Nipponese inefficiency. We used to buy them ourselves for the camp, then the Nipponese stepped in. 'We will handle this.' Result – first, an enormous increase in the number of bad eggs and an increase in price; second – no eggs at all! Now we are being allowed to do it ourselves again and supply is normal, but not the price. Forbes has a bet on – if we are not out before 1.6.43, he wins $100; if we are not out until 1.9.43, he wins another $75; if not out until 31.12.43, he wins another $50. So he wins $225 if we are still here on 1.1.44 (which God Forbid!) Horrid thought! Soccer has captured the camp fancy. A wildly enthusiastic crowd throngs the main exercise yard for the league matches and it has the roar, the advice to players and the invective of the pukka home soccer crowd. Today, one of the backs was rather slow in recovery: 'Christ! Look at the b....' 'Yes, and he's on Marmite too!' One of the small boys comes to me and says 'I'm sorry there will be no more cricket, Mr Kitching.' And why, I ask, 'will there be no more cricket?' 'Well, I'm AFRAID we'll be out before then.' The rice fatigue party went to town today, but there was no rice. Instead, they were given 29 cases of pineapple brandy as a New Year gift from the Nipponese to the camp. Then they were given eight bottles for themselves and, as far as I can gather, the whole lot, including the Nipponese, proceeded to get blotto on it. Anyhow, this was borne out by the two I saw – both completely passed out, asleep on benches with beatific smiles and a ground sheet between their clenched teeth. I am told the fatigue party sang: 'Keep the Home Fires Burning', then the Japs sang it, then the Malays sang it, then the fatigue party sang it again; in fact, it seems to have been a very loving party ere the finish. I have a remarkable dream involving Nora, a motor-bike and Brenda (*Tom's sister*).

30 December: This morning, I weigh myself on the hospital scales – 116 lbs. compared with 133 lbs. on 1.1.42, but J.M. Jackson is 130 lbs. compared with 208 lbs. And on the food the Nipponese are giving us now, it will be worse. The Military Financial Administration Department announces that plans are afoot for the liquidation of former British, American and Dutch banks in Malaya.

31 December: One tin of curried chicken per man has been issued from the store as a New Year treat! I don't suppose mine will be of use to me, but I think at first I'll have a stab at swallowing it. I then swop it with Jack for a tin of meat and vegetables. I am on corridor-cleaning fatigue in the morning and afternoon. With another internee, I sweep up the courtyard. More bloody-mindedness – the Nipponese will not allow husbands here to send ONE letter to their wives known to be in Palembang, Sumatra. Why on earth? It could do no conceivable harm and surely once a year is not asking too much. But they will condescend to send a list of husbands who have wives in Palembang. This doesn't help those of us who have missing wives. All we ask is a list of British women interned in the Dutch East Indies. After 318 days of internment, can we get the list? No; it's all on a par with their all-round inefficiency and, from the point of view of our ultimate success, it is most encouraging! Tiffin! Phew! The dried fish is appalling and certainly represents the lowest type of food we've tried as yet. I cannot look at it. Apart from the stench, the bones make it impossible for me to swallow. Full particulars of the marvellous substitute for milk discovered by the clever Nipponese scientists are now given: take two full teaspoons of sifted rice flour, add three ounces of water and cook for 15 minutes. This, with the addition of some sugar, forms a suitable feed for children under four months. For children from five months on, the quantity has to be greatly increased and little extras such as ripe bananas, fish, liver, eggs and spinach will have to be added, also some red palm oil and fruit juice. God help the babies, say I! At 9.50 p.m., when everybody has stopped his activities, a message arrives: 'Lights out at 11 tonight.' Typical. However, there is certain liveliness in the main yard where they sing 'Auld Lang Syne' and there are some sub-human noises in our vicinity. At midnight, the Crypt makes its presence felt and shouts 'A Happy New Year' to us. So ends 1942. May I, at any rate, never have a worse year! This diary shall now be concealed and I hope to get it away – WHEN we get away!

– VIII –

THROAT PROBLEMS

Tom begins his 1943 diary, using a jotter instead of the pocket diary he had used in 1942. A 1943 pocket diary would not be obtainable in prison, of course! He writes: This paper is good enough to be the medium for my diary for 1943 and I fervently hope that long ere the year end we shall be out of Changi Gaol and the war, in Europe at any rate, over. My camp number is 1071.

1 January 1943: and the 319th day of my internment: I still have $200 cash and, in this, I am luckier than the vast majority here. I know the three children are safe, but have no news whatever of Nora since February 13th, 1942. I greatly fear she may be a casualty. My weight is eight stone four pounds, a drop of 17 lbs. during 1942 and the lightest I have been since I was a school-boy. Physically, I feel very fit, but I doubt if I have much stamina left. I fancy most of the loss of weight is in my limbs and muscles. And I cannot swallow properly. The diagnosis is that this is 'functional'. The doctors gave it up, but Macintyre, the osteopath, is treating me. It is very distressing. However, the present position is that I can get practically anything down if I take long enough over it. I think I should summarise the information about Nora here: She left Singapore on the afternoon of Friday, February 13th, 1942 with many other women who had been working in the General Hospital and, although I did not actually see the vessel she went on, there is practically no doubt it was the Kuala. Next morning, the Kuala was bombed and sunk when anchored off Pompong Island in the Rhio Archipelago. There were some casualties, but not very many, and over 700 people swam or scrambled somehow to the island. Here they remained for two to three days, then 206 women, children and wounded were taken on board a Dutch boat, the Kota or Tanjong Pinang bound for Batavia. The remaining 500 eventually reached Padang on the West Coast of Sumatra by various small vessels, having been taken to the Indragiri River and thence across Sumatra. Nearly all these 500 were taken to India by our Navy and Nora was not amongst these, obviously, or I should not get messages from our children addressed to 'Mr and Mrs Kitching'. Nor, Salmon assured me, was she amongst the few Kuala survivors who were not taken away from Padang by our Navy. Therefore, she was either a casualty in the initial bombing of the Kuala or she left Pompong on the Tanjong (Kota) Pinang. Now, according to the account of a Chinese nurse who was on the Tanjong (Kota) Pinang and later returned to Malaya (published in 'The

227

Syonan Times' of September 17th), this ship was shelled the night after it left Pompong and sank in 50 minutes, 'many going down with it. The Chinese nurse was on a raft with others, of whom the majority died before they were picked up by a Nipponese ship and taken to Banka. No other information is available. The Japanese up to date will not supply a list of women interned in the Dutch East Indies, except for Palembang, and Nora is not on that list, although many of the Kuala survivors are, as far as I can gather, but this is not very certain. There are still many women who left on the Kuala who have not been heard of and it is possible they are interned somewhere in the Dutch East Indies or, I suppose, may have been picked up by the Nipponese vessel which shelled the Tanjong (Kota) Pinang, in which case they may be anywhere. Exchange I personally still believe to be on the cards. If not, it looks as if we shall be in Queer Street for food ere long. I don't visualise release by conquest before the end of 1943, unless Germany collapses. The Nips CANNOT keep a flag over this gaol. An imposing new one went up only a day or two ago. Now it has collapsed under the weather, poor rag, and once again there is no flag. Shoddy, like their currency notes. There is a shemozzle in camp: two days ago, two young Empress of Asia men were discovered to be in possession of stolen camp property, mostly food. They are now awaiting trial locked in a cell by our Disciplinary Committee – who have just been given power by our Camp Committee to inflict corporal punishment. This has aroused a most heated controversy. Most of the Australians, plus the usual contingent of cranks, say that corporal punishment is most degrading and should never be resorted to in any circumstances whatever. Yet I have heard the same people, when their OWN property was interfered with, threaten to push the offender's teeth through the back of his neck and commit other anatomical exercises, if they could only catch him! The Sikh sentry taking these two out for exercise in the Girdle Road remarked to one of our own Camp Police that the penalty for theft nowadays is 'potong kepala!' *(de-capitation)*.

2 January: Another new flag has gone up. *(Tom quotes from Robert Louis Stevenson's* Will O' the Mill*):* 'It is the property of things seen for the first time, or for the first time after long, like the flowers in spring, to reawaken in us the sharp edge of sense and that impression of mystic strangeness which otherwise passes out of life with the coming of years; but the sight of a loved face is what renews a man's character from the fountain upwards.' So we are not to have a tot of brandy after all. The Christmas gift from the Nipponese has been handed over to the medicals who will redistill it to be used as a surgical spirit.

Sunday, 3 January: A notice in 'The Syonan Sinbun' again calls upon all owners of short-wave wireless sets to hand them over for conversion to medium wave only, 'failing which, punishment shall be meted out accordingly.'

4 January: I finish reading the 1942 diary of R.J.H.S. It is an intensely personal document totally unlike mine, though we live under precisely similar conditions and environment. It is interesting to observe how in such circumstances two people produce such entirely different documents – both in their own way (I hope) full of interest. There is fresh fish today. Anyhow, there is not enough to go round, so the women bless 'em, gets it. Hope is out with a fatigue party; a new Sikh sentry expresses the opinion that things are going well and that the British will soon be back. He says, 'A man gets a fair trial with the British, but, with these, if they even think something is wrong, they spit on their hands and beat you up.' An internee was called in by the Nipponese last April; they wanted him to go to Miri in Sarawak. 'You are a diesel engineer' they said. He denied it. 'Then why did you have a sign up in Alor Star: J.J.P.D., Electrical Engineer and Diesel Engineer?' However, he managed to get out of it. The pantomime 'Dick Whittington' is staged largely by our Empress of Asia contingent. It is very good indeed, with topical songs and quips, excellent scenery and outstanding make-up and costumes. I've rarely seen five prettier-looking girls!

5 January: The two thieves get two weeks solitary confinement and are taken off the free list for one month. Brewar gets an extra week and another month off the free list for assaulting the Camp Police – and very right too. Because of overcrowding, we have been forced to put people to live in the well at the foot of the stairs – a dark, gloomy square with no windows, no doorway and a staircase. Twelve men live, sleep and do everything in it. Another group are at the foot of the lift shaft and yet another in the lift permanently jammed halfway up. Surely exchange negotiations must be afoot. Even the Nipponese would not visualise keeping us indefinately under these conditions. In this goal built for about 600 convicts are now herded 2,413 men, 367 women, 61 children and two infants! The truth about the 'fresh' fish yesterday is that the Nipponese, with their usual efficiency, suddenly, without any warning, dumped it on us. Much was found to be already bad; the rest was cooked immediately and served to the women for breakfast next morning, but a lot of that was bad by then. Twenty-seven husbands in this camp have missing wives who were on the Kuala. Life here would be easier to face if only Nora had gone with Joan on January 30th. She would be safe at home and I would know the children had a parent to help them.

6 January: There is a curious sight to be observed any morning; it is one of our doctors smoking a pipe while he has his shower-bath in the exercise yard. He just turns the bowl upside down.

7 January: I am on standby fatigue all day; we may be called upon to do anything from unloading a lorry to moving pianos, but, most probably, nothing except being on tap. One of a fatigue party has his face slapped this morning – he waves to a passing prisoner-of-war lorry. A Nipponese on board the other lorry stops it and performs the ceremony. I'm glad it has never happened to me; I feel I should go berserk. I note an example of curious reasoning: a gentleman wears no shoes (because he hasn't any). He doesn't like to soil his eight-foot by three-foot living space, so he wipes the soles of his feet with his bare hands, then proceeds to toy with his food utencils. Stealing is so easy and so anti-social in this gaol that it should be repressed with the utmost severity. In our room, Strachan has lost a mattress and Gaunt a blanket, which were airing in the yard. Now the material is in the gaol and easily identifiable. If I were in charge, I'd have it somehow. A search organised by floors simultaneously is all that is necessary. The other victim is Australian and was one of the most fervent opponents of corporal punishment in the heated discussion on January 1st. He now explains to me that he is not really against it, but the tactless way in which it was put. This, I believe, is what is known as 'argumentum ad hominem'! Clothing is a very serious problem, Most of us have only the garments we carried in over 10 months ago and they are worn or wearing out. I saw a lovely pair of shorts made out of flour bags today and Jack has just finished with great patience a pair of rope sandals. Sandals with bits of wood and a rag over the instep are common.

8 January: I often wondered how my coolies could eat dried fish; now I know. The Nipponese appear to have decided to supply this instead of meat. We had the stuff today for tiffin and I managed to isolate some flesh from the noisome mess and, what is more, ate it. Question Hour is to be introduced as a camp innovation. The sponsors will endeavour to answer serious questions on why, what or how, if of general interest. No political or religious subjects allowed. Notice must be given and they will try to find the best authority on the subject. Answers will probably be given in 10 to 12 minutes. This should be excellent. Dickson is to go to hospital for an operation. He has no sleeping garments at all. The only sarong in the shop is $9.50 and he has no money. What to do? The camp is undoubtedly getting money from somewhere, judging by the purchases in general. The Nipponese are very anxious to discover where, I am told. I don't know. A German raider has been torpedoed near the Sunda Straits. Excellent! On board were 11 Norwegians and one Swede from a sunken tanker. They arrive here today. They say the Germans on board were depressed by the wireless news.

9 January: There is more comic opera stuff today: Ivor Parrish is now Camp Optician and is allowed to go to Singapore from time to time to collect glasses and hand in further orders. He goes in the lorry today, as usual. He gets to Raffles Square and is proceeding to get out to transact his business, when the guard stops him: 'you can't get out of the lorry.' 'But this is what I've come for!' 'You can't get out. Some other day, not today.' So the lorry brings him back again in due course. No reason is given. It may be mixed up with an 'Anti-White Week' which I'm told they are pursuing. Or it may be mixed up with a notice just put up on the camp boards: 'No member of this camp going to Syonan is allowed to enter any restaurant or eating shop.' This is taken to mean all shops and buildings except those to which members of fatigue parties are escorted under guard. The women give a concert tonight in the main courtyard. The men eligible to see it are husbands, fiancés, relatives and those who were not invited to A-Block at Christmas.

Sunday, 10 January: An internee returns my diary of the first half of 1941 to me. I am most pleased to get it. The Nipponese Military Police or Gestapo have summoned all their Auxiliary Police (householders in charge of groups of householders) and have given them instructions about spies, paratroops and I don't know what else.

11 January: I have promised to give a talk to Rotary next Sunday. We have a five-course lunch today, savoury rice, sardine, fruit juice, peanuts and dried chillies. I can't eat it; the food sticks in my throat. I have to yield it up and throw the balance away. I have an appointment with Macintyre at 12.30 p.m.; I tell him there has been a retrogression. He examines the neck bones and says they have reverted – so I have fairly hefty tweaks. I am on a vegetable fatigue in the kitchen at 2.30 p.m. with Elias. We put all the leaves in a tank and wash them, then spread them out on slabs. It is not an unpleasant fatigue and we are rewarded with a cup of tea with MILK AND SUGAR! Fairy goes to Miyako Hospital with beriberi. Buster Findlay has it too. He has supporting irons clamped from his feet to his knees. Circumstances alter cases: when most people in the room had money and the shop put condensed milk on sale, they bought it. Now the shop has put some more out; 80% can't buy it and they've gone all high-principled and high souled: 'This milk should be kept for the kiddies, God bless 'em! We would not touch it!' And a room vote decides to administer a reproof to the Camp Committee by returning the milk en bloc.

13 January: *(The diary contains nothing of importance for January 12th. When days are omitted from now on, it will mean that there is nothing noteworthy in the entries.)* A squad knock a doorway into the room in A-Block. I am laying it out – eight foot by five foot is recommended. Ventilation is non-existent. I manage to get 75 in, though not with eight foot by five foot each. The room is 78 feet by 42 feet. I am busy most of the day on this. The Camp Medical Reference Committee are very seriously perturbed about our food position. The four Dutch who came in yesterday are engineers from Tanjong Pinang in the Dutch East Indies where they have been working in the bauxite mines.

14 January: The condensed milk controversy is over; it is to be sold as arranged. The Camp has no salt and further supplies are doubtful. I mark the spaces in the new room. The Norwegians move in; they have no beds, but they have more luggage than we had. I am on a fatigue party at 2 p.m. – one-and-a-half miles along the Tampines Road. I stack logs by the roadside for a lorry to collect. We pass 200 troops, British and Dutch – not downhearted! We have a visitation of the gaol by about 30 Nipponese officers complete with jackboots and swords. What a nice-looking lot! Exuding intelligence and Adonis-like! The newspaper reports that the so-clever Nipponese scientists are not only going to eradicate venereal disease, but also discover its causes.

15 January: An internee who came in recently from the Post and Telegraph Office was called up by the Military Police and questioned. 'You enemy,' they barked. 'Yes, I am a British subject.' 'You ENEMY!' and so forth – no rhyme or reason, just a hymn of hate and finally a bark of 'Go away! I will send for you.' Of course, nothing happened. The use of enemy languages will be prohibited in all private correspondence after July 1st! What a move! The Chief of the Military Propaganda Department tells the public: 'There is nothing to be proud of in speaking English, but, on the contrary it is considered to be disgraceful.' The occupation of the warders' quarters (Asiatic) outside the gaol is to be permitted. One hundred will be allowed in the sub-warders' quarters on the Camp Representative's personal guarantee of good behaviour. We are not applying. The conditions are not stated and we prefer the devil we know.

16 January: I was amused by the gentleman who wished they would put the lights on in the morning: 'It's so difficult to dress in the dark.' Dressing equals donning a pair of shorts! On November 1st, the chlorinated water was stopped in Singapore for 'two months'. We have heard no more about it. As cricket organiser, I am a repository for tennis balls. There were two curious requests for old ones today: 1) from Jack who has a broken middle finger; he wants to practise gripping with it; and 2) for the head of the beater for the big bass drum! Forty men have come in (23 municipality officers and 17 engineers). And what luggage! Beds, tables, deck chairs – the poor mutts who came in a year ago with what we could carry on our backs gaze with stupefaction and envy. There is a discussion about the number of clubs we are members of. I can boast the Sungei Ujong, Seremban Golf Club, Negri Sembilan Club, Tampin, K. Pilah, Jelebu, Idris (Kuala Kangsar), Kuala Kangsar Sporting Union, Kajang, Selangor, Selangor Golf Club, Royal Trengganu Golf Club, Johore Civil Service Club, Kulim Club, Malacca, Malacca Golf Club, Malacca Swimming Club, Singapore Cricket Club, Singapore Swimming Club and Royal Singapore Golf Club.

Sunday, 17 January: I should have addressed Rotary at 5 p.m. on the subject of my War Leave, but it was rained off. Try no smoking and the swallow is a shade better.

18 January: Still no flag flies – the Nips seem to have given up the unequal struggle. I report to Macintyre that the swallow seems better than for some time; he thinks the manipulations are working and does nothing. Then comes the worst possible tiffin for the oesophagus: dry rice and dried fish! Ugh! I take about two tablespoons of the rice, mixed with the fish, chutney and vinegar, but it is too much. The swallow refuses to work after I have eaten about three-quarters of it. I ask Coe, who has just come in from the Post and Telegraph Office, if he found the Nipponese incompetent. He says, 'Not incompetent, but they have a different way of doing things.' e.g. Mail bags from Kuala Lumpur to Singapore were handed over by us to the railways in Kuala Lumpur in exchange for a receipt. This is not good enough for the Nipponese; they send a postman with the mail. I attend a fairly interesting lecture by Dr R.B. McGregor on 'The Medical and Health Services.' I do not smoke today.

19 January: An official notice says that eggs, which merely smell, will NOT be exchanged. Jack sells his watch for $65; it cost $32 four years ago. This is indicative of the state of affairs in Singapore. There is absolutely no import of manufactured goods. So it is a great day for both of us; it puts him in funds again and we buy foodstuffs including butter, condensed milk, cocoa and sugar. I try no smoking for a third day, but it seems to make no difference and, when I regurgitate even a banana at 4 p.m., I am so annoyed that I promptly light a pipe in high dudgeon.

20 January: At 7.25 a.m., Jack and I go to the main yard, run half a mile and are not unduly puffed, so I think we will resume daily runs. The sparse spectators at that hour think, of course, that we are completely bats, but I feel it is very good. McMichael has died of diabetes. We played rugger together years ago. Insulin can't be got now, fresh supplies at any rate. Nic mentions a talk the women are given. 'Asia for the Nipponese'. It was not at all popular, I gather. A woman internee sent a wireless message to the Canadian Prime Minister in reply to his Christmas message – through the Nipponese, of course. She said what a wonderful Christmas we'd all had and how happy we all are – disgraceful! One can only trust the outside world doesn't swallow it. It appears our Committee knew nothing of it and are very incensed. Three people arrive from Alor Star; they were two days en route, handcuffed all the way. One was wounded in an attack on his bungalow in Siam. He escaped and made his way to Malaya, but found it was no longer British and gave himself up at Alor Star where he has been until now.

21 January: I am on firewood fatigue in the afternoon. It is very pleasant; the weather is sunny and breezy. I speak to H.C. Clarke, a prisoner-of-war. I shall never get used to the sight of a big, burly Sikh, with a rifle and fixed bayonet, marching up to the bunch of Nipponese – who apparently sit all day long on the verandah of an atap house, all in a row, all wearing topees. He then presents arms, stands stiffly to attention – and performs the regulation bow from the waist! It all looks so comic opera and I always laugh. I expect that one-day I shall be observed and run in for lese Tenno Haiko or something. An internee out shopping met Pawan who asked if he knew me. He runs a stall in the market. He sent me a message. He is anxiously waiting; he wants to return to normal with the British in charge.

22 January: I have curious dreams of Nora two nights running: 1) I am released and we are out walking. Nora says, 'I'm so glad you're out.' 'Good, so am I.'

'You'll be a lot more use, too, on the Western Front.' 'What! The Western Front? And me 53 years old and 30 years in the tropics!' 'But you're not 53 yet.' 'No, but I shall be in less than six weeks.' NB. This implies knowledge of the date in my dream, as I am 53 on March 1st. 2) We are throwing a dinner party. There are a lot of most curious-looking men whom I have never seen before. Our clothes are ragged and filthy. Time passes; there is no effort to wash and change; I get quite hot and bothered. Eventually, about 9 p.m., we make a move. I don evening dress, then find the bottoms of my trousers coated with mud, but Nora comes in and says it doesn't matter and brushes it off, but they're an awful mess! 3) I am ashore in Tristan da Cunha. The population is largely Scandinavian; they speak little English. I talk to a girl in a cottage-cum-shop, but we can't understand each other. I see about four small craft with masts and funnels sticking out of the sea – sunk by a German submarine. I eventually clamber into a small boat; it capsizes at sea, but I find to my astonishment I can swim like a fish and am rescued. I am even unfrightened by the experience. I have no reason to dream of Tristan da Cunha. Wireless messages of 50 words can be sent to Australia via the Nipponese. There are to be no complaints and you can ask for Red Cross comforts, but NOT FOOD. In other words, they are too cocky to admit the truth, which is that they can't feed us and our health can go to the devil. The receipt of a lot of messages saying we are fit and voicing no complaints may deceive the undiscerning; but surely any responsible body will know that the acid test is a neutral Red Cross report and THAT they have not had even after a year.

23 January: 'The Syonan Sinbun' advertises a slogan competition for the anniversary of the fall of Singapore: 'Slogans should clearly show the invulnerable position of Nippon for the successful consummation of a protracted war.' Difficult, one thinks.

Sunday, 24 January: At 5 p.m., I address the Rotarians. I think it is OK. Anyhow, my voice is all right. There is an orchestral concert in the main yard featuring the works of Gilbert and Sullivan; it is a good show.

25 January: Am on standby fatigue all day. We have to move a very heavy machine for rubber rolling. The two top soccer teams, Aberdeen and Leicester City, draw Nil – Nil. Soccer has certainly caught the popular fancy. It is fast and amusing, owing to the vagaries of the ground and, of course, it is skilful. 'The Syonan Sinbun' reports that another clever Nipponese doctor-cum-scientist has discovered that striped mosquitoes convey dengue fever. Our Committee are told: the letter protesting against the solitary confinement of Scott and Morgan over such a prolonged period is 'rude'. The Committee reply that it is not rude, but previously more mildly-worded letters evoked no reply. However, the Nipponese refuse to forward the protest, so that is that.

26 January: Last night's roll was good, but solid. It took me 40 minutes, but I got it down, along with the bully-beef stew. There is a bathing parade for B-Block, but I do not go for the same reasons as before. Our little friends send five lorries into town today for rations. There aren't any, except for a quarter of a lorry-load. In future, there will be no margarine issue, no free bananas and the red palm oil ration will be halved. Asahi said to the Committee, 'What are you worrying about food for? Why don't you grow fruit? That's the stuff' – or words to that effect. The Committee replied that the only feasible quick-growing crop is bananas; other fruit trees take four to five years. This elicited the reply: 'Well, it's going to be a long war, you know.' Which is a fat lot of use in solving immediate food problems. They are a hopeless bunch; they'll crack, I'm sue. The Committee have spent $400,000 on food and other camp necessities.

27 January: I am on a fatigue at 10 a.m., cleaning the exercise yard. It would be more satisfactory if the broom had more than half-a-dozen bristles on it. A survey of the barbed-wire-fenced area outside the gaol is wanted – the vegetable gardens, the pigless pig farm and so on. I am sent for and interviewed. It is arranged that I meet a Nipponese representative at 10 a.m. tomorrow. Asahi now denies ever having seen the letter last August in which we asked for a loan and that he said it would be October before we could get a reply. 'The Syonan Sinbun' reports that the museum authorities in Singapore are busy translating all the thousands of explanatory data from English into Nippon-go. English is to be done away with!

28 January: The Nipponese arrives an hour late for his appointment, as expected, at 11 a.m. He and I go out and he points out the areas which are to be fenced, after which we will be allowed to use them. The biggest is just behind the gaol. We haven't much conversation. He asks my age and how long I have been out here and I ask where he lives. 'In a camp,' he says. H.C.R. Rendle joins us. A lorry goes into town again for rations and comes back empty. Why does this happen? Complete lack of co-operation, I suppose. I meet Norman Dugdale. I thought he was well away, but he has been working in Middleton Hospital (for infectious diseases) which the Nipponese avoid like... the plague! There are absolutely no medical supplies left. The only folk enjoying themselves in Singapore are the Nipponese. Whisky is $120 a bottle. 'But' I say, 'surely no-one will buy it at that price?' The only people who do are contractors, to present to the Nipponese. A wireless message of 50 words can now be handed in to send home.

29 January: I go out at 10.30 a.m. with another internee and a Sikh sentry. I carry a micrometer theodolite with me. It is a pleasant morning. The Sikh sentry brings four young coconuts – very pleasant all round. I send a message home: 'Kitching, 1, Victoria Parade, Morecambe, England. Message: Nora left Singapore February 13th. Ship bombed, sunk. No news since. Am very worried. Just possible interned elsewhere. Have had one letter only from Brian. Hope you both carry on normally until return. Am passably fit. Send tobacco, shoes size six through Red

Cross (Clothing). Love.' To obtain salt, we are trying boiling sea-water. The margarine issue has been reduced from half-an-ounce per head to one-third of an ounce and none with rice cake. A. Newberry of the Fire Brigade has died. He came out the same year as I – 1913.

30 January: I am out on a survey again, but there is nothing of note to report. I get my watch back at last. There is an excellent orchestral concert. I like 'Yeomen of the Guard'; and 'The Quaker Girl' takes me right back to Cambridge days when I saw it with Betty Parfit of Girton. Bugs are fewer, but I get badly bitten by mosquitoes most nights.

Sunday, 31 January: The lorries go into town today, but there is nothing doing. The alleged rice pudding today is a queer do. It makes many feel sick and some actually exude H_2S, apparently due to some chemical action, as it is 'limed' rice. It is certainly most unpleasant. It turns all the spoons black! The Penang internees arrive – 18 of them, with nine soldiers – Leicester's, I believe – all handcuffed.

1 February 1943: My day's timetable: At 7.30 a.m., I rise from my concrete couch. I go to the main yard and trot half-a-mile. I do my laundry, shave, bathe in cold water and return to the room at 8 a.m. I fold up my bedclothes and mattress to make my seat for the hours of daylight, examining everything for bugs the while. At 8.20 a.m., I sit down and eat last night's roll with margarine and jam (my own). It takes 40 minutes, but I get it down without accident. At 9 a.m., I have breakfast – this takes until 9.30 a.m. I wash up Jack's and my own things. I go to the Main Yard Wailing Wall. At 10 a.m., I go to the courtyard with my survey gang and acquire a sentry. At 10.15 a.m., I start my survey round the gaol until noon. Three lorries full of internees wait outside from 10 a.m. to 12.30 p.m. to go to Singapore for food, then they all come in again, having done nothing. At 12.15 p.m., I wash, smoke and read. At 1 p.m., I have lunch – two tablespoons of savoury rice and a modicum of the dried fish (ugh!). I mix it with chutney, vinegar and pickles and succeed in eating it in 50 minutes. At 2 p.m., I do some reading and eat two pieces of nut toffee (my own) and a banana, then I work on crossword number 26. At 3.30 p.m., I go to the library; luckily, there is no queue. I get 'Trent's Last Case' – a grand book. I've read it at least three times in a previous existence. By special permit, I obtain also 'The Ingoldsby Legends.' I drink tea saved from the morning in a thermos, smoke a pipe, finish my crossword and chat with sundry visitors. At 6 p.m., I have my evening meal. I take a little rice pudding and mix it with condensed milk (my own) and get it down fairly easily mixed with two bananas (camp issue). I wash up. At 7.15 p.m., I go to the lecture by Cheeseman in the 'Malaya' series on 'Education'. It is nothing short of excellent in delivery, material and choice of words. At 8.15 p.m., I go back to my seat and take a duck's egg raw to mix with Worcester sauce, but it stinks to high heaven. I go to the yard tap and dispose of it and the smell very thoroughly. I go to the hot water tank near the kitchen, fill a thermos, make cocoa (my own), using gula malacca (my own) and two dessert-spoons of condensed milk (my own). At 9 p.m., I write a chit to the Nipponese and talk to two room-mates. At 9.30 p.m., I put down my bed and drink cocoa, eat three biscuits and clean my teeth at the yard tap. Lights out at 10 p.m. The Penang contingent have had a very bad time. The score mounts. They got rice and vegetables, no books, and no tobacco. Seven out of nine of them are in hospital. The nine were all in one room. They were not even given tea. Coming here, they were not even allowed to bring with them the few clothes they had in gaol. 'The Syonan Sinbun' announces that there are 18 large mailbags in Tokyo with letters from Great Britain for war prisoners in the Southern Regions – that's us. There is also more foolish propaganda in the paper: 'The Malacca rice crop for 1942 was 10 times as great as that under the British in 1941' – flatly impossible.

2 February: I do the office work on the survey. I go to Macintyre at 4.15 p.m. We decide on a diet as an experiment: no rice. I have an idea I am eating more, in bulk, than I ever used to. Now why should Stiven have his spectacles wantonly smashed? He was working on a vegetable fatigue, filling a cart with earth. There was some tripping mishap, the cart slipped and annoyed a Nipponese standing near. He swiped Stiven on the face and smashed his goggles. The Penang contingent – seven Leicester's and two East Surreys – were cut off and made their way to Penang. There they hid in the hills for several months before capture. I would have liked to hear their adventures, but they are removed to a prisoner-of-war camp. There are now 3041 in this gaol; so much for the promises to relieve overcrowding. Including the hospital, there are 2,577 men, 382 women and 82 children. Soccer may have to be stopped. Too many injuries are making inroads on bandages and dressings. Material for making plaster bandages has run out; wooden splints will have to be used in future. Dancing classes are to be started. I don't suppose we shall have a nice instructress!

3 February: As I am having a haircut this morning, I discern at the top of the steps the short, thickset figure and patriarchal beard of our lion-tamer who says he is 87 and don't look it. I am reminded of the story told me by one of our internees. The old man started talking about the war and my informant thought, 'Now, I'm not going to let him pull fast ones over me about what he did in the Great War'. Then the old 'un said, 'Yes, then we advanced on Manila' – and he realised he was talking about the Spanish-American War. I am suddenly told Chuchi wants the survey figures today, so I work all afternoon getting approximate figures. At 4 p.m., Nolan and I visit the den. Chuchi has some champagne in a suku glass – he has been doing well. We converse in Malay via a Nipponese interpreter and I tell him I will try to produce the figures tomorrow. 'The Syonan Sinbun' says that, in India, the British have an army of 'at least' two million Indians whom the British intend to put in the forefront of the battle, while British troops hide behind their turbans in lieu of skirts.

4 February: There is to be a women's concert on the 11th in the 'Rose Garden'. I hope we are allowed to go. Tiffin today is a trial, but I get it down. A roll at 6 p.m. is comparatively easy. Is the tiger changing its whiskers? The nine Penang internees, after a request from the Committee, have been supplied by the Nipponese, with pillows, blankets and mattresses! Now, what about the other 3,000 of us? The salt experiment has been deemed a success – 15 gallons of sea-water boiled down to four-and-a-half pounds of salt.

5 February: I report to Macintyre at 4.15 p.m. I am to continue the 'no bulk' diet another week. A notice is issued: we are still not paying proper respect to Nipponese officers. When we see one, we must remove our hats, stand to attention and bow. I have no hat. The repatriation rumour is very strong. The Nipponese Foreign Minister told their House of Peers that the Nipponese Government is undertaking concrete negotiations with the governments of enemy countries for the repatriation of Nipponese nationals interned in those countries and for the dispatch of exchange ships for that purpose. The Nipponese Government is giving fair and square treatment to enemy nationals, which humane treatment has been thoroughly endorsed by representatives of the International Red Cross who personally inspected the internment camps in Nippon and in the regions under Nipponese control, accordingly reporting the inspection to the world.

6 February: I do a survey in the morning. There is a slight return of the cream crackers at breakfast. I get the sardine and vegetable soup down with difficulty – it takes me one hour, no less. I shall be glad to be out of this, if only for proper investigation and feeding. It is an ironical situation. I probably have more food than anyone in the room and I can't eat it! At 7 p.m., I hear about the Austerhaus affair – he wrote to the Nipponese that he wished to divulge an internees' plot to prove his sincerity and loyalty to them. He has been removed – he is a Dutch subject and pro-German.

Sunday, 7 February: The rations supplied include 350 pounds of dried fish. It's outside the kitchen now – and the smell! We also receive 1,525 lbs. of vegetables, including papayas, 280 lbs. of salt, 332 lbs, of tea, 1,040 lbs. of sugar, 160 gallons of groundnut oil and 515 bars of soap – not much for 3,000 for – is it five days? God help us if we are entirely dependent on Nipponese rations. One of our padres called another gentleman a lazy little bugger which he resented and the case is being investigated! Think he is probably correct in his description, but oh! Padre!

8 February: In the night, what a shemozzle. All I heard of it was heavy boots clanking down the passage after 12 by the clock and I found myself thinking: 'there's a gentleman who reckons nothing of other people's convenience'. It was a Sikh sentry with a Nipponese. They had discovered two Asians in conversation by the party wall between A and B-Blocks and hauled them off. Whether or not they were in actual conversation with wenches transmural is not clear, nor whether they were looking for something else – perhaps a wireless? – As a result of disclosures by our friend Austerhaus. I hear the two boys are being beaten up now – the usual tactics. They are released in the afternoon. An operation for appendicitis on the son of the Chief Medical Officer is done by Chitty, by request. Ledoux has both little fingers permanently bent at right angles to his hands. It is a known complaint, but the doctors can do nothing – very distressing.

9 February: One ton of fresh fish is supplied today by the Nipponese, I hear, plus 1,280 lbs. of rice – wonderful! 'The Syonan Sinbun' reports Tokyo as saying that 'the maltreatment and petty annoyances to which Nipponese internees are subjected in Great Britain and the U.S.A. are in sharp contrast to the warm, sympathetic treatment extended by the Nipponese to enemy nationals and prisoners-of-war.' Why put this sort of rubbish in the local paper, when the inhabitants know quite well how WE have been treated? Warm and sympathetic? Nonsense. Husbands and wives are actually being allowed to meet from 11 a.m. to noon on Thursday – after one year's internment, less six days – very warm treatment. But the meeting is not to be mentioned in 'The Changi Guardian' lest the authorities get to know!

10 February: There is to be no cricket in B-Block yard. The Block Committee say it's too congested – sheer nonsense. I am elected to skipper our side again; I must get up a protest. A Nipponese in A-Block interfered with a woman internee a few days ago under the affluence of alcohol. He has now signed an undertaking not to enter during the night hours unless called. This is unusual tractability – is it because of the impending exchange?

11 February: I am on standby fatigue, but am not called upon. It is another of a series of very wet days and I play bridge for most of it.

12 February: I chat to Doctors Wallace and Hopkins. Dr Johns who is a throat specialist now goes to Kadang Kerbau Hospital and they are most emphatic he should examine me, so I shall have to tell Macintyre tomorrow. I think this is sensible. The Rising Sun absolutely refuses to fly over this gaol while we're in it! The new flag has succumbed. The Nipponese, accompanied by Sikh sentries, are nipping around, perhaps looking for wireless sets as a result of the information received from Austerhaus? Anyway, they annexe electric hot plates, kettles and other possessions, leaving an atmosphere of desolation with those bereft. Celebration Week (of the surrender of Singapore) started yesterday and ho, ho, ho! It's rain, rain, rain! In the paper there is a program of sports and other events and it says: 'The local people will organise parties for the entertainment of the Army and will make courtesy visits to Army and Navy hospitals. They will pay visits to the War Memorials to respect the souls of the dead.' The Sikh sentries are wandering around apparently aimlessly. It transpires that they want to buy watches for resale outside at about 66% of the outside value.

13 February: A year ago today, Nora left and I have heard absolutely nothing of her since. I see Macintyre – my swallow is 'as you were'. I eat soup and a sardine in one-and-a-half hours at lunch! He agrees I should get examined, so I see Johns and he will take me next time he goes to Kadang Kerbau Hospital. He says that it is possible that the mere passage of an oesophagoscope will do the trick.

Sunday, 14 February: In my weekly dusting, I discover a nest of ants in my one good writing pad – interesting. They must have come out of the coconuts in driblets and banded together and formed a colony. They are on top of my wooden box – my library – and were not there last week. I will leave them a bit as they eat bugs. 'The Syonan Sinbun' reports that Yamashita, the conqueror of Malaya, has been promoted to General. 'It is a name that has turned Malaya into Malai and Singapore to Syonan!' A notable feat! Piccadilly is having its weekly airing – the yard is littered with beds and appurtenances. I hear that the home news reveals that the postcards had not been delivered by December.

15 February: I am on a lorry fatigue at 10.30 a.m., pushing a broken-down monster out of the way. Suddenly, two Nipponese and about 30 Sikhs rush in at the double and turn the kitchen, Hudson's Bay and the library upside down. I suppose they are still looking for wireless sets. After a few more abortive rushes, Mr Austerhaus won't be so popular with them! At noon, we have a visitation. I see they have annexed the Victoria House nameboard – the Gestapo gentleman in the lead evidently does not like it – and a microscope, a pair of binoculars, two pairs of handcuffs, a petrol tin, two police belts and a whistle on a lanyard – a really useful bag. Johns, in an interview with Asahi, showed him 'The Syonan Sinbun' with the Foreign Minister's references to the marvellous treatment of internees and asked about a visit from the International Red Cross. Asahi said he hoped to move in this matter as soon as possible! Bunk. I go to a lecture by Linehan on 'The Aborigines of Malaya'; he has a very good knowledge of his subject – interesting, but his delivery is not good. I went to sleep over a palindrome – the best I could do was: Oi! Dark Nip Asahi has a pink radio.

17 February: A year ago today, we assembled on the Padang with, according to instructions, clothing for 10 days and no food. That clothing has, for all the Japanese have done for us, had to last for a year and an indefinite period ahead.

18 February: Repatriation rumours – Asahi is reported to have said to Women's Camp representatives: 'Yes, I can suppy you with banana plants and rose cuttings, but you won't be here to see them.' Passes for those who live in the coolie lines outside are made by a Nipponese with a duplicating machine: 'A Permit for the entree of the INTERMENT Camp.' Things which might have been better expressed! I weigh 120lbs on the hospital scales. Now I am told they are no bloody good. I try the laundry scales – only 112 lbs.! Eight ruddy stones – incredible. I receive four ounces of tobacco via Sell and, from Katherine, some indeterminate tobacco and a tin of condensed milk – very welcome indeed. The flag has collapsed again. Asahi knows no more about an exchange than we do. He cannot get a list of British women interned in Java. He can't write to his vis-a-vis there except via Tokyo. He thinks we all look very comfortable. Ye Gods! Let him try eight foot by three foot for a year, within prison walls on a foul diet. And what 'comfort' we have is no thanks to the Nipponese. Our electric light bulbs are running out now and the Nipponese can't or won't replace them. The passage and the outside lights have gone now and this room, with 100 jammed in, is pitch dark.

19 February: For lunch, I strain the soup and so am able to finish by 1.50 p.m. in time to go on vegetable fatigue. I do watering for one-and-a-half hours between 2 and 4 p.m. (noon to 2 p.m. by the sun) – very hot indeed. How Nora would have rejoiced to see me gardening! I never would do it in Malaya. I always said, 'Wait till I retire.' The vegetable garden is doing very badly, they tell me. The soil is sure to have been worked out by the Chinese in previous years. 'The Syonan Sinbun' for Tuesday and Wednesday surpasses itself. Quoting a 'Nippon Times' editorial (this also shows what sort of pap the Nipponese people are being fed on), it says: in Malaya 'a bright atmosphere exists among the populace, in striking contrast to former days when, under tyrannical British rule, the inhabitants had nothing to look forward to but a lifetime of slavery.... The people are fully cognisant of the fact that Nippon came to emancipate them and not to exploit them, as did the British.' This may be very good for the Japanese people, but to quote it to those of Malaya who KNOW it to be untrue is remarkably bad propaganda. And could absurdity go further than this comment by the newspaper on the progress of the war: 'The stubborn Soviet defence has the Anglo-Americans worried, because they are afraid she will be stronger than they'? *(The Soviet Union at this stage of the war was doing more than just putting up a stubborn defence. The German Sixth Army surrendered to the Red Army on 31 January. An estimated 200,000 Germans had been killed or had died from starvation and the cold since the German forces were encircled at Stalingrad in November. In the north, the German siege of the city of Leningrad was finally lifted on 18 January after 16 months.)*

20 February: At 11 a.m., I can't speak. There is what feels like phlegm in my throat. It is an awful nuisance. I have had it two or three times recently. It is connected in some way with my swallow. Scott and Morgan have been released after practically one year's solitary confinement in separate cells with NO EXERCISE; barbarous. There were no reasons given. Scott, I understand, is very lucky to be alive. He left Singapore on Saturday, February 14th in the Hong Bee. There were about 300 on board. They were intercepted by a Nipponese cruiser, which made unintelligible signals. Four, including Scott, put off in a rowing boat to find out what they wanted.

The ship was shelled and sunk and, as far as he knows, all on board were lost. News has arrived of Edwards; he is in Palestine. News of him came in another internee's letter. As Edwards left in a small boat on Sunday, February 15th with C.T.M. Husband, Goss, Best and Clark-Walker of our department, they are presumably safe too. I am busy on a map of Malaya, showing the progress of the campaign. At 8.15 p.m., I go to a talk by Professor Tratman on 'Digging up the Past.'

Sunday, 21 February: An exchange MUST be on the way! Two more concessions have been made after a year – things which should have been done at the beginning. We can now go outside the gaol and walk in the wired area on Tuesdays and Fridays from 6 to 8 p.m., the women on Mondays, Wednesdays and Saturdays at the same times. There must be no meeting of the two! And the Nipponese will 'endeavour to locate' personal belongings which were left in Raffles, Adelphi, the Fullerton Building and the new Supreme Court.

22 February: We are running in the main yard most mornings at 7.30 and we shave in the laundry. I finish the map of the conquest of Malaya.

23 February: Our first outing from the camp from 6 to 8 p.m. is typical. Food is at 6 so that no one can possibly get out before 6.30. Jack and I go out at 7. It is quite pleasant; there is a nice breeze – but there are still hundreds of men all over the shop! One can't get away from it. The Nipponese are not prepared to provide eggs and palm oil. They are still 'trying' to get soya beans (which we will pay for!) The medics report pellagra-like conditions to the Nipponese (loss of vision). The Nipponese ask for samples! We say to send a medical officer. We ask the Nipponese what has become of a body-disposal squad of six Europeans who have completely disappeared since capitulation.

24 February: I get a haircut today. There is a bathing-parade, but I do not go. I run instead. There are more forms to be filled in duplicate – the same as before. When is anything going to happen? A Fairy Story, showing the immense importance and value of statistics to the Nipponese: Fairy went to hospital six weeks ago with beriberi. A Chinese doctor told him to return to the gaol: 'I am very sorry to turn you out – you are certainly not fit yet – but I have instructions that the number of patients must be less at the end of February, than at the end of January when Dr Landor was in charge. You can come back on March 1st; that will be all right!'

25 February: I have more dreams of Nora. There is a fracas in the laundry. Bull, a magistrate, picks the wrong man to be rude to – Wimbush, an ex-boxing champion – and is taken to hospital. I am on hospital laundry fatigue; we wash blankets, sheets, pillow-slips etc. It is done more efficiently than previously; we use hot water, scrubbing brushes and soap. Jack is on town fatigue to collect 52 bags of rice from St Andrews. He has tiffin in a Chinese coffee shop; it has no stocks at all. Half the cars are running on gas! Co-Prosperity brings you no beer, no nothing. He gets a few cigarettes with considerable difficulty. I start a map of Singapore Island to show the campaign. What I can see of myself in my shaving mirror is 'orrible! Scrawny neck – and torso and arms all shrunk beyond anything I ever thought possible. My size for shirts etc. used to be 40; it's about 36 now. And, when I lie on my concrete bed, I can feel bones all over the place where they were not a year ago!

26 February: The water is now pronounced fit to drink by the Nipponese only two months behind schedule. At 10.30 a.m., I set off for Kadang Kerbau Hospital. There are only 18 in an ambulance built for 10 – 15 inside and three outside with the driver. There are three women, one Nipponese interpreter, one Sikh sentry, two drivers, six doctors, one dentist (Cellan-Jones) and four male patients. I am given an injection of morphia. The back of my throat is sprayed half-a-dozen times with a cocaine solution. I lie on the operating table for one-and-a-half hours, then Johns pushes the oesophagoscope down my neck for about a foot. It is as thick as a finger. It is not very painful, but it is unpleasant. He takes swabs and a 'piece' of something for examination. After this, I rest for two hours on the operating table and wish I could stay there in a state of coma (as I am) for six months. Then I have a cup of tea and wander out into a passage. A nurse says, 'Are you looking for something? Can I help you?' 'No, thanks,' I reply. 'I'm only finding my bearings.' 'Perhaps Mr Johns has them,' she says brightly! I am X-rayed too. The spasms are distinct, but the verdict is – the swallowing difficulty is entirely muscular, subject to examination of the 'piece' removed today. Then I meet Kandiah. He is overcome with joy, all praying to God and all excitement. He asks about 'Madam'. I say I am very much afraid she is gone. 'Oh no, sir,' he cries. 'God would not do such a thing. We must have done some wrong, but God has made us atone for it now; we can expect better things soon.' I have a look at the hospital shop – very expensive, of course. I buy a tin of milk for $2.20, four ounces of tobacco for $7, some biscuits at two cents each and curry puffs at six cents each. I discover that Johns got some insulin on the black market – $245 a pound instead of $78. We return at 4.30 p.m. and I am sick. I am very sleepy and washed out all evening. Impressions – Singapore is three-quarters dead. But most of all I am impressed by the intense eagerness of every Asiatic I meet, including the sentry, to be pleasant and obliging; it is most heartening.

27 February:'The Syonan Sinbun' leader is quite amusing; it tells the people how changed things are for them compared with a year ago and adds in brackets 'for the better' – in case there should be some misapprehension! Our ex-pig-farm-vegetable-garden is now handed over to prisoners-of-war. We will give you another place, say the Nipponese. Three women are to be allowed to take part in our production of 'The Merchant of Venice.' Good gracious! In the evening, I was going to see CHU CHIN CHANGI but it was cancelled because of rain. The illustrated poster is excellent and some of the characters are LOK YEW HUP, a policeman; FOO LING YEW, court magician; CHANG-I-KWOD, emperor of Changistan.

Sunday, 28 February: I play bridge with Coles versus Wiseman and Walker. Walker came out with us on the Sarpedon in 1940. I eat larger helpings of kanji and rice pudding today without great difficulty and get the soup down in one hour.

1 March 1943: Today is my 53rd birthday. What a wasted year! I wonder if Nora is alive. She came to me in a dream very vividly. I open my last tin of cream; it goes well with kanji. I eat last night's roll, so I have a hearty breakfast in one-hour – an improvement. I shall NOT eat dried fish on my birthday. I open a tin of sausages. The camp finances are bad, so eggs go up to 20 cents and nothing will be bought for the store except dietary necessities from day to day e.g. soya beans, rice polishings, peanuts. The camp shop will make at least 33 and a third per cent on everything sold. Medical replacements are restricted to $250 per month; spectacles and other such items to $100 per month; dental equipment to $1,000 in total. Of course, it is iniquitous in the extreme that we should have to do this for ourselves, but it seems quite useless to expect anything from the Nipponese. I receive a most welcome gift of $50, one pound of cocoa, one tin of barley biscuits, one tin of Ovaltine, two sardines and 24 ounces of butter. The Red Cross do their stuff marvellously. I see 'Chu Chin Changi'; it is fairly good.

2 March: 'The Syonan Sinbun' reports that the Nipponese Government has decided not to consider Indians and the other peoples of the Philippines, Hong Kong, Malaya, Borneo and the Dutch East Indies as enemy nationals any longer i.e. as regards property and freezing of assets – providing that they understand Nippon's war objectives and co-operate with her in the construction of Greater East Asia!

3 March: The Nipponese have replied concerning the Body Disposal Squad of six men. They were sentenced to two years imprisonment for 'contravening a military regulation'. There is no news of one of them; Davis and Logan have died of beriberi; and the other three are in prison hospital. Adequate comment is impossible. These men were left outside Changi to assist the Nipponese. They have taken the new vegetable garden from us for the prisoners-of-war and also two-sevenths of the internal prison garden. There is no quid pro quo.

4 March: At 10 a.m., I do a 'light carpenter' fatigue, taking sheets of asbestos-cum-cement on a handcart from the carpenter's shop to the new brine-making shed at the back of the laundry in Girdle Road. It is fairly easy and it is all over by 11 a.m. A German sea-raider called here; it had on board British, Dutch and other prisoners. At the dock, they were maltreated by the Nipponese. The German crew interfered; there was a scrap. I am told a number of Germans are now interned in the prisoner-of-war camp as a result! Asahi informs the Camp Committee that negotiations are now in progress between the Nipponese and British for repatriation. The cards have been forwarded to Tokyo for transmission to London where the selection will take place. Thirty-one internee patients have suddenly been ejected from Miyako Hospital.

5 March: A Roman Catholic priest came back to Changi tight after a visit to his flock! He was in durance vile for 24 hours and an order then came from the Nipponese: 'No internees are to consume any alcohol when out on fatigues or otherwise!' At tiffin, I take a larger ration of kanji and rice pudding and we strain the soup through a perforated tin with a bottle as a squeezer. I take the liquid and Jack takes the solids. This works well as far as my swallow is concerned.

6 March: A fatigue party has to go to the Women's Block to do repairs to the clotheslines. So a notice is put up, asking the ladies to remove their clothes before 2 p.m. I talk to Chipp; he travelled with Nora and Brian on the Corfu in 1934. He says there is a good chance of Nora being interned in Sumatra. I say I do not think so. There is a faint chance, but it is no use buoying oneself up with false hopes, or rather, foolish optimism. Three lorries are to fetch 29 internees from Ipoh tomorrow. I am again asked to stand as Room Representative, but decline. I feel this swallow business is too wearing. Dr Pallister gives his health report on one year of internment: we had again impressed the need for an improved diet on the Nipponese. Beriberi first appeared in May, but the introduction of rice-polishings practically stopped it. There were nine cases of pellagra recently due to malnutrition. There were 49 deaths – 41 men, seven women and one child. This works out at 17.2 per 1,000. This is excellent, but is no thanks to the Nipponese; we looked after ourselves. If anyone should disbelieve this, they have only to look at the rations supplied to us by the Nipponese. There were 726 cases of dysentery, but only 10 deaths. There were 25 cases of diphtheria in the Women's Camp.

Sunday, 7 March: The flag again! It is symbolic; a new one was put-up two days ago; it is now down to half-mast and is in ribbons. The Ipoh crowd arrive. There are very few pure Europeans, I hear.

8 March: I debug my tin box and my small case from 11 to 11.45 a.m. There are not many of them. I write an essay, 'Concrete Cricket' for the 'light essay' section of the Camp Competition. I have a walk outside from 7 to 7.30 p.m. I eat sausages instead of fish – ugh!

9 March: Last night, we got positively the last roll. There is no more flour and no apparent prospects of any. It won't hit me very hard, as I find it difficult to swallow rolls anyway. A gentleman has been telling the Nipponese people that the co-operation in the Southern Regions has been absolutely marvellous and there have been no uprisings against the conquerors! This doesn't fit in with the stories of guerrilla warfare brought down by the Ipohites; they say it is going very strong in Perak. There are 12 men, eight women and nine children and they were in their own homes until six weeks ago.

10 March: This morning prisoners-of-war with relatives, wives and fiancées here are allowed to visit. Asahi asked our Committee for an annual report and he has got it! It details all the beatings, solitary confinement and other grievances and compares the ludicrous rations they give us with what we should get – and mentions no Red Cross visit, no cleaning materials, no hospital supplies, no outside recreation and colossal overcrowding. It also mentions the lack of bedding and footwear and that the majority of us arrived by order over a year ago with clothes for 10 days. On three occasions, women were struck by Nipponese sentries for alleged irregularities in bowing; two women officials of the Women's Camp were struck by members of the Nipponese office staff for reasons which have never been disclosed. One woman was removed on an unspecified charge. She was not permitted to take any luggage and was kept in Joo Chiat Police Station for eight days with no privacy, no bed, no bedding and no provisions for washing and was given nothing but rice and water. She was struck three times during interrogation by Nipponese officials. In the Men's Camp, severe corporal punishment by beating with sticks and knotted ropes has been inflicted on eight internees ... also indiscriminate kicking and punching by Sikh guards. Two men were removed to a penal establishment and kept there for 18 days without bedding or spare clothing. They were allowed no washing, no shaving and no exercise. One was tortured in an attempt to extract information. The Governor, Sir Shenton Thomas, and the Dutch Governor were kept in solitary confinement for some time. There was no trial in ANY of these cases. Four hundred and sixty-five of us AFTER A YEAR have still no bedding or mattresses. Of course, the report does not ignore the very few good points. The swallow – under my non-aggression policy – is behaving fairly well – that is, I am getting down, with care, a fair ration of kanji and rice pudding and the strained soup. Today, just at the end of the rice pudding, a discussion arises about $10 notes. Another internee says the Nipponese note is as good as ours in manufacture and I am so indignant at this that I swallow quickly in order to argue about it and that finishes me. It is two hours before I can swallow my own saliva. However, I am able to drink a cup of pre-bed cocoa.

11 March: I am on wood fatigue and have quite a long walk. As we go along, we are addressed by the inhabitants as 'sahib' and 'tuan.' I am asked to take part in a reading of 'The Rivals' by Sheridan and half-promise to do so.

12 March: I discuss the exchange with another internee. He says we have no business to be interned. He opines we would have a much better chance if we were transferred to Bangkok like the majority of the prisoners-of-war. I can't see it. My own repatriation estimate now is that there is an even money chance of leaving this pestilential hole by the end of June. Among the new internees in A-Block are two Nipponese women! Presumably they are married to men who came in and wish to stay with them.

Sunday, 14 March: I play bridge morning and evening. My swallow is comparatively good.

15 March: I am airing and debugging today and I examine the lock of my cash-box. I am reading 'Haworth Parsonage' by Isabel C. Clarke. I have never read a book on the Brontes before, although I have often passed Cowan Bridge, the noto-rious school, which caused the deaths of Maria and Elizabeth. If I ever see Nora again, she will be interested in this: referring to Bramwell Bronte, the only son, about 1840: 'His sisters saw him depart for Broughton-in-Furness where a Mr Postlethwaite had engaged him as a tutor to his son...' Nora's mother's family were Postlethwaites from Broughton and this would very probably be a relative. Asahi tells us that there are lots more letters from Britain, South Africa and Australia, which we knew a fortnight ago. It will be a week before they reach the camp, because there are so many. Why? It is the first time I've heard it is necessary to sort the whole of the mail for three weeks before you can deliver any of it – and we've been over a year without letters, so anyone with reasonable human instincts would expedite matters. They may already have been censored – if not, God knows when we'll get them.

16 March: Jack had a prolonged tussle with an enormous cockroach in the dark hours. It was walking on the canvas of his camp bed with Army boots on and he heard it. Later, it got on his back. There were a lot of crashes, oaths and bangs, but he never bagged it. I was expecting it to migrate on to me, as I'm on the floor, but I felt nothing, except the usual mosquitoes and a bug or two. Later, at 2 a.m., I emerged into the yard and saw the Southern Cross. A three-quarter moon was shin-ing like a good deed in a naughty world and making the neon light which glares all night to check criminal propensities on the part of Golders Green pale into insig-nificance. Golders Green is where the 'out' people live. They are now to be in-creased to four in a 'house' (there are 12 houses in a coolie line). As the living room is $10^{1}/_{2}$ feet by 14 feet and the verandah five by 14 feet, they still have a lot more room than our eight by three. But the Nipponese won't allow the increase from three to four until the expected arrivals really arrive to increase the congestion in the gaol – which is absurd. It can't make the slightest difference whether 108 or 144 live outside.

17 March: I get my part in 'The Rivals' to copy. There is only one copy of the play in camp. A high-ranking Nipponese came round yesterday; he was in naval uniform and had a guard with fixed bayonets and all the ceremony. Rumour credits him with being a prince. It's St Patrick's Day – there is a reading of 'The White-Headed Boy' by an Irish author and with an Irish cast. There's also a rehearsal of 'The Rivals'. Ambrose Cross is the producer.

18 March: Watson gives an example of military 'intelligence:' a few weeks before the Nipponese descended upon us, a forest officer in Kedah was working in the area of the Alor Star aerodrome and made a map showing all the tracks approaching it through the jungle and rice-fields. He then made an appointment with the Intelligence Officer for the area, duly kept. 'Good heavens!' said this gentleman, 'He's been taking things seriously! He's got a map ... Well, I can give you 20 minutes only – I'm going to the pictures.'

19 March: Kayn is in Singapore today on a shopping fatigue. He brings me back a half-pound loaf for eight cents. It is appalling stuff; it's made of maize flour and rice; my oesophagus rejects it with scorn. The newspaper praises it: 'Bread reappears in Syonan. The doctors are enthusiastic about it; it is more palatable and equally nourishing' (compared with that of the effete and non-prosperous days of British rule!)

20 March: I have a haircut. Today's thought – I have completely shattered the maxim: 'Early to bed, early to rise makes a man healthy, wealthy and wise.' For over a year, I've been in bed at 8 p.m. by the sun and up at 5.30 a.m. and I'm in the worst physical condition ever, poorer than ever and my brain is gradually becoming atrophied! Food deficiency is beginning to show up in diverse ways e.g. many people can't see properly – a focussing difficulty chiefly – I meet four today. And others have no control over their fingers; yet others have no feeling in their feet. I hear that the Nipponese went into every cell in A-Block about 2.30 a.m. Report on my swallow: I see Johns today and he says the specimens they took showed a fairly normal mucous membrane (so there is no growth, I take it.) He has no suggestions for amelioration of the situation. I suggest a diet e.g. a raw egg instead of a hard-boiled egg and soup without solids at midday. He will drop a note to Heron, our Block doctor. There is a variety performance in the Main Yard. It is announced that we are not allowed to sing the National Anthem any more, so, at the conclusion of the performance, they announce, 'Gentlemen, the King,' and everyone stands to attention until the signal, 'Goodnight, Gentlemen.' It's quite impressive.

Sunday, 21 March: The total numbers in Changi now are 3,026 men, 383 women, 77 children and two infants.

22 March: I am on hospital laundry fatigue at 10.30 a.m. I see Dr Heron about my diet. For tiffin, I get strained soup and rice pudding with some resemblance to the real thing. The Nipponese are graciously going to allow us 50 bags of rice polishings per month – to be paid for out of camp funds, if you please! What funds, after a year of buying enough to keep ourselves alive? Air Raid Precautions are typical of the whole comic opera. We are instructed to organise A.R.P. in the camp. We do so and put up six requests:

1) Provision of signals to indicate this is an internment camp;
2) Permission for dispersal outside the walls in an emergency;
3) Permission to dig slit trenches inside and out;
4) Permission for alternative exits;
5) Materials to carry out these works;

6) A.R.P. equipment.

The result is that four, five and six are ignored. Point one receives a flat refusal. On point two, if they are light bombs, we stay in; if heavy, we may be allowed to disperse. (I suppose there's a committee meeting of the Nipponese to decide if they are light or heavy after they've burst.) On point three, no slit trenches are allowed. So what on earth is the use of asking us to organise A.R.P.?

23 March: My rations are kanji porridge and tea, half a pint of milk, soup, custard and Marmite. I get it down, although even the custard is difficult. My weight on the laundry scales is 112 lbs and on the hospital scales $109^1/_2$ lbs. Wilson assures me the hospital scales are correct. There is a rehearsal of 'The Rivals' at 7 p.m. – it is a most amusing play.

24 March: From now on, I shall not chronicle kanji porridge, tea etc., as they are standard. There is a bathing parade for B-Block; I don't go, as we have a rehearsal at 4.30 p.m. I sit silent for two acts, then comes my cue. I open my mouth and emit hoarse croaks, to the intense astonishment of the assembled cast! My voice has completely gone. I shall have to give up the play – a pity, as it is such an amusing one and I think the readers have been excellently chosen for their parts.

25 March: For lunch, I get the usual soup and a pudding with ground rice and macaroni in it. It absolutely refuses to go down. I make three separate efforts at intervals of half-an-hour. My throat gets completely clogged up and I have to eject the food, so I tell Ironside who brought it. He asks the cook what he put in. 'Oh,' he says proudly, 'egg and ground rice and some macaroni to make it nice!' Well meant, but no use to me, alas.

26 March: Jack has sold his old fountain pen for $20. I am seeing what I can get for my old Waltham turnip watch. It must be over 30 years old, but it is gold or rolled gold of some sort. I am trying to hoard any sort of liquid food I can lay my hands on. The Nipponese are still pooping about with the mail. It's absurd, but entirely what one expects. Approximately 5,000 letters arrived today. Now they are going to decide what to do about censorship, for which work they have about one man and his dog. There must be lots more letters somewhere; in 402 days I have received one letter. I see a list of men interned in Palembang – not supplied by the Nipponese, but compiled from the memory of those who have been there. I see Macintyre at 5 p.m. and he details the results of the examination by Johns. He is keen to continue his treatment, so I am to go on Tuesday at 12.15 p.m. I have promised to write a report on cricket in the camp in 1942 for the annual resume.

27 March: The curious betting on soccer matches reflects the Changi Commodity Market – five eggs, two ounces of shag, three rolls and margarine, one stick of gula Malacca, five bars of peanut toffee, two packets of cigarette papers, one Gillette razor blade, one bunch of bananas and three second helpings of soup. The letters are being released fairly quickly, mirabile dictu – about 400 today. Forbes has three postcards; one marked 'Try Singapore, then Batavia'. This shows there must be internees in Batavia and gives me some hope that Nora may be there, although I don't think much of the chance.

Sunday, 28 March: Very neatly put is this from 'The Syonan Sinbun': 'With the return of warm weather, the submarine threat has become a burning question.' My swallow is very coy, but I manage to down a small tin of sardines very, very slowly, except that a kitten nips one in a second while my back is turned. I have a cold; this doesn't improve the swallow or my general fitness. There are – hoorah! – Five letters for me, more than for anyone else in this room. Victor gets one, Jack two and Hope none. It's clearly an absolute lottery what have arrived and what not. There must be 100,000 letters in transit somewhere – 400 days of letters for 3,000 people. At last! Mr Schweizer (a Swiss resident of Singapore) has been notified by Asahi that a Tokyo dispatch gives permission for the International Red Cross to grant relief to the Civilian Internee Camp. The full scope of it has not yet been clearly defined; it is believed to cover the supply of money, food, urgent necessities AND, it is hoped, a visit! But it is typical that Asahi has to cable Tokyo to find out.

29 March: An interpreter told a Nipponese woman married to an Englishman interned here that 600 more internees were coming in. 'Why?' says she. 'To collect you all for repatriation.' 'And when will that be?' 'Oh, next year, or the next ten years,' says he with delightful humour. The father and two boys of this union are in our room. The elder son is huge. I talk to Scott who was in solitary confinement. He says they were so much better off here even in solitary confinement than they were in the criminal prison where they had two months with appalling food, no light, no bathing, no books, no anything. For tiffin, I get the usual hospital soup and a semi liquid custard – the most palatable and easy-to-swallow meal I've had for a long time. The Bishop of Singapore arrives in Changi today – there are seven in his party altogether, including three nuns. As a result, the Three Nuns tobacco joke is obvious, although I don't know if the Bishop is a pipe-smoker. On the subject of humour, Sandy (a Scot, of course) was telling a story of slumming to a circle of six, including a Dutchman. He said he was talking at the front door to the lady of the house when, suddenly, a Chinaman appeared. 'Who is that?' queried Sandy. 'That's my husband.' 'Good heavens – so you are married to a Chinaman?' 'Yes, why not? A woman four doors away is married to a Scot!' The Dutchman thought this extraordinarily funny. Later in the evening, being in another circle with Sandy, he said, 'Sandy, tell that story about the Chinaman.' So Sandy did, but this time he substituted 'Dutchman' for 'Scot'. The Dutchman could not see anything funny in the story at all! I see 'Outward Bound', a play staged in camp. It is excellently produced and the cast without exception is good. It is a most difficult play to put over in these surroundings and one that makes you think.

30 March: I receive two letters – one (undated) from Nellie *(the oldest of Tom's* *three sisters)* in Australia and the other from Amy Hallam in Lancaster, dated 19.7.1942. Both think Nora is here with me. Joan arrived in the U.K. on the 19th (of April?) looking pale and thin. There was much sickness on board and she had helped the doctor a lot. But she picked up quickly. She has gone to St Thomas's Hospital in London to train as a masseuse. Colin is doing the correspondence very efficiently and has suggested to the Colonial Office an allowance of £25 per month. *(This would be for Joan and taken out of Tom's pay.)* They have agreed, I gather; this is excellent news. Colin has got a commission in the R.N.V.R. and is training in Scotland as a Navigation Officer. Brian is well and happy in South Africa. Amy had written a separate letter to Nora, addressed to Mount Rosie Road, Singapore, so they think we are still living in our houses, damn it. Tannie *(Nora's Aunt Anne)* is still at Colinwood. It all makes me long to be home. Oh well, everything points to an exchange, thank God. In the afternoon, there is another letter, this time from Tannie. It is addressed to Mr and Mrs Tom Kitching, 24, Mount Rosie Road and dated 13.7.42. Joan is making good progress at St Thomas's and is a grand girl. There have obviously been previous letters. Macintyre resumes manipulations for my swallow. Later, I walk outside, twice round the gaol – 2,000 yards.

31 March: An internee comes to see me: 'Have I a geological map of Malaya?' He has his eye on the quarries of hornblende granite for road and railway metal after the war. 'It is only a few months now, so I should get busy,' he says! Optimist. There is an appeal in 'The Syonan Sinbun' to stop the black-marketeering in drugs. Quinine is available at five cents per tablet – 'a price well within the reach of the poor.' In the bad old days of British rule, the said poor got it for nothing. I suppose that undermined their independence. Still, it's rather expensive if your wages are 50 cents a day and you need 20 grains, say four tablets, a day. But perhaps the really poor don't have malaria; they just die. I buy six tins of fruit juice for $4.80 to keep me going. There is ground rice and soup for tiffin – I get it down with fair ease. Yesterday's blancmange was overcooked and leathery. I ate it in tiny instalments, every one of which stuck in my gizzard and caused acute discomfort between 1 and 4 p.m. I go to a talk in the 'Malaya' series – Linehan on 'The Malays'. He has a comprehensive knowledge; it is interesting, but he goes on too long at one stretch.

1 April 1943: To mark April Fool's Day, there is a notice summoning all municipal employees to meet the President in C Yard. There is a letter from Joan, Barn Close, Milford, Godalming. It is dated 14.7.42 and addressed to both of us, of course. It is an excellent letter, with the limitations of censorship considered: 'I am well and truly started on my career at last and enjoying it hugely.' It is two-and-a-half years training in massage. She goes to St Thomas's in five months. In South Africa, Joan saw Stanley Jones and Brian; and in Colombo she met up with all the H.M.S. Glasgow crowd. Brenda *(Tom's sister)* has been transferred to London. I see a quotation in 'Jesting Pilate' by M. Arlen who just passed through Japan. He says: 'It is as though there were some inherent vice in Japanese art which made the genuine seem false and the expensive shoddy.' We have seen nothing genuine and everything shoddy! Standby fatigue all day restricted my movements. Peters comes to see me: Have I a map of Malaya? One-inch topographical, for choice! I have not. I haven't seen him since he married the widow in Kuala Lumpur in 1932, 25 years after a boy and girl flirtation. I housed them for the night. We have a very interesting talk; he was in the bungalow-shooting episode in Siam. It was on the Betong-Yala road some 70 miles north of Betong. The people involved were Europeans, men and women, put there under guard by the Nipponese on December 8th. The Nipponese troops came back after an engagement where they suffered several hundred casualties and they were inflamed with booze and bad temper. They overpowered the guard, then threw hand-grenades into the bungalow and machine-gunned it. Peters says the guard did their best. He pushed Mrs Stratton under a mattress and dived under one himself. When the tumult ceased, they came out and he, Mrs Stratton and another escaped. They wandered about in the jungle and lived with the Sakai in the mountains between Perak and Kelantan. They ate appalling food, of course. The Chinese were very good to them, but the Kedah Malays were rotten. They were told by the people in Kelantan and Upper Perak not to trust any Malays lower down the river: 'they'd sell anybody to the Japanese for a dollar, tuan!' They wandered up-river almost to Belum and down to Ulu Temengor and over to Ulu Piah. They heard that Ipoh had been retaken by the British and found this report was false. Eventually, the lady being at the end of her tether and the men almost – and no wonder – they gave themselves up at Sungai Siput on May 9th. Here they were left in the police station for some time. Peters says the front-line troops were excellent and under iron discipline. The venture was for them in the nature of a crusade. They had been impressed with the idea that they were liberators of the oppressed peoples and would be received with open arms. As an example, when he was captured in December, the Nipponese officer said he would give him an armed guard to take him down the village street. 'But I don't need one.' 'But the people will attack you.' 'Of course they won't; they are my friends.' So, reluctantly, he was allowed to go without an armed guard and out came the Chinese towkays and others with refreshments. The officer was astonished, then said he, 'Ah! They are still afraid of you, of course.' By a coincidence, Peters ran into him again at Sungai Siput and he was very friendly and considerably disillusioned about the Nipponese 'crusade'. Peters thinks this disillusionment will have a considerable effect on Nipponese morale.

2 April: The day of the Great Fair in A-Block is upon us. We are actually to be allowed to mingle from 4 to 7 p.m. This, with Christmas Day, makes a total of five hours in 409 days of internment. O warm and sympathetic treatment, how we do appreciate thee! One of our loss-of-vision cases is busy washing his clothes in the laundry. He curses the local-made soap in good broad Scots and no uncertain terms: 'Ah canna get a lather at all.' Someone, sympathising, says, 'Ay, but that's a queer-looking bit of soap you've got.' And it turns out to be a rice-cake. The remaining letters have now been sent to Singapore for censorship. The Nipponese got tired of doing them here, so God knows when we shall see any more. Tomorrow is a holiday, then Sunday and, by Monday, I imagine the receiving authority will have forgotten all about them. Poor Gardner in this room has had bad news; he was in the same position as myself: his wife had left on the Kuala and he had had no news since. Now Charlwood has a letter from his wife which mentions Mrs Gardner as drowned. Livingstone of the police has died, aged 44. I do not find the Country Fair very thrilling, but it is nice to see Nic and Isobel and to speak to a woman again. There are fortune-tellers and Aunt Sally and coconut shies and a portrait for $1 and raffles, darts and doughnuts (ye gods, made of rice!), curry puffs (made of rubber), tea, coffee and dancing. In the middle of it all, the Nipponese come in with Sikhs and clear everyone out of the cells, presumably to stop immorality! What minds! Lady Thomas, the Governor's wife, was sent for yesterday. She went to the office and was confronted by a Nipponese general. 'You're thinner,' he said. 'Yes,' she said. 'the diet, I suppose.' 'You're looking a lot older too' – no reply. 'Well, we have Singapore now and you may be here for another 10 years.' With which gentlemanly sally, the interview ended.

3 April: I have a strange pudding at midday; it is pasty, but I get it all down, then I have cheese and tea. There are no accidents with my swallow. In the Bridge League, I play with Coles against Black and Miles. We lose. I write a poem about 'warm and sympathetic' treatment! I go to a Gilbert and Sullivan concert; it is most enjoyable. There are an orchestra and choir and amusing exordiums by Hockenhull.

Sunday, 4 April: We are asked – at last! – To put in our requirements for bedding, clothing, footwear and toilet requisites. I want a mattress, blanket and mosquito net at the moment. Will the International Red Cross pay, perhaps? The Rising Sun flag went up again two days ago. It is half in ribbons already.

5 April: I am on sweeping fatigue in the corridors and the courtyard drains. There are eight of us working at 10.30 a.m. and 3.30 p.m. Each time, it takes about 45 minutes. I eat three more duck eggs raw.

6 April: I am reading volume four of 'Wonderful Britain'. It is attractively illustrated, particularly to an interned exile! What attracts me specifically, apart from the pictures, are articles on things to see around London, Manchester and Sheffield – Wansdyke and Offa's Dyke, the magic of the Fens. Why I didn't observe more of the Fens when up at Cambridge, I don't know – too busy, I suppose, getting honours degree and college colours for cricket, rugger, hockey and soccer. Any excursions I made were geological. 'The Syonan Sinbun' says: 'What were considered ridiculous prices a few months after the fall of Singapore are as nothing compared to the prices obtaining today'. What a confession! And we are told there is no inflation. The Nipponese inform us that the vegetable and salt ration is to be increased from April 1st. All the letters come back today. Nothing was done to them at all in town, which is precisely what I expected. I am surprised they were efficient enough to send the letters back to us. A list has been pinned up of nearly 200 women for whom there are letters by this mail (addressed to Malaya) whose whereabouts are not known. They are presumably not at large, so they must be interned or killed. A few letters are released today. I get my fifth and last – it is from Amy addressed to Nora at 24, Mount Rosie Road and dated July 19th. It contains no new news. I chat to Dr Ainslie; he was on the Sarpedon in October, 1940. *(The Sarpedon was the ship on which the Kitching family sailed from Liverpool to Singapore in 1940.)* He expressed horror at the change in me; he hasn't seen me since, so it's a good criterion. I was too heavy then at 150 pounds; now I am 110. The flag has given up the ghost again.

7 April: There are some new arrivals today. 'what a collection,' someone remarks. 'It's like the East End.' They are Jews – 110 of them – and the manner of their being taken into custody is disgusting. They were roused at 5 a.m. today with no previous warning and torn from their wives and families. They have come in with wardrobes and Heaven knows what junk. And their conditions in here are disgraceful – 110 in the rice store. There is one toilet in the room and they are locked out of the gaol proper at 10 p.m. The Nipponese are at it again – no men's fatigue parties are to be allowed in the Women's Camp. Why, God knows. They can't be expected to manhandle their own food, firewood etc. And last night, the tall interpreter tore up the credentials of the men's quartet and threw the pieces at them after they had been given permission to go over to the Women's Block to sing in their concert. Is it the new broom showing his authority? He has replaced Naito. The score mounts; it is all unnecessary. We are amused by a true story told by a patient just back from Miyako Hospital. A Chinese boy there told him that a new type of bedpan was introduced at the General Hospital where the Chinese boy worked at the time. The Nipponese did not know what it was for. They at last decided it was for table use, so they used the bedpans for serving the officers' food. I go to a talk by Linehan on 'The Malays'. At the end, he puts up a spirited defence of the Malays and the way they have behaved in this war, to contradict the many ill-informed criticisms rife throughout the camp. No doubt there was some treachery, he said, but it is not British to condemn people without hearing the defence. We failed in our protection of them; anything they do now is in the same category as our signing the oath a few months ago not to escape. And he gave specific examples of the excellent behaviour and fortitude of Malays right up to the capitulation. He also read tributes to the conduct of the Malay Regiment by various British officers. He certainly put up a very good case.

8 April: At tiffin, the soup is OK, but I can't eat the rice pudding. It is solid; I take it to the doctor and complain. Nevertheless, my swallow is better than yesterday. Walker tells me his mother-in-law had exactly the same thing; her voice was affected too. And the ailment disappeared in due course. I am on firewood fatigue from 2 to 4 p.m. – nice exercise. It is very hot, however. We have ONE clinical thermometer left in the hospital. There is an appeal for internees to hand over any. There is no hope of getting any out of the Nipponese, of course. More Nipponese visitors are shown round; I suppose the Nipponese blow about the wonderful organisation etc. which, of course, is entirely due to our own efforts, considerably hindered by theirs. I am convinced they are utterly incompetent as colonisers. They rule by force only and have not the personality nor the qualities, which inspire respect and affection. There is great speculation about why these 110 Jews have been brought in and why their wives and children are left outside. What are the said wives and children going to do? It looks like deliberate persecution. The probable object is loot.

9 April: 'The Syonan Sinbun' reports a speech made by Colonel Okabo to a meeting of Mohammedan delegates. He tells them to warn the population against the lying and malicious propaganda of the British and Americans about retaking this part of the world. It is absolutely impossible, and, even if it isn't, it will be 'thousands of years' before they can even dream of 'staging a comeback'. Compare the difference in fighting spirit, he said; Nipponese soldiers will never surrender e.g. a Nipponese unit in New Guinea, up against superior forces, held a conference with its officers, decided it was hopeless, all shouted, 'Ten-no, haika, banzai!' and committed hara-kiri. Somehow, I don't think the thought of a unit disembowelling itself would appeal much to the Malay delegates and, anyway, if the Nipponese in the unit all did it, HOW DOES HE KNOW? The peroration was good; it stigmatised us as 'these devils of the Earth – the Anglo-Americans. Banzai!' The interview Lady Thomas, the Governor's wife, had with a Nipponese general:

Nipponese General: You Mrs Thomas?

Lady Thomas: Yes.

N.G.: I come here special to see you.

L.T.: That is very kind of you.

N.G.: You told them to hang out the white flag at Government House, so Singapore had to surrender.

L.T.: No, certainly not. I did not want to surrender.

N.G.: (insisting): But you told them to hang out the flag at Government House.

L.T.: Certainly not, nothing of the sort. You have been misinformed.

N.G.: Then who surrendered? Your husband?

L.T.: The military were in command; we had to do what they advised.

N.G.: Oh, so you did not surrender, but Perçival surrendered Singapore. Singapore – you know what that name means? Lion's city.

L.T.: Yes, the British Lion, it means.

N.G.: Now you have lost it. It is no more British. It is now Syonan – the shining in the south – and, after a little time, it will become the brilliance in the south. Now it is no longer British; it is Nipponese.

L.T.: Yes, temporarily.

N.G.: Temporarily?

L.T.: Yes, only temporarily.

N.G.: During the British regime, Singapore was a very dirty city.

L.T.: No, it was very clean.

N.G.: No, it was very dirty.

L.T.: As a matter of fact, it has less epidemic disease than any other city in the East.

N.G.: It has no parks.

L.T.: Oh yes. It has the Botanical Gardens and others.

N.G.: You have children here?

L.T.: No, none here. My daughter and my grandson are in England.

N.G.: Oh, you do not like to be here. Here it is very tiresome.

L.T.: Yes, very true. No one likes to stay in prison.

N.G.: I think you stay here 10 years. The food is very bad.

L.G.: Yes, it is not at all nice.

N.G.: You are very thin. How old are you?

L.T.: I am 56; my husband is 63.

N.G.: You are very old and you are getting older every time. Where is your husband?

L.T.: My husband was sent to Formosa. I asked to go with him. I was not allowed. Do you know?

N.G.: Yes.

L.T.: Do you know how my husband is looked after? Is the food good?

N.G.: Yes.

L.T.: Better than here?

N.G.: Yes.

L.T. What sort of house?

N.G.: I don't know.

L.T.: Really, you don't know that?

N.G.: You have been bombed?

L.T.: Oh yes, we were bombed.

N.G.: Government House was quite safe. Only the Chinese and poor people were bombed?

L.T.: No that is not at all true. Government House was bombed and shelled and badly damaged. Many of our people were killed.

N.G.: You ran away?

L.T.: No, I did not run away. I stayed here. You see I am here now.

N.G.: Why did you stay here?

L.T.: I wished to stay with my husband and friends.

N.G.: Your friends are only Europeans?

L.T.: Not at all. I have many friends who are Chinese, Indians and Malays.

N.G.: How long you stay here?

L.T.: I have been here seven years. In seven years you make many friends.

N.G.: You are connected with Churchill?

L.T.: Well, not really connected. I admire him very much.

N.G.: You admire him? Churchill and Roosevelt are postponing the war, you know. They postponed the war. *(He meant 'prolonged'.)* They postponed the war 100 years. They all the time make preparations.

L.T.: Yes, I am sure they are preparing quite a lot of things.

The Nipponese General then questioned a doctor about the children in the camp and said Lady Heath would be returning here soon. What an extraordinary talk! Thinking it over, I am inclined to the view that the Nipponese General had imbibed a lot of his ideas from the local paper; and this puts a new idea into my head: I never thought of the newspaper as an instrument for propaganda amongst the Nipponese themselves, but, of course, it must be. This also explains why there is so much in it about the former regime, which the locals know to be false. The general physical condition of the internees is certainly deteriorating. Our poker group of six is an example: I cannot swallow and my voice is going; Menzies can't see; Forbes gets black-outs and fits of dizziness; Barron's circulation is all to blazes and he has no feeling in his feet; and Ivery has been in hospital with dysentery. That leaves Laville, unscathed as far as I know.

10 April: Young Rusk has had bad news from home – his father has died. Robinson, whose wife was on the Kuala, has heard she is interned (in Batavia?) and the people at home have seen her name on a list. (There is just a chance for Nora.) S.W. Jones is working at the Colonial Office.

Sunday, 11 April: In the bridge league, I am partnered by Coles against Courtney and Knox. We get the foulest cards and haven't a chance.

12 April: I receive another letter from Joan, dated June 30th. She had just started the massage course for which the fee was 142 guineas. And she hoped that, when the course was finished, we would have no objection to her marrying John M.! My swallow is the same as yesterday.

13 April: I am given a mixture with some eggy substance atop; it's not bad. I eat it all. *(Tom is now getting special food for his condition.)* After 7 a.m., I have a most extraordinary dream, even for me. I am interned, but allowed an outing. The scene is in Manchester and simultaneously Lancaster. I am staying with friends and my mother is there too. Two men come in; we talk golf. I say I won't be able to play any more – I've lost my wry-necked mashie, which is irreplaceable. At this stage, I notice a stranger – a dark, low-browed and humorous-faced gentleman. He has, deeply imprinted on his face from forehead to upper lip: 'Per Goffo ad Libo'. *(The pseudo-Latin motto could mean 'Through God to Liberty.')* We discuss this and I remark, 'I see you pronounce it Goff'. I awake at 7.40 and rush to the laundry for my bath and shave! I am supposed to be on a fatigue sweeping the yard, but Hamilton offers to do it while I investigate letters for members of the Survey Department. Letters have arrived for Bridges and Clark-Walker from their wives in Australia. The evidence for their being at Padang is Salmond and that is uncertain. There is no news of Best or Goss, but Edwards is definitely in Palestine! There is also definite news that C.T.M. Husband is missing; his wife is in Australia. The new arrivals have paid $44,000 to the Camp Fund. This is good news.

14 April: Dr Johnstone has a letter from Bunny dated September 3rd; there is still no news of Nora in it, nor am I mentioned. At 5 p.m., Jack gets his first letter at last – sent from Australia in June. And on the 421st day of internment – it's a wonderful job the Red Cross are doing! There is another very sudden death – Finch, at the age of 51. He just conks out in the middle of his normal activities. I go to a lecture by Trevor Hughes in the 'Malaya' series on the subject of the Eurasians. He handles a difficult subject tactfully and well. There are no fatigues today; the benevolent Nips have decided on a belated holiday for the Sikhs in commemoration of the Amritsar Massacre on April 13th, 1919.

15 April: The new broom shows its bristles, apparently just to show its presence. There is to be no fair as arranged at the end of the month. The much-vaunted 'recreation' ground outside the gaol is rapidly being ploughed up for vegetables. Jack gets his second letter – his wife is working in the censorship department. Stanton Nelson has been removed to Miyako Hospital – off his head, I fear. The flag is in bits again! It has been removed and we have no flag now. My voice is worse.

16 April: I am given custard; it is very good. Our numbers are now 3,181.

17 April: For most of the morning, I am airing my clothes, mattress and bedding. T. E. Edmett has died, aged 69. He came out in 1898. His wife has been in hospital since the date of their internment.

Sunday, 18 April: I am growing accustomed to not speaking. I can now never make a normal sound. It's not unbearable and, if I have to be deficient, I'd rather be dumb than deaf or blind. I wonder if all this will clear up when I get out. Anyway, when you can't converse, you do at any rate realise that three-quarters of what you normally say is quite unnecessary. The world and your companions will get along just as well without it! In the bridge league, Coles and I lose again to Venables and Wakefield.

19 April: I see Hugh Wallace who tells me Asahi has gone to Sumatra on a visit. He still retains his job in Singapore, but has no longer anything to do with us. The Free List credit has been increased from $3 to $4 per man (as a result of the Jews' contribution to the Camp Fund). Internees who have not smoked for three months have been asked to come forward for eye testing to prove or disprove a theory that the muck we have to smoke affects the eyes. I am still on English to-bacco and am smoking very little, about five ounces a month. April 29th is the Emperor's birthday. We ask for permission to send a postcard to relatives; it's not much use if they aren't sent off, of course. There is trouble in camp: Johns has been locked up, is allowed no food and is deprived of his position as Camp Command-ant representing the internees. The problem began when we asked and got permis-sion to send four men to Miyako Hospital. They were necessary cases and our hospital was full anyway. Before they went, a Nipponese came round and found one empty bed (just vacated and going to be filled). He waxed indignant and re-fused to allow the ambulance to go. He further made allegations about our treat-ment of the sick in New Delhi. Johns said, 'I can't believe it.' Nothing happened then, but, by the afternoon, the Nipponese had evidently chewed it over and de-cided Johns had called them liars, so they locked him up.

21 April: Johns is still locked up and was allowed nothing but rice and salt until Monday night, when a meal was allowed to be sent in. He is back on rice and salt today. The Nipponese say: 'We are very anxious about him, but you see, the man who had him locked up has toothache and can't come to the camp.' Ye Gods! Words fail! I study the undeliverable letters for the Survey Department. A cover addressed to Miss J.Y. Thomson (who is not known) has a long superscription saying she left Singapore on February 13th on the S.S. Kuala. The Kuala sank on the 14th; she and others were captured by the Nipponese on February 24th, according to a Nippon-ese broadcast, and TAKEN BACK to Singapore. This raises new hopes in me for, if Nora's name was amongst those broadcast, this would account for letters being addressed to both of us in Singapore.

22 April: Some loathsome vandal has deliberately poured water into the piano and done other minor damage to it. Inexplicable! If caught, he should be treated with the utmost severity, but he won't be. Johns is still incarcerated; he is now allowed ONE square meal a day. The Jewish Passover is on; they have managed to get unleavened bread from the synagogue in Singapore. The Church is giving an

Easter gift to every internee – you take your choice – cheroots or gula malacca, value 25 cents.

23 April: It is Good Friday and St George's Day, so the celebration of the latter has been postponed. Easter is as late this year as it ever can be, I think. The kanji porridge is full of dirt and grit – from lower grade rice polishings, I think. Johns is released. Asahi has been transferred to the Dutch East Indies permanently. Our new bugbear is very military, bless him. I finish reading 'Gone with the Wind' by Margaret Mitchell – A most remarkable book. I enjoyed it very much, but what a little bitch Scarlet O'Hara is! Vic's invariable comment is: 'What a wonderful book for a WOMAN to have written!' I say I imagine the woman who wrote it would be extremely angry to hear him say that! In the evening, I attend 'The Crucifixion' by Stainer; the choir sings well.

– IX –

MIXED BLESSINGS AT EASTER

As Tom contemplates another Easter in Changi, news from the outside world is steadily growing more heartening for the internees and more depressing for the Japanese. The camp rumours of Japanese threats to shoot prisoners if Japan is bombed probably reflect a very real fear that more and more of the Allied air-forces are coming within range of vital Japanese targets, together with a general Japanese malaise about the progress of the war. Possession of the airstrip and harbour at Guadalcanal would now provide first-rate facilities for U.S. forces within range of Rabaul, Japan's main base for the area. And on 11 April, U.S. forces landed in the Aleutian Islands. On 20 April, with the threat of invasion long since lifted, Churchill announced that the country's church bells could be rung regularly once again. The bells of York Minster were broadcast to the nation on Easter Sunday. The spirits of the Allies were rising indeed. Tom Kitching, however, was still faced with the grim reality of a Japanese internment camp. The internees' Camp Committee listened to the departing Japanese Commander telling them that he hoped it would not be long before peace came and that they would all be friends again. Tom's comment was: 'Friends! My God!' Asahi had called up the Committee on 22 April to tell them he was leaving Singapore for Sumatra. There he would be in charge of a number of civilian internment camps where the internees were mostly Dutch. Asahi asked where Johns, the internees' Camp Commandant, was and, after some fencing by his Japanese subordinates, was told. Presumably Asahi did not know of Johns' recent treatment.

24 April 1943: Asahi said Lieutenant Suzuki would replace him as Controller of Enemy Civilians in Singapore, which includes us. He said the internment of civilians was a new practice and he could find nothing relating to it in Oppenheim's 'Manual of International Law.' Japan is not bound by any treaty regarding the treatment of internees – then neither are we to Japan, but they do not appreciate that. But, Asahi said, Japan would treat civilian internees with justice and give them fair play!! He should ask what Johns, Morgan, Scott and others like them think about that! He said he had visited a number of internment camps and Changi was the best. God help the others, then. We have pianos, music and daily newspapers ! and letters!! – two sketchy mails in 430 days! He said there were some problems remaining. One was the meeting of husbands and wives. The best would be for them

261

to live together, but restricted accommodation made that difficult. By letting us keep our money instead of pinching it, we had been able to buy food for a year. Now, he said, we had a loan from the International Red Cross and the Jews had brought in $100,000. Later, he said to Worley who is acting for Johns, the Camp Commandant, 'Exchange is a Foreign Office matter, but I hope it will come soon. The Nipponese do not wish to keep enemy civilians; they are no use to the Army and the Nipponese internees cannot be of any use to Britain and the U.S.A.' The kitchen now have orders to feed me with chicken essence, vegetable soups, raw eggs, tomato and fruit juices, full cream and other such items. H.M. Gregory has died at the age of 64.

Sunday, 25 April: I fear a rumour that the Nipponese are going to execute publicly two U.S. airmen is correct. If so, words fail. They have done nothing that Nipponese airmen did not do in Singapore. Vengeance will be ours.

26 April: I receive two raw eggs – both are bad! A.E. McDonnell has died aged 75. The new flag put up on April 24th for Yasukuni (more shrine-worshipping) is in bits! I repair my mattress; the ticking is getting very thin. No wonder! It is sat on all-day and lain on all night. I am on lorry fatigue and we unload lashings of cases of sardines and corned beef, boots (canvas, with rubber soles) and maize – all bought by Salmond (with International Red Cross funds?)

27 April: Macintyre has gone to hospital with appendicitis, so there will be no more osteopathic treatment for a long time. The Nipponese refuse to reinstate Johns, so we are to have an election.

28 April: What a day, what a day! I have a busy morning, airing and cleaning. The new broom bristles most ferociously. The new Japanese Commander assaults Arnold in B-Yard for not standing up. Arnold had not observed him. He walks all round the camp with a Sikh guard and an interpreter. In the main yard, an unfortunate who did not see him is struck on the face, jabbed in the stomach, felled to the ground and kicked while prostrate. Several others are beaten up. The V-sign on the stage arch arouses his ire. The whole superstructure is knocked down by this afternoon by his orders. The stage manager, MacDermott, and four electricians are arrested. All outdoor strolls are cancelled, as are the gymkhana arranged for May 2nd and all communications between husbands, wives and relatives. Ours is a 'appy 'ome, ours is. One bright spot – the Sikh accompanying him refuses to strike when ordered. Now he's tied up in the Guard Room. I receive my Church of England present from the Bishop.

29 April: There are no outside fatigues; it is Tenno Haika's birthday. This matter of the V-sign is worth recording as an example of Nipponese methods, in case I ever emerge with this diary. This sign was erected last year over the top front of the stage – not strictly a V, but in the form of brackets – () – composed of two neon lights. Some months ago, they conked out and were removed, but an irregular black mark of the same shape was left on a white ground. It has been seen scores of times by the Nipponese in charge of the camp. Now, in addition to yesterday's assaults, the Nipponese have thrashed and released the electricians and MacDermott, but arrested Worley and Penseler, commandants of D and B-Blocks. Tominara is the new officer-in-charge of Changi and Suzuki is not here. I hear the prisoners are being allowed no food or water and have been tied up and beaten. Worley is a judge and Penseler is manager of the Raub Gold Mine. Neither has had anything in the remotest degree whatever to do with the stage or the V-sign. I understand that the underlying cause (apart from a wound Tominara got from a British bullet in Shanghai) is that he attaches an exaggerated importance to the sign. He says someone in authority is responsible, so he seized the two block commandants of longest standing. The Sikhs have also been beaten up and what is happening in that quarter I don't know exactly. Worley has naturally withdrawn as a candidate in place of Johns! All this on top of Asahi's speech in which he prated of friendship after the war! The spirit of Hakko Ichiu is said to be the mainspring of Nipponese actions. Well, we know what their protestations are worth now, if we did not before. We are powerless to resist. Doubtless, they would welcome a real incident. We have removed any remotely possible cause of offence – maps on walls, even the Piccadilly Underground sign! I am amused as I pass another internee in the corridor. He is muttering 'Damned swine', so, thinking he has some fresh atrocity to report, I ask, 'What is it?' 'They've taken away the wet refuse bin before 2 o'clock,' he replies. Yet another internee I chat with presumes I am going to destroy my diary; I am going to do nowt o't sort.

30 April : There are no outside fatigues, I don't know why. There is an amusing sidelight of the 28th strafe: the Nipponese spotted a copy of 'The Escaping Club' by A.J. Evans and confiscated it! The Sikh who refused orders to beat internees was badly beaten up himself and came to our hospital for dressings. When the Nipponese saw this, they tore the bandages off and would not let him have any. I go to see 'The Rivals' and it is really excellently done. It is a pity the laundry acoustics are so very bad.

1 May: Today's bombshell – all Golders Green (those accommodated outside the prison) are to be ejected and are to be back within the prison walls by 5 p.m. There are over 100 of them. No reason is given. This makes the congestion even worse. Five have to be squeezed into our tennis court room, making 108 in there; it's scandalous. And the Golders Green people have worked so hard on the vegetable gardens and rearing poultry outside the coolie lines. Katherine sends me a sago pudding. I eat it all with surprising ease. A Tamil is very badly assaulted just outside the gaol by a Nipponese with the steel shaft of a golf club. His face is cut to ribbons and he is left half-dead by the roadside. I don't know why. Worley and Penseler are still locked up; they are allowed no washing or shaving, although they get some food. They have been made to kneel on concrete for one hour with bamboo tied at the back of their knees – it must be excruciatingly painful.

3 May: I am on a curious fatigue today – plaiting leaves of the nipah palm to make thatching for the salt factory. It needs practice; it takes me one-and-a-half hours to do one leaf; I should do better next time. Worley and Penseler are still in solitary, but they are being allowed to wash, shave and have books. Adrian Clark has been elected Men's Representative with 1,164 votes. Collinge got 968 and Stone 329. Johns, Worley and Penseler are not eligible. The candidates for B-Block Commandant are Bill Adams, Harper Ball and Gridley. The Golders Green lot are in trouble. When they moved into their coolie lines, no inventory was taken. Now that they have been thrown out, with characteristic acumen an inventory HAS been taken and they are ordered to replace every missing fixture – brass taps, electric light bulbs, switches and so forth. This is quite impossible. Although there has been SOME scrounging, a lot of fittings were missing ere ever they moved in. So what will be the end of it, God knows. We witness another comic opera situation: a firewood fatigue party goes out today with a lorry. When passing a Nipponese post, only the party leader bows, in accordance with orders. The group is roundly rated by a Nipponese officer for not all bowing and the Sikh guards also get it in the neck. On the return journey, all bow, but it is another officer who knows the orders and all again are sorted out for bowing. This makes life difficult!

5 May: The new broom seems to be settling down. Our orchestra was allowed to perform in A-Block yesterday and A-Block residents are allowed to walk outside. I listen to election addresses by our three block candidates.

7 May: Patients from Tan Tock Seng are sent in to Changi today. There are no Europeans left there now. Yesterday, Jewish wives arrived in force to see their interned husbands, bringing their children, a permit and parcels. Tominara, the new Commander, tore the permit up and sent them away with fleas in their respective ears. Today, they are back again with another permit, presumably from a bigger noise. Anyhow, they are allowed to see their husbands and deliver parcels, but talking is not allowed.

8 May: Johns examines me by appointment. There is a hold-up in one of my vocal chords, perhaps caused by the strain of swallowing over the last nine months. There is nothing pathological, which is satisfactory. More mail has arrived – about 4,000 letters; the list says there is only one for me. C.E. Jordan has died.

Sunday, 9 May: News begins to trickle out from the mail. One wife writes: 'I expect you are getting your Sunday golf as usual.' Hells bells! There is another quite unnecessary pinprick from our captors: 'The Changi Guardian' has now to go up to the powers-that-temporarily-be for censorship. It is as a rule a single typed sheet of foolscap. Five minutes would be ample time to censor it; it is kept for three or four days. So the issue is now irregular.

10 May: I get my letter; it is from Pip (*Tom's sister, Phyllis*) and is dated June 21st, 1942. She says Colin looks absolutely splendid and is fighting fit; he is proud of us. Joan is well too. The letter goes on: 'Tobruk has again fallen ... things don't seem to be going too well for us in Libya.' What a contrast now! Of course, she thinks Nora is here. Macintyre has heard that his wife is interned; she was on the Kuala. O'Malley's wife says she hears we are being treated badly. This is good news from our point of view. Vic and I have the old argument again. He'd rather the folks at home thought we were living on the fat of the land and amusing ourselves, 'then they won't worry.' I say they SHOULD worry and we should be got out as soon as possible otherwise a lot will never recover their health. W.H. Palmer has died, aged 62.

11 May: Last night was the hottest we have had. It was most uncomfortable. I was sweating, twisting and tossing on my concrete couch. We gather from the latest letters that our postcards have been received. Full lists of the internees were expected by the end of July. 'How glad we are to know,' one correspondent writes, 'that the Commander-in-Chief, Singapore is a kind Roman Catholic. This means you will be well treated.' Another letter says, 'We see by the newspapers you chaps are being treated well.' And another: 'I am wondering if you are able to carry on your business at all. Reports here of treatment of civilians in Singapore are very good.' Snooks, one of our cricketers, is sentenced to 21 days solitary confinement for theft and assault in the kitchen. I discuss this with Joe, another Empress of Asia lad and a cricketer. His point of view surprises me; he is sympathetic to Snooks. He says the man who reported him for theft and was therefore assaulted should just have told him to put the nine sticks of gula malacca back again and all would have been well. An internee has gone very queer; I do hope his brain is not giving way. He has aged ten years in appearance in the last four months.

12 May: I am told the reason for the confinement of Worley and Penseler was our Mock Parliament; it is considered highly suspicious by the Nipponese! But later, we are told that the Camp Committee have asked why they have been punished and how long they will be in solitary and have been told: 'The matter is under investigation!' J. Phillip has died, aged 62. Recently, we opened one of our few remaining tins of cheese, but my swallow didn't like it, although I did; nearly all of it came back again. Speech is also difficult, so I don't like having to say a thing twice, therefore I try to croak very clearly and, when people say, 'What?' I wait. And now I know that half the time they say, 'What?' they have heard what you said, because they produce the goods within a very short period afterwards, whether it's a reply or action or what-have-you.

13 May: Bedlington who was on a fatigue party in Singapore says the price of an empty Johnny Walker or Dewar bottle with intact label is $15! This is because, of course, the contents can be faked. A full bottle costs $100. Adrian Clark, the new

Camp Commandant representing the internees, gives an address in the yard. He speaks excellently, mostly on matters of discipline as a result of the meeting of the Committee with the Nipponese this morning, which was very successful. But he contrasts British methods (appeals to higher authorities successively in cases of imagined injustice) with the Nipponese methods (no appeal – the man above takes no notice whatsoever. The man in immediate charge has practically a free hand. If his superior officer doesn't approve, he strafes HIM, but the underdogs get no redress.)

14 May: Nine women and children have arrived in Changi from Palembang – I don't think they are European.

15 May: I sleep on Jack's camp-bed, but there is no mattress; it is about the same as mine.

Sunday, 16 May: I had a pleasant dream last night: met Nora on a repatriation ship and it was an East Asiatic, the Fionia – a Danish ship. I wish it could come true! At the meeting of our Committee with the Nipponese the other day, although all present could speak English, the communiqué was made in Nipponese and translated into Malay by the Nipponese interpreter. English is obviously beyond the pale as a means of communication, which strikes me as cutting out your tongue to spite your intelligence!

17 May: The Saturday newspaper has part of a column cut out. As there is no war news from Europe elsewhere, you can put omission and excision together and make Tunis. *(The Allies entered Tunis on 7 May. By 12 May, all organised resistance by German and Italian troops in North Africa had ceased. The Allies made prisoner 110,000 Germans and 40,000 Italians. By coincidence, the day on which Tom Kitching noted this victory – 17 May – another cause for Allied rejoicing was taking place over Germany – the Dambusters' raids on the Eder, Mohne and other dams.)*

18 May: I hear that two internees came to blows; one had said the Nipponese newspaper news was as reliable as ours. The wireless after a hectic career for three nights, has been out of action for two. Worley and Penseler are released.

19 May: The doctors are very concerned about this tobacco blindness and they advocate no smoking. The poor diet plus smoking is the probable cause of the illness. There are now 66 cases; the numbers have doubled in the last five weeks. There are no cases among non-smokers who make up 15% of the camp's male population and there are no cases in the Women's Camp. We receive an issue from the local Red Cross of washing and toilet soap, tooth powder and four clothes pegs each! They are all local make, of course. I am called away at 8 p.m. from a lecture by Jordan on the Chinese in Malaya. I am summoned to the Nipponese office. I hear that others are also sent for, including the Bishop of Singapore and Colonel Lord of the Salvation Army.

20 May: Wonderful news – from today we are to receive through the Red Cross an eight to ten-ounce loaf baked in a Nipponese bakery. This is Co-Prosperity. I can't eat mine; it peeves me intensely, as I long for solid food, although it's most inferior bread made out of sago flour. And the joke is that, when the diet squad bring my special diet at 5.30 p.m., they say, 'Ah! We've got a special treat for you' and produce another eight-ounce loaf with a pat of butter on it. I eat one thin slice, but it almost chokes me and isn't worth it. I finish reading 'Walking in the Grampians'. If Nora's alive, I swear we will do some of them WHEN this bloody war is over.

21 May: I am in the yard at 1.30 a.m. The Southern Cross at an elevation of about 15 degrees twinkles out of a glorious vault more conspicuous than I've ever seen it before. There is scarcely another star visible, but the full moon shines on the sleepers and the grim grey walls. The latest order is that there will be no more cutting of rubber trees for firewood until we have taken all the stumps out! Of course, we've no jacks or tackle to get them out with. I hear that Worley and Penseler were freed with the remark: 'Well, you know what you've been confined for – don't do it again.' And, of course, they have no idea and have never been told. The vegetable garden we worked so hard in and were then ordered to abandon is now derelict – wonderful organisation!

22 May: My swallow is very poor this morning. I manage with difficulty to swallow two doubtful eggs, drowning the taste with vinegar and a dash of my remaining spot of real Worcester sauce. I am beginning to have the theory that whatever I try to swallow last remains on top until either forced into my stomach by the next instalment, or, if it can't be so forced, brought up again and remains there more or less indefinitely. Each morning the passage is choked with saliva, so I get no comfort in swallowing anything until I have stuck my finger down and brought that up. I manage to swallow half my loaf, boil it up with milk and water until it is a fair mush, then push it through my filter tin – the residue is like glue! And it goes down with some ease. The Red Cross issue fruit – I get one-fifth of a large papaya and a banana. Emboldened by my success with the bread, I try to eat the fruit and think I am succeeding, but oh no! They stick and I have a miserable time. I don't get the tubes clear until 1 a.m. in the Main Yard. 'The Syonan Sinbun' Thursday and Friday editions are much cut about by our gaol masters! There are no less than four excisions. I can't think what they'd allow in the rag which is good for Malayans to read, yet not for us.

Sunday, 23 May: I acquire a camp-bed, unfoldable except longitudinally. Where I shall put it in the daytime, God knows.

24 May: Sixty men are out with six lorries for rice. Four return empty; the other two have no tarpaulins and the rice gets soaked in the very heavy rain. I see Salmond and he promises to approach Schweitzer of the Red Cross and I may get some·

special liquids for my diet via the Red Cross. I hand in four letters to be forwarded to Java in case Nora is there. I initial each letter, so she will know I have had them. We have asked for a copy of the broadcast about the capture of the Tanjong Pinang or a list of those captured. The bed is much more comfortable than the concrete floor.

25 May: I receive an issue from the International Red Cross of a whole bar of washing soap and a cake of toilet soap.

26 May: I filter custard and eat it all. I shave and bathe as usual at 7.30 a.m. and feel better. Nic sends me a sago pudding with coconut juice and I eat it all, all the soup at 1 p.m. and the custard at 4 – 5 p.m. At 6 p.m., I eat an egg, a quarter-of-a-pint of milk, condensed milk, sugar and cocoa. At 8 p.m., I have tomato juice and liquid Marmite. And I have no accidents! At 9.30 p.m., I take my last Phanodorm sleeping pill, crushed, in condensed milk. I sleep soundly until 2.30 a.m., then I awake with a mouthful of saliva which bubbles up. There is butter on top of it, seemingly. I try to cope with this for one-and-a-half hours, with no success. So I go out to the main drain at 3 a.m. and bring up water in spoonfuls – the last thing I drank, after the condensed milk and Phanodorm. I go back to bed and I am OK.

27 May: We are graciously allowed to send another postcard. On it is printed: 'Enemy Civilians Internment Camp No. 1, Malaya'. We must give no date. We must not mention the war or the conditions of internment or political matters or Syonan or Malaya – only personal matters. I write mine to Pip (*Phyllis, Tom's sister*) and hand it in. It is Nipponese Navy Day. The wireless is working again and gives the most amazing exhibition of blatant conceit it has ever been my lot to hear. All this is received in a decorous silence by us, but, when the raucous voice of the loudspeaker goes on to say that the Italian Fleet has our Mediterranean Squadron bottled up in the Mediterranean, even the ranks of the poor bloody infantry can scarce forbear to jeer. This is instantly suppressed, of course. We are told a 'very high officer' is visiting us tomorrow. Everything is to be scrupulously clean. This always gets my goat. There are 3,260 in a gaol for 600 and the Japs have never given us a thing to keep it clean. Yet they loftily issue their orders. I prop my head and shoulders up a bit in bed and have no saliva trouble or bubbling in my mouth.

28 May: I eat everything I'm given today. The big noise arrives – he's nowt to look at! He just whizzes past. This story is unsavoury, but too good to be forgotten: in the library queue, I am next to a man painted with mercurochrome from head to foot; he is all abrasions. It transpires that he was watching soccer yesterday and the ball went into a drain – a main drain and very deep. He nobly went after the ball and, while he was down there, the sluice was opened! It washed him right down to the outlet, about 50 yards away, through all the filth and excrement. 'And,' asks an inquisitive individual behind me, 'were there any people squatting over the drain as you passed underneath?' 'Yes,' says he with feeling. 'There were!' Ugh, how horrible! Of course, the drain is as slippery as ice.

29 May: Approval has been given to get supplies – fresh fish for the hospital only, fresh and frozen meat, sweet biscuits, jam, honey and margarine, among other things, all paid for by the Red Cross, no doubt. Unfortunately, I can't eat any of them.

Sunday, 30 May: I arrange cash for my $440 loan receipt which is backed by the Government. Two Jews will give cash at the rate of $75 per $100; this suits me well.

31 May: My swallow is rather better than for some time. I eat everything and nothing is returned. A real Changi situation at breakfast: a squad is bringing rations to table, two carrying tea on a bamboo pole. People are in the way. One at the end of the pole, being the polite sort, says, 'Gangway, please.' The other, an Aussie, says, 'Get out of the bloody way.' Both – or should one say 'united' – they achieve their object. The latest atrocity concerns a Jew. He has in his home some canvas which he thought might be of use to the camp, so he consults Meredith, his block commandant. Meredith says, 'Write to the Nipponese and ask permission to get it in', which he does. He is sent for and badly beaten. Then Meredith is sent for and also assaulted. No reasons are given. Hakko ichiu! Our own bit of excitement is a room election for shopkeeper. Coles objected because Jack, the incumbent, would not weigh out tobacco for him at 4.50 p.m. Jack had announced earlier he'd be ready at 5 p.m. Coles moved off, vowing he'd have him out of the job, but no-one else would stand, so Coles stood and Jack was re-elected by 68 votes to 14, which shows what the room thought about it. I get $330 cash for my $440 camp loan receipt.

1 June: The Nipponese tell us that Austerhaus *(the suspected spy)* is at liberty to walk anywhere he likes in the camp and, if he is molested, the offender will be most severely punished. Who wants to molest the rat? But the trouble is he has only to say he has been molested and that will be quite sufficient.

2 June: Last night, five brothers of a Roman Catholic order arrived from Kuala Lumpur. They have been told they are here for repatriation. Today's excitement is the locking-up of the orchestra! They were busy practising in their usual position in the south- east corner of Girdle Road. They are accused of talking to the women who work on the duck farm – with what truth I know not. Anyhow, there's the orchestra languishing on top of the gaol tower – six of them – and apparently there for the night anyhow.

3 June: This is the 24th anniversary of our wedding day. We can't celebrate, Nora, but we will next year. Is Austerhaus locked up now? He was in the courtyard last night (the women's night for the wireless) so a Sikh sentry said, 'Out!' He said, 'No. I can go where I like, see Article 76 etc.' So he was reported to the Nipponese and judged. All electric gadgets are to be handed in to the Nipponese by 2.30 p.m.

And all fatigue parties into Singapore are cancelled. In both cases, I don't know why. The orchestra is released at 5 p.m. They have been grilled on top of the tower since yesterday morning. They had nothing but a blanket up there. Luckily, there was no rain. There was one casualty – Beverley. He collapsed and is in hospital. Both Tuesday and Wednesday editions of 'The Syonan Sinbun' have bits cut out – one-and-a-half columns then one column. I buy a blanket via Elias for $12.

4 June: There is another visitation due; we have orders that no beds or clothes airing are to be on view in any yards and mosquito nets in rooms have to be taken down! It is comic in the extreme. I do not see the 'high' officer myself.

5 June: Today is earmarked in memory of Admiral Yamamoto, so we have strict instructions that we are not to revel (!) and not to laugh, sing, whistle, dance or play. Ah me! Gone are the days when one honourably mourned for a gallant opponent. There is no chivalry left in war – not when dealing with the Axis, at any rate!

Sunday, 6 June: There is more censorship of the newspaper. It is cut about all over the place.

7 June: I see Johns at 10 a.m. He says that, if my weight continues going down, I'll have to have a stomach tube. Ugh! Upton, who is chairman of the messing committee, is getting my tins on Saturday and will put sugar in the custard. I am on a fatigue at 5 p.m., unloading a lorry-load of fruit – bananas, papayas, limes and oranges. It is quite heavy work, but I can still do it. H.M. Parry dies this afternoon. I am very sorry. He was a man who seemed perfectly fit when we came into internment. We are to get $5 cash each on the 15th of each month. I don't know if it is coming by way of the Red Cross, but I think so. My talk on the development of surveys in Malaya should fall due about six weeks hence, so I must get busy.

8 June: At 10.15 a.m., I attend the funeral service for H.M. Parry. It is a strange scene: the body is in a coffin in the mortuary; the padre stands at the door and 50 of us line a passage outside. Then we go out to Girdle Road. Five Nilai planter friends and the padre leave in the ambulance for the cemetery – R.I.P. I listen to the wireless news soon after 10; it is utter drivel.

9 June: We are printing 27,000 postcards for prisoners-of-war. I hope they are to go with us on the repatriation ship! The rumour is strong that we are to be away by the end of the month! There are various sources, including the usual interpreter and Dr Green, who is still not incarcerated. All dogs in the camp have been destroyed, by order of the Nipponese. And I say they are quite right. With 3,190 bipeds in this gaol, there's no room for quadrupeds. I get an enormous bottle of Horlicks via Salmond and the Red Cross.

10 June: At 9.30 a.m., I go to hospital where they take a tube of blood from a vein in my right arm. By 2 p.m., I am outside the prison on firewood fatigue, picking up wood chips – quite a pleasant occupation. Blakemore and other health officers have been brought in to Changi at last. I have Horlicks in the morning with last night's rice and again in the evening. Earlier, I had spoken to the chairman of the Messing Committee about my midday custard pudding having no sugar in it every other day. Today, as they are handing it out, he comes up and says to the server, 'Any sugar in that?' 'Oh no. I quite forgot – I'll put it in tomorrow.' 'Oh no you won't. You'll put it in now.' And it is done. It is very regrettable, but one is forced to the conclusion they were doing me down and keeping the sugar for themselves. The latest order is that no notice of any kind whatever is to be posted anywhere in the camp without a Nipponese stamp of approval on it. That is quite unnecessary e.g. a list of names or a football team or a price list! Or X wants to exchange a pair of socks for a razor blade.

11 June: I play league bridge all morning; we are fighting for promotion to Division One! At tiffin, there is actually some fresh beef in the soup, I understand. I discover a new Nipponese word in a newspaper report: 'Three of our planes committed jibaku' i.e. deliberately dived into objectives.

14 June: A young Sikh has his hands tied and is then very badly beaten up. I don't know why. After we have tried for 16 months to arrange regular meetings for husbands, wives and fiancés and received innumerable promises, in comes a message at 11.20 a.m. that they can meet at noon in the courtyard for 15 minutes! Typical! Half the people eligible for this concession are out on fatigues and will miss it. Kayn amuses me with this statement: 'you know this place brings out the worst in everybody. Here's a man in my cell; he hasn't a tooth in his head and he left his dentures in Singapore. Yet he is moving heaven and earth to get a toothbrush, just because there's a free issue from the Red Cross today.' I got one. It is official that there are to be no more fatigue parties going into Singapore. The Nipponese are evidently cutting all possible contacts with the populace. Miss M. Aitken and A. Urmossi have died. He was 46. As a Rumanian, he should not have been interned. Soccer is going very strong again. There is to be a cup competition. Seven-a-side hockey is also being organised.

15 June: We all receive $5 cash from the International Red Cross. What can I spend it on apart from foul tobacco?

16 June: I hear that the head boy at Miyako Hospital – a Chinese – died of a beating received for getting a tin of Klim for a patient, but I can't vouch for the story. I go to a talk by Dickinson on the Malayan Police; it is rather inconsequential and disappointing.

17 June: An article in 'The Syonan Sinbun' headed 'RED CROSS SAYS SYONAN PRISONERS WELL-TREATED' reports that the International Red Cross representative in Tokyo has told Geneva: 'The representative of the International Red Cross in Syonan is satisfactorily carrying on HIS ASSIGNED DUTIES' – which is quite true, but they do not include an inspection report! Jewish internees playing a card game for money (there is no rule against it) are seized by the Nipponese and taken to a room, where they are made to stand to attention for a few minutes, perfectly still, to be flogged if they move, then they are asked how they would like that for three hours. At last, they are allowed to go, but warned not to offend again. This is childish in the extreme, but it's not funny being subject to the whims of children.

18 June: My puddings at midday are much better since I registered my protest. They are liquid or semi-liquid and I can eat them without straining them. I play bridge most of the day. There are four divisions and a graduation league – ten teams of five pairs in each, an excellent institution.

19 June: I watch the Empress of Asia play the Malaya Cup Players at seven-a-side soccer. The Asia team win 3 – 2. One or two exhibitions of bad temper by the Asia team are not so good. The padang is much improved and must be the only instance on record of a playing field on the Equator being levelled and all earthwork done by entirely European labour. I shudder to contemplate the cost per cubic yard in salaries!

Sunday, 20 June: Miller sells a sovereign for $42.50; this must be an all-time record! He stuck out for his price for weeks. The buyer says, 'Don't let it be known, as I'm getting these for $17 from others.' The Nipponese want a list of internees who had any connection with intelligence work in Malaya, no-one knows for what reason. I imagine they'll get an almost nil return. And, of course, the list must be finished by 11 a.m. The latest victim of aggression is the ladies' Commandant. Tominato discovered an electric cigarette lighter which hadn't been rendered up to the Nipponese in accordance with orders, so she is in durance vile, though it has nothing to do with her as such. My big Horlicks bottle reminds me of Nora, she used to keep silk stockings in one.

21 June: I see Johns at 10 a.m., but there is nothing to report. Something went wrong with the blood sample taken on the 10th. There is no report, so they take another tube full. After 490 days, the Nipponese have agreed to 'consider inquiries regarding missing relatives!!' 'Warm and sympathetic' treatment indeed! At 8.30 p.m., I go to a meeting about forming a circle concerned with 'Sporting Reminiscences.' Though I can't talk, I can listen. We arrange to meet on Mondays at 8.30 p.m. I take dope and sleep fairly well.

22 June: There is another example of unnecessary Nipponese brutality: one Walker is found guilty by our own Disciplinary Committee of embezzling the proceeds of a raffle and gambling it away. The sentence and other details are handed to the Nipponese to be approved under the new ruling about notices. The Nipponese say, 'Ho! What's this?' send for Walker and beat him up. And three new and unnecessary afflictions are promulgated today: 1) all gunny sacks with a green stripe are the property of the Nipponese and must be given up at once. So 40 women and a number of men, whose beds have been made out of these sacks, have to yield them up and sleep on concrete. Our secretary, who innocently asks what the women are going to sleep on, gets his face smacked and is cast into solitary confinement; 2) No lights will be allowed after 9 a.m. or before 8 p.m. As a result it will be impossible to do anything in these dark rooms on dull days. 3) No internee will be allowed to make ANYTHING without a permit from the Nipponese. There is a bathing parade for B-Block, but I do not go. There's a new arrival today – Strachan from Malacca. He is married to a Nipponese woman and is confined to the compound. Is this another exchange pointer? It is two years ago since we heard that Germany and Italy had declared war on Russia. Bet they regret it. What a difference between the situation then and now! Then, we stood alone.

23 June: Yesterday, I bought three cracked eggs, but the shells were otherwise intact. I put them in an open tin. This morning, a piece of shell had been removed from two and some of the contents had gone. It can only have been done by huge cockroaches, which inhabit the closed cupboard. So I eat the three eggs before more theft can take place. I start writing my talk on 'The Development of Surveys in Malaya'. As I can't speak, I have to write it and Sworder will read it.

24 June: I see Tiny Smith; he can get some liquid foods via the shop and will do so. And I see F.W. Douglas about the early days of surveys from 1890 to 1910.

25 June: Although I take dope, I don't think I get more than four hours sleep; there is more regurgitation. After her recent afflictions, Dr Cicely Williams, the Women's Camp Commandant has naturally resigned and has been replaced by Mrs Nixon. 'The Syonan Sinbun' announces that Nipponese is to be the future lingua franca of Malaya, but do not be perturbed – English will be permitted as a medium of expression for some time yet. How magnanimous is this. There is also a notice to say we are to give up all steel helmets, whistles, daggers, stilettos and binoculars.

26 June: Thirty years ago today, I arrived in Malaya. I wish I was out of it now. In the bridge league, Morgan and I win our match. At 8.30 p.m., I go to a talk by Professor E.K. Tratman on 'Caves and Cave Exploring'. It is interesting; the talk largely concerns the Mendips, but he also speaks of some Yorkshire caves I know. Of course, 'Nippon knows no class or racial distinctions which were so hateful under the British,' says a leader in 'The Syonan Sinbun'. Yet a railway notice in the paper says, 'Owing to current exigencies, first-class tickets will only be issued to certain specified people.' Well, well! We never descended to that.

Sunday, 27 June: At 5 p.m., I go to hear F.W. Douglas's 'Reminiscences'. He came out to Malaya in 1895.

28 June: I see Johns at 10 a.m. He is going to see if he can get the oesophago-scope from the other hospital at Kadang Kerbau. We are not allowed to go there now, so I suppose people who need these things just die – an intolerable position. Johns says that my blood test was negative. I gather he was testing for syphilis! He says he wishes it wasn't negative, then he would know what to do! (Syphilitic lesions!) The Nipponese are examining all documents in A-Block (the Women's Block). The door is not locked now; the Nipponese go in any time day or night and look into the rooms. I'm told they watched bathing under the showers the other day. At 8.30 p.m., I attend a meeting of the Conversation Circle on 'Racing in Malaya'. It is not enlightening, but interesting; it passes the time until 9.30 p.m. Twelve people attend.

29 June: Nic sends me some sleeping pills. I make a cocktail of papaya juice, vinegar, tomato juice, soya bean sauce, lime and water; it is quite drinkable! I can't talk, eat, sleep or smoke now, so I must do something. Husband and wives now meet regularly twice a month. 'The Syonan Sinbun', under the heading 'No Room For Criminals', reports on the new regime's effective campaign against crime. The paper reports: 'A gang of twelve armed Chinese robbers in Singapore have confessed and are to be executed.' Their ringleader said how well the public co-operation with the police was under the wonderful leadership of Nipponese officials. (I bet he did poor devil.)

30 June: Two incidents yesterday demonstrate the Nipponese mentality yet again: 1) a fatigue party is coming in as usual with bamboo. One is sent for and escapes a beating by the skin of his teeth. He is informed that the bamboo pole he is carrying is pointed and could be used as a spear. Instructions are given that all bamboos in future must be hewn off square. Yet, daily, our fatigue parties go out armed with axes and other sharp implements. 2) Some days ago, orders were given to hand over all keys of 'sleeping places'. This was done. Yesterday, a fatigue party was observed working on the flat roof of the gaol. 'What's this?' It was pointed out that this was a regular fatigue engaged in tarring, that written permission (produced) had been obtained for it, that the roof was not a sleeping-place and that evidently there was a misunderstanding of the instructions if they wanted the key. N'importe! Adrian Clark, Camp Commandant, gets 10 days' solitary confinement. Optimists point out that, for the first time, we have been given a period to the confinement and we know what the 'crime' is; and The Commandant, in being incarcerated, has not been compelled to resign. Wonderful progress!

1 July: This is the 500th day of internment. The Nipponese are reported to be searching the whole camp for various articles, including torches, watches, diaries – with what truth, I know not. *(In a paragraph headed 'New Esperanto', Tom Kitching uses code to report Japanese actions, including beating and solitary confinement.)*

3 July: The ladies perform for us 'Pow Wow Circus'. It is very amusing: there are freaks such as a bearded lady, a giantess and Siamese twins; there are clowns, tightrope walkers, performing elephants, horses etc. I see Kath; she looks fit. Of course, no women except performers are allowed and all our captors are on the roof balcony with their refreshments. It finishes at 8 p.m. and I open a tin of sardines; I eat two in one hour, but it is hopeless. They block up the swallow in spite of my chewing every morsel to dust. I have to fetch it all up again. I take dope and sleep well until 4 a.m.

Monday, 5 July: I see Johns; there is no change. If he gets the oesophago-scope, he hopes to be able to do quite a lot. The population of the camp is now 3,038, 398 women and 80 children. I go to see 'The Wind and The Rain' in the laundry; it is most excellently performed under great difficulties. I enjoy it – it is real entertainment.

7 July: The royal coat of arms over the main gate is finally coming down – and in a hurry. Is this on account of Tojo? J.H. Winters has died, aged 67. The ladies are making cakes for 25 cents each; they are no use to me, alas.

8 July: At moments, I think my voice is a shade better. I get more Virol from the dispensary. Orders have gone out that there is to be no revelry and no noise after 8 p.m. yesterday and today. The only reason we can think of is the Double Seventh, the sixth anniversary of the outbreak of the 'China Incident.' *(Japan attacked China in 1937 from the puppet empire of Manchukuo.)* The doctors are alarmed at the increase in what for want of a better term they call 'tobacco blindness'. In the last six weeks, the cases have increased from 66 to 112. The consumption of local tobacco was higher in June than in any previous month. The flies are very bad again. The utmost care is necessary to avoid another outbreak of dysentery. The latest commandments from the Nipponese: thou shalt not: walk on the flat roof; look out of the grilles on the fourth floor; look out of any grille when Nipponese officers are about; affix maps or plans to any wall; possess tools except by permit; retain any axe, parang, fork or hoe after use. We are informed by Nipponese radio that our messages have all been sent.

9 July: During the night, there is a cat under my camp bed after something.

Monday, 12 July: We have an issue of soap from the Red Cross – five tablets! – and an issue of 14 oz of sugar from the Nipponese. I go to see Johns – the second blood test is negative. I have finished the Horlicks in 32 days. It is doubtful whether I shall get any more. It was in perfect condition. I still get Virol but that is not so much of a food as Horlicks.

14 July: Franklin asks if I would like to be in charge of exchange and mart for the block, but I can't talk and I have to spend such a lot of time preparing my food and eating it. I go to a talk by Gordon Hall on the duties of a District Officer. He outlines them thoroughly, although I think a little light relief would have been an advantage.

15 July: Today is pay day – $5 per person per month! It is Ladies' Day at the osteopath's. About half a dozen of them arrive, closely guarded by a Sikh and a camp policeman lest they are spoken to. They sit in a corridor outside his door and a portable screen is carefully placed all round them. I see Macintyre myself. He would like to restart the manipulation if the oesophagoscope has not arrived by Monday and if it is confirmed that my trouble is not pathological. 'The Syonan Sinbun' reports a wonderful bit of news – there is heavy fighting in Sicily; we have landed on the coast. Of course, we are being blasted and annihilated, but, still, we have landed. *(Allied troops went ashore in Sicily on 10 July.)* A new session of the bridge league has started. There are now four divisions of 12 teams each. Morgan and I beat Imrie and Hudson.

16 July: The wireless last night mentioned the Sicily landings for the first time. 'The Syonan Sinbun' says the Axis have won the first round in Sicily, but doesn't explain how they let the Allies get there. We have no whistles for the referees at soccer matches. The Japanese have taken away all our whistles. We made one; it was also confiscated. So we have made a rattle.

17 July: I took dope last night. It gave me the best sleep since internment. I did not go outside at all. I was awake at 3 a.m., but only for a brief spell. I had some vivid dreams, one involving me opening the batting for England versus Australia at Manchester! I spend most of the morning debugging my camp bed. I find the breeding places between the lath which fastens the canvas to the frame and the frame itself. I fill them with beautiful pink soap locally made. The last few nights, I have killed several bugs crawling on me. I go to a reading of 'The Importance of Being Earnest' in the laundry. I enjoy it, but it is a pity to introduce Changi gags like, 'Yes, I smoke, even if it does give me amblyopia!'

Sunday, 18 July: The ration strength is now 3,152: 399 women and 80 children. My daily diet and the preparation of my food has settled into a routine to cope with my difficulty in swallowing. This is the routine: first, I drink very slowly half a cup of tea to clear the toobs, so to speak. While doing this, I mix gula malacca, hot water and one dessertspoon of Virol in a pint mug. Then I put the rice into a perforated tin and grind it through with a fork, using skimmed milk to wash it through. This gives about a pint of liquid with bits of rice floating in it. Then I filter it all through another tin, which is more finely perforated. I add santan (coconut water) mixed with white liquid expressed from the coconut. This gives more than a pint of liquid containing some solid in suspension and, as a rule, I can swallow it in an hour. I regurgitate at 11 p.m. Sometimes I regurgitate again at 3 a.m.

19 July: I go to see Johns; there is no change. He is to send another message concerning the oesophagoscope. Their opinion is that my swallowing problem is definitely spastic, which is what Macintyre wanted me to confirm. Married men see their wives for half-an-hour and fiancées also meet. In the queue, I notice one married man aged 60 whose wife is away. I suppose he is there as a fiancée; I know he has a girlfriend aged 30 on the other side. A. Gow has died, aged 74. At 8.30 p.m., I go to the Sport and Reminiscences Club; Harvey gives a talk on 'A Game Warden in Tanganyika'. The material is interesting, but it is difficult to hear at times because of his very quick, staccato method of talking.

20 July: 'The Syonan Sinbun' reports a spokesman of the Nipponese Army Board of Information as saying Britain has sent warships to the Indian Ocean from the Mediterranean. This is good news, as it means that we can spare them. Wonder if Colin is involved. The fourth session of the Central Co-operative Council of the National Service Association vows to defend 'our sacred land to the last man' This is not very optimistic, surely.

21 July: My talk on 'The Development of Malayan Surveys' is read by Sworder. It goes very well. Many people come and congratulate me on it.

22 July: At 3 a.m., wind and rain sweep through the room. Stanton Nelson is back from Miyako Hospital. I fear his reason is gone. He is parked at the end of the Sanctuary in a hut just built and has two internees with him. I hear him about 4 a.m. cursing them: 'why the hell don't you do as you're told? Have YOU received the Holy Spirit?' It is very sad; he has a wife in A-Block too. I am told that Miyako Hospital is to be avoided at all costs now. There is no discipline at all; it is go-as-you-please, there is petty jealousy among staff and it is dirty. The wireless last night told us of a meeting between Mussolini and Hitler in North Italy at which they discussed the terrific Russian onslaught and the Sicily situation. It sounds good. Allied 'vandals' have bombed Rome. And Premier Tojo tells the assembled Governors in Nippon that the British-U.S. counter-attack is 'by no means negligible.' Black-out practice details are given in the newspaper; nuisance raids may be expected! I am told this story of 'Arry Hesp of the Asia. 'Arry was reading a book when one of the usual Nipponese visitors was being shown round. He asked politely, 'Is that a good book?' 'Arry, not knowing what fate was in store, handed it over. The Nipponese had a look and handed it back, saying, 'Arrigato' *(thank you)*. 'No,' replied 'Arry, not knowing the language. ' 'Arry Hesp!' In the bridge league in the afternoon, Morgan and I beat two Dutchmen from Piccadilly. We as a pair have played nine and won seven.

23 July: We are all to assemble on Monday in the main yard to be counted; no-one knows why.

24 July: I have no breakfast. I try last night's rice, twice filtered, but the swallow will not look at it and it gets stopped up immediately. What a day – very wretched, most wearing and I am very hungry.

Sunday, 25 July: I go to see Macintyre at 11 a.m. He still thinks he can deal with the swallow. He gives me several tweaks on the neck and spine.

26 July: The great census arrives! The whole camp is in the main yard. Breakfast is at 8.30 a.m. and the parade at 9.30 a.m. – in our respective blocks. The Nipponese walk round while our representatives read out the names and each man springs up as his name is called. There are no incidents and all is over by noon. I see Heron and arrange for a supply of Marmite. Mine was stopped with the general stoppage. Some Horlicks has come in, but Bowyer is keeping it in reserve.

27 July: I took dope last night by a very effective new technique. I crushed and mixed it with tea and saccharin and swallowed it at 9 p.m. On top of it, I took a layer of tomato juice in order not to lose the dope by regurgitation. On top of the tomato juice, I took a layer of tea, so as not to lose the tomato juice. This sequence was completed by lights out at 10 p.m. Then I went to bed and regurgitation started. I went outside, stuck a finger down my throat and regurgitated the tea. I then got a decent night's sleep. I regurgitated at 6 a.m. I get my Marmite issue. The gentleman serving me, because I can speak only in a hoarse whisper, thinks I am deaf and shouts. I find this a common delusion. Actually, my hearing is particularly acute. I go to Macintyre at 12.30 p.m. He gives me a good spinal twist. The Nipponese wireless reports that Mussolini has resigned on account of 'ill-health'. The King of Italy takes over, with Badoglio as Prime Minister. Martial law has been declared throughout Italy. A dictator has gone at last – banzai! *(Mussolini was deposed on 25 July, at a time when Italian soldiers were surrendering in their thousands in Sicily.)* Black-out starts from today and we are allowed no lights from 8 p.m. to 8 a.m. The nights will be long and dreary when I can't eat, talk, smoke or sleep. 'The Syonan Sinbun' says a cable from Lisbon on July 22nd reported the arrival in London of 20,000 postcards and letters from the Pacific theatre. I hope ours are amongst them.

28 July: The air-raid precautions are not so bad as I expected – we are allowed lights between 8 and 10 p.m., except for the duration of a warning which tonight was from about 9 to 9.30 p.m. The latest prohibition is that we are not to use the stage more than twice a month. Nic sends sago pudding which I liquefy with Gula Malacca and Santan.

29 July: Jack and I still rise at 7.30 a.m. and bathe and shave in the laundry. There are no lights until 8 a.m., so it's darkish. The air-raid precautions practice is postponed indefinitely! Why, on earth? And there's been such a fuss and palaver about it on the wireless and in the paper. We wonder if, coming simultaneously with the Italian news, they've decided it would have a very bad propaganda effect. They have just dropped it like a hot brick and not a word why, either on the wireless or in the paper. I should have gone chipping with the wood fatigue party, but it was rained off.

30 July: In the bridge league, Morgan and I beat Folliot and Rayman.

31 July: I hold a sewing bee for myself this morning. I patch my shorts, sew on buttons and contract my garters in accordance with my leg contraction. My shorts are getting very decrepit – no wonder! They have been worn constantly for 530 days! Our eight Changi-born babies are beginning to celebrate their first birthdays, starting with Victoria Scott on July 23rd and ending with Mervyn Shorthouse on October 23rd. His mother says he doesn't want his first birthday here, nor do I think he'll have it here, although the latest rumour is that Eden says they still have no information about us.

Sunday, 1 August: Another month gone – how much longer? There is a very strong rumour that 900 are to go; a list has been received from London. I finish reading 'The Escaping Club' by A.J. Evans; it is very interesting, but what a contrast to our lot and treatment. He got so many food parcels from home, plus what he could buy (his pay from the Germans was 100 marks a month), that he never touched the German rations. And when they got dried fish, they threw it away. Evans writes: 'Our letters and postcards came regularly and quickly and only those who have been prisoners can understand what that means.' We can indeed – 531 days and only eight letters, all old, and NO parcels. Evans also says: 'X was truculent when captured and I admired him for it.' (Try being truculent to the Nipponese!) At a hotel in Damascus, Evans says: 'I absolutely refused to enter the room in spite of all threats.' Lights Out times were absolutely ignored. They told the commandant exactly what they thought of him and, even after escape and recapture, there was no punishment! He describes his feelings when a Turkish officer hit an unresisting Turk sentry several times; I know these feelings too.

2 August: The dope gives me my best sleep for years – 10.45 p.m. to 6 a.m. I go to see Johns. One vocal chord is still out of action, but the other is showing signs of compensation. I see him again at 6.45 p.m. He overhauls my chest and everything is OK He says the swallow will be easy to deal with once instruments are available. I also go to Macintyre; he gives me three tweaks on my spine and one on my neck.

3 August: To my list of curious sights seen in Changi, I must add: the Bishop of Singapore pushing a pram round the gaol.

5 August: I take dope and have an excellent night. The newspaper reports that two Chinese Communists have been captured; they are leaders of the Malayan Anti-Nippon 5th Independence Corps. So there is still guerrilla warfare.

6 August: In the bridge league, Morgan and I beat Carmichael and Wood. The Nipponese inform us that the postcards written 'recently' (!) are still in camp, but an 'effort' will be made to dispatch them this month. There will be no further men's concerts given in the Women's Camp and vice versa.

7 August: The soccer is going very strong now. A team of married men draw one-one with a team of single men at seven-a-side. The ground is as true as a billiard table, but it is a very hard gravel surface – very dangerous – so there is no robust play and no charging. It really ruins it as soccer. The goalkeeper is quite immune and can do what he likes.

Sunday, 8 August: The dope last night gave me an excellent sleep – from 11 p.m. to 2 a.m. and from 2.30 to 7 a.m.

10 August: There is no water this morning; it's an appalling nuisance. I get enough for shaving, but you can't wash and there's no tea or aught to drink and idiots WILL use latrines. There is to be no fishing or bathing round Singapore Island or in the Straits of Johore until further notice and the public are warned not to eat raw fish. The authorities fear an outbreak of cholera for some reason not stated.

11 August: There is no bath for me! The laundry opens at 11.15 a.m. There is a shortage of water in Singapore. The latest prohibition: the residents of the kitchen are not to use the boiler-room roof any more except to air clothes. They used to sit there to watch the soccer and other activities. There is no reason one can see. I hear we are getting no more eggs; the price is up to 30 cents. This seems to me to put my diet below the irreducible minimum to maintain my already attenuated frame, so I see Dr Heron who gives me a chit to Dr Bowyer. The result is that I am to get one pint of full-cream milk per day instead of three-quarters of a pint of skimmed milk; and five tins of soup and two tins of tomato juice per week, instead of three and two respectively. Official announcement: the Nipponese here have 'promised' to make 'further' inquiries about the survivors of the Kuala and the Tanjong Pinang

12 August: I receive two tins of tomato juice and one of Brand's chicken essence from Nic – very welcome. I go to Macintyre in the morning. I tell him about the retrogression since last Monday. I also tell him that I have more regurgitation in daytime and more difficulty in swallowing liquids. He gives two tweaks to my neck and one is a real snorter. At 7.30 p.m., I go to see 'French Without Tears' in the laundry; it is excellently acted and produced. What a pity the Nipponese won't let the women see it.

13 August: I am asked by an internee to make 25 maps of Sicily. It's a bit of a sweat, but I can do four at a time, using carbon copies.

14 August: The clock goes on striking every hour and continues halfway through the night. It usually does not strike between 11 p.m. and 7.30 a.m. Water is still very short; there is none this morning. It's horrible being in a tennis-court-size room on the Equator with 100 others and not to be able to wash your face in the morning. In the bridge league, Morgan and I win our match, but our team loses again.

16 August: There is a beautiful eclipse of the moon. I view it at 4 a.m. – it is a full moon two-thirds obscured in a cloudless sky. I wonder if Chinatown has frightened it away in the customary manner. I expect Bushido, Hakko Ichiu and Kultur have eradicated all that. I see Johns; the Nipponese have asked for a list of all who have been on the sick list for two months or more and I am on it. Does this presage an exchange? A young hopeful in the Women's camp, aged five, asked what he was going to do when he grew up, said, 'Go over to the Men's Camp.' Comment of 'Pow-Wow', the ladies periodical is: 'WE can't even look forward to that.'

17 August: Dick Hewitt has dysentery now; there is a recrudescence. As for the cholera scare, the Nipponese have reported a suspected case in this part of the island, so we are all to be inoculated. All drinking water must be boiled no Gula Malacca, peanut toffee or fresh fruit will be bought and bread will be re-baked. Mrs L. Edmett has died aged 57; her husband died recently.

18 August: Adrian Clark makes an excellent speech, dealing with finance, supplies and a letter just communicated to the Camp Committee by the Nipponese. The 'Neutral Agent' (which is what we are instructed to call the Red Cross representative who has been supplying us with food, money etc.) has inexplicably been told from Geneva that he has to stop paying money out on our behalf at the end of August. So there will be no more cash advances of $5 per month to internees and rations will be cut down to the minimum necessary for health. There will be half a loaf a day, no fruit and so on. After taking 16 months to get help, we are having it cut off after two months and we understand the Nipponese here are as much in the dark as we. Supplies are becoming impossible too – and prices. The Red Cross paid $57,000 for food last month; and half a bar of washing soap and one cake of toilet soap each would cost $5,000 – if you could get it, which is very doubtful. We are woefully short of water and firewood; and such things as axe-handles, cobblers' nails and cloth for shorts are absolutely unobtainable in Singapore. We are even finding difficulty in making coffins for our dead. Adrian Clark also speaks of discipline and how the camp deals with offenders. His voice cracks – he asks for water and someone rushes off and gets a mug full from the tap. There comes a voice from the crowd: 'It hasn't been boiled!' But the letter is a very bright spot: it is from Schweitzer (the Neutral Agent) to the Nipponese and is dated July 20th. He says that exchange negotiations are proceeding successfully. He expects one or two ships here 'in the autumn'. He expects they will bring supplies and presumes that women and children, the aged and sick will go first. So we all feel very bucked about this except the usual pessimists, for Schweitzer would not write like that without some cause.

19 August: I go out in the afternoon on a firewood fatigue collecting chips. It's a long walk now. At 9 p.m., we are peacefully playing bridge when a Nipponese interpreter and two large Sikhs rush into our room carrying a stick four-foot long and one-and-a-half inches in diameter. Luckily, someone at the door shouts, 'Stand up!' and everybody does. The interpreter glares all round, can discern nobody not standing to attention and rushes out again. But other rooms and floors are not so lucky and altogether he assaults about 10 internees. Some have to go to hospital for attention. For example, on the fourth floor of C-Block, two men are in a cell, one dictating from a book, the other taking it down in shorthand. Engrossed in their work, they hear nothing. The interpreter rushes in and beats them up. Old Captain Barton, aged 75 and stone deaf, is sitting in his cell, having heard nothing, of course; the fiend rushes in and beats him with the stick several times. Also Baker, who is lying down in his cell, is kicked in the eye and is lucky not to have lost it. The interpreter also visits A-Block, where he strikes four females, although not seriously. A total of 31 men and women are struck for not leaping to attention. One is a crippled old lady and another an old lady asleep in a chair. The interpreter is tight, of course. Words fail.

20 August: 'The Syonan Sinbun' says goods supplied by the Nipponese will be distributed today; the goods include crockery, glassware, earthenware, vases, beer mugs, cutlery, buckets, needles, lunch boxes, toys, stationery and trays. I see Dr Evans of the Messing Committee about eggs, meat juices and warming my soup in the kitchen now that the Dover stove hours are restricted. The immediate result is that I am apparently to get two raw eggs a day. At any rate, I get them today. The same interpreter who went berserk yesterday rings up this evening: his car has conked out, so we have to send the ambulance driven by one of our men to bring him and his prostitute back! The Camp Committee have protested. The Nipponese authorities say they will inquire! On a par with this strange state of affairs is the fact that the whole of the Nipponese and Indian staff of the camp came to our doctors for anti-cholera injections! GERMANS VIA GOEBBELS ASK FOR PEACE *(in code – this information appears to be false).*

21 August: Dr Ted Lawrie has committed suicide in the camp hospital; he cut his throat; I knew him well; he leaves a wife and two children in Australia. I buy a Gibbons stamp catalogue for 1940 for $5; it will help to pass the time. I buy it from a Scots tin miner from Puchong. Official details are available concerning the money and other matters mentioned in Adrian Clark's speech on August 18th: the telegram was from Geneva via the International Red Cross in Yokohama before July 20th, 1943, instructing the Neutral Agent to cease purchases on behalf of internees and prisoners-of-war. (It is surmised that this action has been taken pending adjustment of payments between London and Geneva.) I go to Ted Lawrie's funeral – it is very impressive. All the nurses attending are in uniform. Of course, we are not allowed outside the prison walls. The latest disciplinary order: when visitors are being shown round and internees are standing at attention and the visitor says, 'Sit down' or words to that effect, internees must remain at attention, unless the Nipponese member of camp staff confirms the order. At 8.30 p.m. I go to a talk by Dr Amstutz on the Batak tribes round Lake Toba in Sumatra. It is interesting, although he is not an expert. Morgan and I lose our bridge match by 750 points.

Sunday, 22 August: My swallow is very fluctuating just now. Liquids alternate between being quite easy and very difficult. My voice is no worse, but anything like prolonged talking is very exhausting, so I don't do it.

23 August: I see Macintyre; he gives me several tweaks, but he says I am rather tense today. He thinks he now knows how to deal with it, so will start on Thursday and go ahead. Borrie, leader of the wood fatigue party, is beaten up and given seven days' solitary confinement. This morning, the Sikh soldier out with the party tells them not to stop and rest when they have pushed the heavy cart full of wood to the top of a steep hill, when a rest is always taken. Borrie tries to argue against this, I gather, but only very mildly, and they obey the order. But the Sikh reports the incident and that's the result. Sheer savagery *(the last word in code).*

24 August: We all have a cholera injection this afternoon – a very sharp process. I think our doctors did the 100 in our room in five minutes.

25 August: The latest rule is that not only the leader, but everybody in a group must now bow when passing a sentry and, when the Nipponese visit the camp, everyone must not only stand to attention, but also bow when the Nipponese enter a room. When our 100 perform simultaneously, I anticipate some head-on collisions. A new inmate, a Norwegian – Thiel Marstrand – has been employed at Batu Arang coalmine and latterly on vegetable cultivation in the Cameron Highlands. I'm told he was five days en route and had no food; when he arrived here, he was given a handful of rice in a newspaper. Eighteen months ago, one would have said that story was nonsense. I am much weaker now than when I first came in. I noticed it particularly yesterday when walking up the slight gradient from laundry to kitchen.

26 August: I go to Macintyre in the morning and he gives me a super-tweak; the reaction runs down my right arm to my fingertips like a red-hot poker. He expects marked results. Last night, I went to hear Cheeseman talk on 'Some Malayan Books' – an excellent talk. I enjoyed it immensely, although it brought back acute memories of the Malayan books I have lost. Damn, damn, damn. I had a goodly selection, many out of print and rare, but it is no use repining; only two things matter at the moment: is Nora alive? And to get out of here.

28 August: I go to a talk by Ogilvie on the Che Wong Sakai of Krau Game Reserve – a part I've always wanted to visit; it lies east and south of the summit of Benom. He has good material, but his delivery is poor and he has that very bad habit of dropping his voice so that you miss vital words. The latest prohibition is that internees must stop talking when passing a sentry. Here are a couple of good uns from the Norwegian, Marstrand. At Batu Arang, Tamil coolies were going in for petty theft in a big way, particularly of nails, which fetched a high price. All efforts to stop this failed, so at length a Nipponese arrived on a bicycle to turn them from their wicked ways. He delivered an address full of 'co-operation', 'bushido' and other lofty, highly laudable sentiments, ending as usual with the iron hand jutting out a cubit from the velvet glove. Then he turned for home, with something accomplished, something done; he went round the corner – no bike! The Tamils had stolen it! In Ipoh, the Nipponese distributed free ice-cream to the Tamil coolies. They were told to bring their pals next day for more, which they did, then again they were told to 'bring more tomorrow', which they did. They were then all rounded up and sent to a labour camp in Siam.

Sunday, 29 August: Our last batch of postcards is still being censored here. On his, Jeans wrote: 'this is the third postcard I've been allowed to write. I don't suppose you've got either of the other two and I don't suppose you'll get this.' He was sent for, we thought for the high jump, but no, Tominara was quite affable and gave him another postcard. They are absolutely unpredictable.

30 August: The shortage of firewood causes short hours for Dover stoves, therefore they are crowded out and I find it difficult to warm my soup, so Jack makes a stove with tins and we burn sacking in coconut oil – very satisfactory, but we cannot put it out. Eventually, we smother it with a sack and raise a most pungent smoke, which fumigates the room!

31 August: We get our second anti-cholera injection. I am busy drawing a map of interesting parts of the Russian front. I am also working on a new crossword called 'Plus Fours' in which the answers will, I hope, consist entirely of words to which the solver has been given no clue.

1 September: There is a variety concert on the stage in the main yard. Jack and I sit apart and enjoy the music. I spend most of the day on my map. A radio message to an internee via the Red Cross indicates knowledge that we are in Changi and he is well. The inference is that some of our postcards of last November have arrived. Two-and-a-half bags of mail have just arrived in camp. I wonder what date they are and if I'll get news of Nora. A census of occupations shows that we have here 226 seamen and 876 government officers and amongst the other 1,883 civilians of 24 nationalities are 331 planters, 302 merchants, 188 miners and mining engineers, 153 engineers, 144 medical and associated professions (102 government), 103 municipal officers, 85 accountants, 59 bankers, 35 brokers, 37 lawyers, 50 clergymen and other religious workers, 6 farmers, 12 entertainments and catering staff, 16 managers of hotels, boarding houses and clubs, 8 musicians, 32 retailers and 11 horse-trainers and jockeys. Of 402 women, 70 are nurses, 258 housewives, 6 doctors, 13 teachers and 11 typists.

2 September: We are to continue to get $5 a month. The letters have been sorted – as I expected; they are a complete lottery. There are about 9,000, I should say, dumped into bags by the Nipponese Red Cross in Tokyo – entirely haphazardly – seven for me, one for Hope, none for Jack and 28 for Jimmy Crick! Now the 'censoring' begins. As they are approximately a year old, it seems rather a work of supererogation. What on earth they do with them in Tokyo except delay, I can't imagine. Nic sends a sago pudding, all jellyish. I get the first portion down with small difficulty, liquidated of course with milk and santan. This is an improvement. I get no ground rice today; I gather that the kitchen forgot it.

THE END IN SIGHT?

3 September 1943: I am reading with intense interest the government blue book of documents prior to the outbreak of war on September 3rd, 1939 – four years ago today. And the most pessimistic prognostications as to the world scope of the war and the wholesale destruction have been more than fulfilled. But it is strangely heartening to read this book. It proves beyond the shadow of a doubt that we fight for the Right and demonstrates the utter irrationality of Hitler; and irrationality is a weakness; and this weakness will tell in the long run. Well, the Allies are on top now after months when they were all but down and out and the end of the long run is not far away, I think. At 7.15, there is a combined service in the Main Yard. It is a good one; special prayers are most excellently and tactfully worded and there is a sermon by the Bishop. He speaks well and has a really remarkable voice.

4 September: At 8.30 p.m., I go to a talk by Molesworth on 'A Naturalist in the Shetlands'; it is most fascinating, as he talks of skuas, eider duck, puffins, guillemots, basking sharks, seals, whales and sea otters. I must certainly go next summer!

Sunday, 5 September: The recent mail comprises 10,334 letters, mostly from the U.K. The latest date is early November. And there are a few from Australia, New Zealand, Africa and India dated early December. Of course, none has been released yet. Cholera inoculation is now compulsory for us by order of the Nipponese. At 6.30 p.m., I watch Plymouth Argyle beat Spurs by four goals to one at soccer. At 7.45 p.m., I listen to the election speeches for the post of Commandant in B-Block by Harper-Ball (the present Commandant) and the Rev. R.K.S. Adams. Either would be satisfactory, I think, but Harper-Ball points out that he took over four months ago at a very difficult time, with Blocks B and C Commandants both in the jug. Things are improved now – why change your experienced man? I agree.

7 September: I go to Macintyre at 12.45 p.m., but he is hors-de-combat with 'flu, so I do not get the intended manipulation. Still, the swallow for liquids is improved, although very far from normal; nevertheless, I down ground rice in suspension every teatime. I go to a performance of Shaw's 'Arms and the Man' in the laundry; it is excellently done; the diction is exceptionally good. The Changi Quartet appropriately play selections from 'The Chocolate Soldier' which takes me back to Cambridge days. Jack and I enjoy it very much. To get your seat into anything like a decent position, you have to park it in the queue at 6 p.m. for the 7.20 p.m. opening of doors.

8 September: The ban on swimming and fishing because of the cholera is lifted. Those with next-of-kin in Australia can hand in wireless messages to be sent from the S.B.C. They must ask for a reply to be broadcast and the S.B.C. want any information about reception in Australia, which probably accounts for the milk in the coconut. But any propaganda put across can do no harm, so the Committee decides in favour of sending the messages. I may get one to Nellie *(Tom's sister)* later. There is a 'flu epidemic. The flag flies today, being the 8th; every 8th is now a day of celebration, the 'mensersary' of the 8th December, 1941, when Asia was liberated and acquired all this freedom which is being so lavishly distributed just now. G.N. Magill has died, aged 59; he was a Penang trainer. I go to a lecture by Shebbeare on 'Malayan Fauna'. It is most inconsequential, but interesting and amusing. He is a staunch advocate of a National Park in the remotest portion of the Malayan jungle, I am glad to hear.

9 September: I hand my Waltham turnip watch to Meyer to dispose of for cash. It won't fetch much, but it is worth whatever it fetches to me, converted into raw eggs. I go on firewood fatigue this afternoon, collecting chips. It's a walk of three miles there and back now and I'm quite tired at the end of it. To think of it. Three miserable miles tiring ME! I send a wireless message to Nellie in Australia and ask about Nora, Colin and Joan. I say I am not very fit. The radio announces the surrender of Italy to the Allies. That's one Axis partner hors de combat *(in code)*!

10 September: My crossword 'Plus Fours' is an excellent soporific. Whether it is possible to complete it, I don't know. The Nipponese ask for the addresses of people in Singapore who have our clothes – they will 'try' to get what we want! R. Williamson has died, aged 57. He was a senior partner with Drew and Napier. He could have left in February 1942, but elected to see things through. The pudding is solid again; I register a protest and open a tin of milk. AT LAST! A letter from Brenda *(Tom's sister)* dated July 27th, 1942, with some news of Nora: 'I expect Joan has told you of the letter she had from Mrs Noble giving an account of Nora's adventures – it upset us very much. I do hope she is not suffering any ill effects from what must have been an awful time.' Mrs Noble was on Joan's ship; Noble was on the Kuala and he is at large and has written to his wife telling her of the sinking of the Kuala. That is what I read into it, so the inference is that Nora was safe after the Kuala bombing, but what happened to her after that is still a mystery. The other news is that Joan is well and she and Brenda see each other frequently. Colin is also all right and is still in Scotland. All seems OK at Colinwood *(The house in Morecambe)*. Brenda, who is in the Censorship Office in London, evidently thinks the mails are coming through regularly!

11 September: I get a beauty of a papaya from Katherine – home-grown. It is a

3 SEPTEMBER 1943 – 31 DECEMBER 1943

pity I can't eat it, but I will try the juice. I get $20 for the Waltham watch; it will never stand me in better stead and it won't go anyway. I am busy on the Burma map and expect it to be interesting in the near future. I'm wearing shoes and stockings; they do feel queer. In the bridge league, Birkinshaw and I beat Westrop and Brockett.

Sunday, 12 September: We bought 10,000 eggs yesterday – for $3,000 or £350! So, for the first time in history, there are two hard-boiled eggs for breakfast! F.L. Horth has died, aged 68, also Mrs D. McIntyre.

13 September: The Nipponese issue instructions that even urgent cases cannot be sent out of camp to hospital; no reason is given.

14 September: In future, wives and relatives are to be allowed to meet once a week for one hour! Ye Gods – a wonderful concession! When are we going to get more sugar? It's well over a month since we had an issue of 16 oz. The food is falling off; today's menus are: rice, tea, vegetable soup, half a loaf; rice, tea, peanut butter. I receive a letter from Pip *(Tom's sister)* dated September 23rd, 1942, addressed to Nora and myself: 'I do hope our letters are reaching you.... Colin has just been here, after his return from Dieppe. *(He was on the Dieppe raid.)* How well he looked! I hope you are both keeping fit and that things are not too bad for you...' I go to Macintyre, but he does not give me any tweaks. He has another gambit in store, but the time is not ripe for it.

15 September: Two thousand letters are out; information in them shows that they had no news of us to the end of 1942! (e.g. letter from India, dated December 10th, 1942: 'Still no news of you, but a few names are filtering through.') There is a letter to both of us from Joan, dated July 28th, 1942. She is enjoying her work 'hugely'. She writes, 'I feel that I am at last working to attain something.' Her billet is excellent: 'I cannot think of a more delightful household to be in.'

16 September: I receive another letter from Joan, dated October 13th, 1942 and numbered two. She is full of enthusiasm for her work; she has started on real patients in hospital and moves to London next week. She will live with Brenda – excellent. She writes, 'I am horribly well and as happy as I can be in the circumstances.' I partner Smith at bridge in the evening. By curious coincidence, when I see one of our opponents, Ladell, I remark, 'Oh, you came out on the Maloja with me in 1913.' 'So did I,' says his partner! So three out of four had come out together.

17 September: I take dope and sleep very well. I go to Macintyre; he says, 'Ha!' Apparently, something he manipulates in the neck has slipped back, which accounts for the difficulty in swallowing liquids for the last three days. Certainly, something goes with a click when he manipulates today. Wilson gives me two tins of condensed milk – extremely noble of him. They will be most useful. He will not hear of me paying; he says he cannot take money for food. I very much fear the food situation will be very bad in Singapore 'ere long; it's bad enough now. Bathing resumes today; I don't go. I hate being regimented to the beach by sentries and the sea is full of jellyfish. Our initials are checked; the Nipponese think they might send a nominal list of internees to London by the exchange ship, which has left Nippon and will call here. I wonder if there is hope of its taking the sick.

18 September: I receive two letters from Brenda. One dated June 22nd, 1942 says she was just moving to London and was going to do all she could for Colin and Joan. She says she will 'take your place to the best of my ability', which is extraordinarily nice of her. She goes on 'Colin looks marvellous in his uniform and is growing really handsome; he is a son to be proud of.... They are two fine youngsters.' So that's excellent. In the letter dated October 19th, 1942, she says Colin sent a message via the BBC. All the letter writers assume their letters are reaching us regularly, so we miss a lot of news. They little know our conditions! C.T. Davies has died, aged 44.

Monday, 20 September: H.J. (Ronnie) Ridgwell died last night after an operation. He was 55. He was the brother of the famous 'Punch' artist. Ronnie had no reserves of strength at all. That is another from our room. I knew him in 1913 when he was on the Sungei Mahang estate. Before coming out here, he was private secretary to Pemberton Billing. I attend the funeral service at 10.15 a.m.

21 September: Taking soup last night at 10, I had a brief spell when it went down almost normally – I wonder if this portends a change, an improvement? I also thought I was going to have no regurgitation, but I woke at 3 a.m. to it. When the locust swarm has been dealt with, the rehabilitation of Malaya is going to be an interesting job. I'd like to be in on it, but I don't propose to part from the family any more. In this mail, I've had no letters addressed to Nora. I wonder if they've been sorted out by the Red Cross in Tokyo and sent to a different destination? The Nipponese have given permission for the banana fatigue to buy 'gula batu' – a locally-made sugar in large chunks. And the rice shortage now appears to have vanished.

22 September: I am on corridor-sweeping fatigue; I find I soon tire these days. There is a new restriction on going to see wives and children: internees are not allowed to take a book. Why, oh why, and how long, O Lord, how long? Surely our government are doing something to get the women and children, if not us, out of Nipponese clutches. I go to the talk by C.C. Brown on 'Malay Dialects!' He has a comprehensive knowledge of certain dialects, but not of the southern states. An advertisement for the Japanese film of the fall of Singapore, 'On to Singapore', announces 'Syonan – City of Peace, Plenty, Prosperity'.

23 September: I go out with the wood fatigue party, collecting chips. We were told we could get more rice, hence rationing was not introduced, but now we haven't got it, so rationing starts! Typical! *(In a paragraph inserted at this point in code, Tom appears to be reporting the mission of Rudolf Hess to Britain, offering peace terms which would include the return of Britain's colonies and giving Germany a free hand in Europe. Tom goes on to describe the latest air-raid precaution prac-*

tice.) There are no lights from 8 p.m. to 8 a.m. The practice continues for several days. It is much boosted in the Press, with columns of details. At 9.30 p.m., the lights are turned on and we're told it's been postponed indefinitely – once again! I am offered $150 for my watch today by a Jew. It cost $40 two-and-a-half years ago. It is tempting – I can buy eggs with it.

24 September: There was a pep talk on the wireless last night: 'Why aren't people going to places of amusement at night? There's nothing in these stories of people disappearing and being taken to labour camps. Contradict them and roll up! It's not playing the game at all, when the authorities are racking their brains to amuse you, not to turn up and be amused! Very few people go shopping; amusement parks and cinemas are well-nigh deserted.' (And only a few days ago, they said a propaganda film broke all records for attendance, including those under the British regime!) 'This is due to the absurd rumours about the GUNSEI (the military administration) taking people away for forced labour.' (The nice, kind GUNSEI would not do anything like that.) 'Anyhow, people should voluntarily respond to the necessary calls for labour... and anybody who obstructs the GUNSEI will be dealt with.' (Out peeps the iron hand again!)

25 September: I have a hell of a struggle at tiffin. I cannot swallow my food in spite of diluting and filtering it. I have four separate chokes, then give up. I am very distressed and hungry. So I go to the kitchen and tell them for the nth time that the puddings MUST be liquid. I receive a letter from Brenda, dated September 18th, 1942. She writes: 'We are hoping it won't be long now before we have news of your safety. Colin and Joan had been in town for a weekend with Brenda. They went to see Gordon Harker in 'Warn That Man'. Brenda sent a model plane from Selfridges for Brian's birthday. It all sounds so VERY normal.

Sunday, 26 September: I ask the Rev. Amstutz about R.H. Young, the doyen of surveyors in Malaya. He was about 90 and came out about 1875. This harmless old man was settled in Singapore with his children and grandchildren. To my horror, I hear he was interned here just the same as anyone else. He died early on in the occupation in Miyako Hospital. Of course, the hardships killed him. Verdict – unjustifiable homicide amounting to murder, say I. There is an appeal for subscriptions to buy footballs, price $50.

27 September: The postcards written late June are still here. If, as a result of recent mail, we wish to rewrite them, we can do so, but we are limited to 25 words.

28 September: The Nipponese have taken mattresses from the hospital, so we are 10 short and there is an appeal for them. Letters received mention a book about the attack on Singapore by one Gilmour in which he says anyone could have got away as he did, but people were cowering terror-stricken in their houses! *(Gilmour, Oswald Wellington, Singapore to Freedom, London: E.J. Burrow, 1943)* If true, we shall have something to say to him. In the bridge league we are promoted to Division 1. There is a brown-out and a black-out tonight. With no lights, it is so very dull. I can't talk much or smoke, so I sits and thinks and sometimes just sits.

29 September: I see 'The Amazing Doctor Clitterhouse' in the laundry – it is excellently done. The scenery is marvellously contrived out of nothing and there is a curtain for the first time – it moves off horizontally! The standard of Changi productions is very high and this lives up to it. It passes the evening very pleasantly, although one can't help reflecting on the oddity of being part of the audience in a Changi theatre. We are in shorts and nothing else and smoking the foulest of shag and cheroots.

30 September: Lady Thomas has received a letter, a year old, from a friend in the Colonial Office. They are doing all they can to get internees exchanged. At 7.15 p.m., I go to a new series of readings from famous authors on the English countryside – selections from Mary Webb, D.H. Lawrence and Adrian Bell. The commentary, is read by the Bishop of Singapore. I go to bed very tired after struggling all day to swallow various meals.

1 October: There are two new internees from Alexandra Power Station; they have lots of luggage. One has a mincing machine; I wonder what he's going to mince in it! I play poker this morning. I am offered four ounces of English tobacco for $25! There's nothing doing, of course. J. Kellie has died, aged 56. Of his effects, I buy a 12-oz tin of cheese for $4.

2 October: There is a terrific wind and rain in the night; everything gets wet in our room and Bewsher gets into a cupboard with the bugs and spiders. At 8.30 p.m., I go to hear Shebbeare on 'Everest'. He was transport officer for more than one expedition. He thinks that Mallory and Irvine slipped and fell on the way up, although it is possible they reached the top.

4 October: The exchange ship Teia Maru is here – in the roads. She is taking nobody from Singapore. She has mail on board for us, but, as she is officially not here, this will go to Goa and come back again! Typical! No doubt there will be lashings of mail put on at Goa for us, which will go to Tokyo and come back God knows when. At 7.15 p.m., I go to Dr Poynton's talk, '100,000 Miles in a Year,' mostly as a surgeon on the Empress of Britain – very amusing indeed – and interesting. I am extending my map of Russia west to the Polish border. There is something very much wrong with my right arm and thumb in particular – can it be rheumatism? I have never had that before. I think it is a result of the manipulations, as that's exactly where I felt the sensation running down the arm like a red-hot needle. At 10 p.m., the swallow is blocked again. I cannot drink my tea with sugar and milk, which I take from the thermos. I give it to Jack. 'What is it?' says he, after taking a sip. It is so long since he tasted tea with sugar and milk in it!

5 October: A note from Nic says that, if I send a coconut weekly, she will send sago pudding – very nice of her. I can't see Macintyre about my swallow and my thumb; he is off colour.

6 October: A Red Cross representative who visited the camp yesterday was a real live Nipponese prince – Prince Shimada; let's hope there are results. He agrees to receive a statement of our troubles; it has been given. I go to hear Cowgill's paper on Emerson's 'Malaysia' – very interesting, although noises off make it difficult to hear.

7 October: My thumb is much better; I have a fair night. Last night, the wireless told us that a party of journalists was here to 'decimate' the news. I presume 'disseminate' was meant, but the word was apt. Suzuki, the Japanese Camp Commander, has told the Camp Committee that the camp must be patient; another repatriation ship will be here and, in his opinion, it will be soon. He is confident that supplies of insulin will arrive with others on the exchange ship from Goa. I go on a wood fatigue at 1.40 p.m. We now parade in Girdle Road and eventually march out in twos, about 50 strong, pushing three carts and in the charge of Sikh sentries. We pass a shell dump – many hundreds of them. To me they look about six inches in diameter and nearly two-foot long. I think they are ours, as they look old and are being brought from Changi. A one-and-a-half-mile walk brings us to where our woodcutters have been at work on the rubber. I fill my sack with chips and the more able-bodied stack logs and load carts. And so we return at 4 p.m. I feel the walk is a good thing to keep up, but I've no reserves. If we move at a quick pace, I'm soon in trouble.

9 October: Nic sends me a sago and santan pudding, which causes a complete blockage, even diluted. It is lunchtime before I recover and can start swallowing again. Late at night, it is sprung on us that there is to be a roll call of the whole camp in the main yard as before and we are all to be there by 9 a.m.

Sunday, 10 October: What a day! We are up at 7.15 a.m. and are paraded and in place in the yard well before 9 a.m. We have nothing to eat or drink. The Nipponese appear a bit before 10 a.m. They make a harangue in Nipponese, which is then translated. It is inaudible where I am; all I hear is 'will be severely punished'. Then lots of names are called out, apparently haphazardly – electricians, merchants, doctors, Eurasians, a ship's butcher – all are removed. At 11.15 a.m., our Block returns to B-Yard. The place is full of sentries with fixed bayonets. An intensive search of all rooms is carried out. My maps of Russia and Sicily and others are found. I am sent for to acknowledge ownership and they are taken away. We get some tea at 3.15 p.m. It is very hot, then there is rain at 6 p.m. We are not allowed shelter. At length, I get back to my room at 8.45 p.m. I have gone 26 hours without food; I am very weary and sun-scorched. My possessions are all over the place, but only biscuits are missing. I sup off milk, two raw eggs and soup and go to bed very weary. The object appears to have been mainly to find any evidence of connection with the outside, but typewriters, torches, medical bags, maps, documents and, in some cases, money were impounded. Those whose names were called out were searched, questioned and, in some cases, taken away, for what fate we know not. *(This infamous day is now known as the Double Tenth. On 27 September 1943, seven ships in Keppel Harbour were sabotaged by Australian and British commandos. The raid by the Japanese Military Police or Kempeitai on the internees were carried out because the Japanese suspected that prisoners in Changi were not only receiving information over hidden wireless sets, but were also relaying information to Allied Forces, resulting in the successful mission. Fifty internees were interrogated, of which 15 died from torture. Suspected Asian civilians were not spared. Choy Kun Heng, the ambulance driver and his wife, Elizabeth, referred to in the diary entry of 28 September were among those arrested and tortured.)*

11 October: The Gestapo *(Tom refers to the Japanese Military Police, the Kempeitai, as the Gestapo)* are again carrying on the good work. All fatigues and lectures are cancelled. It is otherwise a normal day, though what's going on I do not know. There are 9,400 letters in; six of them are mine.

12 October: The Inquisition continues and a new order says no activities of any kind are allowed after 5 p.m. Should have seen Johns today, but he was removed with the others. There is a kingfisher actually making a nest in a silt pit surrounded by 3,000 internees – brave bird. I hope he gets away with it, but it will be almost impossible; there are too many bad hats. In B-Block, they even tear up important notices on the board – to make cigarettes, I suppose – so one can't expect them to respect a mere kingfisher. There is no communication at all at the moment, so, as a precaution, the rice rations are reduced.

13 October: I have not smoked for a week now, but it makes no difference to my swallow. It's a wet morning; the camp is very dull; all activities are suspended; there is not even a newspaper. M. Johannes has died, aged 62.

14 October: The investigation proceeds – R.J.H. Sidney was taken away for questioning yesterday. We don't understand what it's all about. It looks as though wireless and communication with the outside are the main objectives, but why take camp funds, torches typewriters and so on? Of course, we have no wireless. *(This was wrong.)* The latest restrictions are that no letters or postcards are to be sent to the Women's Block until further notice.

15 October: There is only five days firewood left and fatigues are still not allowed.

16 October: There has been no newspaper for over a week now. We are completely cut off; there was no wireless allowed last night.

20 October: Sidney and seven others return from their period of detention; Sidney has lost 12 lbs.

22 October: At last, a fatigue party is allowed out – the first since October 9th – a lorry and five men to collect firewood.

23 October: I get five tins of kidney soup and am told that is the end of the stock of tinned soup in camp – so what happens to me? The rice lorry returns, but the fatigue party were told it's a holiday, so there will be none till Monday, but they get vegetables and dried fish. All tools have been taken away, so, though we are desperately short of food, there's the big vegetable garden (opened by us) completely neglected just outside the walls and 3,000 people inside straining to get at it. It is a very bad day for me. I manage with the utmost difficulty to get soup down (after straining it through a bit of chemise) and the pudding, but I regurgitate, have difficulty in breathing and have congestion all day, although I clean the passages out half a dozen times by sticking my fingers down my throat. I eventually get some tomato juice and my ground rice solution (partly) swallowed, but it is all most distressing and I go to bed completely washed out. There is no wireless allowed again tonight.

Sunday, 24 October: It is a fortnight now since the raid and there are no activities of any kind, except soccer. Last night, the Bald-headed Men beat Scotland by two goals to one before a large and vociferously amused crowd. With nothing else to do, the library queue has grown beyond all bounds. It took me an hour yesterday to get 'The Silk Stocking Murders' by A. Berkeley – quite a good detective yarn. There is no rice – only enough for tomorrow morning – so there will be none for lunch tomorrow, it is announced. Macintyre has been taken for questioning.

25 October: I see Worley about the advisability of an interview with the Nipponese about my food. I am to wait a day or two. Both my medical advisers are now in durance vile. But, if there is no improvement, something will have to be done. The book, 'History of Malaya' by Winsted, should be in the library, but it was being read on the day the Japanese raid on the camp was made. It was snatched away and has not been seen since. My swallow improves as the day wears on and I go out at 10 p.m. and smoke three pipes – first of the day – and have NO REGUR-GITATION – the first night for months I have been clear of that trouble.

26 October: The latest order from the Nipponese: there is to be a general clean-up in rooms of tins, bottles and other items. No dry clothes are to be put on lines. They must be put into containers. So the war goes on; where we are to get containers from and, having got them, how we are going to put them in a space eight foot by three is not specified.

27 October: I see Dr Bowyer about rations for me. Five more people have been taken by the Nipponese, including Jelani and Chettle. The latest restriction is that there are to be no lights at all, except between 8.30 and 10.30 p.m. This means that nothing is possible from 7.45 to 8.30 p.m. and this will kill evening bridge and of course reading during that period. A fatigue recently introduced is cleaning the latrines of the Sikhs as part of cleaning the guardroom.

28 October: It is Colin's 23rd birthday – ah me, we are missing some valuable years. We are in a poor way – almost no food, no light, no matches, no tobacco, no lectures, no entertainments, no fatigues, no tools, no newspapers, no wireless last night, no clothes, no beds, no letters, in fact, almost no anything. Vive la Hakko Ichin. I see Bowyer; I give full details of my diet. He will see what can be done. He decides to do nothing, except give me four tins of tomato juice instead of two per week. So how can I can keep my weight up even to its present ridiculous level, I don't know. What I have to live on is one pint of milk, half an-ounce of Marmite, three-quarters-of-a-pint of vegetable soup, about half-a-pint of liquid pudding at midday, one dessertspoon of Virol, a quarter-of-an-ounce of butter, about three tablespoonfuls of ground rice, eight ounces of tomato juice, tea and four ounces of Brand's essence of chicken on alternate days.

29 October: Henceforth, no water is to be used on the vegetable garden unless we dig wells for it. We receive 14 days' supply of rice from the Nipponese (98 bags), 734 lbs of tea, 3,046 lbs of crude salt and 3,111 lbs of sugar – enough to give us an issue of 12 oz each to last one month! And we had none for well over a month. Light bulbs have to be taken out and reduced by 40%. Heigh ho!

30 October: We parade for a roll call at 8.45 a.m. The call starts at 10.15 and we are back in our rooms at 11.30 a.m. My swallow behaves today.

Sunday, 31 October: What a vogue there is for bridge! One hears the most unlikely people discussing forcing calls, slams and so forth, people who in ordinary times would no more have thought of playing bridge than polo at Hurlingham. Some letters are slowly trickling out at last. We were allowed the wireless again last night, but there was no mention of Europe.

1 November: Dr Bain comes to see me about my rations. I am to get an extra half-pint of milk, making one-and-a-half pints a day; this is good. And I have a disappointment: I open a 1,700-gram tin of margarine bought a long time ago and find I can't take it; it congeals somewhere in the toobs. I spend the rest of the day regurgitating it and spitting it out. So I'll try to swop it for condensed milk or other liquid foods. There was no wireless allowed last night. Since it is All Souls Day, memorial services are held for the 89 who have died in this camp. Winter is to make a cloth filter for my food when he can get to work again; he has been locked out since October 9th in common with all other craftsmen – tinsmiths and so on. And how can those taken away be faring? I have a long talk with Day – a surgeon – about my swallow and my voice. He will see if he can examine me without butting in on the work of the other doctors. The condition is well known; a mercury bougie is the method of treatment, along with a change of climate.

2 November: Graft is rampant in this camp: A gets baccy, because he knows the shopkeeper; B gets tea at 7.30 a.m. and a cup for his pal because he's on the Messing Committee; C gets a coconut a day because he's in the police – and so on ad infinitum. This refers to the present moment when everything is frightfully short.

There was no radio last night again. And there are still no supplies. The position is serious; even our own vegetables are nearly finished and they are only leaves. Some people are smoking papaya leaves in lieu of tobacco, but I understand they are not very satisfactory!

3 November: There was no radio yet again last night. The utter absence even of enemy news at a time like this is a great deprivation. We are doing water divining in the garden now! The camp can even produce a dowser; it's a wonderful camp.

4 November: We get a storm every night; it makes it cool, but blows in the sleepers-out with much noise in the small hours. There was again no radio. The surgeon, Day, advises me to sing; it will possibly rectify the vocal chords; he recommends a medium note. So I decide on 'O, Who Will O'er the Downs Go Free' and produce extraordinary cacklings in the main yard to the intense astonishment of 2,999 other internees.

5 November: Brian is 11 today. Alas, we had planned never to leave him. The supply of insulin is almost finished; the diabetes patients are in a bad way. I hear they are all being kept in hospital and starved as much as possible. Surely, surely, the women and sick, at any rate, will be repatriated soon. Day examines me: there is nothing to be done under these conditions except carry on. There will be a roll-call tomorrow and every Saturday in future, we are told. There is no radio. There is no bread, just rice, rice, rice. I am trying cooking mine – using coconut oil in a tin as fuel (around the rice) and the last two days have got the liquid mixture down with some difficulty.

6 November: The roll call passes off without incident, but I can't see that it serves any useful purpose. We are up at 7.30 and in position by 9.30. We are back in our rooms at 11.30 a.m. There is no radio again. I wonder how things are going; and our prisoners have been away four weeks now. We are now on a half-ration of rice and some very thin vegetable soup.

Monday, 8 November: It is Joan's birthday today. What a shame – no parents to celebrate the occasion. Indeed, it is doubtful whether she knows yet whether Nora is alive or dead. There is no radio and still no newspaper. Our rations are now down to less than the minimum to exist, if prolonged like this. There is no bread. I weigh 101 lbs. on the hospital scales. I am to weigh weekly and report to Dr Bain on November 22nd. An internee at the outside garden fails to greet a Nipponese soldier properly – his bow is too perfunctory. He receives the usual beating as punishment. The dustbin parade is reorganised, to avoid any possible contact with the Women's Block. Now the women bring out their bins and retire, then our fatigue party goes along and collects the bins. A supply of 160 bags of rice has come in – sufficient for 20 days.

9 November: We have stocks of rice polishings for 14 days, sardines for $12^1/_2$ meals and chicken curry for $30^1/_2$ meals. I consult Day and he says it's not worthwhile swallowing the ground rice and irritating the swallow, so I will try dissolving what I can in hot water and straining off the liquid only, though, with my weight, I don't like losing ANY of my present diet. There is a terrific furore about five lorries which have arrived with tobacco, cheroots and cigarettes! There are also eggs, gula batu, onions, peanuts and other items – our own purchases. It is astonishing how mad people are over this very inferior tobacco. Personally, I have practically given up smoking without any difficulty, although I still have an occasional pipe of English tobacco.

10 November: There are no eggs for me, I am told, because 'diets' don't get any. But I am not on a diet in the general sense, being unique, so I inform Bain and leave it at that. I open my tin of 'Colombia Milk' not condensed, so it won't keep – lovely stuff. And I open my last but one tin of jam – raspberry and apple. I put a spoonful in the milk, dissolve the sugar etc, filter it and use it as flavouring for my mixture of ground rice, water and milk – the result is satisfactory.

11 November: It is a quarter of a century since Armistice Day and what a mess the world is in. There is now a Nipponese Orderly Officer each day and anything we want to ask about goes through him. I am told we proffered our first requests yesterday: 1) to send a change of clothes to those in Singapore *(those taken away on the Double Tenth),* 2) to hold a service in commemoration of Armistice Day; 3) to have our letters released. The replies were 1) no, the military are looking after them; 2) no, it means nothing now; 3) this question should never have been asked.

12 November: We are desperately short of clothes and utensils and it seems the height of folly to close down our tinkers and tailors for so long. Our washing-up bucket is now out of action; it has sprung a small leak. Food theft is so prevalent that all private stoves are to close down and it will be an offence to possess a sweet potato. This legislation is by our own committee. I must get a special dispensation for my little tin can and coconut oil. A Red Cross lorry has come in with BEEF(!), honey, gula batu, tobacco, cheroots and cigarettes; there is great excitement.

13 November: The roll call goes off without a hitch. There is beef stew for tiffin! I have soup. And how all enjoy the beef – such a fuss – and, when worked out, it totals five ounces per head including bones and other debris! Ye Gods! Our private supply of coconuts has now run out and none has been allowed in since the upheaval.

Sunday, 14 November: A building is to be put up in the main yard – we don't know the details or why.

15 November: I have a long talk with Day about my swallow. He says the cure will probably be effected, not by instruments etc., but by a change of climate and environment; and the condition is caused by worry. Well, I'm not conscious of it, but he says that's quite likely. What good can I do by worrying? That's my creed and therefore I don't. But I suppose I do it subconsciously. I am offered 15 cents a sheet (= fourpence) for Jeyes toilet paper. The buyer wants to roll cigarettes. I think this must be a world record. I do not take it. The Nipponese inform us that the main yard will be closed for us at any moment. Some building is to be put up, but we know nothing. What we shall do for defecation, swill-pits and charcoal burning, I don't know. And exercises anywhere will be out of the question. We have a visit from a large noise this afternoon – he is said to be General Yamashita, but I don't know. We have to remove all beds from yards, take all clothes off the lines and be in our places in our rooms at 3.30 p.m. He arrives about 6 p.m., but comes not near us.

16 November: It seems that C workshop was inspected yesterday and afterwards there was some noise. Today, they are being punished; I don't know the details yet. It is not likely anyone would deliberately mock, knowing what we know. The Assyrians came down again like a wolf on the fold, turned out Hudson's Bay neck and crop, searched, excavated bore holes in the main yard and D yard and dug holes. The result – nil. Now I am composed of skin, bones and a few hairs, I feel the cold much more easily. A Red Cross lorry comes in with more beef, eggs, biscuits, dried peas and tobacco – hurrah!

17 November: Stoves will be abolished tomorrow. I get permission to use the hospital hot plate for my ground rice. The explanation for yesterday is that C-Block started talking when the inspectors left. The four youngest were arrested and are being punished. Our Men's Representative and all concerned have been severely reprimanded and warned that such an incident must not recur. It was grave disrespect to the distinguished visitor.

18 November: I debug my mattress; there are not many, but some eggs.

19 November: Further restrictions are: at weekly inspection everything must be in barrack-room order. All clotheslines in rooms must be parallel and the same height. Everything must be clean, neatly folded and put away. There must be no smoking at roll call and no books may be taken. All lights are to be shaded, but no materials for this are provided. This may be a permanent brownout. If so, it is goodbye to any reading, bridge and the like between 8 p.m. and 9 a.m. – 13 hours.

November 20th: Tominara walks along our ranks as roll call takes place this morning. The censoring of our letters may start on Monday; they have been kept only six weeks. The mosquitoes are much worse now, caused by the cessation of our outside anti-malarial activities, I suppose. I hear of several dengue cases. Husbands and wives are still not allowed to meet or correspond; it has been six weeks now. Boiling ground rice on the hospital stove is very successful. Surely I will not have lost weight this week? On sale from the shop are goods sent by the Red Cross in Singapore: biscuits at $1.70 a kati, sweets at $3 per kati, gula batu, local baccy, cheroots and cigarettes. There is to be no brown-out after all, but most rooms have obscured their lights and people cannot see.

Sunday, 21 November: The latest order says that all lights will be switched off at the mains at 10 p.m. The latrines have been moved to the main drain behind the laundry, but there are not so many and they are much closer and therefore even more unpleasant.

22 November: I held my weight this week, but only just. But, alas, Bowyer comes along and says that, as I get two eggs a day, my milk is reduced from one-and-a-half pints to one pint a day. I point out that a pint is all I get, but he counters that a Changi pint is eight pints to a pound. I realise that this is reasonable, but why call it one-and-a-half pints of full-cream milk a day, when it isn't? It gives a wrong idea of the diet values one is getting. Bowyer also says that children aged one to three years need the milk; it is life and death to them. (It may be for me too, if I don't stop the loss of weight.) The room lights were all shaded last night; it was impossible to read or anything. From 10 p.m. and through the dark night, the only illumination was a small coconut-oil lamp for our 100 on a tennis court. It was a feat to get out without falling over somebody or something. The mysterious building in the main yard is to begin.

23 November: Rumour has gone mad again in the absence of news. The latest instruction from the Nipponese is that all rope is to be given up. Is it intended for making beds, since they are strung with it? Yesterday, I watched the last soccer match; it was played by the Empress of Asia team versus the Malayan-Born. The result was two goals to four – the best game I have seen.

24 November: It is Nora's 46th birthday; shall see her ere the next, I am convinced. I read 'Golden Horn' by F. Yeats Brown. He was a prisoner in Turkish hands for two-and-a-half years. As in all these prisoner biographies, they had much more latitude compared with us: they had money, luxuries (e.g. drinks and good smokes), individual purchases of food and other commodities, opportunities of escape and a reasonable rapport with their captors. My swallow is very bad. Twice today, I am within an ace of choking.

25 November: Two more come in to Changi; they have been working in the breweries. Jack gets a piece of wire gauze and makes me a new filter for food. There is a black-out from 4 p.m. to 9.30 p.m. The four scapegoats from Block C workshop are still incarcerated.

26 November: Last night, my swallow was again completely out of action, so, as I still had three-quarters of a pint of pudding and milk left, I had it put in the kitchen refrigerator lest it turned sour in the night. I go for it this morning, but the diet cook has eaten it – barefaced robbery. He uses much foul language and cheek too to the member of the Messing Committee who is looking after it for me. So I breakfast off milk and Virol and manage to get it down. My swallow is a bit easier today.

27 November: There is a sensation today – Room IV in Block D is to be evacuated by Tuesday. Where, oh where, can we put 130 people? The why is unknown, we surmise the reason is structural alterations. A lorry was upset yesterday with eggs, honey, gula batu and other supplies – what a mess! And, of course, we lost our eggs and most of the honey.

Sunday, 28 November: Our room lavatories are to be closed and two men are to sleep in the spaces so created. This overcrowding is incredible. A long hut is going up in the main yard, built by Chinese labour. We are of course completely cut off from them. I am much weaker; carrying a tin of tea about 50 yards makes me gasp and breathe painfully.

29 November: I feel dicky after breakfast, although I have yesterday's two eggs; honey and milk, all mixed. We reorganise our space on account of the two men in the place where the latrines used to be. Some people have been handed cables, sent from Great Britain about July, 1942 via Geneva, I believe. There is no sign of any of our mail. There was a black-out last night and there will be one again tonight.

30 November: It's St Andrews Day, but even the Scots are silenced.

1 December: Worley, Middlebrook and others have been taken in for questioning. So we are again minus a head! There's not a scrap of news – we have had no newspaper or radio for two months now. *(On the Burmese frontier, the Japanese lost 100,000 men in an attempt to invade India. Their air forces based at Rabaul were destroyed by the Allies in a series of fierce air-battles throughout October. The main American naval forces, under Admiral Nimitz, had begun to concentrate for his drive through the island groups near the Equator, which were the outposts defending the Japanese fleet base at Truk in the Carolines.)*

2 December: Harper Ball is sent for by the Nipponese and told he is the Men's Representative, Worley having been removed from the post. The Nipponese announce that the Camp Committee have behaved very badly. The whole camp has been made to suffer for their delinquencies. What has been done amounts to mutiny and, if it occurs again, there will be dire consequences.

3 December: Huts spring up in the main yard. They are very temporary structures; there are three long ones; we can see roofs and Chinese labourers on top. The hope is that this will be a gathering of clans prior to repatriation. What we shall do meantime about cooking, water, sanitation, God knows. Dr Gibson-Hill foolishly slept in Room IV in D-Block after it had been cleared. He was discovered, sent for and punched six times in the face.

Sunday, 5 December: I see Bain about the midday soup which I cannot get clear with filtering and it seems to upset the swallow almost daily, so it is decided to give me an eight-ounce jar of Marmite weekly instead of every 14 days and two extra eggs daily, making four eggs a day. So my daily food may be said to consist of: one ounce of Marmite, four eggs, eight ounces of tomato juice, three-quarters of a pint of milk, ground rice, about half-a-pint of pudding, whatever it is, plus some sugar and Virol, cod liver oil emulsion, tea and honey. This should be enough to keep going on, but not to put weight on. The camp generally is no better off; the rations are rice, tea; rice, vegetable soup; a bun, margarine, tea. At times, there is a sardine at tiffin or one-tenth of a tin of chicken curry. The loss of weight is great and common to all. Room IV in Block D is still empty, while our overcrowding is appalling. Three long huts are well under way in the main yard and I hear some are to go up in the Women's Camp. It is two months now during which husbands have not seen their wives, letters have been held up, there have been no meetings, lectures, classes, entertainment's or news and the unfortunates are still with the Gestapo in town. The camp is all agog again – the main courtyard has been closed. Arrivals are expected – who?

6 December: The new internees have arrived. I think they are both male and female; I don't know yet. From Singapore itself, the newcomers number about 50 – some Europeans including a Dr Green, Jews, Eurasians, some locals and a man called Storch from Chile. But why should Room IV, Block D have been turned out for them? Why should THEY not have been pushed into holes and corners? At 9.30 p.m., all lights are suddenly put out – a black-out – whether practice or the real thing, we do not know. I feel very weak now; even carrying the washing-up bucket full of water is a trial.

7 December: D-Block is again closed; more arrivals are expected. There is an election of B-Block Commandant, consequent on the elevation of Harper Ball to the steerage *(the Camp Commandant's post)*. The candidates are Gridley, Gutsell and Smith, all of our room!

8 December: Today is the great anniversary of the liberation of East Asia and the inauguration of the Co-Prosperity Sphere. There were more arrivals yesterday – locals, I understand. They were addressed by the Nipponese Officer Commanding in Nipponese, translated into Malay. An imperfectly stationed ear-witness tells me the gist of his speech was that, as subjects of the Great Nipponese Empire, the new arrivals had not fulfilled their obligations.

9 December: I feel queer every morning after breakfast lately and can feel my heart pumping away. I wonder if it is due to the very rich mixture of two duck eggs, honey and milk. I am OK after half-an-hour or so. But Jack nobly does the washing-up now. The holiday to celebrate the anniversary of the Japanese invasion appears to have lasted only one day this year and that's the length of time the flag flew. The Nipponese ask for a list of husbands who wish to meet their wives for one hour on Christmas Day. We are to submit a program of any entertainments or religious services we want at Christmas. Any presents we wish to order for Christmas must be done via the Camp Shop i.e. Mr Suzuki.

10 December: I get no raw eggs today – a very big hole in my diet. I report it to Bowyer and I am to get a four-ounce tin of Brand's chicken essence in lieu, daily. I hear there will be no more eggs until Tuesday. The reason? 'The lorry is occupied bringing in new internees.' Zoological books are continually stolen from the Reference Library. If I had my way, I'd search everyone's belongings and inflict corporal punishment on transgressors. It is such a crime in here – and they are possibly only taken to make cigarette papers, being thin paper in many cases.

11 December: There is a roll call again today, but, of late, I have been going to the camp hospital during roll call. I do the same again today and have no trouble. Joynt and others are in hospital with fainting fits – caused by the diet again, I understand. There is a strong rumour, whence I know not, that Hitler is out and Rommel is in charge, asking for terms.

Monday, 13 December: No tins are to be thrown away, by order of the Nipponese. They are to be kept, we are told, for the use of the new internees. The huts in the main yard seem almost finished. There is one going up in the Women's Block. I see a list of the new internees: they are nearly all Eurasians – 59 men, 53 women and 51 children. We have asked if prisoner-of-war husbands, fathers, relatives and fiancées will be allowed to see their loved ones at Christmas. The request has been refused. The latest rumour is that a ship will take away women, children, and the aged and sick before the end of December. I fervently hope so.

14 December: Tominara says that censoring of the mail has started. The Block C hostages are still confined in town. One becomes sick today and another is delivered to town in his place. We are now told that the Nipponese will not be satisfied until the culprit who laughed is produced. It's the first one has heard of this. I get four eggs again today and my swallow is not so bloody as yesterday. We get an issue of 14 ounces of sugar per man – a Nipponese ration. I buy a Gibbs shaving stick for $5. Victor says it will last a year! Not with me.

15 December: The Gestapo pay a visit to the hospital laboratory; they poke about in nooks and crannies and take something away, whether of import or not, I do not know. Some American internees have received Red Cross parcels. Where are ours? There is no supply of coconut oil coming in for night lights and smoke lights. If we don't get some soon, we shall be entirely out of it.

16 December: There are generous concessions for the Christmas season. Families can meet for one hour, from 2 to 3 p.m. on Christmas Day. There will be Protestant and Roman Catholic services of half-an-hour each, but there will be no sermons and no arranged carol singing. There will be a concert in D-yard from 6 to 8 p.m. on December 24th. Finis! Passages must be swept prior to roll-calls on Saturdays. We are IN POSITION by 8 a.m., so it is not so easy, especially as there is nothing to sweep with.

17 December: Waiting in the library queue, I ponder on the lengths people will go to get tobacco – and that of the most inferior type. I have practically eschewed tobacco. Some swop their sugar ration for it, even on their present feeble diet. And what a lot of varicose veins and hammer toes one sees now that no feet and legs are covered! The only effect on mine in two years has been to make all my toenails normal and not almost atrophied as my little toenails used to be. We ask permission to walk in the barbed-wire enclosure outside the gaol on Christmas Day; the request is refused.

18 December: The latest instruction from the Nipponese concerns smoking: the camp, they say, is strewn with cigarette ends and ash. There is to be no smoking in the corridors or in the yards when moving about; no ash or ends must be dropped anywhere except in ashtrays and those must be kept clean. The Gestapo were busy again yesterday interrogating several people, but all were returned.

Sunday, 19 December: The Nipponese issued a new instruction at roll call yesterday: all must bow in unison when the Nipponese arrive and when they depart. You can keep your hats on when you bow, but you must not cross your knees when sitting. At last, some mail has been given out, including photos. Old Natrass has received one of his wife, son and daughter-in-law; he is as proud of it as Lucifer and as pleased as Punch. The letter is dated August 1942!

20 December: It is real Northeast monsoon weather these days – incessant rain, damp and cool. My weight has struck a new low of 96 lbs. The Christmas Day menu is to be a secret, but we are assured officially that it will be better than today's, which is rice, tea; rice, vegetable soup and fish paste made from dried fish contaminated with diesel oil; a maize bun, four ounces of Kreamoline and tea. Yet another list is being made of folk without bed or mattress. They have been without these necessities for only two years.

21 December: The bridge league session has just finished; we keep our place in Division 1 by the skin of our teeth and our 'Cubs' are promoted from the Graduation League to Division 3. This league is a marvellous success and excellently run by Brooks.

22 December: An interpreter tells someone in the Women's Camp that there is to be a pleasant surprise for them on Christmas Day and a very good one for the whole camp on New Year's Day!

23 December: All the letters have been distributed; they have been here only two months. I get my six: two-and-a-half from Joan, two-and-a-half from Brenda and one from Pip, with dates from 2.11.42 to 29.1.43. A 'Post Early For Christmas' postmark on a letter of 1.12.42 strikes an ironic note when I receive it on 23.12.43! The gist of the news in the letters is: there is no news of Nora or me. Colin is still going strong; he is an acting lieutenant. Joan is liking her work immensely. Brian was about to start as a boarder at St George's Diocesan College in Rondebosch in January 1942 *(should be 1943)*. On 4.1.43, Brenda wrote separately to Nora, as she didn't know if she was here or if I could forward letters – and that letter has not arrived, so POSSIBLY Nora has got it and is alive. But nothing is certain – scores of letters are missing. There is a distribution of one banana each for Christmas! It is welcome, as it is the first fruit for two-and-a-half months, but, of course, I can't eat mine; I give it to Jack. There was an unheralded black-out last night and again tonight. Although our feeble coconut oil glims had been approved as brownout lights, tonight they are ordered to be put out, so all is pitch black and our room with 100 people a scene of indescribable confusion.

24 December: We receive a Christmas gift from the Nipponese of one packet of Cycle cigarettes. And from camp funds I get a choice of tobacco or gula batu; I naturally take gula. I read 'Peril at End House' by Agatha Christie; it is excellent. I don't stand in the library queue now; I have special permission to go straight in owing to my feeble condition. I have a lot of regurgitation of food and saliva – at least a quart a day – and the swallowing of ANY liquid is very difficult and painful. I wonder how much longer I can carry on. The camp numbers are now 3,398 including 24 at Miyako Hospital and 38 detained in Singapore. Supplies have come in from the American Red Cross – I don't know what – but they must have been here for some time – 536 parcels and medical supplies. The Nipponese Camp Commander directs that one parcel should go to each American (there are 22 of them) and the rest will be distributed to all – milk, prunes, cheese and so forth – good. Katherine has sent me a godsend – a one-pound tin of Klim which equals six pints. Nic has sent me a tin of tomato juice; and Mrs Gregory a card. I have sent Nic biscuits and cigarettes and Katherine cigarettes. The mail discloses that a list of internees was published in the U.K. early in May, 1943 and that our November, 1942 postcards were received in August, 1943!

25 December: The Christmas Day Menu is: breakfast – extra rice, tea; tiffin – rice, vegetable soup, half-a-tin (six ounces) of chicken curry, beans; tea: maize bun, sweetened rice pudding, one sardine, one spoonful of honey, Kreamoline, tea. Hilarious! Having extra milk, I am going to eschew ground rice for a day or two and see if it makes my swallow easier. I get nothing extra for Christmas. They might have given me a tin of Brand's essence or a couple of eggs! I speak to a member of the Messing Committee about it and he arranges for two extra eggs. Good, but when tiffin arrives, I get two extra eggs, but no pudding or ground rice! So much for the Christmas feast. The prisoners taken away for questioning and held in town have been released, presumably as a Christmas gesture! An uproarious Christmas Day closes with all lights suddenly plunged out at 9 p.m. – and so to bed.

Sunday, 26 December: The contents of the Red Cross parcels vary. A typical one has nine packets of Chesterfield cigarettes, ten packets of cold-water soup, four of hot-water soup, a quarter of a pound of cheese, a pound tin of powdered milk, four ounces of coffee, twelve ounces of cocoa, 34 ounces of orange juice, two cakes of soap, seven-and-a-half ounces of chopped ham and eggs, seven-and-a-half ounces of corned pork loaf, three small tins of butter, four ounces of diced sugar, one packet of prunes, one tin of pate (soya and chopped liver) and one packet of biscuits. We are still not allowed to put notices up e.g. the bridge league tables! And no classes for children are allowed.

27 December: There is to be an extra-special inspection next Thursday. The camp, says the C.O., is to be as clean as a new pin. Parcels are to be divided among groups of seven, with the milk taken out.

28 December: I am moved to the camp hospital where I can be given a bigger and a better liquid diet. I write a screed explaining exactly what my diet is. The first thing they offer me in hospital is a fried tomato! I receive a wireless message from Helen Bell in South Africa via the Red Cross: Brian is well and happy; he hears from Joan and Colin and he loves school. The latest internees include Dr Ryrie, whose life work was the leper hospital in Kuala Lumpur.

29 December: Our parcel has been divided: I get one packet of cigarettes, two four-ounce tins of Kup-Kofi and a chocolate iron ration. And Jack, Hope, Victor and Elias very kindly give me four packets of soup. The parcels are beautifully got up and the things irreproachably packed in tins etc. – U.S. Army stuff. There doesn't look like any shortage of tins or any-thing over there! I send a wireless message to Nellie. *(The message was not sent to Tom's sister until 19 June 1944, more than five months later. It was picked up by several people in Australia who passed it to Nellie. It read "Still existing, please send me news of Nora by radio. Had wireless from South Africa. Colin, Joan and Brian well. Have had some letters. Wish Brian to return to school in England when advisable. Grateful if radio message possible. Love, Tom." The following which Tom included was omitted: 'I am very unfit and swallow only liquids with much difficulty; my voice has gone; and my weight is six stone 10 lbs.')* We hear from a new internee that the local paper said that all arrangements for the repatriation of Europeans in the Dai Toa are complete. I am allowed to go where I like, so hospital will not be intolerable.

30 December: Four more soups are given to me by various people in our room. I try one tonight; it is very good, but salty. The camp spend the day sitting on their bottoms according to orders, waiting for The Big Noise inspection which never comes.

31 December: I get most of my food down, but there are one or two upsets and I think the midday soup causes them. So ends 1943, infinitely the worst year of my life in every possible way.

– XI –

BAD NEWS

Sunday, 1 January 1944: I have a very bad day: I get nothing down from 10 a.m. to 5 p.m. I regurgitate all day and stick my fingers down my throat six times to force everything up. Finally, I take dope prepared by the chemists, but it has no soporific effect whatever. My mattress is made in gaol, stuffed with corn and very hard, so are my bones on it. It's a peculiar thing – if you say you are constipated, people understand what you mean, also if you can't urinate, but the opposite process – you can't swallow – they seem totally unable to grasp. It is very hot now and the spectre of thirst which I can't quench because I can't swallow is very real. There is a shortage of water too; it's off about 16 hours out of the 24 and this with 3,400 people in such a confined space makes bathing, washing etc. very difficult and, in hospital, with dysentery and other ailments, even worse. There were no letters for Nora herself in recent mail; some must have been written, so I take this as negative evidence that she may be interned elsewhere and her letters have been sent there from Tokyo.

3 January: In spite of all the efforts to supplement my diet, my weight is down one pound, to six stone $9\frac{1}{2}$ lbs. Of course, I regurgitate a lot, but it seems hopeless. I move to a corner bed with a softer mattress and more space for things. I say 'more space'; I should say 'less lack of space'! I get my breakfast down again, but I have trouble with my swallow and regurgitation for the rest of the day. My neighbour here hails from Lancaster – his name is Yates and he's from a brewer's family. We talk of cricket and Lancaster's palmy days.

4 - 6 January: I get my food down, but it is a hell of a job.

7 January: Mr Chitty, the surgeon, comes to see me. He thinks an operation is desirable, with a feed direct into my stomach; I agree. So I move to a downstairs bed and go to the operation room at 3 p.m. Mr Chitty does the operation with Dr Grove-White; I get a local anaesthetic. The operation takes an hour and I find it an ordeal. Being conscious, you hear everything. 'If you feel anything, don't move – just shout,' is not reassuring! And remarks such as 'Hand me the tubular cutter' or 'I want that drag-hook now' do not make for serenity. And, of course, I can feel various instruments flopping on to my anatomy. However, it passes over without any serious discomposure and now I have a tube into the tummy and closed outside by a clip. Of course, one is in no condition for operations now. A curious development is that my tummy has contracted to such an extent that it will hold only five ounces. My first feed at 4.30 p.m. is two ounces of tomato juice and at 6.30 p.m. I get egg, milk and sugar poured into a glass funnel and thence via the tube. I feel absolutely nil. I pass a fair, but rather sleepless night despite an injection.

8 January: I have regular feeds all day, but at 11 a.m., I have an appalling thirst and can't drink. I get an injection at 10 p.m., and then I fall asleep at 11 p.m. I awake at midnight and regurgitate saliva until 5 a.m. – a dreadful night. At 5 a.m., I wedge myself upright in a corner wall-bed and get a little sleep. At 9 a.m., of course, I am not allowed to move off my bed. I succeed in drinking two ounces of water, but it is a night ghastly in the extreme, with pains all over my torso. I have no sleep despite an injection and I lie and regurgitate on my side. From 9.45 p.m. until midnight, I bring up saliva only and I have a raging thirst. At midnight, I prop myself up as erect as possible and sit regurgitating steadily until 8 a.m. It is the most miserable night I can ever remember. There are times when, if I'd had an overdose of some lethal liquid handy, I would not have answered for my acts – if I could have swallowed it, that is. I daren't clear my throat of saliva as I used to for fear of straining the operation wounds.

Sunday, 9 January: Chitty thinks that to use my fingers to regurgitate will not cause strain, so, with considerable pain, I regurgitate stale saliva day and night. I then have no more regurgitation, then injections of morphia and atropine to check the saliva flow give me an excellent night.

10 January: I have a visit from a member of the 'Distant Healing Circle'. They concentrate on a certain person and wish him well being and I am the choice for tonight at 11. If I'm awake, I'm to do the same for myself. I thank him profusely and say I will. Parcels can now be received from and sent to the Women's Block on Tuesdays and Fridays. All medical and dental books are to be given in on Nipponese instructions. Anyone not doing so will be severely punished – it's business as usual. The books will be kept in the hospital library. Today I drink about one pint of water in small sips – nectar! A sum total of one-and-three-quarter pints of solid and liquid per day on the Equator is obviously not enough even for a shrivelled hulk like poor Tom Kitching.

11 January: Last night was good again after injections. I had very many dreams of an unusual type for me – is it the injections? The diabetics are in this room; they look fairly fit. I wonder how much longer the insulin can be eked out? *(By May 1945 all the diabetics had died due to the Japs refusal to provide insulin.)*

12 January: My tummy will still not hold more than five ounces, they tell me. Reading 'Forbidden Journey', written by Ella Maillart in 1936, I am interested in her remarks about our friend, the enemy: 'Once again, I saw the military supreme, not only over civilians of their own country who often have different ideas, but also over the natives who are full of hatred for their brutal masters. But, above all, I was struck at every step by the hatred of the Japanese for us. They detest us all, us whites.... And they miss no opportunity of maltreating us....'

13 January: I slept well with the aid of regurgitation and two injections.

14 January: I have only a moderate sleep. The old Eurasian Yzelman makes a lot of noise in pain in the night and dies this morning, a happy release. He should never have been in Changi, of course. The Nipponese come into the hospital to make an inventory. My rations are up to six ounces. I am drinking more, for two reasons: 1) I think two fluid pints a day into my tummy are not enough, as I regurgitate about a pint of saliva, then other natural losses make the outgoing of the body well over two pints a day; and 2) if I don't drink, the oesophagus gets full of nasty, offensive saliva.

15 January: I get my stitches out; it is not painful. Chitty thinks I've put weight on. I hope he's right. I don't think so. There is no roll call. There are orders for a general clean up yet again for a forthcoming inspection.

Sunday, 16 January: After hanging around all day, with all clothes taken off the lines and the usual precautions, the inspection is declared off, but the Gestapo take Bowyer and Gorsuch and give Macnab one for the road for no ascertainable reason.

17 January: My weight is now six stone $7^1/_2$ pounds; I thought my weight had gone down. The capacity of my tum-tum is up to 10 ounces, which equals three-and-a-half pints a day. I sit out in the sun for an hour this morning. It now appears the military are taking over the running of this camp, but we don't know for certain.

18 January: The Nipponese are trying to push someone into my place in our room (WS2) which is a swindle. Ask Chitty about the probable course of events. He won't commit himself; Johns did the examination. But I am likely to be here many weeks and this rubber tube into the tum is the only one they've got. It will have to be taken out and sterilised and put back again – a bright prospect indeed. However, my operation wound is doing splendidly. I should not take any food through the mouth and as little as possible liquid for thirst quenching. Ah me! Wot a life! Is it worth it? The kingpin of the 'Distant Healing Circle' sees me basking in the sun at midday and says this is no good; the vegetation is now absorbing all the sunshine and giving out noxious emanations; I must come out at dawn. I take a 12-ounce ration with no difficulty, but my tummy feels rather full after it.

19 January: There is a roll call; no one knows why. I get no breakfast; tomato juice is on offer, but it will not go down the tube. Chitty comes along after roll call at 11.30 a.m. It transpires that the tube leading to the tummy is blocked. He washes it out with a syringe and all is well again. Heigh-ho! How galling to watch others eating and drinking, smoking and talking – and I can do none of these things!

20 January: At 11.30 a.m., I take 18 ounces of food in the space of two minutes and positively cannot move for a bit! But my tum must be expanding. Many police internees are summoned by the Nipponese and harangued. There is no apparent objective, but they are treated very politely.

21 January: I get no eggs; there have been none coming into the camp for a week now. This makes an enormous hole in my diet. The bandage is taken off and a contraption rigged up fastening the tube in with two safety pins and elastoplast and a clip-end suspended from my neck. First, the entrance end breaks off and soup runs all down me. They cut that off, fix the funnel and again it runs all over – the tummy end has come out! And this is the second attempt at setting up the apparatus! I am also told today that some saliva must be mixed with the feeds – I had wondered about this.

22 January: There are still no eggs coming in. All the new regime has achieved is more regulations, the chief being to ban smoking from 10 p.m. to 8 a.m. and we must bow to ALL Nipponese, including privates.

Sunday, 23 January: This Changi cameo must be recorded: it is 8 a.m. and at the bed on my left two feet away, Padre Bennitt is conducting Holy Communion. There are four people round the bed. Across the room, an elderly man lies, probably dying; his cries of pain are incessant. In comes the orderly with a basin of water and a chair for me to wash my face. Outside, our whistling optimist bursts into 'The Flowers that bloom in the spring, Tra-la'. There are still no eggs – it will be hard to regain weight on this diet. My ration of milk is still three-quarters of a pint per day, but I think they must increase it when there are no eggs.

24 January: I weigh six stone $9\frac{1}{2}$ lbs. – a gain of one-and-three-quarter pounds, which is very good considering the shortfall of eight eggs a day for half the week. NOTHING is coming in and we are short of everything, even rice. The tummy contraption is intolerable; it holds my tum tight, it can't expand when a pint is poured in and I get severe pains. So I get them to release the lower half, but now I have to move carefully lest the tube drops out of my tummy. It has been appalling the last two nights; old Ramsay roared all night and we got no sleep. There are about 200 letters from South Africa, dated September, 1943. They had just got our November, 1942 postcards, but not the cards dated April 1942 – the first ones, that is! Several letter-writers express the conviction that they will see us in a few months and we hope this means repatriation. They speak of trying unavailingly to send food parcels. One says the news is miraculous and hope has changed to certainty.

25 January: One Nipponese internee returned from the U.S. says that every day they got 20 cigarettes, one large beer, two eggs, ham, cereals, fish, meat and bread. He is the one interviewing the police here. This morning, I tell Dr Cameron that I am convinced the bandage is harmful as it is at present; I have far more pains than a week ago and nearly pass out after each feed. So he puts on a longitudinal bandage instead of a lateral one and it seems much better. Now almost my biggest trouble is saliva; constantly swallow it and it seems to stay in the oesophagus, then that gets fuller and fuller. I get more uncomfortable until I have to fetch it all up with my fingers – and it is foul smelling too. I don't think I'm swallowing anything at all now. The Nipponese orderly officer comes in this afternoon and says that a Nipponese doctor is coming tomorrow; he gives no explanation. We naturally hope it is in connection with the repatriation of the sick at any rate.

26 January: Ramsay dies this morning – a happy solace. Aged 70, he was a retired captain, formerly with the Straits Steamship Company. I talk to the orderly who gives me a bed-bath. He was in Kuala Lumpur until seven months ago. He came across the same idea there as I had i.e. that the Nipponese thought their invasion of Malaya was a crusade to release the oppressed Malayans and they got a shock. A few supplies have come in at last, but there are still no eggs. I observe blood in my regurgitated saliva, so I hand a sample in.

27 January: 340 lbs. of fresh fish have been received from the Nipponese! The fish is reserved for women, children and hospital patients, as there is not enough to go round the whole camp. All say that the Nipponese attitude has grown more tolerable. My throat and my swallow are most uncomfortable all day; all last night I had no sleep, so tonight I get the usual dope and two injections of atropine which seem to dry up the saliva and I sleep.

28 January: The Nipponese doctor is at work and promises to see to medical requirements; I wonder if he can get an oesophagoscope. My throat is awful – I wonder how long I can go on. The stomach tube is working well. I suffer excessive thirst, but that can be endured if I can only get over this saliva business. Eggs and other supplies have arrived at last.

29 January: There is no roll call! They are tired of it, one presumes.

Monday, 31 January: My weight is now six stone $10^1/_2$ lbs. – an increase of one pound. But today the blow falls and I fear it is a death sentence. Dr Cameron tells me my trouble is a tumour in the oesophagus. Johns knew last February when he examined me with the oesophagoscope – or was practically certain. He took a piece of tissue. I wonder why he not only didn't tell me, but assured me on several occasions and in reply to point-blank questions that the trouble was SPASTIC. I would rather have known. So I shall probably never even see Nora again (if she's alive), nor Colin, Joan, Brian, Brenda and Pip. Well, it can't be helped, but, if it is to be so, I would rather not have died in misery in a Nipponese internment camp; and I'd have liked the pleasure of seeing the forces of Evil beaten to the ground.

1 February: There is a new regime in charge. The Nipponese Commanding Officer is full of promises again. There is actually some meat in too, with some queer kind of Nipponese dried fish.

2 February: I have another chat with Dr Cameron. He rightly does not buoy one up with false hopes. Nothing can be done in here except feed into the stomach and thereby deprive the tumour of material to grow on. Even outside, the operation would be more than I could stand, he thinks. Radium is the only chance. The growth is low down in the oesophagus, I gather.

3 February: The recent visit of a Nipponese doctor and others was the result, I understand, of representations that the really incapacitated should be repatriated as soon as possible. I fervently hope so; it would be worth a lot to me if I could get home and see the family before I die.

4 February: A wireless message has been received in Australia sent from Tokyo by a Mrs Shaw who was on the Kuala – the first news of her. So Nora may be there – how I hope she is for the children's sake. I fear I can't last long enough to hope to see her again. Still, one never knows and I don't give up yet. Saliva which I can't swallow is still my biggest discomfort, although life would not appear to be much use when you can't eat, drink, talk, smoke, take exercise or do anything! Still, the motto is 'nil desperandum.'

5 February: There has been a permanent brownout since February 1st. It makes the nights very long in bed.

Sunday, 6 February: Wireless messages to Great Britain of 25 words are to be allowed. You must ask for a reply by radio. I send mine to Pip, saying there is still no news of Nora and that I am seriously ill. Today, I have a congested feeling about my throat in the region of the windpipe. There is some shemozzle in the Women's Block today – we do not know what, but the Nipponese refuse to allow supper to be sent in at 5.30 p.m.

8 February: I walk to the B-Block workshop – my first walk since the operation.

9 February: Roll call at 9 a.m. turns out to be another search, but a perfunctory one. Byron and Kelly have been taken in for questioning. Those removed on October 10th are still in Singapore and there is no news of them whatever. We are also still entirely deprived of news, even the local newspaper, and no meetings, entertainment's or assemblies of any kind are allowed, not even lessons for the children.

11 February: Those doing fatigues are to be paid at the munificent rate of 15 cents a day (fourpence). Thus we progress, after two years.

12 February: Byron and Kelly are still in close confinement. They are interrogated daily; they cannot answer a question, so they receive no food until they give the right answer. They have been without food since 8 a.m. on February 9th.

Sunday, 13 February: It is two years since Nora left on the Kuala. I feel very muzzy and depressed all day. I wonder how long I can keep this up – not much longer, I fear. It is very wearisome disgorging saliva literally every two to three minutes the whole day. I fill up another form today – name, age, birthplace, family details and so on. A lorry came in yesterday with coconuts, bananas, eggs and two pig carcasses for 3,400 people! The Jews are not pleased.

15 February: Coles and I win our bridge match and are now top of the league with a clear lead of five points and a match in hand. Byron and Kelly, still in solitary, get their first meal today since February 9th.

16 February: I hear the Nipponese have given orders that all food in stock has to be finished by the end of the month and we are to go on pukka prisoner-of-war rations – whatever they are. Later, we find they are quite substantial, including sugar, vegetables, meat or fish – don't we wish we may get them!

17 February: Two years of internment have been completed. Byron and Kelly have been released. One of the most tantalising things in my present predicament is the smell of food – it makes me simply long to eat!

18 February: The rice-grinding fatigue party is all under arrest now; they are alleged to have disposed of rice to the Sikhs. So all the Jews are pitched out of Aldgate, which is to be used as a store, and the unfortunate Jews are to occupy one of the long huts in the main yard. As they have no floor bar the football pitch and only partial sides, they will be in considerable discomfort in wet weather.

19 February: I now have a daytime injection of atropine to dry up the saliva; it makes my mouth very dry, but I can't go on getting rid of saliva from 8 a.m. to 10 p.m. – it's too wearisome.

Sunday, 20 February: There are wonderful rumours of landings all over the place, but they are obviously untrue.

22 February: The rice-grinding fatigue party has been released without a stain on their characters!

23 February: We should have had our weekly sugar issue, but no. My diet today has more body in it – cornflour, rice polishings and other more solid foods being mixed in with it. I think this roughage is what I need to send my weight up.

24 February: The Gestapo took Hugh Fraser some days ago to join the throng in Singapore. *(He died after torture by the Kempei-tai.)*

25 February: The Nipponese have discovered yet again we should grow more vegetables for our own support, so yet again steps are to be taken! In the bridge league, I hold a Yarborough seven high – the lowest hand I've ever seen.

26 and 27 February: Without warning, there is an acute water shortage. There is no tea, no cleaning of teeth, washing or anything.

Monday, 28 February: My weight today is $93\frac{1}{2}$ lbs. *(This is the lowest Tom reports and compares with 133 lbs. before captivity, a 30% loss.)* I can't do any more to keep it up; I get severe tummy ache after each feed.

29 February: Edwards had a very bad night; he was making awful noises. He dies today.

1 March: Today is my 54th birthday and what a wreck I am and as weak as a kitten. The Nipponese celebrate by assaulting S who is sitting peacefully at the hospital reception table writing and smoking, having an ashtray as per orders, but they say he might have set the table on fire.

2 March: I had a wonderful dream last night in which I actually ate crumpets with lashings of butter.

3 and 4 March: The camp is on starvation rations – there is no rice available.

Sunday, 5 March: There is a sudden incursion by the Nipponese to stick labels on all the hospital beds announcing that they are the property of the Nipponese Government.

6 March: My weight is now $95^1/_2$ lbs. – up two pounds. I still have tummy-ache after each feed and the flow of saliva all day and night is incredible. Only an atropine injection stops it; I have one-hundredth of a grain at 2 and 10 p.m. The effect lasts about three to four hours. A. Mustard is brought to the hospital at 10 p.m., suffering from a wound to the head; several stitches are necessary. There have been only about 250 lbs. of root vegetables this month; otherwise, no vegetables of any kind have been supplied, so the ration scale is not much use, inadequate as it is.

7 March: I pass a very bad night; the saliva is incessant from 3 a.m.

8 March: Harper Ball resigns as the Men's Representative – the strain is too much. Dr Glyn Evans is elected.

(There are no entries in the diary for 9 - 12 March 9th.)

13 March: I now weigh 97 lbs. We are officially informed that Stevenson and Buchanan, who were taken to Singapore by the Gestapo, have died of dysentery and beriberi.

(There are no entries for 14 – 17 March. There are frequent gaps in the diary from now on.)

18 March: There are no more eggs, except perhaps for special cases like mine. The neutral agent thinks they are too dear, I hear – a duck's egg costs 95 cents and a hen's egg 70 cents!

Monday, 20 March: I now weigh $95^1/_2$ lbs. I am very weak. I doubt if I can carry on much longer. The saliva is most wearing day and night. I get a sort of obstruction with it – over the windpipe – and getting rid of this shatters me to bits very often. Food is a mockery and every feed a penance. I sleep very badly. A quick exchange seems the only hope.

22 March: Dr McGladdery is now in charge of my case. He says he will see if anything can be done about the saliva. He later prescribes one hundredth of a grain of atropine four times a day and mixed with the food, not by injection. This certainly almost abolishes the saliva, but I get a very dry throat and can scarcely speak at all!

24 March: About 7,500 letters have come in. They have been sorted by us, but we are not allowed to make a list of recipients or anything. Their release will be very slow, I imagine! I have another very bad shaking – I want to vomit, but I can't. A few eggs still come in and my quota varies between eight and nil.

25 March: At last, we are allowed a newspaper. 'The Voice of Japan', printed in Java 'for prisoners-of-war and internees only'. I haven't seen a copy.

Monday, 27 March: There is an even more comic request than usual: all works of Somerset Maugham are to be handed in to the Nipponese at once! No one has an inkling why. Two women and seven men return from the clutches of the Gestapo in Singapore. They all come in to hospital; they look a weary lot. We are now told that Adrian Clark and Bryning are also dead.

March 28th: I weigh $96^{1}/_{2}$ lbs.

1 April: Robertson in the bed opposite me has died. There was a post-mortem – I don't know the verdict. They suspect it was meningitis or a tumour. Tominara puts up a questionnaire asking our opinions on our treatment as internees: 'Answer as if you were answering your father; there will be no punishment.' 'Nuff said. About a dozen internees are putting up answers. We thought the 'Double Tenth' inquisition was over, but today they take three more, I am told, including Rendle and Kerr?

– Postscript –

TOM AND NORA'S LEGACY

The last entry in Tom Kitching's prison diary was dated 1 April 1944. The war ended with the dropping of atom bombs on Hiroshima and Nagasaki, followed by the Japanese surrender on 14 August 1945. Freedom came for the internees in Singapore on 5 September 1945, but for Tom it came too late. Many went home; Tom died on 14 April 1944. He was buried in Bidadari Cemetery in a suburb of Singapore.

On 12 November 1945, a memorial service organised by the Survey Department was held at the cemetery and attended by the department's European and Asian staff. W.K. Wilton delivered this eulogy:

Appreciation of life and work of the late Thomas Kitching

I have been asked to express the high regard in which Thomas Kitching was held by all who knew him throughout his 30 years in the Malayan Government Service. Joining the Survey Department in 1913, he served in almost every part of Malaya, attained to a senior administrative post, and was at the fall the most senior officer of his Department remaining in Singapore. It is particularly tragic that so long and meritorious a career should end in suffering in the depressing atmosphere of a Japanese internment camp. We would like Mr Kitching's family to know not only that his European acquaintances were proud to call him friend, but also that the Asiatic Staff who were working under him at the end showed their appreciation by risking the direst forms of punishment in order to smuggle to him in internment medical and other aids to alleviate his suffering.

His name will always be associated in our memory with good fellowship, good sportsmanship, and a very fine sense of duty in his dealings with the personnel in his Service.

Only a solitary clergyman was allowed to attend the last Christian rites at the burial in the dark days of 1944 and we have now joined in liberated Singapore to honour the memory of a friend and convey to the bereaved family our very deepest sympathy in their loss of a devoted Father.

Ten years later, a Mr Menon from the Survey Department, took Brian Kitching to see his father's grave while Brian was serving with HM Forces in Malaya. On the gravestone is inscribed:

Thomas Kitching,
Malayan Survey Service,
1.3.1890 – 14.4.44
A tribute from his brother officers.

The Singapore Housing and Development Board has plans to exhume and cremate the remains of all the 140,000 buried in Bidadari Cemetery. Tom Kitching's ashes will be place in an urn within niche A01/08/106 of the proposed columbarium. Tom's diary was preserved throughout the war in internment and is now safely in the Kitching family's hands, but its survival is something of a mystery. The Jack with whom Tom shared so much in those years in Changi – Jack Snoxhill – is the person who had it in his possession at the end of the war. But it is not known exactly where the diary was between the date of Tom's last entry in April 1944 and its appearance in Jack Snoxhill's hands in 1945. Less than a month after Tom's death, all the civilian internees in Changi were moved out to Sime Road Camp, once the headquarters of the RAF in Singapore and latterly a prison camp for the Allied forces captured during and since the fall of the city. Either Jack or some other friend had moved Tom's diary notebooks to Sime Road or they had been hidden in Changi and retrieved by Jack Snoxhill at the end of the war.

Jack Snoxhill handed the diary to Hugh Bryson, also interned in Changi, shortly before the latter sailed for home in 1945. The Brysons had been friends of Tom and Nora since the 1920s when they met in Trengganu. In London, Hugh sought out Joan Kitching and handed the diaries to her. They are now kept by Brian Kitching.

Brian was at the time of his father's death in Stellenbosch, near Cape Town, South Africa, being cared for by a family acquaintance, Mrs Helen Bell. He was nine years old when he last saw his parents in Singapore and he did not learn of his father's death till about 6 months afterwards. When the war ended, he was brought to the U.K. by Mrs Bell and entrusted to the care of his elder brother, Colin, who was Brian's legal guardian until he was 21.

Brian completed his education at Sedbergh School and Loughborough College. He subsequently carved out a successful career for himself as a chartered civil engineer, eventually settling in Perth, Scotland. He married Moira in 1959 and they have three children – Trevor, born 1961, Dawn, born 1963, and Neil, born 1966. Brian is now retired and all three of his family are themselves married, Brian and Moira now being proud grandparents to seven grandchildren.

Joan reached the U.K. safely in 1942 on the ship Nora was to have taken. After training as a physiotherapist, which Tom was delighted to learn she enjoyed very much, Joan married Edward Hague, a Canadian Army officer, in 1945 and settled down with him in Montreal. Joan and Edward had two children, Nora, born in 1947, and Richard, born in 1950.

Colin had an eventful, if not hazardous, career in the Royal Navy during the war, taking part in both the Dieppe raid and the Normandy landings. At one point, he served aboard the ill-fated cruiser Edinburgh. Luckily, he had been transferred before the Edinburgh met her miserable end in Arctic waters. Colin married Betty in 1943 and they have two sons, Alan, born in 1945, and Ian, born in 1958. Colin and Betty are now retired in Repton.

Tom would have been delighted to know that his family had overcome the difficulties and the grief occasioned by their parents' deaths to be able to carry on in the cheerful, active Kitching tradition, which comes through so strongly in his diary. He would have been even more pleased if he had known that members of his family have been back to Singapore and Malaya to visit the places remembered from their childhood days.

Brian did part of his national service in Singapore and Malaya from December 1955 to August 1956. It was during this time that Mr Menon from the Survey Department took him to see his father's grave for the first time.

Brian and his wife, Moira, paid a fleeting visit to the city in December 1990 when they visited Tom's grave and went to see 24, Mount Rosie Road, where Brian had lived with his parents and sister in 1941. Brian and Moira returned to Singapore and Malaysia in February and March 1995. Accompanied by Catherine Small (Hugh Bryson's daughter), they revisited Tom Kitching's grave and Mount Rosie where they visited the house that Catherine had lived in as a schoolgirl and to which Brian used to cycle as a boy.

Catherine and Brian climbed Gunong Angsi where Tom and Nora had spent their honeymoon in a bungalow at the top – 2,700 feet up – in January 1920. The party also took a boat out to Pulau Kapas, a small island off Trengganu, and Brian walked across the island as Tom and Nora had done about 1929.

At times, Tom Kitching doubted whether it was worthwhile taking the trouble to keep a diary. On 26 October 1942, he asked: How can I write something worthy of being written every day? It can't be done. Earlier, on 8 October, he had written: The deterrent to taking infinite pains with this diary is that always at the back of one's mind is the thought that one may never be able to preserve it.

On both counts, Tom's doubts were unfounded. He did write a great deal that was worth recording and keeping for posterity. He has provided his family and others, fortunate enough to have enjoyed the fruits of his labours, with an invaluable insight into the horrors of existence amid the death throes of a great city under siege and during his subsequent internment in a Japanese prison, with all its attendant cruelties, deprivations and forebodings. And he need not have worried about what would happen to his diary. It did survive and with it a valuable record of one man's cheerful determination to lead a civilised, humane and organised life amid the chaos of a war-battered world – an inspiration to us all.

– Index of Internees –

Names of internees, their ages, occupations and nationalities given in this index are as they appear in the Changi Register held by the Imperial War Museum. It would seem that the Register lists only those who arrived in Changi in early 1942. Attention is drawn to differences in spelling between diary and Register by underlining. The introduction to the microfilm of the Register says that it 'has certain lacunae'. In matching names from the diary with the Register, reasonable assumptions have been made. For example, the 'Nic' mentioned in the dairy is assumed to be Jean Hamilton McCulloch Nicholson of the Register. There are no other listed female internee with Christian or Surname starting with 'Nic' and from the entry of 8 November 1942 it is clear that she was a nursing sister, the occupation of Jean Nicholson. Where there are more than one person with the same surname in the Register and it cannot be reasonably ascertained which the diary referrs to, just the surname and the number with that surname is given. M.C.S. is Malayan Civil Service. Dates of death are largely given according to the diary entries.

Abang Braddon. *See* Braddon
Adams, Bill 264
Adams, John William Earnest (46, transport company manager, Australian) 70
Adams, Sidney (45, missionary) 189, 192, 285
Adkins, Edward (39, M.C.S.) 100
Ainslie (doctor) 254
Aitken, John (56, judge) 70, 160, 178
Aitken, Marion (71, private music teacher, died June 1943) 271
Alexander, Norman (35, Prof. of Physics Raffles College, New Zealander) 84, 100, 118, 141, 151, 154
Allen, George (48, medical practitioner) 102
Allen, Hugh (36, planter) 99
Allen, L.A. 128
Allen, Mrs. L.A. 128
Amstutz, Hobart Baumann (45, missionary, American) 100, 282, 289
Anderson, Conrad (57, Master Mariner, Norwegian) 183
Anderson, David (the Register lists 2) 144
Arnold (the Register lists 3) 262
Austerhaus 238-240, 269

Bagot, Edward (49, Inspector General of Police) 75
Bags 167
Bailey, Frederick (33, merchant seaman) 199
Bain, Mathew (41, medical practioner) 69-70, 294-296, 299
Baker (the Register lists 7) 281
Baker, J. 143
Baker, M. 54, 187
Barraclough, Frank (47, Malayan Educational Service) 169
Barron, George (51, surveyor) 33, 74, 76, 78-79, 81, 138, 198, 219, 257
Barton, William (65, Master Mariner) 281

Baumann, John (66, mining engineer, South African) 128
Bayley, Sidney (48, planter) 119, 126, 134, 138, 179
Beale, Raymond (24, Chartered Accountant, Australian) 125
Beasley 195
Beattie, David (35, surgeon) 122, 127
Beavis, Stephen (36, merchant) 130
Beck, Ewald (47, Police) 151
Beck, Helen (45, housewife) 151, 220
Bedington, Guy (53, civil engineer) 187, 189, 191
Bedlington, Keith (45, Senior Surveyor, Malacca, Canadian) 47, 68, 76, 103, 180, 265
Belgrave, William (51, Advisor & Director of Agriculture, Malaya, British West Indian) 70, 99, 151, 168, 176, 211
Bell, James. *See* Bell, Raymond
Bell, Herbert Haviland (55, planter) 175
Bell, Raymond (also referred to as James, 37, Police) 19, 72, 74, 83, 93, 170, 201, 220
Belloch 70
Benham 147
Bennitt, Albert (also refered to as 'Padre', 34, priest, Church of England) 69, 79, 81, 83, 87, 96, 108, 111-112, 211, 308
Beverley, Henery (37, Police) 270
Bewsher, John (57, planter) 290
Bidlake 111
Billing 147, 150
Bingham, Robert (39, M.C.S.) 156
Birkin 151
Birkinshaw, Frank (55, Chief Field Officer, Malayan Agricultural Service) 70, 108, 114, 287
Birnie (the Register lists 2) 164
Bishop of Singapore (Church of England). *See* Wilson, John Leonard

– General Index –